D1566491

SUCCESS WITHOUT VICTORY

JULES LOBEL

SUCCESS WITHOUT VICTORY

*Lost Legal Battles and the
Long Road to Justice in America*

New York University Press   *New York and London*

NEW YORK UNIVERSITY PRESS
New York and London
www.nyupress.org

Library of Congress Cataloging-in-Publication Data
Lobel, Jules.
Success without victory : lost legal battles and the
long road to justice in America / Jules Lobel.
p. cm. — (Critical America)
Includes bibliographical references and index.
ISBN 0–8147–5112–1 (cloth : alk.paper)
1. Law—United States—Anecdotes. 2. Justice and politics.
3. Political activists—United States—Anecdotes.
I. Title. II. Series.
K184.L63 2003
349.73—dc21 2003012365

New York University Press books are printed on acid-free paper,
and their binding materials are chosen for strength and durability.

Manufactured in the United States of America

10 9 8 7 6 5 4 3 2 1

To my parents,

Paul and Lena Lobel,

with gratitude and love

Contents

Acknowledgments

I COULD NOT HAVE COMPLETED THIS BOOK without the loving support of my wife, Karen Engro, and the continued grilling of my three children, Michael, Caroline, and Sasha, as to when I would be finished.

Without my colleagues at the Center for Constitutional Rights and the National Lawyers Guild, particularly Michael Ratner, this book could not have been written. They gave me the opportunity to be a part of wonderful organizations that are in the forefront of the legal and political resistance to oppressive government policies. They also taught me a lesson that is at the heart of this book—that progressive legal work must be tied to a political movement.

I thank all the people who graciously agreed to be interviewed for this book. Congressman Ron Dellums and Congressman Tom Campbell gave time from very busy schedules. Staughton and Alice Lynd, Lee Halterman, Robert Brauer, Michael Ratner, Elisabeth and David Linder, Charles Houston Jr., Beth Stephens, Dorothy Brooks, Oliver Hill, Arthur Kinoy, Victor Rabinowitz, Ruth Wald, Juan Williams, and Dan Snow also generously provided insightful interviews that enriched this book.

I particularly want to thank Sara Miles for her invaluable editing of my draft manuscript. I also am grateful to my editors at New York University Press for all the help they gave me in producing this book. My work was also enormously aided by my friends and family members who read my drafts—my sister Myra Lobel, my wife, Karen Engro, and my friends George Lowenstein, Todd May, Art McDonald, Margaret Randall, Michael Ratner, Elisabeth Linder, Lee Halterman, Staughton Lynd, and Arthur Kinoy.

I have benefited from the generous institutional support of the University of Pittsburgh Law School. I particularly want to express my appreciation to the members of the Document Technology Center at the law school, LuAnn Driscoll, Karen Knochel, Darleen Mocello, Barbara

Salopek, and Valerie Pompe, who went to extraordinary efforts to prepare the manuscript. My research assistants at the law school, particularly Carrie Dunn, and Aaron Milke assisted in finding difficult sources.

This book continues the work that I started by publishing, in the Cornell Law Review, an article entitled "Losers, Fools, and Prophets: Justice as Struggle." While nearly all of the analysis and the writing in this book are new, I would like to thank the Cornell Law Review for permission to excerpt some materials from the original sources.

I

Introduction

Losers, Fools, and Prophets

ON A BRIGHT, sunny November morning in 1990, my fellow lawyer Michael Ratner and I stood on the steps of the Federal District Courthouse in Washington, D.C., listening to members of Congress explain why they were suing the president of the United States to prevent him from going to war against Iraq. More than a hundred national television newscasters, radio commentators, newspaper reporters, and free-lance journalists thronged the patio below us, but they appeared little interested in the constitutional issues that Michael and I were poised to explain. Instead, their eager, zealous questions to us and the legislators we represented focused on one issue: Could we win?

The journalists' concern reflected a deeply rooted American value on *winning*—the belief that, as Vince Lombardi once put it, "Winning isn't everything. It's the only thing."[1] And any realistic, rational, hardheaded American could easily see that Michael and I had only a slightly better chance of winning in Court than of having God suddenly appear in Washington to halt the impending war. What did we think we were doing?

Since that fall day, I have been intrigued by—even plagued by and obsessed with—the question of what "success" means. American culture constantly identifies success with winning and draws a sharp line between victory and defeat. In politics, business, and sports, we have a passion to win and a terror of losing. Professional sports leagues eliminate tie games, preferring clear winners and losers. The American entrepreneurs who brought European soccer to this country changed its rules to avoid dreaded ties. Our political elections are based on a winner-take-all model, unlike those in many European nations that prefer proportionate representation. Our law eschews mediation, where both parties give a little and receive something in return, preferring a courtroom drama designed to produce clear winners and losers.

I

In contrast, I seem to thrive on losing. With equally "unsuccessful" colleagues in places like the Center for Constitutional Rights, a non-profit law firm that works on issues of international human rights, civil rights, and social justice, I've litigated an impressive number of lost cases. My brilliant losing streak on behalf of what I consider to be important political causes has caused me to ponder the winning metaphor in American life and, more specifically, in American law. Why do we remember Clarence Darrow, F. Lee Bailey, and the mythical, always victorious Perry Mason, yet forget great losers like Albion Tourgée, who unsuccessfully litigated *Plessy v. Ferguson*? Is there such a clear line between winning and losing, success and failure, or is reality more complex? Are success and failure really mutually exclusive, as we're taught, or do they exist in dialectical relationship to each other?

Most of my thinking about these issues grows out of a quixotic, decade-long effort, undertaken by the Center for Constitutional Rights (CCR) in conjunction with the National Lawyers Guild (NLG) and other legal groups, to litigate against U.S. military and economic intervention abroad in the 1980s. The Center, founded in 1966 by several civil rights lawyers, views as its mission the development of creative legal strategies to serve progressive political movements. Similarly, the National Lawyers Guild, founded in 1937 as the nation's first racially integrated bar association, is dedicated to the need for basic change in the structure of our political and economic system. During the Reagan and Bush presidencies, the lawyers at CCR, working with NLG and other lawyers, applied the creative approaches they had learned from the domestic civil rights struggles to challenge U.S. foreign policy in the courts.

This band of progressive lawyers brought almost a dozen cases challenging the U.S. government for sending military advisors and aid to El Salvador; launching a covert contra war against Nicaragua; prohibiting travel to Cuba; invading Grenada; and planning to attack Iraq without congressional authorization. We litigated on constitutional grounds, on international-treaty grounds, with innovative human-rights uses of old tort laws, and in almost every way we could dream up. We brought in co-plaintiffs from Congress, co-counsel from leading legal organizations, and students from prestigious law schools, all of us working around the clock. We joined with community groups and activists, carried out media and educational campaigns, and organized politically around our cases. Our foreign-policy litigation became a sort of Sisyphean quest as we maneuvered through a hazy maze cluttered with gates. Each gate we unlocked led to yet another that blocked our path, with the elusive goal of judicial relief always shrouded in the twilight mist of the never-ending maze.

Over the years, we were spectacularly unsuccessful in court. With a few exceptions, we lost every case we litigated.

By 1991, I was an experienced, accomplished, and well-polished loser. I turned forty, had a child with a serious disability, and avoided to some degree the quest to reflect on what, if anything, we had accomplished during those intense, exciting years of the 1980s. I wanted to understand not simply why we lost but what the value of our losing might be and what our legal battles might teach us about the bigger values of "success" and "failure" in our culture.

The mainstream legal milieu in which I taught and practiced law offered relatively easy answers. Losing cases have no effect on the law, which is seen as a collection of rules and precedents. While lawyers might have some respect for well-crafted losing arguments, most of them can't be bothered with lost causes.

Even within the law-reform community, many, such as the former NAACP Legal Defense Fund general counsel Jack Greenberg, argue that the main result of losing cases is the creation of bad legal precedent and that, therefore, test cases generally "should not be brought if they are likely to be lost."[2] My friend and fellow progressive lawyer Michael Krinsky once questioned whether our losing foreign policy cases "had the effect of validating the government position."

This prevailing view of the law is utilitarian, as is the dominant American view of success. To succeed means to win concrete results, to change the legal rules, to win damages for your client, or to obtain a court injunction. The utilitarian perspective is premised on a sharp divide between winning and losing, which in turn relies on a separation of law and politics. The success of a lawsuit under traditional doctrine depends on its legal result, not on any subtle and nuanced political effects it might create. The traditional lawyer seeks to win some judgment for her client, the law-reform litigator to achieve some structural change through a successful court challenge. While traditional public interest litigation may use concurrent political action to create a favorable climate for court victory and to implement that victory, it considers politics only a predicate to the courtroom drama.

In our losing efforts, however, we took a different view. First of all, the primary point of many of the cases we litigated was to inspire political action. While we believed that the law was on our side and hoped the courts would agree, we used law not merely to adjudicate a dispute between parties but also to educate the public. Even though the political contexts of our challenges made courtroom success highly improbable, we persevered because our purposes were broader than victory alone. We were speaking to the public, not just to the court.

But, while we tended to use political action, not courtroom victory, as a marker for success, I have always been unsatisfied with justifying these cases as political agitation or defending our choice to persevere on purely political grounds. Some law-reform litigators ask whether the time and energy we spent on these cases could have been better expended on more productive political activities. As one lawyer friend recently claimed, "You wasted a lot of time, energy, and legal talent," litigating these hopeless cases. Other scholars, including many associated with the Critical Legal Studies Movement, question whether reliance on courts and litigation unduly narrows and restricts the political movements we sought to aid and even legitimated the very system we were challenging. So, while I believe our cases did help inspire public debate, dialogue, and political action in positive, albeit limited ways, I still had to question whether political "success" was any more valid as a criterion than legal success.

As I pondered these issues, I began instead to reevaluate the philosophical utilitarianism itself that underlies the mainstream view of success in law and life and to look at different traditions that critique it.

One view, perhaps expressed best in our country by Ralph Waldo Emerson and Henry David Thoreau, replaces "success" with expressive individualism, a kind of self-reliance that doesn't depend on the rewards of the outside world. In this view, work is a calling, an expression of oneself, and a way to cultivate moral sensibilities, not merely a utilitarian activity that leads to winning. "[We should] measure a person not primarily by the virtue of his actions," writes Thoreau, "but by the free character he is and is felt to be under all circumstances."[3] Their focus on the inner, expressive self led Emerson and Thoreau to view success and failure not as dichotomies but as existing in dialectic tension and unity. "My entire success, such as it is," writes Emerson, "is composed wholly of particular failures."[4]

The Emersonian self-expressive mode has informed a tradition of American protest. In recent times, the example of Derrick Bell comes to mind: the distinguished legal scholar sacrificed his teaching job at Harvard Law School in protest over its refusal to hire a black woman professor. As Bell wrote, "At its essence, the willingness to protest represents less a response to a perceived affront than the acting out of a state of mind. . . . Often, the desire to change the offending situation which is beyond our reach may be an incidental benefit and not the real motivation. Rather, those of us who speak out are moved by a deep sense of the fragility of our self-worth. It is the determination to protect our sense of who we are that leads us to risk criticism, alienation, and serious loss while most others, similarly harmed, remain silent."[5] In a similar vein, when former Supreme Court Justice William Brennan was questioned about the utility of his repeated dissents opposing capital punishment, he proffered not a utilitarian defense but an explanation that these dissents were expressions of his own conscience; his main purpose in writing them was to define himself and not to change society.[6]

For many of us who struggled in losing cases for decades, convinced of the morality and justice of our cause, it never really occurred to us to do anything different; our lives' meaning was precisely in carrying out this calling, whether it led to success or failure. We spent thousands of hours trying to succeed—we wanted to succeed—but our motivation was self-expressive and lay in the fight itself. My own moral and ethical outrage at the U.S. government's actions in Central America, for example, and my feelings for the victims of those actions compelled me to act. I had talked, made friends, and fallen in love with people whom I wanted to help. I was a lawyer, so I utilized my legal skills to express this desire. I did not undertake the calculations of a tort attorney as to the likely outcome of any case: it was the very act of challenging the injustice that I felt gave meaning to my life.

Yet, this self-expression rationale, a powerful antidote to the success culture of America, left me dissatisfied. For many years I had focused on working to better society, and I remained troubled by focusing on the self to justify what I did. The Emersonian critique, insightful as it was, still was an individualist one; although it extolled the expressive self rather than the ambitious, achieving self of the success-mongers, it was still an uncomfortable position for me to take. I wanted to look more deeply at community, not individualism, as a way to step outside the prison of winning and losing.

Digging deeper for answers, I began to look back to history, culture, tradition, and my own roots. I began with the uniquely American tradition of radical movements that sought to litigate their aspirations in

6 INTRODUCTION: LOSERS, FOOLS, AND PROPHETS

court. Throughout the nineteenth century, litigation as a means of protest was common—and most of those early litigators were losers.

Virtually hopeless test cases brought to challenge unjust policies is a recurring thread in the tapestry of American law. Radical abolitionists challenged aspects of slavery in American courts in the 1840s and 1850s, to no avail. Members of the post-Civil War women's movement advocated a broad interpretation of the Fourteenth Amendment and litigated women's rights in the 1870s in a series of cases that were uniformly unsuccessful. *Plessy v. Ferguson* was a test case brought in the 1890s by several civil rights lawyers who had strong doubts about their chances for success in that period of reaction.

One hundred years ago, Albion Tourgée, the lawyer who argued for Homer Plessy before the Supreme Court, agonized over issues of success and failure. In his best-selling autobiographical novel, titled *A Fool's Errand*, Tourgée argued that an individual is often both a fool and a genius, with only history's thin line separating the two. For Tourgée, there was no inherent difference between success and failure, prophecy or foolishness: historical circumstance was the determining factor.

In our era, I found others who continued the tradition of the nineteenth-century litigators like Albion Tourgée and struggled not simply for self-expression but in order to protest and to build movements. Most of them were losers, too. Labor activists have proposed innovative theories of employee property and contract rights to avert plant closings, although courts thus far have given these theories short shrift. Countless lawsuits challenged the constitutionality of the U.S. war in Indochina, with meager results. Lawyers for Haitian refugees sought to enjoin the Coast Guard's interdiction and return of Haitians, knowing that the Supreme Court was likely to uphold the government's policy.

This is the tradition of which I began to feel part. These cases have helped to create a community and a culture dedicated to litigating the constitutional aspirations of oppressed groups. Paradoxically, that culture survived and persisted in spite of, or maybe even because of, the failure in courts. Or, to put it differently, the current commitment of civil rights groups, women's groups, and gay and lesbian groups to a legal discourse and to legal activism to protect their rights stems in part from the willingness of activists in political and social movements in the nineteenth century to fight for rights, even when they realized the courts would be unsympathetic. I began to see how communities often gain their identities not in celebrating their victories over oppression but in remembering their defeats.

And I began to see how "failure" could not really be measured adequately by the winner-take-all model of American law. Certainly, on the face of it, the legal tradition I studied was unsuccessful. Many of the early nineteenth-century cases seem to have disappeared from our history, playing virtually no role even when the Court eventually reversed itself decades later. For example, Chief Justice Earl Warren's opinion in *Brown v. Board of Education* did not cite Albion Tourgée's argument in *Plessy* or even Justice John Marshall Harlan's ringing dissent in that case. The women's rights arguments before the Court in the 1870s were never cited or even referred to when those arguments were revived in abortion rights and women's rights litigation one hundred years later. If success can be measured only by direct result, immediate change, or easily perceived impact, then these earlier cases were unmitigated failures. But, if success can be viewed like the pentimenti of a painting, as an unseen underside necessary to the final perceptible painting, then these cases take on a different hue. Success inheres in the creation of a tradition, of a commitment to struggle, of a narrative of resistance that can inspire others similarly to resist.

The American success culture is invariably concerned with the present, with immediate accomplishments.[7] In our view of success as individual achievement, we isolate the individual from community and from tradition. A society that so emphasizes success as immediate accomplishment lives almost exclusively in the present, with only tenuous ties to past generations or concerns for future generations.

An alternative model of success must place individual actions in the context of history and forge links of solidarity with communities and traditions. Most oppressed peoples have not cultures of success but, rather, cultures of remembrance where individuals view "success" not by present accomplishment but by their tie to past memories and future hopes and dreams. Such communities of memory, writes the sociologist Robert Bellah, tell "painful stories of shared suffering that sometimes create deeper identities than success."[8]

For example, African American culture in the United States has developed in large part out of the unifying shared memories of oppression and resistance. The historian Vincent Harding writes that the terrible vision of a black man being killed becomes a symbol and a source of truths for the future. For Harding, "the river of struggle" is the connection between blacks living today and the history of the African American people, and it is within the context of that river that the failed slave revolts, the unsuccessful individual acts of resistance to slavery, and the losing legal resistance to slavery can all be understood.

My own Jewish culture and heritage provide another example of this tradition. The most powerful symbol of my childhood was standing for a moment of silence at the Passover Seder to remember the Warsaw ghetto uprising that commenced on Passover night in 1943. The narrative of the Jewish Warsaw ghetto uprising against the Nazis might be interpreted as a reminder that overwhelming force prevails against poorly armed resistance fighters or that the Jews were abandoned by the Poles and Allied nations. However, the message I took away from those Seders is that people can struggle even when faced with overwhelming odds and that, through struggle, they may achieve a spiritual victory over their oppressors.

I found links with that popular tradition in the action of lawyers like Helmuth James von Moltke, a German who was legal adviser to the High Command of the German Armed Services until he was executed by the Nazis in 1945. In battle after losing legal battle to protect the rights of Poles, to save Jews, and to oppose German troops' war crimes, he made it clear that he struggled not just to win in the moment but to build a future: "The most irritating part," he wrote, "is that I consider all the work being done now as having no chance. But it has to be done with all due care all the same, so that others, and we ourselves, can't blame ourselves for having missed any chance."[9]

The pentimenti of political protest, like those of art, are often imperceptible in the present tense. When I considered history, I began to see my litigation as part of a community of memory. When I used the law to protest, I remembered the abolitionist, suffragist, antisegregationist lawyers whose actions helped construct a uniquely American culture of litigating broad political issues in court. I remembered courageous lawyers like Moltke, whose failures inspired others. And my community of memory also included the more recent anti–Vietnam War litigators who brought every imaginable lawsuit to try to bring that catastrophic war to an end and who lost every case—but who laid the groundwork for all the work we did at the Center for Constitutional Rights and the National Lawyers Guild in the 1980s.

Moreover, my community of memory was not limited to a legal tradition. It included the aspirations and values of people—black people in the Americas in the "river of struggle," Jews in Warsaw who refused to surrender, and many, many others—whose lives informed not only my legal work but also my spiritual and moral choices. Their example was like the words from the Old Testament that began to resonate for me: "But let judgment roll down as waters, and righteousness as a mighty stream."

Our society's central metaphor for justice, the traditional scales of justice, connotes the ideals of balance, equipoise, detachment, and congruence. But the prophetic vision of justice articulated by Amos in the Old Testament calls forth the image of a mighty, turbulent, cascading river. This justice is not merely the technical legal process employed to reach a decision, nor even the set of norms that might constitute a just society, but also the continual, turbulent process of struggle. To maintain its meaning, substantive justice must be linked to movement. And, if justice is the mighty stream of struggle against oppression, then losing efforts constitute some of the myriad rivulets that constantly feed that stream and inspire further struggle.

Those who view justice not as a mere norm but as a turbulent river, "a fighting challenge, a restless drive,"[10] are continually operating on the fault line between current reality and human aspiration, between what is and what ought to be.[11] Success in navigating the river requires maintaining the tension between reality and aspiration, between what is and what ought to be, between our reach and our grasp. It requires not getting stuck on either bank of the river, neither the muddy bank of reality nor the high cliffs of our dreams.

I am still not sure whether our efforts were successes or failures. They were successful if they inspire others to struggle, to resist injustice together, and to eschew the easier, more "successful" path. They will be successful if they help others, as they helped me, to understand the meaning of our lives as more than winning or losing.

2

Can Law Stop War?
The Constitution and Iraq

IT WAS LATE OCTOBER 1990 in Washington: the colors of autumn were fading, the leaves falling, and members of Congress finishing up their business before leaving town for the holiday breaks. But Congressman Ron Dellums, a tall, slender, distinguished-looking black man who had represented California's Eighth Congressional District since 1970, was not thinking about his Thanksgiving plans. The congressman was very worried by the rumblings he had heard in Washington corridors on the edges of official briefings about Operation Desert Shield and "the military defense of Saudi Arabia." Dellums was convinced that the Bush administration had decided to go to war against Iraq.

Ronald V. Dellums was born in a working-class neighborhood of Oakland, California, in 1935. Raised by his father, a longshoreman, and his mother, Willa, who worked as a clerk in a government office, he graduated from high school in 1953 and, soon thereafter, enlisted in the U.S. Marines. After two years on active duty, Ron Dellums went back to school, eventually earning a master's in social work from the University of California at Berkeley. He spent several years as a social worker and community organizer, finding a political identity that combined antiwar activism with racial justice issues. Elected to the Berkeley City Council in 1967, by 1970 he won a seat in Congress, defeating a six-term liberal in the Democratic primary and handily beating his Republican opponent. In his victory speech, Dellums thanked "my public relations expert,"[1] then-Vice President Spiro Agnew, who'd attacked him as "an out-and-out radical."

A month after he entered Congress, Dellums caused a minor sensation by displaying on the walls of his office photographs that depicted war crimes perpetrated by U.S. forces in Vietnam.[2] Although, as a poverty worker, Dellums had hoped to be assigned to the House Committee on Education and Labor, he was named instead to the Foreign Affairs Committee.

Dellums recalls the political battles that led to his career as a foreign policy leader who eventually rose to be chairman of the powerful House Armed Services Committee: "My first term I was really disappointed I wasn't on Education and Labor but by the time I was reelected in 1972, I'd decided that the key requirement for social justice was to divert money from the military budget to meet people's needs. So I put in for the House Armed Services Committee, which oversees the military budget and has direct power over the military. And no black person had ever served on it."[3]

The chairman of the Armed Services Committee, F. Edward Herbert, an old-style southern reactionary from Louisiana, hit the roof. "That damn radical pinko Dellums will never serve on my committee," he reportedly vowed to the Democratic majority leader, Carl Albert. "How would we be able to hold closed session hearings discussing sensitive military secrets—Dellums would leak everything to our enemies!" After a series of meetings, Albert called Dellums and offered the plum he thought sufficient to buy him off. "You want the Education and Labor Committee, right?" asked Albert, a master dealmaker. "Well, just drop your request for Armed Services, and you got it."

Dellums thought it over a while and decided not to cave in. He called Louis Stokes, a mild-mannered man who was then the head of the Congressional Black Caucus, and asked him to request a meeting with Albert and the leadership. "And, Louis," said Dellums, "make sure you invite Bill Clay, who will act mean, tough, and black." Stokes, Clay, and Dellums sat down with the leadership. "As a matter of principle, Dellums should get Armed Services," Stokes calmly stated to start the meeting. When Albert demurred, Clay's shrill angry voice cut him off: "There's never been a black on Armed Services, and now that Dellums asks for it, you tell him no," said Clay, sounding disgusted and militant. "You wouldn't want us to charge racism, would you?" Albert, thinking fast, proposed Barbara Jordan, a black woman freshman from Texas who the leadership assumed would be pliable. But Dellums had anticipated Albert's ploy and pulled out a letter from Jordan saying that she wanted the Judiciary Committee. Albert gave up, launching "that pinko radical" on a twenty-year career on the Armed Services Committee and catapulting Barbara Jordan into the national spotlight for her part in the Judiciary Committee's 1973 hearings on Nixon's impeachment.

Dellums remained a passionate voice against involvement in Vietnam and subsequently led campaigns against military involvement in Grenada, Mozambique, Nicaragua, El Salvador, Honduras, and Afghanistan. He worked closely for years with many of us at the Center for Constitutional Rights and National Lawyers Guild, lending his name, his prestige, and his energy to our lawsuits and strategizing with us about how to have the greatest possible impact in Washington. "Maybe I am an idealist," said Dellums once about his never-ending struggles against U.S. intervention abroad and injustice at home. "Maybe I am just a black Don Quixote chasing windmills. But I would like to think that this country needs some Don Quixotes, because we have had too many people caught up in their own aggrandizement."[4]

In October 1990, Dellums was poised for one of his greatest challenges: trying to prevent what he believed was an unconstitutional, immoral, and unnecessary war against Iraq. Sitting alone in a hotel room, watching TV, and not getting much sleep, he stewed about his gut feeling that Bush was going to war and his dismay that even his progressive constituents didn't seem to recognize the urgency of acting to oppose the president's plans. Suddenly, a light bulb clicked on in his head. He jumped out of bed and called one of his key aides, Lee Halterman. "Lee, I've got an idea," Dellums barked into the phone. "Do you think those guys at the CCR would sue Bush to prevent him from going to war over Kuwait without congressional authorization?"

Dellums had several reasons for thinking that a lawsuit might be worthwhile. First, he wanted to "throw a monkey wrench into this situation," to slow the march toward war. He strongly believed in the integrity of the constitutional process that required Congress to vote on whether to go to war. And Dellums also opposed going to war against Iraq. To sue Bush now might buy some time and get enough attention to allow the substantive issue of whether the United States should go to war in the Persian Gulf to emerge.

Dellums also believed that a court might rule in his favor, for the president was flagrantly violating Congress's right to declare war. But winning or losing in a traditional sense was not what motivated him. "Society measures worth based on producing or being effective," Dellums told me. "For me, winning is being persistent, being faithful to one's cause." Dellums's view of victory is based on the long haul, not immediate gratification. "My son once told me that if he was to write a book about his father it would not be entitled *Seize the Moment.*" Rather, said Dellums, "it would be a book about my tenacity and persistence." His persistence now had led him to think of creative ways to challenge Bush's drive toward war. The next morning, Lee Halterman called Michael Ratner at the CCR to see whether the Center was interested in pursuing Dellums's idea.

One hundred miles south of Washington, Sergeant Michael Ange was about to make the most difficult decision of his life. Ange, a short, stocky, twenty-six-year-old white man with short blond hair, had dreamed of being a soldier when he was young. His mother, Patricia, remembers him constantly playing soldier as a kid;[5] while in high school in Greenville, North Carolina, Ange joined and later commanded the school's ROTC battalion. After graduating, in 1982, Ange signed up for the National Guard Reserves because, he said, "people have an obligation to give something back to the country." He was a good soldier, rising to the rank of sergeant; in his civilian life, he worked as a sheriff's deputy and as an undercover narcotics agent in North Carolina.

When Iraqi troops invaded Kuwait, Ange was majoring in criminal justice at Appalachian State University in Boone, North Carolina, and serving as a reservist with the National Guard 1450th Transportation Unit. Ange's unit was called to active duty on October 11, 1990, and sent to Fort Lee, Virginia, three days later.

Ange and his twenty-three-year-old fiancée, Dorothy Brooks, were hardly political activists. Brooks, the deeply religious daughter of a Southern Baptist minister, scorned sixties activists as "radical, uninformed, and inconsiderate." She resented antiwar protestors whom she'd seen throwing tomatoes at the troops during the Vietnam War. "I always had a great deal of respect for the White House and our ideas of democracy,"[6] she explained. A law student at Campbell University in North Carolina, Brooks was a political conservative.

Yet, Dorothy Brooks and Michael Ange, people who would seem to have virtually nothing in common with Ron Dellums, were nonetheless headed on a path of conscience that would soon lead Ange to sue the president of the United States.

In August 1990, when Iraq overran Kuwait and President Bush sent troops to the region, ostensibly to defend Saudi Arabia, Ange supported that decision and actually volunteered to go. The year before, the army had denied him an ROTC commission and started the process of dropping him from the program, finding him medically unfit due to serious problems with his knee, leg and foot. With the crisis, Ange thought, maybe the army would need volunteers and make him an officer after all. But the army turned him down, finding him not medically qualified for a commission on active duty in Saudi Arabia.

Yet, just five weeks later Ange and his unit were called up for active duty. Consistency apparently is not the army's strongest virtue, and Sergeant Ange, medically unfit for a commission, was nevertheless held eligible to be sent overseas on active duty. When Ange questioned this decision, he was told that the policy was to deny virtually all requests for medical discharge. "If you're still breathing," an officer told him, "you'll go." Moreover, the company commanders, apparently peeved by Ange's audacity in questioning their decisions, assigned him a new job as a driver for heavy fuel transport trucks, a position for which he had never been trained and that would exacerbate his knee and leg problems.

While waiting to be deployed at Fort Lee, Ange picked up disturbing information from other NCOs who were with army intelligence: the U.S. military, they said, was going to take offensive action to drive Iraq from Kuwait. One particularly well-placed friend with access to intelligence information told Ange that war with Iraq was definitely coming, probably by mid-January. The reports that were making Congressman Dellums nervous had also filtered down to Ange.

Ange was upset. He had been willing to go to the Middle East to defend Saudi Arabia, although as an MP and not as a truck driver. But now it seemed that offensive action was planned—and that seemed wrong, maybe even illegal. Like dozens of other soldiers he talked to, Ange was troubled about the new mission in the desert. He was moving toward action.

Ange's fiancée supported and even encouraged him to question his military orders. Brooks's deep religious convictions, long the foundation for her conservative politics, now led her to question President Bush's actions. "I was listening to a voice deep inside my head," Brooks recalled. "If I was going to sleep at night with a clear conscience, I had to act on my principles."

Brooks had generally looked at world affairs the way most people do, with a surface understanding gathered from a few minutes spent watching the nightly news. But this event touched her personally. She felt that her life, and Ange's, was threatened. So she worried and prayed and studied everything she could get her hands on about the politics, economics, and legal issues involved in U.S. policy toward Iraq. Ange called his professors to ask them about the economics and politics of the Middle East. Ange, who had done a research paper on the War Powers Resolution in college, thought about his studies of the constitutional issues involved in the Vietnam War. He believed that Congress must authorize war in order to prevent the kind of divisiveness that had engulfed the American public during Vietnam, and he was worried by Bush's unilateral action. The two concluded that the president's motivation was not humanitarian or democratic; with great disgust and sadness, they decided that Bush was interested only in protecting certain economic and political interests.

So, in early October 1990, Michael Ange asked his fiancée to call the ACLU for legal help: the two had decided to challenge Ange's deployment to the Gulf in court. The ACLU referred them to the Center for Constitutional Rights—a relief to Brooks, who mistakenly assumed from the CCR's name that it was a more politically moderate organization than the ACLU. She called the CCR and told a staff attorney, Jose Morin, that Ange wanted to bring a constitutional challenge to his deployment.

That mid-October, the CCR was in its usual state of pandemonium. Beth Stephens, Jose Morin, and Michael Ratner were bent over their desks, roaming the halls of the CCR, or sprawled in the conference room eating takeout food and arguing. Beth had attended Berkeley Law School and then clerked for the controversial liberal California Supreme Court justice Rose Bird. Forsaking a conventional legal career, she moved instead to Nicaragua and spent six years working in support of the Nicaraguan revolution before returning to the United States in 1989 and landing a job with the CCR. Jose, also a fairly recent addition to the CCR legal staff, had worked previously at the Puerto Rican Legal Defense Fund and the Latino Rights Project. Jose was preparing to fly to Hawaii to represent Corporal Jeffrey Patterson, a member of the Marine Corps, at his court-martial hearing for refusing to go fight in the Gulf. Michael Ratner was the experienced member of the team to whom Beth and Jose turned for advice. Michael, a brilliant lawyer and a dedicated political activist, graduated first in his class from Columbia Law School and, after clerking for Judge Constance Baker Motley, was hired as a professor at the prestigious New York University Law School. After a year, Michael decided that the relaxed, insulated academic life was not for him and left the law school for a bustling, tension-filled life as a litigator and political activist. He had been either at the CCR or in private practice since 1971 and for a time in the 1980s was the Center's legal director. Michael and I had already worked together on several cases challenging U.S. intervention in Central America and in Cuba and were close friends.

Beth, Jose, and Michael were hard at work writing a brief to be submitted at the court-martial hearing for Corporal Patterson. For Ange was not alone. Like Patterson, dozens of other solders were petitioning for conscientious objector status, going AWOL, refusing to serve in Desert Storm, or seeking some legal means to avoid being transferred to the Gulf. Many of them had been referred, as Ange was, to the CCR, and the lawyers were trying to figure out who they could help and which cases they could best use to challenge Bush's intervention. Meanwhile, the CCR was also considering working with Dellums on his constitutional challenge. The pace was frantic, and the lawyers could not work on Ange's case immediately, but they promised to get back to him quickly.

One afternoon in late October 1990, my phone rang. "We're swamped," Michael Ratner said. He was calling to see whether I was interested in representing Dellums.

I was wracked by conflicting feelings. I was both mentally and physically worn out, sick of bringing unsuccessful legal challenges to the government's foreign policy. Tilting at windmills can be very frustrating, and constantly losing in the courts had taken a toll on my psyche. I knew that the Dellums case would consume a substantial amount of time and energy; I was tired of litigating losing cases in addition to writing scholarly articles and teaching and wanted a break. Moreover, I now was the father of a year-old child and knew that representing Dellums would keep me working until late at night, away from my family. "I know," said Michael, who had two young children of his own. "I can't bear leaving my kids any more."

But I couldn't refuse Michael's request. I was furious that President Bush was leading us into a war that could cost thousands of lives and that he was doing it without getting the consent of Congress, overriding the Constitution one more time. I opposed Bush's policies on both moral and constitutional grounds and felt an obligation to try to stop yet another war: it was a matter of human life, not just of legal principle. If Dellums could get a substantial number of other members of Congress to support him, I figured, his lawsuit, while probably a loser in court, could affect the national debate.

I thought about the chance to be involved in a historic moment, to feed my ego by doing something important, and to work again with Michael. I knew I would be frustrated and overtired, but I told him yes.

We talked over the situation. In many ways, Bush's actions against Iraq presented the best opportunity we'd had to challenge a president's usurpation of congressional war powers since the Vietnam War. Our prior cases had all involved murkier situations where the line between presidential and congressional war powers was arguably hazy: the sending of fifty-six American advisers to El Salvador, the covert war against Nicaragua, the surprise attack against Grenada. The case Dellums was proposing was different. If President Bush could launch a major war in the Persian Gulf without the approval of Congress, the constitutional distribution of war powers was meaningless.

But, in order to take advantage of the moment, we had to decide how best to frame our case. "There's a guy called Michael Ange in the National Guard," Michael told me, "whom I think we could put in here." Ange clearly had standing to sue in court, while a member of Congress might not. Michael outlined Ange's story to me, and we discussed whether to bring Ange and Dellums together in a single case.

Michael and I, along with Dellums and his staff, leaned toward bringing two separate cases. Congressman Dellums wanted to raise only the constitutional issue of who had the power to initiate war. He did not want to base our case on whether there had been compliance with the 1973 War Powers Resolution—an act that Dellums had always opposed, arguing that it gave the president too much power to use U.S. troops abroad. Dellums had taken flak from fellow progressives at the time for his view; the flamboyant congresswoman Bella Abzug had "read the riot act" to him for his vote. But Dellums believed that the Resolution improperly allowed the president to initiate warfare unilaterally as long as he got congressional approval within sixty days; even Abzug many years later told him he had been right. He now was not about to litigate on the basis of the Resolution. Yet Ange needed to rely on the Resolution, since he was challenging his assignment to the Persian Gulf, not only the pending war.

Besides not wanting to base his case on the War Powers Resolution, Dellums also had a practical reason for wanting the cases to be brought separately. His office was seeking to get other representatives interested in the lawsuit. Many moderate members of Congress who might oppose the president's initiating a war without congressional approval would not want to be associated in the same lawsuit with a serviceman who was objecting to his assignment to the Persian Gulf. We decided to separate the two cases.

With that decision made, our legal team at the CCR began to work. Michael became the lead attorney on *Ange*, and I took *Dellums*. Beth Stephens, an excellent writer and editor, would be responsible, along with Jose Morin, for developing the facts and for writing sections of the brief, particularly in the *Ange* case. Peter Weiss, one of the founders of the CRR who had litigated prior war powers cases with Michael, gave us invaluable advice, and Franklin Siegal, an experienced attorney who had recently joined the Center, helped pull together the myriad statements we would need.

Beth met with Ange in Washington on November 5. Arranging a meeting had not been easy, but we felt we had to explain the legal situation to him in depth and get his consent to go ahead in person. Beth was impressed with Ange. He seemed very serious, "clean-cut," and genuinely interested in the issues of presidential and congressional powers and the War Powers Resolution. Beth said Ange had diligently worked within the military system in raising his medical claim before he contemplated court action. And, Beth felt, Ange believed in the constitutional issues in a real way. "He's not a flake," she told us. "This guy isn't going to change his mind halfway."

Ange was also favorably impressed with Beth. He was generally cynical about lawyers; most of the lawyers he had run into took cases either for money or for publicity, and he doubted their sincerity. In contrast, he thought Beth was professional, not self-promoting, and sincere. "Beth never once was condescending to me or Mike," Brooks would later recall. "She was concerned for Mike and his safety, and we felt she really cared about the person behind the case." That Beth was constantly available and would accept collect calls at two or three in the morning helped establish a personal rapport that made the couple comfortable with the CCR.

But Brooks and Ange had also found out more about the CCR and began to realize that it was a much more leftist group than they originally had thought. They had basic political differences with many of the CCR's positions and worried about being represented by "radical" lawyers. Still, Ange was impressed with the fact that even the CCR cases he disagreed with were serious endeavors, not just publicity stunts. Brooks went to the law library and actually read some of the court's decisions in other cases we had brought against intervention abroad. Even when the CCR lost, the couple decided, the organization and its lawyers had integrity. They would stick with us.

The next week, Beth, Jose, and Michael stayed late at night working on a complaint and motion for a temporary restraining order enjoining the military from sending Ange to the Persian Gulf. Beth was very tense; Ange's departure for the Gulf was imminent, and the case had to be filed before he was sent. In an effort to preserve some sanity and get some sleep, she asked Ange to try to find out when his unit was leaving. He called her back. "Beth, it's a military secret," he said, still the obedient soldier. "I can't tell you." Finally, Ange admitted that it would be safe for her to delay filing until the following week.

The complaint in the *Ange* case, titled *Michael Ange v. George Bush*, was difficult to draft, raising a potpourri of issues, including whether Ange's deployment violated Article I of the Constitution, the Fifth Amendment to the Constitution, the War Powers Resolution, and the army's own procedures for evaluating medical fitness to serve abroad. One senior attorney at the CCR came to Beth after reviewing the draft complaint to ask, worriedly, why the medical claim was put in: including it, he thought, suggested that Ange's interest was merely in getting out of the army, not in challenging the constitutionality of President Bush's orders.

To Beth, the answer was clear and showed why Ange had decided to trust her. The CCR represented not only a cause, she said, but an individual. That individual felt strongly about the Constitution and the law, but his primary goal was not to be sent to the Gulf, and we were responsible for finding the most effective argument to help him achieve that goal. Our obligation to Ange meant that, when tensions existed between the individual case and our broad constitutional objectives, those tensions were going to be resolved in favor of the individual claims.

On Friday, November 8, President Bush announced a significant increase in the Persian Gulf deployment, raising the total troop level far above the 230,000 already present. At his press conference, the president divulged the change in mission. The goal of the additional 150,000 troops was to provide "an adequate offensive military option" should that be necessary to achieve the withdrawal of Iraqi forces from

Kuwait.[7] Bush praised Prime Minister Margaret Thatcher's statement that Iraq must get out of Kuwait soon, "or we and our allies will remove him by force."[8] The president was preparing for war.

Less than a week after announcing the new offensive option, the president met with key members of Congress. When Senate Majority Leader George Mitchell and House Speaker Tom Foley raised the issue of Congress' constitutional prerogatives, the president pulled a copy of the Constitution from his suit pocket and admonished them. "I know what the Constitution says," he lectured, "but it also says I am commander-in-chief."[9] Less theatrically, Secretary of State James Baker claimed that the president had the authority to commit troops to combat without congressional approval,[10] pointing to actions in Grenada, Panama, Libya, and Vietnam as supporting his position. A presidential aide was quoted as saying that Congress would "receive the usual phone calls after the bombs start dropping."[11]

Even prior to the president's announcement, eighty-one members of Congress, organized by Dellums, had issued a statement of concern demanding that the administration not undertake any offensive military action without the full deliberation and declaration required by Congress.[12] The November 8 announcement and the ensuing fallout gave us fresh impetus to file our cases immediately. On November 13, Michael, Beth, and Jose took the 6 A.M. Metroliner from New York to Washington to file the *Ange* case and their motion for a restraining order preventing the army from transferring him to the Persian Gulf.

The CCR team navigated through the maze of bureaucratic rules for filing in the District of Columbia District Court—an unbelievable tangle, including strict rules about the proper method for stapling the papers—and drew one of the worst possible judges to hear this case. Royce Lamberth had been appointed to the Federal District Court in Washington by President Reagan in 1987. A graduate of the University of Texas Law School, he had enlisted in the army in 1967 and had served for several years in Vietnam, rising to the rank of captain with the Army JAG. Awarded the Bronze Star and various other medals, he left the army in 1974 to become an assistant U.S. attorney with the Washington, D.C., Civil Division office. In 1978, Lamberth became the chief of the office, a position he still held when he was nominated for judge in 1987, over the objections of Senator Howard Metzenbaum, who was concerned about Lamberth's views on civil rights. Lamberth did not seem at all the kind of judge who was likely to sympathize with a war resister's claims.

Judge Lamberth scheduled a hearing on Ange's motion for a temporary restraining order for that afternoon. As we expected, Lamberth denied us the TRO, yet we were encouraged that he treated the case seriously, agreeing that it raised a difficult legal question and setting an expedited hearing for December 10. The suit, and the widespread media coverage it attracted, had one immediate practical effect: the army decided to review Ange's medical claim. Beth was guardedly optimistic.

The next day, the 1450th National Guard Transportation Unit left for the Persian Gulf. Michael Ange was not shipped out with the unit but was left behind for further medical tests and to allow review of his civilian medical records. After several days of review, the army ordered Ange to report for active duty in the Persian Gulf.

Ange and Brooks were in a quandary over whether he should refuse to go. When they had made the decision to file the suit, they had realized the potential consequences and difficulties that might await them. But now things were heating up. Brooks had started to receive nasty mail; military officials had begun harassing Ange; he was confined to his barracks and intermittently denied access to the phone. During the next few months he would receive fifteen "reports," complaints that could lead to court-martial, from the officers in his company.

Brooks and Ange felt that the harassment could get worse in the Persian Gulf; Brooks feared that her fiancé would be assigned the most difficult and dangerous jobs, those most likely to get him killed or wounded. She wanted him to refuse to go, even though that meant court-martial and jail. But Ange thought his protest should be a legal one and felt that a decision not to go would undermine the validity of his actions. He had always worked within the system, and the court action, as radical as it might seem to other soldiers, was consistent with that philosophy. Civil resistance to his deployment orders was not. The two talked endlessly with each other but told their lawyers they were still undecided.

Ange was no martyr, but neither was he an obedient, docile soldier. If he was to go to the Gulf, he still wanted to protest Bush's actions. His affirmative lawsuit afforded him an opportunity to do just that. Affirmative litigation allowed accommodation to state authority while still challenging the State's law.[13]

If Ange chose civil resistance, his "success" would not be measured by whether he won in court and eventually escaped jail. A resister's success is determined not by the state's response but by the fact of his acts, which express his own personality and leave a record of protest for future generations. Similarly, if Ange was to go to war, he still wanted to leave behind acts of resistance, such as his lawsuit, that recorded his alternative view of the law.

On November 19, Ange drove to the air base where a plane was waiting to take him and other soldiers to the Persian Gulf. Neither we at CCR, the press, nor the military brass knew what his decision would be. In the car, he dictated an emotional statement that Brooks scrawled out on a piece of scrap paper. "To remain within the provision of the law," he wrote, "I have been forced to obey an unconstitutional and unlawful order." The rest of his statement urged lawful and peaceful protest. He urged every member of the armed services to use "whatever lawful means possible to insure that American lives are not wasted in order to support the economic interests of the major oil companies or in support of political feudalism." He added, "I hope and pray that the American people will affirmatively act to stop this intended immoral aggression and return American service people to their home." With that statement, Michael Ange got on the plane to the Gulf.

While Ange was making his decision, we at the CCR had shifted our focus to the *Dellums* case and were hard at work drafting a complaint, a motion for preliminary injunction, and a brief with supporting factual appendices. It was not a complicated case. Our sole legal claim in *Dellums v. Bush* was that President Bush's initiation of an offensive military attack against Iraq without having obtained a declaration of war or other explicit authorization from Congress would violate Article I, Section 8, Clause 11, of the Constitution and deprive plaintiffs—Ron Dellums and fifty-four other members of Congress—of their duty to debate and vote upon whether the United States should initiate a war against Iraq.[14] We asked the court for declaratory and injunctive relief, declaring that the president could not unilaterally launch such an attack and barring him from doing so.

We wanted the brief to show that the case posed a question of supreme importance to the nation, one for the courts to decide. "If the President takes it upon himself to initiate a war without the unequivocal consent of Congress, the victim of Iraqi aggression will be not just Kuwait, but the Constitution of the United States," we wrote. Our argument emphasized the narrowness of the legal case *Dellums* was bringing. We did not question the legality or morality or wisdom of the present deployment of U.S. forces in the Gulf, nor did we ask the court to require the president to seek immediate congressional approval for any use of force—only that he do so before taking the country to war.

We opened our legal memorandum with what we felt were the strongest arguments: those put forward two hundred years ago by James Madison, Alexander Hamilton, and other participants at the Constitutional Convention. The framers were concerned with ensuring that the judgment to initiate war not be made lightly.[15] James Wilson, one of the most important participants at the Philadelphia Convention, explained the rationale for giving Congress the power to initiate war thus:

> This system will not hurry us into war; it is calculated to guard against it. It will not be in the power of a single man, or a single body of men, to involve us in such distress; for the important power of declaring war is vested in the legislature at large: this declaration must be made with the concurrence of the House of Representatives: from this circumstance we may draw a certain conclusion that nothing but our national interest can draw us into a war.[16]

We believed that this unambiguous constitutional mandate giving the question of war and peace to the legislature was intended to ensure congressional debate and authorization prior to entry into war, except in case of sudden attack. The framers were quite clear: they did not assign the president the power to start a war and then give Congress power to withhold funds once the fighting had begun. They did not suggest that the president could launch a war and then, at some unspecified later date, face a congressional override. They certainly did not give the president authority to initiate a war without congressional authorization.[17]

Once the bullets are flying, once soldiers have been killed, patriotic appeals to the public to close ranks against the enemy can make it extremely difficult to "chain the dogs of war." The framers believed that war was an issue of such gravity and consequence that, as Hamilton wrote, "it is the duty of the President to preserve the peace till war is declared [by Congress]"[18] and to make sure that the question is fully and openly debated before hostilities are initiated.

By focusing on the framers of the Constitution, we hoped to push the administration hawks into a corner that would at least be politically awkward for them and point up as well the contradictions in their legal reasoning. Both the Reagan and the Bush administrations had long taken the position that the courts should strictly apply the original intent of the Constitution's framers and deny any expansion of rights beyond those explicitly recognized in the eighteenth century. However, when confronted with the framers' original intention in the matter of giving Congress the power to initiate hostilities, Reagan and Bush maintained an embarrassed silence. Secretary of State Baker avoided the framers' intent altogether in contending that the president did not need congressional authorization to go to war with Iraq and insisted instead that the president could ignore congressional approval simply "because [presidents have done it this way] going all the way back, I think, to World War II."[19] One might think that the interpretation of our Constitution for the more than 150 years before World War II would be relevant to an administration that held such a fundamentalist view of the authority of the original scriptures and prophets. But apparently the theory of the framers' original intent was to be discarded if it yielded the wrong results.

Meanwhile, even as we were drafting our legal memorandum, the president was seeking authorization for military action from all fifteen members of the U.N. Security Council. His secretary of state embarked on a trip around the world in which he met with high-level officials of Bahrain, Kuwait, Saudi Arabia, Egypt, China, Turkey, the Soviet Union, Great Britain, France, Canada, and others. If the president had the time to seek U.N. approval, what plausible reason could he have for not seeking the required constitutional approval of Congress?

A military offensive designed to drive Iraq out of Kuwait must surely be considered "war." Bush, we said, was not embarking on a relatively minor and short military action like the invasion of Grenada, nor was there any element of surprise or emergency that might justify the president's failure to obtain congressional approval. While we at the CCR believed that other, shorter interventions should also require congressional consent and, in fact, had sued the president over Grenada, the Persian Gulf action was a military action of a totally different magnitude. Whatever the authority of the president to initiate uses of force short of war, ordering nearly half a million American soldiers to attack an Iraqi army of at least that size had to be considered a war for constitutional purposes.

We also felt it important to address the political argument that requiring the president to seek congressional authorization would unduly constrain his options against Saddam Hussein. I could see that if Congress refused to authorize the use of military force, the military option would at least temporarily vanish, leaving the president to rely on diplomatic, political, and economic measures. But if the American people did not support a war with Iraq, our brief argued, then the Constitution, basic common-sense policy, and our tragic experience in Vietnam would dictate that the time was not right for the military option.

Our team then turned to the jurisdictional hurdles we knew were awaiting us at the courthouse door. Most of those obstacles were issues we dealt with constantly at the CCR in our cases against intervention. I felt that I knew them so well as to feel them old acquaintances: "political question," "congressional standing," "equitable discretion." I groaned to myself just thinking about jumping into these battles one more time.

We knew the government's favorite jurisdictional argument would be the political-question doctrine, but here we thought that precedent was on our side. A number of court decisions from the tail end of the Vietnam War[20] had held that, where the opposing armies are of such magnitude and significance as to present no serious question as to whether war exists, the constitutional issue of whether the president must obtain congressional approval does not present a political question. Certainly, an armed conflict between Iraq and U.S. forces would meet that standard. I was happy to think that those Vietnam War cases, while losers, had something to contribute to our ongoing fight and could now be used in support of Dellums's claim.

The District of Columbia Court of Appeals had also been pretty good on congressional standing. Michael's 1985 El Salvador case challenging the president's pocket veto of human rights legislation was very helpful.[21] That case, and another similar decision from 1984,[22] held that congressional plaintiffs could sue when their complaint alleged that the president had violated some specific constitutional procedure requiring congressional action. That was precisely the case here.

That left a last major jurisdictional hurdle, one that was relatively new to us and that posed the most serious problem: ripeness. In constitutional parlance, a dispute is not "ripe" when the threatened injury to the plaintiffs is not real and immediate but speculative.[23] Here the government would argue that war was not sufficiently imminent or certain and that thus the *Dellums* case was not ripe for decision. It would suggest that we wait until after the president had definitely decided to go to war without congressional approval, at that point, there would be an injury the courts could evaluate. But the time between the president's public announcement of a decision to attack Iraq and the actual attack was likely to be extremely short. And, once any attack has been decided upon—that is, as soon as it becomes "ripe"—the issue of whether Congress must give prior consent is likely to be moot, since U.S. armed forces will be in combat before plaintiffs can get into court. It seemed to us that the question of whether the Constitution mandates prior consent is never, in a technical sense, ripe; it is either unripe or overripe.

In a practical sense, we knew this case was as ripe as any could be. There were 400,000 U.S. troops in the Gulf to develop an "offensive" military option. The U.N. would shortly authorize the use of force if Iraq did not withdraw from Kuwait, and the president was emphasizing the urgency of the situation. How much more of a realistic threat did we need?

We worked around the clock the weekend of the 17th and 18th and Monday the 19th to prepare everything we needed. Beth and Jose were faxing new drafts of the brief so fast to my office that it was hard to tell which version was the latest. At least once a day Peter Weiss, Beth, Michael, Jose, and I would get on a conference call to discuss or argue about a paragraph we had written, trying to perfect our argument. In one conversation Peter quipped that, once the bullets start flying the battle cry is "rally 'round the flag," not "rally 'round the Constitution." We immediately wrote it into the brief. By the end, we were sick of looking at the same pages over and over again: our drive for perfection was in conflict with our desire to be done.

We had agreed with Dellums that we would file the case on Tuesday the twentieth, and his office was rounding up members of Congress to join the suit and sending out press releases. It wasn't easy. Even many members of Congress who sympathized with Dellums thought a suit would be "too far out in front." Some didn't want publicity, others wanted to stay within Congress and not go outside the institution to the courts; several thought a court action would simply be an ineffective "gesture." Dellums and his staff emphasized to other members that they were not simply gesturing or engaging in political theater, they thought they could win. But, win or lose, they were sure the lawsuit would shake people up and provide an opportunity to educate the public. The lawsuit would be controversial, but controversy allowed Dellums to be educative. Ron Dellums had always viewed his role as Congressman as involving more than drafting and voting on legislation, he saw himself as part of the educative process. "I told them even if we don't win in court, maybe we'll win in the courtrooms and living rooms of America, where this case will eventually be tried."

Dellums's basic attitude was that we have to make our constitutional system work for us; we can't accept that the system will not work. As a young man, he had been profoundly influenced by Martin Luther King's statement that "the most revolutionary act that our people can engage in is to assert the full measure of our citizenship." Dellums tells people to say to themselves, "I am a citizen and I will be dealt with." He followed that philosophy through many a lonely and frustrating year in Congress, when many members ignored him as a pinko-radical, easily dismissed.

Now he and his staff were asking members of Congress to assert their rights and to demand to be dealt with. "I emphasized the process point to other Democrats," Dellums recalls. The Constitution grants Congress the right and duty to decide on whether to go to war. Dellums was simply asking other members of Congress to go to court to assert that right, to demand that Bush follow the constitutional process. Success for Dellums inhered in adopting the attitude of asserting one's rights, of demanding to be dealt with, and of refusing to accept that the system would not work. That sense of self, not victory or defeat, gave one a sense of power.

By Monday, Dellums had succeeded in getting forty-five representatives to sign on to the lawsuit. We were ready to file.

Early on Tuesday morning, Michael and I flew to Washington, with Michael lugging a heavy lawyer's suitcase filled with court papers. We went to Dellums's office and were met there by three of his aides: Bob Brauer, George Withers, and the irrepressible Max Miller. Max, an old Brooklyn Dodger fan, was a veteran of the U.S. army and had served in Korea before becoming Dellums's press secretary. He believed in three things: God, the Bill of Rights (with the possible exception of the Second

Amendment), and baseball. That morning, Max regaled us with political commentary interspersed with baseball stories as we waited, anxious and overexcited, sipping coffee and trying to appear calm.

Dellums's office was a beehive of activity. A *New York Times* photographer who proudly proclaimed that he'd taken a famous picture of President Kennedy arrived to take ours. After the photo session, Michael and I went into Dellums's office and traded stories about everything but the case. The tension was extreme.

At 9:45, we straightened our ties, left the office, and went to the courthouse to file our case. Three plaintiffs from Congress accompanied us: Dellums, Don Edwards, also of California, and Marcy Kaptur, of Ohio. We arrived at the courthouse, where Michael had mastered the torturous and picayune rules for filing. Every staple was in its proper place, holes punched at the right intervals, documents in order. We waited tensely for our judge to be selected.

Probably the one key page in the massive pile of documents we had so carefully collated, stapled, hole-punched, and filed was the cover sheet to the complaint and summons. On that sheet was a box for attorneys to check whether the case was related to any other currently pending case. Michael and I had agonized over whether we should check that box, since CCR's *Ange* and *Dellums* cases were closely linked. If we did, though, then the case would be automatically assigned to Judge Lamberth, who was hearing *Ange*. If we chose not to check the box and drew a more sympathetic judge, we risked having the government claim that the *Dellums* case was related to the *Ange* case, in that case, we would probably get bounced back to Lamberth anyway. Michael and I decided to take a gamble and leave the box blank, hoping that we'd draw a better judge than Lamberth.

Our gamble worked. A few minutes after ten, Judge Harold Greene's name was picked from among the judges of the D.C. District Court to preside over *Dellums v. Bush*. We were elated. Greene was considered an excellent judge—smart, fair, and in control of the courtroom. Appointed to the federal bench in 1978 by President Carter, by 1983 Greene had established himself, according to *American Lawyer* magazine, as the best district judge in the D.C. Circuit. The son of a German-Jewish jeweler, Greene had escaped from the Nazis with his family in 1939 and come to the United States. After the war and his service in Army Intelligence, Greene attended law school and joined the Justice Department. His most lasting contribution there was his role in drafting the Civil Rights Act of 1964 and the Voting Rights Act of 1965. A former clerk told us that Greene, while liberal in domestic affairs, was an admirer of former Senator Henry "Scoop" Jackson's hawkish views on foreign policy.

A month after his appointment to the federal bench, Greene was assigned his first, and probably most important, case, *United States v. AT&T*. For the next six years, Greene presided over litigation that led in the end to the breakup of the AT&T's monopoly over the telephone industry. He masterfully handled the complex case, which some antitrust experts thought was too difficult for any single court, rising to the challenge and dominating the courtroom. We felt that Greene's assignment to our case boded well: he was independent, not afraid to take on the government, and undaunted by a big political case.

At exactly 10:29, we got into formation, and Dellums, Edwards, and Kaptur, flanked by Michael and me, began what felt like a choreographed procession down the long, dark courtroom corridor. As we walked out the door, I was startled by the glare of more than twenty-five television cameras and the buzz of more than a hundred reporters waiting for us.

Dellums could always be counted on for an elegant, quotable public statement in a pinch. He stepped in front of the dozens of microphones strapped together at a makeshift podium and introduced the lawsuit, eloquently explained its basic purpose, and turned the platform over to me. I stepped forward and froze. I said a few fumbling words and flashed on *The Honeymooners* episode in which the bus driver Ralph Kramden gets his big chance on television. When asked, "What work do you do?," Ralph falls apart, sputtering, "I bribe the dust!"

I steadied myself, feeling quite the dust briber myself, and turned the mike over to Michael, who rescued my inarticulate effort and made a cogent explanation of our case. Don Edwards and Marcy Kaptur then spoke. Edwards, seventy-five, a very articulate, distinguished Democratic representative in his fourteenth term, a former FBI agent, and a leader of the California Young Republicans, had been transformed by the McCarthy witch hunts and had become a staunch defender of the Constitution, earning the enmity of J. Edgar Hoover and becoming known as a voice for civil and constitutional rights.

Edwards was eloquent, but the real surprise was Congresswoman Marcy Kaptur. Max Miller at Dellums's office had tried hard to get Kaptur to attend. She was a forty-three-year-old moderate Democrat from

Toledo, Ohio, whose parents were both auto workers. Kaptur was the first family member to attend college and had worked fifteen years as a city and regional planner before winning an upset victory in her bid for a seat in Congress in 1982. She presented a very different image from that of the radical Dellums. In a very low-key, calm manner, Kaptur read a prepared statement full of conviction. "As a member of the Vietnam generation," she said, "when I was privileged to be sworn in as a member of Congress I promised myself I would never be a part of any undeclared war. I join this suit on behalf of every mother, of every wife, of every husband, and father, and any relative who has a loved one serving our country faithfully in the Middle East. They and you have a right to a Congress that does not shrink from its responsibilities."[24]

After Kaptur finished, Dellums asked for questions, and the reporters went wild. As a law professor used to the orderly decorum of a constitutional law classroom, I was taken aback by the spectacle of reporters cutting one another off, yelling questions from various corners of the crowd, and generally being as obnoxious as possible. Out of the chaos, two basic questions emerged. One was whether our lawsuit was helping Saddam Hussein by making it more difficult for the president to use the war threat as a bluff. Weren't we inconveniencing the president, even giving aid and comfort to the enemy? We were prepared for this, and the members of Congress all answered that the U.S. government must operate under law despite the law's inconveniences. "The Constitution," said Dellums dryly, "is designed to inconvenience one person from taking us to war."[25]

The second theme of the questioning was summed up by a reporter who asked bluntly, "What makes you think you have a snowball's chance in hell [of winning the lawsuit]?" Edwards responded by arguing the constitutional case and praising our team as "the best lawyers in the country."[26] It was flattering, but the response that meant the most to me came from Ron Dellums. His words were inspirational and reaffirmed for me why I was standing there, in front of that unruly crowd. "That's an incredibly cynical question," Dellums said firmly, "and cynics don't change the world. Those of us standing here are idealistic enough and optimistic enough to believe that we have a responsibility to try to act. If we simply said we don't have any chance, then we would not act."[27]

On the plane ride back to Pittsburgh, Dellums's words stuck in my head and made me briefly reflect more deeply on the meaning of our

Persian Gulf cases. Yes, it was true that I worried about my performance, and of course we all worried about winning. But winning wasn't
everything. I began to think about the long tradition that—win or
lose—this case belonged to.

Every time Beth and I shared a joke about "ripeness," every time
Michael used a precedent from Vietnam-era litigation, every time someone like Ange turned to other lost courtroom causes to justify his own
resistance, I could see the practical impact of decades of "losing" litigation. Obviously the CCR's work on war powers and the constitutionality of intervention abroad was the most immediately relevant: our work
on these previous cases formed the body of knowledge that we drew
on, again and again. But, in significant ways, I also saw how the Vietnam War had shaped the environment, both legal and political, in
which we were now bringing this case.

Vietnam represented the first time in American history that a radical movement had made use of litigation to mount a sustained challenge to American foreign policy. Antiwar protest widened the forums
for struggle against U.S. military intervention abroad to include the judiciary. But the lawsuits brought by citizens, soldiers, reservists, state
governments, and members of Congress against the Vietnam War had
all lost: the courts had refused to interfere with the political branch's
handling (or mishandling) of the Indochina conflict. That failure should
have led Ange and Dellums to avoid the courthouse.

Yet the Vietnam litigation seems to have had the opposite effect.
Ron Dellums was spiritually, legally, and politically following in the
footsteps of Parren J. Mitchell, a black congressman from Baltimore
who had, along with twelve other members of Congress, including a
young Ron Dellums, filed suit in 1972 to end the Vietnam War. The D.C.
Circuit Court of Appeals had held that Mitchell had standing to sue,
that the question of whether Congress had to authorize the war was not
a political question, that the Constitution requires that Congress ap-
prove warfare, and that, in the absence of approval, the United States
must withdraw. As with all the Vietnam litigation, the court refused to
issue an injunction, in this case holding that Nixon was publicly committed to withdrawal and that whether he was doing it rapidly enough
was a political question that the courts could not decide. Nonetheless,
Mitchell's failure in court resulted in a precedent that was to prove very
helpful for Dellums in his battle.

And Michael Ange also had ancestors lurking in the Vietnam era. While the early cases filed by soldiers seeking to avoid the war on constitutional grounds were summarily dismissed, by the 1970s soldiers were beginning to fare somewhat better. In the summer of 1970, Malcolm A. Berk and Salvador Orlando, both members of the armed services, sought federal court injunctions barring their assignment to Vietnam. While both lost their cases, the Second Circuit Court of Appeals did hold that a soldier had standing to challenge the constitutionality of a war in which he was being sent to fight.

But the more important consequence of Vietnam-era and other radical losing litigation, I began to see, went far beyond the technical lesson, or the ways we could use legal precedent. When Dellum chastised the reporters for their cynicism, it reawakened in me the sense that our goal, in its broadest sense, was not to win a court case, or even to stop this particular war. Our long-term goal was the creation of a community based on shared values and the articulation of a tradition of resistance. It was the political, moral, and even spiritual dimensions of this tradition that I wanted to understand.

If we focused on winning and losing, it was easy to despair. The repeated failure of the justice system to enforce legal restraints on presidents' misconduct of foreign policy made cynicism the logical response. Why should anyone break his or her head one more time against the brick wall of the courts? But logic is not often the engine of change; as Oliver Wendell Holmes once said, "The life of the law has not been logic." Rosa Parks's decision not to move from her seat on the bus in Birmingham, Alabama, was not a logical act. Neither was Ron Dellums's decision to file this lawsuit: it was simply a result of his belief that "someone needs to do something."

A community that supports individual acts like these, and locates them inside a collective set of values, is one based not on logic but primarily on faith. That faith, whether or not it is explicitly religious, has allowed cultures as different as the Jewish, the African American, and the Serbian to survive catastrophic defeats that should turn any modern, rationalistic person into a cynic. It is concerned less with short-term victory than with creating a community of resistance and memory. And it was precisely that type of faith, expressed in the legacy of other antiwar legal battles, that motivated Ron Dellums and Michael Ange, made them feel part of a meaningful tradition, and in turn inspired others to challenge an unconstitutional war.

I realized that I didn't expect the attitude of the federal courts toward restraining the president in foreign policy to change markedly in my lifetime. But that didn't have to change my determination to fight. What could change was the political and moral environment of our country— if we nourished and helped a community of resistance to grow.

To Ron Dellums, his interchange with that reporter that day also had a profound impact. "I never forgot that question," he later recalled. "I ran into that reporter a few years later, and she was rather apologetic about her question to me. I told her you can't operate from a position of cynicism. My job is to believe it is possible to win." Dellums defines victory as staying in the fight—as not allowing cynicism to defeat us. Or, as Dellums's aide Bob Brauer put it, "Often times in history, people will confront similar choices to those we faced in that fall of 1990. Our example might help them to decide to do what we did."

It would be a while, however, before I could consider these questions more deeply. Every day, our country was moving closer to war, and our cases were barreling ahead.

I got home from filing our brief in Washington desperate for rest. The past few days had been brutal, and all I wanted to do was take my son for a stroller ride and get a good night's sleep.

But as I rolled my toddler son to the park, I didn't know that the Justice Department had immediately filed a motion to declare the *Dellums* case related to *Ange* and transfer it to Judge Lamberth. Judge Greene's response was faxed to the CCR, and I discovered, when I called my office later that afternoon to get my messages, that Greene was requiring that we fax our response to the court by noon the next day. My mood sank as I realized that, tired as I was, I had to go back to work. I remembered Victor Rabinowitz, my good friend and former boss at the law firm of Rabinowitz, Boudin, Standard, Krinsky, and Lieberman, saying that, in his opinion, the most recent invention that had improved the practice of law was the telephone, and he wasn't even sure about that. I agreed: fax machines and computers merely increase the amount of work to be done in a shorter period of time. This fax from Judge Greene was a perfect example.

Despite the hectic timetable, Michael, Beth, Jose, and I agreed that our response to the motion to consolidate the cases before Lamberth was probably the most important document we would file in the case. If *Dellums v. Bush* went to Lamberth, our chances of getting anywhere were dismal.

I worked until 5:30 the next morning, drafting an argument explaining why the cases should not be considered related. After editing and revisions by Michael and Beth, we faxed the document to Greene's chambers. Later that same day, we got surprising news. Greene had decided that the *Dellums* and *Ange* cases were not related and that he would keep the *Dellums* case. Greene ordered the government to respond to our motion for a preliminary injunction by the next Monday and gave us a court date of December 4. Greene's schedule meant that the Justice Department would have to work through the Thanksgiving holiday to draft its response, a prospect that I have to admit pleased me.

The news energized Dellums's office and the CCR lawyers: Max Miller enthusiastically went back to work rounding up more members of Congress to support our case (eventually, fifty-four representatives and one senator signed on). Greene obviously was serious about the case; we had a chance.

I felt that an amicus brief from law professors supporting our case could be helpful. I called Michael Glennon, a professor at the University of California, and Professor Harold Koh, of Yale—both excellent legal minds—to see whether either was interested in organizing such a brief. Koh said he'd try.

It was a very difficult task. Koh quickly drafted a basic statement addressing two key issues: whether the president could go to war unilaterally without congressional approval and whether the case presented a nonjusticiable issue. But getting top law professors to sign on was the hard part. Several professors said they would sign, but only if other, more conservative professors did. Another told Koh that he would sign, but only if the signees were limited to professors at the most prestigious universities.

By the end of the Thanksgiving weekend, after considerable tinkering, cajoling, politicking, and persuading, Koh had enlisted the support of a politically and jurisprudentially diverse group of eleven well-known constitutional law professors from elite universities. They included conservative scholars such as Philip B. Kurland, of the University of Chicago, and Erwin Griswold, a former dean at Harvard Law School and solicitor general under President Richard Nixon. Several other scholars identified with the philosophy of judicial restraint also signed on: John Hart Ely, a former dean at Stanford Law School, and Gerald Gunther, another Stanford professor, author of the most widely used constitutional law text in the country. The other signees, along with Koh, were Professor Louis Henkin of Columbia, probably the most prominent expert on foreign policy and law in the country; Harvard's Lawrence Tribe; Abram Chayes, of Harvard, formerly President Kennedy's State Department legal adviser; Bruce Ackerman, of Yale; William Van Alstyne, of Duke Law School; and Lori Fisler Damrosch, of Columbia.

The filing of their amicus brief, along with a second amicus prepared by Michael Glennon and Kate Martin for the American Civil Liberties Union, created quite a stir and was reported extensively in the press. Apparently the Justice Department was concerned enough that it tried to organize conservative law professors to file an opposing amicus brief, but the effort failed, probably because of a dearth of support for the government's position, even among conservative scholars.

But, even as the legal maneuvers around our case continued—with all of our team still seriously lacking sleep—the political situation in the Gulf was rapidly evolving. When we first filed, the administration's policy had been in serious trouble. President Bush, meeting in Paris with President Mikhail Gorbachev of the Soviet Union, had failed to gain Soviet agreement on a U.N. resolution authorizing the use of force to drive Iraq out of Kuwait. At home, the public was wary, with a *Times*/CBS poll reporting that almost half of the American people believed that the administration was too quick to get American military forces involved in the Gulf. Bush's approval rating for his policy toward Iraq had dropped from 75 percent to 50 percent. The Senate Armed Services Committee had opened hearings on the Persian Gulf crisis, and its hawkish chairman, Senator Sam Nunn, had questioned the need to rush into combat with Iraq, as a parade of high-level witnesses from the defense establishment expressed doubts about a U.S. military attack.

Against this background, our lawsuit added to the administration's growing problems. The press coverage was far flung and generally sympathetic. The president's top advisers, his press secretary, Marlin Fitzwater, and Attorney General Richard Thornburgh were forced to respond publicly to the case. Dellums's demand "to be dealt with" was getting a public hearing. But the situation was evolving rapidly and would take several dramatic turns before we argued our case in Judge Greene's courtroom.

On Thursday, November 29, the United Nations Security Council voted 12–2, with China abstaining, to authorize the United States and its allies to use "all necessary means," a euphemism for force, to expel

Iraq from Kuwait. It was a triumph for Bush. As Thomas Friedman, of the *New York Times*, reported, he had lined up other nations behind the resolution by a deft combination of arguments, rewards, and a few veiled threats.[28]

Bush and his secretary of state must have hoped that the U.N. show of support would in turn sway Congress. But getting Soviet approval proved much easier than getting congressional approval: after all, the Soviets were backing only the deployment of U.S. troops. Their own soldiers were not being sent, since the Soviet executive admitted that it would need legislative approval before committing troops to battle. This was an ironic twist: the Soviets had appropriated the fundamental principle of separation of powers that the framers of our Constitution believed vital to a republic at the very instant that a U.S. president was preparing to abandon it.

In Baghdad, a defiant Iraqi president proclaimed that his nation was ready for war. In Washington, continuing congressional opposition made the president decide against calling a special session of Congress to vote on authorization for U.S. action. But on Friday, November 30, President Bush dropped a diplomatic bombshell. At a news conference, Bush said that he had invited Iraq's foreign minister to Washington, and offered to send Secretary of State Baker to Baghdad "to reach a peaceful solution" to the Persian Gulf crisis.

This flurry of diplomatic activity had important consequences for our legal argument. We knew that one key issue in our case was whether the lawsuit was ripe. The Security Council resolution, with its forty-seven-day countdown, had helped us with this, showing how perilously close war was. It had the effect, according to the *New York Times*, of "igniting a fuse under the Persian Gulf crisis."[29] That metaphor fit right into the legal definition of ripeness. Unless the court acted quickly, the fuse would burn to the end, igniting a war.

But now Bush's diplomatic overture to Baghdad cut the other way. It reintroduced uncertainty, speculation, a way out of war. While Congressman Dellums and other observers saw the diplomatic maneuverings as mostly show, nonetheless, a judge would be reluctant to issue an injunction while diplomatic efforts were under way. What if a court's injunction stiffened Hussein's resolve and led to the breakdown of negotiations? Any judge deciding the case would shoulder a heavy burden.

At approximately 3:15 on the afternoon of December 4, 1990, Michael, Beth, Jose, Jim Klimaski (our local counsel in Washington), and

I walked into the federal courthouse in Washington, D.C. By the time we arrived, the courtroom was packed with reporters, and a line had formed outside. We settled into our places, "close shaves and briefcases . . . on one side, the facial hair and backpacks on the other," as the *New York Times* columnist Anna Quindlen described the scene.[30] Four members of Congress—Dellums, Tom Foglietta, James Moody, and Marcy Kaptur—joined us at the counsel table, providing a much-needed veneer of respectability. Dellums cut through our tension with a story about a letter he'd just got from Texas calling him a coward for his position opposing the Gulf War and for filing the lawsuit. The Texan was shocked when his phone rang and Dellums greeted him personally. After almost an hour of conversation, the man agreed that Dellums was no coward and, moreover, that his position was right. "But," the man complained, "must you protest so publicly!" We all laughed, but in a sense the Texan was on to something. By so publicly and aggressively protesting, instead of taking a discreet, insider approach, Dellums had chosen struggle over respectability. It was this contribution to a culture of resistance, and not his substantive views, that made the Texan object to Dellums.

Judge Greene's arrival in the courtroom cut short our laughter, and I approached the lectern to begin the argument.

Our strategy was to hammer away at the merits, to focus on which branch had the power to place the country at war. The government's brief focused almost exclusively on the jurisdictional arguments in the case—standing, ripeness, political question—and we wanted to draw attention away from those issues and to a dialogue on the fundamental question of who can send us to war.

We did this for two reasons. The first was legal; our strongest arguments were on the merits, while our weakest were jurisdictional. If we could focus the judge's attention on the bankruptcy of the president's constitutional argument, the court might want to reach the merits and dispose of the jurisdictional arguments in our favor. The second reason was political. The political importance of the case lay in its contribution to the national debate over whether to go to war against Iraq. If the case focused on standing or ripeness doctrine, rather obscure issues for most nonlawyers, it would lose most of its political significance.

I started with the lines Michael had written for me just an hour before. "Your honor," I said, "the question before this court is straightforward: can the president initiate a war against Iraq for the purpose of driving it from Kuwait without first obtaining the prior authorization of Congress? The president says he can; the Constitution says he cannot."

After responding to some questions by Judge Greene on issues of ripeness, I returned to the constitutional issues, seeking to goad the Justice Department by being as provocative as a mild-mannered law professor could be. "The government's argument," I summarized mockingly, "if accepted by the Court, would in essence read Article I, Section 8, the war powers clause, out of the Constitution. If the clause does not apply in this case, I would like the defendant to tell me in what case it applies."

The Justice Department and the judge bit at this bait. Assistant Attorney General Stuart Gerson began his side's argument by responding to my constitutional goading, but he had barely started when Greene interrupted him: "Are you suggesting that the war powers clause at Article I, Section 8, Clause 11, means nothing? When does it apply?" Gerson argued that the court could not define a war. Greene responded by picking up our line of argument that if a march into Iraq isn't war, what is it? Gerson deftly sidestepped the question by saying that the administration hadn't definitively decided to attack Iraq.

Greene persisted. "What I am interested in finding out," he said calmly "is whether a clause in the Constitution, not some blank space in the Constitution or some interpretation but an actual clause in the Constitution, can be enforced, or is it simply up to the president either to ignore it or abide by it?"

After some farfetched conjecture about Congress's right to declare war in the event a president refused to, Gerson wound up his argument by describing the contexts in which a court could legitimately decide whether or not there is a war. "For example," he began, "when the case involves whether an insurance payment ought to be made, whether a policy kicks in . . ." Greene, somewhat incredulous, stopped him. "Isn't there historical evidence," asked the judge, "indicating that the reason for this clause was to make certain that one person does not get the country involved in a war? They were not talking about insurance payments; they were talking about getting the country involved in war."

At our table, there was controlled but genuine optimism. We were following the judge's comments intently, and so far our strategy seemed to be working. I rose to respond.

With only a hint of sarcasm showing, I summarized the government's argument that the purpose of the declare-war clause was: "One, to tell us whether there was a legal status of war after the president initiates warfare so that insurance companies could pay claims and merchants would know who to trade with; and two, in case we have a pacifist president who doesn't want to go to war, don't worry, Congress can declare it for him." Greene quickly and ominously proffered a third purpose: to permit the political branches to struggle over when there should be a war.

Overall, we considered the hearing before Judge Greene a success. Max Miller's admittedly nonscientific poll of the journalists in the room concluded that seventeen of eighteen thought we had won. And it was clear that our attempt to use the lawsuit to open public debate on the war was succeeding: there were stories on all the major networks and in the newspapers. We had forced the Justice Department to articulate its constitutional argument for executive power, and the *New York Times* and other newspapers had attacked "extreme" presidential claims that interpreted the war clause as "a one-way, pro-war clause."[31]

A week later, Michael argued the *Ange* case before Judge Lamberth. We expected a hostile court, yet Lamberth was surprisingly friendly and even seemed sympathetic to Michael's arguments as he made them. But this friendliness turned into comradeship when it was the turn of the Justice Department attorney. I whispered to Michael that the judge and the government lawyer were discussing these issues as if they were colleagues at the Justice Department. It was amazing: Lamberth fed the government's attorney leading questions, suggested answers, and generally acted as an advocate for the president's position. We left that courtroom gloomy about *Ange*'s fate. For Dorothy Brooks, who had come up from North Carolina to attend the argument, the judge's comradely chat with the government's attorney was an eye-opener about her future profession. "It's not the judicial neutrality you learn about in law school," she remarked after leaving the courtroom.

On December 14, Judges Greene and Lamberth both announced their decisions. As we'd expected, Lamberth dismissed Ange's case on the broad grounds that war-powers issues present a nonjusticiable political question.[32] Judge Greene's decision was more nuanced.[33] Greene wove his way through a thicket of complex jurisdictional obstacles like a savvy basketball point guard dribbling a ball downcourt. Until the very end of his opinion, it read as if we would win—but after we had pushed the Sisyphean rock up the hill, and when at last our goal was in sight, Greene utilized the ripeness doctrine to send the rock tumbling down upon us.

Greene's support for our constitutional arguments was hopeful. He decisively rejected the Justice Department's political question defense, stating:

> If the Executive had the sole power to determine that any particular offensive military operation, no matter how vast, does not constitute "war-making" but only an "offensive military attack," the congressional power to declare war will be at the mercy of a semantic decision by the Executive. Such an interpretation would evade the plain language of the Constitution, and it cannot stand.[34]

He agreed with us that a U.S. assault on Iraq would be war, within the meaning of Article I, Section 8, Clause 11, and announced that "the court is not prepared to read out of the Constitution the clause granting to the Congress, and to it alone, the authority to declare war." He went on to hold that our plaintiffs had standing and that the court had the equitable power to grant relief and concluded that, in principle, a court could issue an injunction at the request of members of Congress to prevent the conduct of a war that was about to be launched without congressional authorization.

And then it all fell apart. The court concluded that the plaintiffs were not entitled to injunctive relief because the controversy was not ripe. Greene held that the president was not so clearly committed to military action against Iraq as to make the case ripe for injunctive relief. More important, Greene said that the judicial branch should not decide issues affecting the allocation of power between the president and Congress if only a minority of Congress seeks relief. Only where a majority of Congress has disapproved a president's claim to use force does a ripe controversy exist, for only then, Greene held, are the president and Congress locked in such deadlocked conflict that a court should intervene.

But at least Greene did not dismiss our case; he only denied our motion for a preliminary injunction. He seemed to invite congressional action disapproving Bush's move to war and stated that, should Congress take such action, we could come back to court.

Both sides claimed victory: on *Nightline*, Dellums praised Judge Greene's rejection of the Justice Department's sweeping war powers claims.[35] Beth Stephens termed the decision a "Pyhrric victory" for the executive branch.[36] Harold Koh, the author of the professors' amicus brief, termed Greene's decision an unappealable declaratory judgment against the government. Even in courtroom defeat, our team was trying to keep public attention on the constitutional issues, once again hoping that a losing case could still have a positive political impact. I struggled to maintain a sense of victory, even as the government crowed that Greene's decision imposed no limit on the president' prerogatives. "The bottom line," said Gerson, "is we won."[37]

And, as a technical, legal matter, Gerson was right. While Gerson probably recognized that we could use some of Greene's dicta to our political advantage, he didn't really think it mattered that much. For him, and for those who share his mainstream, mechanical view of law, the only significance of cases lies in their final legal consequence—who won and who lost. But the history and development of American law has always been about much more than winning or losing. In 1803, Marbury lost *Marbury v. Madison*, and Jefferson technically won.[38] In the process, though, Chief Justice Marshall established certain critical foundations of American constitutional law that in essence went against Jefferson. Much more recently, the Supreme Court's infamous *Korematsu* decision upholding the internment of the Japanese during World War II was a terrible loss for civil rights lawyers. But it also explicitly articulated for the first time the principle that racial and ethnic classifications were to be given strict scrutiny by the judiciary.

Moreover, the consequences of *Dellums* could not be measured in purely legal terms. Our purpose in bringing the lawsuit had been, in large part, to spur political action. From that perspective, Judge Greene had written a masterful decision, probably the best he could have rendered.

Greene had told the president that he couldn't go to war alone. But his decision also took Congress to task for avoiding its responsibility and for contributing to the constitutional crisis through its refusal to vote on Bush's war. In effect, Greene was telling Congress to show some backbone of its own if it wanted him to enjoin the president. The whole decision put political and legal heat on both Congress and the president to act, and the fact that Greene had not dismissed our case meant that, if Congress did show some courage and vote to stop Bush, we could be back in court. We decided not to appeal Greene's decision.

But, as the U.N. deadline drew closer, Bush still would not ask Congress to authorize his war. Would the Greene decision, and all the political efforts resulting from our case, help at all to persuade President Bush to finally seek congressional authorization? While some State Department lawyers have told us that the case did have an impact on Bush's decision to do so, the fact remains that the president to the end maintained his position that such approval was unnecessary. Bush was committed to war even if Congress voted against him. As he later explained, "I wasn't going to let some old goats in Congress tell me whether I could kick Saddam Hussein out of Kuwait."[39]

On January 11, 1996, by a narrow margin, Congress voted to authorize the president's war. By stalling until the last possible moment, Congress had essentially preordained the result; its vote had come too late. The deployment of half a million troops, Bush's public ultimatum to Saddam Hussein, and military plans to carry out his threats made it almost unthinkable for Congress to oppose the president. Congress should have voted in October or November, not in January, when the momentum toward war was virtually irreversible.

The aftermath of a decision always invites rereading and reinterpretation; in the months to come, we reflected on whether the *Dellums* and *Ange* cases had been "successful." Nobody had won, in the sense that one team wins the Superbowl, a defendant is acquitted or convicted after trial, or a politician wins an election. The media couldn't declare a clear winner to the *Dellums* case, juxtaposing headlines like "Judge Finds Bush Can't Go to War Alone" with subtitles, in smaller type, reading "But Says It's Premature to Order President to Get Congressional OK."[40] The *Los Angeles Times* reversed the captions, starting with "U.S. Judge Refuses to Block Bush from Starting a War" and then adding "But He Also Says Only Congress Can Authorize an Attack on Iraq."[41] The *New York Times* noted that, while Greene had rejected the legislators' request for an injunction, "his ruling was also a significant rejection of the Bush administration's position that it need do nothing more than consult with Congress before going to war."[42]

For Ron Dellums, however, the lawsuit was a clear success. He focused on the political climate the case had helped create. "I'm convinced that the main reason Bush eventually came to Congress was because of our lawsuit," Dellums emphatically told me. "The lawsuit brought our struggle front and center, brought the Constitution front and center, and brought the Persian Gulf buildup front and center." Judge Greene's holding that "the Court is not prepared to read Congress' war powers out of the Constitution" gave us momentum to force

Bush to come to Congress. "Everyone felt buoyed by the decision." The congressman's aide Lee Halterman felt that a "sea change" took place in Congress after Greene's opinion was announced. While Dellums had not stopped the war, Bush was forced to come to Congress, and Congress debated and voted on whether to go to war. "For me that was a victory," Dellums claims.

Michael and I publicly maintained that Judge Greene's decision was a victory. Privately, we felt Greene's decision was legally problematic, and we were not confident that the case had had the political impact Dellums attributed to it. I did not object so much to Greene's denial of our claim on ripeness grounds; any injunction he issued would have been quickly reversed by the Court of Appeals. But his decision was weak on the basic constitutional issue.

Greene stated that congressional approval is required to start a war but then added ominously "if Congress desires to become involved." The last phrase was the basis of his determination that, if Congress is silent, then the dispute is not ripe. If Congress was content to let the president go to war without authorization, Greene would not intervene.

What Greene meant by this phrase is ambiguous. He could have been agreeing with us that the president does not have the constitutional authority to go to war but nonetheless holding that a court ought not issue an injunction absent a mandate from a majority of Congress. However, Greene could have been arguing that the Constitution permits the president to act when Congress is silent. This reading of the Constitution rejects the extreme Bush administration position that the president can go to war irrespective of Congress but accepts that the president can go to war where Congress expresses no opinion.

That latter perspective as applied to war powers was very disturbing to Michael and me. In our view, the president has no constitutional authority to introduce troops into combat absent affirmative congressional approval, a point Greene seems to accept elsewhere in his opinion. If Congress is silent, than a sufficient consensus does not exist to go to war. Only where our national interest to go to war is so compelling that a normally slow-moving, dinosaur-like Congress votes affirmatively should our country take the drastic and potentially devastating step of initiating warfare. Congress ought not be able to decide that it need not vote on whether to go to war, any more than it can abdicate its duty to vote on the U.S. budget or on whom should be appointed a federal judge. Congress cannot decide that, because the decision is too politically difficult, the president should make the decision alone. Congress cannot abdicate its responsibility to decide on whether to go to war—despite its twentieth-century predilection to do so.

For these reasons, I was not sure whether Greene's decision really was a victory. But I was beginning to feel somewhat removed from the kind of detailed legal discussions I'd previously loved so much. The bigger questions, for me, were becoming more political and moral ones. What was the real value of our losing cases? What were we contributing to "the river of struggle" with our efforts? And how could we use our defeat on the legal terrain to build a community with a long-term vision of justice?

I returned to teaching; it was a period of reflection, and I kept turning these questions over in my mind. It became clear to me that the long-term effects of the *Dellums* and *Ange* litigation were often imperceptible at the time. One day, a year or so after the *Dellums* case, I got a call from John Hart Ely, a signer of the law professors' amicus brief. A former dean at Stanford Law School, Ely told me that he wanted to start a clinic for litigating war powers and other foreign-policy issues. I asked him why a man of his prestige and legal talent would want to litigate losers. "It's my turn," he said. "Even if it looks like we can't win, I need to do my part." Ely never established his clinic, but the *Dellums* litigation helped motivate Professor Koh to establish a clinic at Yale and to collaborate with Michael and the CCR in litigating important human-rights cases involving Haitian refugees who were seeking asylum in this country.

More than six years after we filed the *Dellums* case, I had just finished teaching my last class in constitutional law for the year, when two of my students came to see me. They were both Japanese and spoke English haltingly. The man pointed to a sheet of paper, eight and a half by eleven inches, with Japanese printing on it, that he held in his hand. "What is it," I asked, totally perplexed. "This page is a page from the largest Japanese newspaper, the *Asahi Shinbun*, of November 15, 1990. Its a report on the *Dellums* and *Ange* cases," he told me. "I was a leader of a Japanese peace group," he continued. "And this article gave us tremendous inspiration. Up to that point, we had believed that there was very little protest against the Persian Gulf buildup. But when we saw that members of Congress and the U.S. military were suing the president, we became bolder. We, too, filed a lawsuit, challenging

Japan's giving $8 billion for bombs, planes, tanks to be used against Iraq. We lost, but since that time peace activists in Japan have filed more lawsuits challenging the Japanese government."

I considered the surprising and unpredictable ways in which movements can grow. Our Persian Gulf cases were built on losing efforts to challenge the constitutionality of the Indochina war and on losing efforts to curtail illegal executive actions in the covert wars of the 1980s. They in turn became part of a long, long narrative that urges soldiers, members of Congress, citizens, law professors, and lawyers to step forward and stop the executive if it is unilaterally making war. Perhaps, in decades to come, such challenges will be treated with the legitimacy accorded constitutional-rights cases today. If so, however, it will not be primarily because of the sagacity and wisdom of the courts. It will be because individuals like Sergeant Ange and Congressman Dellums, emboldened by their identification with history, have spoken out and demanded that the courts act. The *Dellums* case was not a tale of defeat but the story of citizens challenging the breakdown of democracy. The lasting lesson from these cases may be that the heart of a constitutional democracy lies not in the institutions established by the Constitution but in the determined drive for justice of the people.[43]

3

A Tradition of Resistance

Antislavery Litigators and the Fight for Freedom

WITH THE *DELLUMS* CASE FINISHED, I entered a new, more reflective period of my life. The prior decade had been an intense, exciting period of legal and political struggle. For almost a decade, we had fought Reagan and Bush's foreign policies in the courtroom, in Congress, and on the streets. Michael and I counted close to twenty cases the CCR had litigated challenging the United States's interventionist policies.

Our work had taken us beyond the courtroom. We felt ourselves part of a broad movement in solidarity with people in Central America who were seeking social justice and revolutionary change. We spoke at countless meetings and rallies around the country. We testified before Congress. We protested in the streets, joining almost 100,000 people in a 1983 Washington demonstration.

In 1985, I was arrested during a sit-in at the Federal Building in Pittsburgh protesting U.S. aid to the contras and spent a night in the Allegheny County jail, an act that must have caused consternation among some of my respectable law school colleagues. I still vividly recall the testimony at the subsequent trial of the fifty-five protesters with whom I was arrested. One testified in a thick German accent that she had been a little girl in Nazi Germany and had asked her father after the war why he had done nothing against the Nazi genocide. She now had a young son, she said, and she didn't want him to ask her the same question about her complicity in U.S. policies toward Nicaragua when he grew up.

By 1991, I was tired. I also now had a young son who was diagnosed with a serious developmental disability. At the age of forty, I went into temporary semiretirement, needing to spend an enormous amount of time and energy with my two-year-old and wanting to reflect on the past decade of intense legal and political activism.

This semiretirement also reflected how discouraged and frustrated I was with putting tremendous energy and effort into losing cases. I felt tremendous self-doubt, wondering whether I was just a failure, and the political and social environment fueled my doubt. When I began my legal activism with the CCR, it was a time of optimism: the Sandinistas had won in Nicaragua, there was a nearly successful revolution in El Salvador, and strong insurgencies in other countries in Latin America seemed poised to sweep away dictatorships and injustice. Popular revolt was on the rise, or so it seemed. But, by 1991, the insurgencies in Latin America had stalled, the Sandinistas had lost power, Cuba was in crisis, the so-called Socialist world had collapsed, and the United States had just bombed Iraq "back to the stone age," as one U.N. report put it. The international arena looked bleak for progressive change.

I turned to history to find solace: my own personal history and the struggles of others who had had similar experiences. From early childhood, I had identified with the underdog who struggled against overwhelming odds. My litigation history was probably foreshadowed by an irrational switch in allegiance, in 1964, from the then–world champion New York Yankees to the hapless New York Mets. The late 1960s for me were dominated by two movements: the rise of the Mets from perennial losers to world champions and the Vietnamese struggle against a colossal, powerful, and, in my opinion, monstrous U.S. government. When I graduated from New York University in 1972, I foreswore the life of a professional and became a bakery worker, organizing a rank-and-file movement of bakers against both greedy employers and corrupt union officials. My flight from professionalism was temporary; my attraction to underdog struggles turned out to be a permanent character trait.

This predilection stemmed in large part from my Jewish culture. Three thousand years of Jewish history of oppression and resistance, from enslavement in Egypt to the Holocaust, can breed a determination to struggle against great odds, even if victory is not the likely outcome. My maternal grandparents were both idealistic Jewish leftists. In my youth, my grandmother would regale me with romantic stories of attending Jewish socialist meetings in Russia and hiding out from the Czarist police. So I began to study Judaism, particularly the prophetic tradition of the Old Testament. The aspect of the prophetic tradition that appealed to me was not the prophet as a clairvoyant or seer but the prophet as a passionate "advocate or champion, speaking for those who are too weak to plead their own cause."[1]

Reflecting in this way on the prophets made me recognize a deep spiritual connection to the travails of the Jewish people, and to their spirit of resistance. I had never been a religious person, although my grandfather was an Orthodox rabbi, on New York's Lower East Side. I associated all spirituality with organized religion and so for a long time did not pay much attention to my spiritual life.

But I began to view spirituality as encompassing much more than religious doctrine, or a belief in God. My spirituality became located in a faith in human potential, a sense of connection to other people's struggle and history. This stems not from rational study but from a deeply Jewish identification with people's suffering and resistance.

The Jewish tradition and its prophets gave me a metaphor of struggle to substitute for society's emphasis on success: the image of a cascading, turbulent river. But, as I reflected on my own history and my culture, I also turned to my legal ancestors. Poring through American history, I discovered nineteenth-century litigators who, much to my surprise, had faced dilemmas and frustrations similar to my own. The kind of test-case, law-reform litigation the CCR was doing is not a new phenomenon in American history, as most lawyers presume, but dates at least back to the abolitionist movement in the nineteenth century. The abolitionists, the woman suffragists of the post–Civil War era, and the advocates of full equality for the freed slave all relied on test-case litigation. Virtually all these litigators lost in court. Indeed, as one noted historian has commented, "[the] work [of the constitutional-reform litigator] has often been heroic and sometimes successful. Yet, it has failed frequently enough that historians may wonder whether clients might not have sought better weapons in [their] struggles for respect and legitimacy."[2]

That they lost in court, however, does not mean that these litigators were failures. The American obsession with winning and losing has clouded the meaning of these cases. Success for these lawyers and their clients was not synonymous with court victories. Their work often generated substantial public debate on the issue; at times, the losing judicial decision galvanized the political process to remedy the injustice.

As I looked more deeply into history, I uncovered a more spiritual aspect to these cases and to what I was feeling. Spirit resides in history, in the connection between our ancestors' struggles and our own hopes and dreams.[3] My ancestors, these nineteenth-century litigators, created a culture of constitutional struggle by reading their aspirations into the Constitution and by refusing to accept the mainstream interpretation held by the courts, government, and most of society. By resisting and not accepting the mainstream view, these litigators chose struggle over winning, just as Ron Dellums did a century later. By doing so, they helped create a tradition of challenging injustice in courts, of utilizing the courts as a forum for protest. Their "winning" was spiritual in that they had a spiritual impact on future generations.

These litigators I studied were much more than "winners," even when they won cases. Winning is temporal and definite, located in the present. America's obsession with winning is premised on immediacy of result. Struggle, on the other hand, is historical; like a river, it cannot be cordoned off into a neat box, or moment, but occurs over years and involves temporary victories and defeats, ebbs and flows. For me, a spiritual life requires the elevation of struggle over short-term success. The spirit resides in memory, not only in the present; in connectedness to past and future generations, and not just in individual happiness.

Many of the nineteenth-century litigators I studied were deeply religious people. Their litigation was motivated by a "simple undoubting faith" that led them to believe in the righteousness of their beliefs.[4] Their faith bred optimism, the foolish optimism of those who believe they can change history in the face of insurmountable odds. These litigators left two major legacies, apart from their court victories or defeats. First, they brought oppressed groups' constitutional aspirations into the courtroom, fostering what has become a deeply ingrained American belief that the courtroom is an arena of struggle over basic constitutional values. Second, these litigators interpreted the Constitution as granting the natural rights to liberty and equality. This reading of the Constitution as incorporating the aspirations of oppressed groups has "justified continued struggle by groups in the face of (presumably temporary) judicial and political defeats."[5]

These litigators thus contributed to the creation of a uniquely American culture of constitutional faith that constitutes what has been termed our "civic religion."[6] That quasi-religious, spiritual faith, supplementing or even replacing traditional religious reverence, is premised on the belief that the Constitution cannot be read narrowly or textually but rather incorporates our vision of a just society and that the courts are arenas where those aspirations can be articulated and sometimes achieved.

Some progressive scholars and activists question whether bringing the constitutional aspiration of oppressed groups into the courtroom is counterproductive in that it encourages undue faith in lawyers, Constitutionals rights, and the judicial system, and because it tends to channel broad movements into a narrow, confining, legal terrain. Certainly, these dangers and tendencies exist, as some of my own cases attest to. To the extent that the courtroom battles dominate or control the political movement, are overly technical, or are not inextricably tied to a movement, this critique does have validity. But to the extent that these litigators used the law and courts to create a new arena of struggle that drew people into the political movement, and to inspire, motivate, and convince their own generation and future generations to resist and not passively accept injustice, their efforts must be valued.

My work, in a sense, has been a cultural and spiritual byproduct of these litigators' struggles. My legal story thus starts with the antislavery attorneys, whose work represents one of the earliest American efforts to utilize the courts to carry out major political and legal reform. It is a tale that begins with one of the most harrowing and traumatic narratives of American history—the capture of fugitive slaves.

On March 10, 1837, a troubled James G. Birney appeared at attorney Salmon Chase's office. Birney, a former Alabama slave owner turned abolitionist, told Chase a heart-wrenching tale that exposed the inhumanity and hypocrisy of slavery. His maid, twenty-year-old Matilda Lawrence, had accompanied her master and father, Larkin Lawrence, to Cincinnati. The light-skinned Matilda had begged her father to free her. Her father refused, and she ran away, first finding refuge with a black family and then taking a job as a maid with the Birney household. Her father briefly looked for her and left Cincinnati for his home in Missouri, hiring the notorious slave catcher John M. Riley to find Matilda and return her to slavery.

Riley located Matilda in March 1837, and she was arrested pursuant to the federal Fugitive Slave Act of 1793. Birney considered helping Matilda escape but quickly realized that his only viable option was to challenge Matilda's return to slavery in court, even though Birney viewed the local judges as "appointees of the slave power" and unlikely to be sympathetic.[7]

Birney was a lawyer, but he could not represent Matilda because of his personal involvement in the case. So he asked Chase, a respected, twenty-nine-year-old antislavery lawyer who also had good ties to Cincinnati's conservative proslavery elite, to handle Matilda's case. Chase agreed to take the case.

Chase, born in New Hampshire in 1808, moved to Ohio after his father died. After graduating from college, he served a legal apprenticeship with U.S. Attorney General William Wirt from 1827 to 1829 and returned to Cincinnati in 1830 to practice law. Cincinnati, known as the Queen City, was a booming, bustling gateway to the West. As a rapidly growing northern city bordering the slave state of Kentucky, Cincinnati was conservative, deeply racist, and hostile to abolitionists. The Ohio legislature had, in 1804, adopted legislation known as the Black Laws, which discouraged black residency in the state and denied to blacks rights of citizenship such as the right to vote, to testify in court, to serve in the militia, or to receive a public education.

Cincinnati's location as a sizable free-state city, separated from the slave state of Kentucky only by the Ohio River, made it an attractive magnet for fugitive slaves. Controversy over the recapture of fugitive slaves fed the city's cauldron of explosive tensions.

A precocious young man, Chase at first steered clear of the slavery issue. He followed a conservative and traditional career path, marrying the daughter of a prominent Cincinnati family, cultivating wealthy and elite friends, and accumulating business clients, including the Cincinnati branch of the Bank of the United States. He established himself as a diligent, effective lawyer, albeit not a great one. His prepared briefs and oral arguments were clear, forceful, and well reasoned, although not impassioned or dynamic. He was uneasy speaking in public, reportedly breaking down on his first important argument and never mastering the art of persuading a jury.[8] His lack of humor probably hampered his ability to appeal to a jury. As one of Chase's friends recalled, "Chase was not a great lawyer, but a great man who had a knowledge of law."[9]

Chase's ambition was, however, great. His life was driven by the tension between ambition and moral principles. The Republican Party orator Carl Schurz noted in 1860 that he had never met a man more "possessed by the desire to be President."[10] Abraham Lincoln reportedly remarked in 1864 that "Chase is about one and a half times bigger than any other man I ever knew," probably a reference to both Chase's ability and his ego.[11] Most who knew him spoke of his "burning ambition," "love of power," and "cold, selfish" personality.[12]

But Chase also held strongly felt moral principles that he acted upon, principles that probably more than anything else denied him his ultimate ambition of becoming president. A deeply religious man, Chase had been raised from age eleven to age fourteen by his uncle, the Episcopalian bishop Philander Chase, who imbued him with an unshakable faith in God. His religious faith was the compelling motivation behind Chase's condemnation of and agitation against slavery.

In the mid-1830s, both Chase and the abolitionist movement were at turning points. Until then, abolitionism had been mainly a moral and religious crusade that sought to abolish slavery by means of moral persuasion, not legal or political action. Antislavery societies often resolved to use "no weapon but reason and truth" in their campaign against slavery.[13] Antislavery litigation was utilized mainly as a "practical necessity" to defend abolitionists against mobs and riots, not as an ideological opportunity.[14] But reason and truth had not worked. Southerners had not been moved by moral persuasion to end slavery, and, by the 1830s, political abolitionists like James Birney were developing constitutional theories that would provide legal and political means for restricting and ending slavery.

In 1837, Chase was also at a crossroads. He had built a stable, prosperous commercial legal practice. He had also just suffered personal tragedy: his wife had died in December 1835, just a year and a half after their marriage and several weeks after the birth of their daughter. Personal tragedy was to continue to afflict Chase, who by his forty-fourth birthday had lost three wives and four of his six children. That personal pain may have driven his political ambition to even greater heights.[15]

Chase had, however, been drawn into the cauldron of antislavery activities, not through sympathy with slaves but through moral revulsion at mob attacks on abolitionists. His brother-in-law Isaac Colby was a leading abolitionist in Cincinnati and introduced Chase to the Cincinnati abolitionist community, probably helping Chase to fill some of the void he felt when his wife died. In the summer of 1836, a mob had broken into Birney's office, destroyed his printing press, and then rampaged through town, systematically looting black neighborhoods. Chase's sister Abigail Colby fled to his house for safety. The next day, the mob was out again, looking for Birney at the hotel where he was rumored to be staying. Chase hurried to the hotel, and, although Birney was not there, the mob was. Chase refused to be intimidated, stood at the doorway, and firmly refused admittance. One of the mob's ringleaders asked who he was. "Salmon P. Chase" was the reply. "You will pay for your actions," said another voice. Chase firmly replied, "I [can] be found at any time."[16] The mob didn't attack him and a while later dispersed. The incident, Chase later recollected, made him "a decided opponent of slavery and the slave power."[17] What had motivated Chase to antislavery action was not the ill treatment of slaves but the impact of slavery on the rights of whites. "I was opposed at this time to the views of the abolitionists," Chase wrote, "but I now recognized the slave power as the great enemy of freedom of speech, freedom of the press and freedom of the person."[18]

Chase chose to represent the abolitionists in damage suits against the mob leaders. He took those cases reluctantly, for "I had just begun to acquire a pretty good practice for a young man and among the gentleman to be sued were several of my personal friends."[19] Chase worried about the effect on his law practice: "Wealth, influence, position, were all on the side of the slave owners, and the worst reputation a struggling young man could get was that of an abolitionist."[20] He vigorously and effectively litigated the cases and was disappointed when, at the end of the trials, minimal damages were awarded.[21]

Now Chase was poised to act on principle to defend a fugitive slave—to develop a courtroom strategy and to articulate a constitutional position that would take the movement to another level. Chase's decision would begin a long crusade that would earn him the nickname "Attorney General for Runaway Slaves,"[22] and, though that crusade would result in mostly losing cases and very few freed slaves, it would catapult both Chase and the slavery issue to national prominence. Chase would in time become the antislavery leader most responsible for the success of the transition from moral outrage to political action. As the New York Tribune later would write, "To Mr. Chase more than any other one man belongs the credit of making the antislavery feeling, what it had never been before, a power in politics. It had been the sentiment of philanthropists, he made it the inspiration of a great political party."[23]

When Birney appeared in Chase's office in the early afternoon of March 10, 1837, Chase already knew Birney and his theory that the federal Constitution was an antislavery instrument. Now he had to act quickly: that very day, a local Ohio justice of the peace, William Doty, was to review the slave catcher Riley's claim that Matilda was Lawrence's slave. Knowing that Doty would quickly send Matilda back to slavery, Chase, assisted by his partner Samuel Eels, requested a postponement, arguing that they had been retained as counsel only hours before. Doty granted a one-day postponement.[24]

But Chase didn't want to return the next day to argue the case before Doty. Local magistrates such as Doty had a reputation in Ohio for speedily delivering alleged slaves to their masters.[25] Moreover, Chase did not want to base his claim primarily on technical arguments: he wanted to test the constitutionality of the federal Fugitive Slave Act, under which Matilda had been seized. A local magistrate was unlikely to even consider those constitutional arguments. So, the same day, Chase and Eels were back in court, this time before David K. Este, an Ohio common pleas judge, requesting a writ of habeas corpus on behalf of Matilda. Este granted the writ but set a trial date for the next morning.[26]

A large crowd awaited Chase, Eels, Birney, and Matilda as they entered the courthouse the next morning. Matilda, attractive and white in appearance, and Birney, an outspoken abolitionist, added to the public interest in the case. Tall and awkward, Chase stood up before the court and, in a clear, rather dry, conversational tone, commenced a three-hour argument that was really more of a lecture. Because of the limited time available for preparation, it was not his most effective argument.[27]

Chase's main strategy seems to have been to utilize Matilda's case to challenge the constitutionality of the Fugitive Slave Act of 1793. While he did raise a number of technical, legal arguments, he discussed those quickly. He did not focus on the fact that Matilda had not escaped from her master while in a slave state but had escaped when voluntarily brought to Ohio—a point that was later to become a major issue in fugitive-slave litigation. Chase focused instead on broader constitutional points of natural rights, federalism, and the Fourth and Fifth Amendments. He did so over the objection of opposing counsel and amid clear signals from the judge that Chase's discourse was not pertinent.

Chase started by claiming that he wanted only for the court to do its legal duty and that he did not seek the "aid of feelings" on behalf of Matilda or question the validity of slavery. Yet his opening and closing arguments were attempts to infuse the Constitution with broad natural rights and an egalitarian moral perspective. He "perceived" the court's responsibility as not merely to the individual and community "but to conscience and to God." The argument's major premise, foundational to the rest of Chase's fugitive-slave litigation, was that "slavery is admitted . . . to be contrary to natural right." Thus, he argued, a slave brought by her master to a free state was "legally free, legally restored to her natural right."[28] Chase based his argument on the famous English case known as Somerset's case, in which the prominent English judge Lord Mansfield held that, since English law did not recognize slavery, an American slave traveling in England with his Virginia master was free.

Chase then argued that the Fugitive Slave Act requiring free states to summarily return runaway slaves was unconstitutional because (1) the federal government had no power under the Constitution to require states to return runaways, (2) it violated the Northwest Ordinance, which had made Ohio a free state, and (3) the Act violated both the Fourth Amendment's prohibition against unreasonable search and seizure and the Fifth Amendment's due process clause. Chase undoubtedly realized that he would lose his constitutional argument but believed he would be vindicated by history. "I feel assured that though my reasoning may fail to convince this court," he stated, "other courts, and perhaps this court at another time, if not now, will pronounce this act unconstitutional, repugnant to the ordinance of 1787, subversive of the first principles of civil liberty, and therefore null and void."[29]

Chase concluded with several broad themes critical to his constitutional thinking for the next four decades. He argued that the natural right to freedom required that the Constitution and laws be strictly construed in favor of liberty unless some clear and explicit exception denied liberty. That natural right to liberty, reiterated by the Declaration of Independence's "self-evident" truth that all men are created equal, mandated that Matilda "be regarded free, until it be shown by the fullest and clearest evidence, that her case falls within some exception to the universal law of human liberty." Let "every provision, unfavorable to liberty," argued Chase, "receive a strict and rigorous interpretation." Relying on this principle of interpretation, Chase demanded Matilda's discharge "in the name of justice, of liberty and of our common humanity."[30]

Judge Este listened patiently to Chase but quickly ruled against him on the basis of the current state of the law. After a quick hearing before magistrate Doty, Matilda was pronounced to be Lawrence's slave. The slave catcher Riley quickly rushed Matilda across the Ohio River to Covington, Kentucky, while she wept and begged for her freedom. Matilda and Riley boarded a ship bound for New Orleans, where Lawrence apparently had arranged for her sale. Matilda was "sold down the river" and disappeared into slavery and history.

The historian William Wiecek has termed Chase's Matilda argument "a noble failure."[31] Chase was saddened by the outcome of the case and felt that his legal position had been "treated with ridicule or disregard."[32] Yet, despite Matilda's personal tragedy, Chase's mentor, Birney, believed that the case had "done much for the cause in this city."[33] The litigation had stirred considerable debate over fugitive slaves and slavery in Cincinnati. Birney and Chase had worked out the legal theory that, while it lost in court, was eventually to become the constitutional basis of the Republican Party program.

The courtroom struggle had other unseen, pentimento effects that became apparent only many years later. In the courtroom that Saturday was a young medical student who, unknown to Chase, was particularly moved by his antislavery legal argument. After graduating from medical school in Europe, Dr. Norton Townsend came back to Ohio and became an antislavery activist. Elected to the Ohio legislature, he would cast critical votes in favor of repealing Ohio's oppressive Black Laws and electing Salmon Chase to the U.S. Senate.[34]

But, at the time, the losing case dramatically altered Chase's career. He increasingly became a political lawyer, using the courtroom to further the antislavery movement. Eventually, he gave up the full-time practice of law for politics; his legal failure in *Matilda* led to personal success.

The *Matilda* case did not vanish with the unfortunate woman's return to slavery. Birney was prosecuted for harboring a fugitive slave and was found guilty and fined. Birney decided not to pay the fine, and Chase filed an appeal. Chase quickly realized that Judge Este had made a technical error when he charged the jury to consider only whether Birney had harbored Matilda and not whether he did so knowing that she was a slave. But both he and Birney agreed not to raise that issue on appeal, even though they knew they would win if they did. Their interest lay in arguing the broad constitutional issue of whether Matilda had become free the moment she entered Ohio with her master, not in "winning" the case and avoiding the fine.

The Ohio Supreme Court's decision disappointed Chase. The court reversed Birney's conviction, but only on the technical grounds, not argued by Chase, that the jury had not considered whether Birney had known Matilda was a slave. Chase's disappointment with the court's avoidance of his argument was tempered when the Ohio Supreme Court took the unusual step of ordering the publication of his arguments in the case. In all likelihood, the court agreed with Chase's arguments but was unwilling to adopt them given the political climate in Ohio in the late 1830s. So it signaled its leanings by having the argument printed and widely publicized.[35]

For the next decade, Chase actively represented fugitive slaves in Ohio courts. His cases usually drew large crowds to the courtroom. Most of his efforts lost, although occasionally he was able to win his client's freedom. Equally important, Chase's arguments were reaching a wider national audience, touching a chord with northerners who wanted to dissociate free states from slavery.

The 1845 *Watson* case was one of Chase's most dramatic and well-publicized cases. Henry Hoppess, transporting a slave named Sam Watson down the Ohio River, had been assured by the boat's captain that they would not stop in Cincinnati, a city that by then had a reputation for freeing slaves. When Hoppess discovered that the vessel would indeed dock there overnight, he unsuccessfully attempted to transfer Watson to another boat. When they docked in Cincinnati, Hoppess panicked and sought to obtain a magistrate's order requiring Watson to leave with him.[36]

Chase and his co-counsel immediately filed a writ of habeas corpus for Watson's freedom. Nathaniel Read, Chase's opposing counsel in the *Matilda* case, who by then was an Ohio Supreme Court justice, heard the case. Read personally disliked Chase, but the two men respected each other professionally.[37] Read was smart and political, and his views on fugitive slaves had evolved with changing public opinion since his confrontation with Chase in *Matilda*.

Chase presented his familiar litany of constitutional arguments, which he had honed since the *Matilda* case, arguing principally that, since slavery was against natural law, a slave was automatically freed when brought to a free state. Judge Read began with the bane of a test case lawyer's existence: a compliment that the case had been "argued with distinguished ability, much learning and great eloquence."[38] When judges say that, losing is usually in the cards—unfortunately, Chase's and Watson's fate that day.

Read went on to acknowledge that "the great principles of natural right asserted in the Declaration of Independence, and lying at the foundation of our institutions, if permitted to operate, would liberate all."[39] But, continued Read, "the question is not, what conforms to the great principle of natural right and universal freedom—but what do the positive laws and institutions . . . command and direct."[40]

Read then ironically launched into an extended discussion of policy, not law. "I regret deeply that slavery exists." But "ours is a government of white men." Read's solution was removal of the "whole race of Negroes . . . to a country of their own." With that political discussion of slavery, Read proceeded to reject Chase's constitutional arguments.[41]

But Read did accept one of Chase's major contentions: that a slave brought by his master to a free state is automatically freed. Acknowledging that he had once held the contrary opinion, Read now explicitly held that the Constitution recognizes the right of recapture only of a fugitive slave who has escaped into a free state. But Read still refused to free Watson, holding that Watson had not been brought into Ohio since the boat had only docked in port. Slave owners had a right to take their slaves down the Ohio, he said, and, since stopping overnight is only "incident to the right to navigate, it does not," according to Read, "change the relation of master and slave."[42] Chase had vigorously argued that Ohio jurisdiction began at the middle of the Ohio river, but to no avail. Read believed that the spirit of "that great compromise" of the slavery issue, and the continued harmony between the states, required that slave owners be accorded totally free navigation rights on the Ohio.

Chase had lost another case and was disappointed with the result. But Cincinnati's black community viewed the case—despite the unfortunate result for Watson—as a victory. While the court had held against Watson, "yet some principles were recognized of the most vital importance to the free states."[43] They accurately saw that Read's acceptance of Chase's argument that slavery was a local and unnatural condition and that slaves brought to Ohio by their masters were automatically free was of great importance to their security and status in Ohio. What Read had ridiculed in 1837 he accepted in 1845. Judge Read's conversion, albeit limited, reflected the growing white discomfort with the practice of returning fugitive slaves to their owners, and was viewed by abolitionists and blacks as progress.[44]

In a gesture of gratitude, the Reverend A. J. Jordan, the pastor of the African American Baker Street Church, collected donations from his impoverished congregation to present Chase and his co-counsel with gifts to show their appreciation. Chase was given a silver pitcher with the inscription "From the colored people of Cincinnati for his various public services in behalf of the oppressed and particularly for his eloquent advocacy of the rights of man in the case of Samuel Watson."[45] In his speech accepting the gift, Chase eloquently stated that "there is no reliable security for the rights of any unless the rights of all are, also secure," a theme he was to constantly reiterate as a Republican politician.[46] Chase was not surprised that Judge Read had not accepted many of his broad arguments on behalf of Watson, but nonetheless he expected "to live to see [his arguments] recognized in all Courts as sound law."[47]

Chase's most famous case stemmed from his representation of an abolitionist involved in the underground railroad. On April 21, 1842, John Van Zandt, a farmer who had left Kentucky because of his hatred of slavery, was conducting nine fugitive slaves north when his wagon was stopped by two slave catchers. The slave driving the wagon fled, but the other eight were captured and rushed across the Ohio River to Covington, Kentucky, where their owner, Wharton Jones, reclaimed them and paid the slave catchers $450.

Jones then sued Van Zandt for harboring fugitives in violation of the fugitive slave act. The old, stooped farmer appeared one day at Chase's office to request that he represent him for free. Chase was now thirty-five years old, his second wife was in poor health, his third infant daughter had just died, and his political activities in the antislavery Liberty Party (one of the precursors to the Republican Party) were consuming much of his time. He agreed to take Van Zandt's case and, as usual in his antislavery litigation, accepted no fee. He asked former U.S. Senator Thomas Morris to aid him in the defense.

Chase was optimistic about the *Van Zandt* case. He recognized that, whatever the outcome in Court, the case would get wide publicity for his antislavery constitutional views. Moreover, he thought he could win in court, despite the substantial evidence that Van Zandt was transporting slaves he knew to be fugitives. Chase was an eternal optimist, a common characteristic of those who take on losing causes. One biographer wrote of Chase that "Perhaps what he most lacked was healthful pessimism; he had always too much preliminary confidence that everything was to be for the best, and a corresponding sinking of heart when his plans miscarried."[48] He believed in the righteousness of his cause, and his religious faith combined with a substantial ego led to an over-inflated confidence that he could rationally convince others of his position.[49]

But Chase did have some good reasons to be optimistic about the *Van Zandt* case. First, the case would be tried in federal court before a U.S. Supreme Court justice, John McLean, who was assigned to the Ohio District. McLean, an impressive-looking man whose features and reserved demeanor resembled those of George Washington, had strong antislavery views. McLean had ruled in favor of fugitive slaves when he was an Ohio Supreme Court justice and in 1842 had set forth his antislavery views in the U.S. Supreme Court case *Prigg v. Pennsylvania*. Moreover, McLean was Chase's friend and future uncle-in-law: Chase's third wife, whom he married during the course of the Van Zandt litigation, was McLean's niece by marriage. It would be hard to find a better federal judge to try *Van Zandt*.

Moreover, Van Zandt was well liked in Cincinnati, and the case generated much interest amid a growing antislavery mood in Ohio. The large audience that attended the trial generally believed Van Zandt would be acquitted. Even the plaintiff, Wharton Jones, admitted to Chase at the trial that he had been poorly advised to bring what he had come to believe was a futile quest to recover damages from Van Zandt.

To the surprise of most spectators, McLean rejected Chase's motion to dismiss the case, and a jury ultimately awarded Jones $1,200 in damages. McLean believed that the duty to obey the law overrode natural rights, his antislavery views, and individual conscience. He charged the jury:

> In the course of this discussion much has been said of the laws of nature, of conscience, and the rights of conscience. This monitor, under great excitement, may mislead, and always does mislead, when it urges anyone to violate the law.[50]

Chase moved for a new trial, continuing his by then increasingly futile constitutional challenge to the fugitive slave law. McLean again decided against Chase. While he agreed with Chase's view of slavery and the presumption in Ohio that every person was free, McLean's view of the Constitution's necessary compromise with slavery made him object to Chase's natural-law argument and his appeal to conscience. To

McLean, the immorality of slavery was irrelevant. He repeated his old charge to the jury: "The law is our only guide."[51]

Chase, however, remained undaunted and appealed to the United States Supreme Court. Perhaps his optimism came from the encouragement he got even from a slave owner who wrote him that his legal argument "seemed to have the right of it."[52] Or maybe Chase's hopeful outlook stemmed from his unbounded faith in an argument that he had repeated so many times and so deeply believed in that he felt sure he could convince others to accept it. That faith, combined with tremendous drive and ambition, motivated Chase to articulate arguments that eventually moved thousands of northerners to view the fugitive slave law as unconstitutional. But that faith didn't move the Supreme Court. After the Court unanimously ruled against Van Zandt, Chase wrote to the prominent New York abolitionist Lewis Tappan that "I regret the decision in the *Van Zandt* case, and, I confess, did not expect it."[53] If he didn't, pretty much everyone else did.

But even Chase must have recognized that the chance of winning Van Zandt's appeal in the Supreme Court was minuscule. The Court had upheld the constitutionality of the Fugitive Slave Act in *Prigg v. Pennsylvania*, decided in 1842.[54] The only Supreme Court justice with antislavery views was Justice McLean, and he had already ruled against Chase. Although McLean had urged the Court to hear oral argument in the Van Zandt case, Chief Justice Roger B. Taney objected to hearing oral argument, for he thought the constitutional question was already settled. Taney persuaded the rest of the Court except McLean, and Chase was relegated to submitting only a written brief, an ominous omen. Perhaps Chase subconsciously recognized that he could not win, for his *Van Zandt* brief comes the closest he ever was to come to adopting a pure higher-natural-law theory. His brief straddled the fine line between "urging disregard of positive law and urging incorporation of natural law within it."[55] Chase's argument was designed to test the limit of law, to put before the country and court the conflict between humanity and prevailing law.

The brief opens by tacitly admitting that current legal precedent may be against him. Chase argues, however, that "such authority may stand for law" but does not always represent the law. Reason and truth "will ultimately prevail."[56] Other well-established legal doctrines have been overturned in time, and Chase urges the Court to consider his arguments dispassionately and openly. Fifty pages of technical legal argument follow to prove that Van Zandt could not be liable unless the slave owner had actually notified him that the persons he was transporting were fugitive slaves. Chase's argument is logical, well researched, and persuasively argued, but his interpretation of the law would have made it virtually impossible to prosecute underground railroaders, a result neither the South nor the Supreme Court was willing to countenance.

If the first part of Chase's argument was technically sound but judicially unattainable, the second half descended to utter futility. His argument that the Fugitive Slave Act was unconstitutional defied legal precedent and current political reality. Yet the brief brilliantly sets forth Chase's antislavery constitutional philosophy. The future Massachusetts senator Charles Sumner considered Chase's *Van Zandt* brief to be the best he had ever read, and he borrowed Chase's arguments when he condemned the fugitive-slave law in the Senate a few years later. "It is a triumph of freedom," said the retired Justice Joseph Story of Chase's argument, and he predicted that "his points will seriously influence the public mind and perhaps the politics of the country."[57]

That was Chase's aim. His biographer argues that Chase's point "was simply to put before the country a solemn protest against making the free States share in slavery."[58] Chase reprinted the brief as a pamphlet that he widely distributed to every member of Congress and to other leading politicians irrespective of their views on slavery. The case attracted national attention. Chase used the forum to publicize the antislavery cause and to help his own political ambitions. He had astutely secured the prominent governor of New York, William Henry Seward, to act as co-counsel in the Supreme Court, in order to help the case achieve national prominence. Seward's argument to the Court was also published, in the *New York Tribune*.

Chase's argument, which eventually became the constitutional bedrock of the Republican Party, was that the Constitution intended the U.S. government "to be kept free of all connection" with slavery and to exclude slavery from the territories.[59] Slavery was a local institution, confined to the slave-holding states.

Chase drew on several key principles to support his constitutional position, principles that were to undergird civil rights litigation throughout the nineteenth century. First, he drew on the Declaration of Independence and on other extraconstitutional sources such as the Northwest Ordinance to inform his view of the Constitution. To antislavery advocates like Chase, the Declaration's self-evident truths were not "empty flourishes of rhetoric"[60] but proof that slavery was not constitutionally "to be fostered or sustained by national authority."[61] To Chase, either the "Declaration of Independence is a fable" or the Constitution must recognize all inhabitants of the United States as persons with rights.[62] Chase also relied on a rule of interpretation that holds that the Constitution must be interpreted consistently with natural, God-given rights, and that slavery was a violation of a natural right. Reaching its highest rhetorical note, Chase's brief argued that

> No legislature can make right wrong; or wrong, right. No legislature can make light, darkness; or darkness, light. No legislature can make men, things; or things, men. Nor is any legislature at liberty to disregard the fundamental principles of rectitude and justice whether restrained or not by constitutional provisions, these are acts beyond any legitimate or binding legislative authority.[63]

The Court is obligated, therefore, to avoid interpreting the U.S. Constitution in a manner

> which will bring its provisions into conflict with that other CONSTITUTION, which, rising, in sublime majesty, over all human enactments . . . finds its "seat in the bosom of God."[64]

Chase's real plea in *Van Zandt*, as in many of his other cases, was not to the Court but to the public and history. For Chase, the final arbiter in cases of a "moral and political nature" is not the court's judgment but "public opinion, not of the American people only, but of the Civilized World."[65]

Antislavery lawyers like Chase, and their southern counterparts, understood that an appeal to the Constitution had the same kind of force on public opinion as the equally common appeal to the Bible, and therefore they tried to read into the Constitution self-evident natural rights. As the son of one of Chase's friends later recounted, the appeal to fundamental rights, "however little it might convince a court, was the most effective of all the antislavery arguments, because it brought back the discussion to the absolute incongruity of democracy and slavery, and emphasized both the question of moral right and the social expediency of upholding the moral law."[66]

Nobody was surprised—except possibly Chase—when the Supreme Court unanimously ruled against Van Zandt, holding the Fugitive Slave Act constitutional despite "its supposed inexpediency and [the] invalidity of all laws recognizing slavery or any right of property in man."[67] But, despite losing,[68] Chase wrote that he was "thankful" to have brought the case. His arguments were widely publicized, and he was "satisfied" with the public discussion the case generated. Abolitionists praised his arguments, and the respect he won in *Van Zandt* and other fugitive-slave cases helped propel Chase to election to the U.S. Senate in 1849 and to the governorship of Ohio in 1855 and 1857. Chase helped found the Republican Party and sought its presidential nomination in 1856 and 1860. Lincoln appointed him secretary of the Treasury in 1861, where he served as the most radical Republican in the wartime cabinet. Chase could not contain his presidential ambition and quietly tried to run against Lincoln in 1864, leading to his removal from the cabinet.

Lincoln, however, recognized his dedication and skills and nominated him to be the fourth chief justice of the Supreme Court in 1864. Chase at first found the position boring. His first love was tackling broad political matters, and as justice he was "working from morning till midnight and no result except that John Smith owned this parcel of land or other property instead of Jacob Robinson."[69] Chase recovered from the boredom and served ably as chief justice, briefly flirting with the Democratic Party presidential nomination in 1868, until his death in 1873.

While Chase went on to a national career, the poor, old abolitionist farmer John Van Zandt, who had found "special gratification in aiding fugitives from the oppression of slavery,"[70] died in 1845, while his case was pending in the Supreme Court. The old man had suffered emotional and financial losses from the suit against him, even though Chase and his co-counsel had represented Van Zandt for free. Chase believed that the stress from these problems was enormous and probably contributed to Van Zandt's untimely death. But Chase also thought that Van Zandt's struggle lived on in the hearts and minds of others. He considered the underground railroader John Van Trompe, in Harriet Beecher Stowe's *Uncle Tom's Cabin*, to be modeled on Van Zandt and hoped that, "even though my poor old client be sacrificed, the great cause of humanity will be a gainer by it."[71]

The main long-term legacy of Chase and other fugitive-slave litigators was their contribution to a culture that encourages political movements to use courts as vehicles of political protest. That litigation aided the rising tide of northern public opinion against slavery and eventually contributed to the nomination by the Republican Party of a man whose attacks on the Supreme Court helped him win the presidency. As the prominent Wisconsin newspaper editor Rufus King, wrote in 1855, the judicial controversy over the constitutionality of the Fugitive Slave Act "must provoke, everywhere, discussion and agitation, and Liberty and Right must profit by these."[72]

The two decades before the Civil War erupted saw a legal war fought in state and federal courts over whether the Constitution nationalized slavery. To the narratives of slave resistance to slavery, of the underground railroad, of John Brown's raid, was added another—the legal struggle waged by Chase and many others in the courtroom.

While Chase and his compatriots were fighting a difficult, uphill battle in the courts and in the political arena to remove federal and free-state legal support for slavery, another group of abolitionists was waging a more utopian battle to constitutionally extinguish slavery everywhere in the United States. These abolitionists also read the Constitution to conform with the Declaration of Independence and the natural right to freedom but drew the much more radical conclusion that the Constitution required the abolition of slavery both in the North and in the South. They did so in the belief that northern reverence for the Constitution required the abolitionist movement to develop an antislavery constitutional interpretation in order to gain adherents and spur antislavery sentiment. Like Chase and the more moderate antislavery movement, the utopian constitutionalists used test-case litigation as one means of publicizing their constitutional doctrines.

In 1844, the utopian constitutionalists created an opportunity to litigate their broad constitutional theories in court. That year, New Jersey ratified a new constitution that included a Declaration of Rights providing that "All men are by nature free and independent, and have certain natural and unalienable rights."[73] Although the framers of the New Jersey constitution had ignored the issue of slavery, the New Jersey Antislavery Society nevertheless resolved to initiate a test case to "settle the question of the existence of slavery under the new Constitution."[74] They genuinely hoped to win in court, but the abolitionists' primary goal was to focus the attention of an indifferent public on their cause.[75]

New Jersey was the last northern state to provide for the gradual abolition of slavery. In 1804, the legislature provided that children born to slaves after July 4, 1804, were to be free but to remain servants until twenty-five years of age (if male) or twenty-one (if female). As a result of this act, the New Jersey slave population dropped from 12,422 in 1800 to only 674 in 1840, most of whom were more than fifty-five years old.[76] Several thousand servants awaited adulthood and emancipation.

The New Jersey abolitionists realized that their constitutional challenge to the remnants of slavery in New Jersey would be difficult, and their leader, John Grimes, was openly dubious.[77] Yet, in challenging slavery pursuant to the free and independent clause, the New Jersey abolitionists were not without some legal authority. Sixty years earlier, a similar clause in the 1780 Massachusetts constitution had been reportedly construed by Chief Justice William Cushing, of the Massachusetts Supreme Judicial Court, as being incompatible with slavery, thereby ending slavery in that commonwealth. In 1806, Virginia's venerable Chancellor George Wythe, a prominent abolitionist, a respected judge, and the law teacher of Thomas Jefferson, held that Article I of Virginia's 1776 Declaration of Rights, the ancestor of the Massachusetts and New Jersey provision, made all men in Virginia presumptively free. Wythe, approaching eighty, had just written a will leaving most of his estate to a black former slave, and might have been trying to apply judicially the noble experiment of promoting freedom that he had undertaken personally. Both attempts ended badly. Wythe's nephew and heir murdered both him and his former slave to obtain his inheritance, and the Virginia Supreme Court repudiated Wythe's view of the Declaration of Rights. While Virginia was obviously not ready to abolish slavery by judicial fiat, the New Jersey test case would have some respectable authority from Massachusetts and Virginia on its side.[78]

In the spring of 1845, cases were initiated on behalf of Mary Tiebout, a nineteen-year-old black servant girl whose mother was a slave, and a black man named William, born before 1804, who was still a slave. One week before the scheduled argument before the New Jersey Supreme Court, a remarkable change occurred in the litigation strategy. Several prominent New York abolitionists appeared at the Antislavery Society's quarterly meeting, including Alvan Stewart, a dynamic, eccentric New York lawyer. Stewart was one of the foremost proponents of the theory that the U.S. Constitution prohibited slavery. He convinced the Society to argue broadly that the U.S. Constitution barred slavery in New Jersey, and not to base the case solely or even primarily on the New Jersey constitution. He also agreed to argue the case the following week before the New Jersey Supreme Court.

Stewart, born in upstate New York in 1790 to parents of modest means, attended Burlington College in Vermont before settling in Cherry Valley, New York. For many years, Stewart dabbled in politics, often without much success, because, according to a contemporary observer, "he always managed to enlist in the weaker and unsuccessful side."[79] Nonetheless, Stewart won election as mayor of Cherry Valley at the age of thirty-one, his first and only elective office.

Stewart did establish an immensely successful law practice. "'It was proverbial of Stewart as a lawyer,' a close friend and former law partner recalled, 'that he always succeeded in every suit commenced by himself.'"[80] His commanding stature—tall, dark, and muscular—and his large, piercing eyes, coupled with his tremendous wit, charm, and immense learning, captivated juries and, later, antislavery audiences. Unlike Salmon Chase, Alvan Stewart was a witty, comic lawyer who used his eccentric personality and biting wit to win over juries. "No man ever excelled Alvan Stewart in wit," wrote Stewart's former law partner, "and this was his great weapon with which he demolished all his adversaries."[81] While Chase relied on carefully constructed legal arguments, Stewart was the master of arguments ad absurdum, "in which," according to the great abolitionist orator Theodore Dwight Weld, "he had no peer."[82]

By the mid-1830s, Stewart had moved to Utica, New York, and given up his law practice.[83] He devoted himself full time to the causes of abolition and temperance. Motivated by a devout Christian faith, Stewart became one of New York's leading abolitionists.

Stewart's embrace of abolition brought him scorn and opprobrium.[84] The Convention of the New York State Antislavery Society, held in Utica in October 1835, was broken up by a mob, and Stewart was physically and verbally assaulted. Upon learning of rumors that his house would be attacked that night, Stewart armed a number of friends to help him protect himself. The mob, hearing of Stewart's conversion of his house into a fortress, abandoned the attack.[85]

Stewart is remembered by history mainly for two key contributions to the abolitionist cause: his leadership in creating an antislavery third party and his creative, eccentric constitutional theories. Yet, Stewart's most important legacy, according to his friend and prominent abolitionist ally William Goodell, lay not in the public's adoption of his positions but in his *"proposal* of them."[86] For Stewart's proposal set off a chain of struggle, and, for Goodell and Stewart, that struggle, and not victory, was of utmost importance.

Stewart was one of the earliest abolitionists to propose the formation of a separate antislavery party, and he worked tirelessly to create the Liberty Party, the forerunner of the Republican Party. His call for independent political action was linked to Stewart's theory that both Congress and the courts had a constitutional duty to abolish the "peculiar institution" of slavery.

Stewart dramatically launched his career as a constitutional theorist by arguing the new and startling position that the Constitution, far from safeguarding slavery, required its abolition. He based this claim upon the Fifth Amendment's due process clause, which provides that "no person shall be deprived of life, liberty or property without due process of law." Stewart argued that slaves were persons because the term covers "all humanity" and that other references to slaves in the Constitution, such as the fugitive slave clause and the three-fifths compromise, referred to them as "persons." Since slaves were persons entitled to due process and since due process required judicial proceedings before a person's liberty could be taken, Stewart concluded that all slaves were constitutionally free and could be declared so by Congress and the courts.[87] His argument, as one sympathetic legal scholar has noted, was "characterized, on the one hand, by bold imagination and, on the other hand, by an illuminating disregard for historical fact."[88] Indeed, four years earlier, the U.S. Supreme Court had held that the due process clause did not apply to the states but only to the federal government, a ruling that Stewart either did not know of or conveniently ignored.

Undaunted, Stewart moved to amend the American Antislavery Society's charter at its annual convention in 1838 to remove the clause recognizing that the Constitution gave the slave states exclusive control over slavery within their own territory. For two days, Stewart argued vigorously against most of the other leaders of the society, who, Stewart reported in a letter to his wife, "came down upon me like a thunder shower."[89] The vote on the motion was 47–37 in favor of the change, which Stewart proclaimed "an immense victory," although in fact the motion was defeated because a two-thirds vote was necessary to amend the charter.[90] Stewart saw victory not as winning the motion but in getting his argument accepted by a substantial number of abolitionists.

Stewart's speech was published widely and discussed throughout the abolitionist movement.

Now Stewart was ready to make his arguments to a court. For both Stewart and the New Jersey abolitionists, the New Jersey Slave Cases, as the newspaper accounts termed them, were ideological cases "undertaken for purposes of the movement, to dramatize the inconsistency of slavery with underlying principles of a democratic state."[91]

Stewart's argument before the New Jersey Supreme Court on May 21 and 22, 1845, was a classic performance of wit laced with sarcasm, of erudition intertwined with avoidance of precedent and historical fact. He spoke for six hours on May 21, and then, after the defendants' argument, replied for almost five hours on May 22, ending at 10:30 P.M. with an impassioned, spellbinding plea to the justices. "Such was the impressiveness with which the closing appeal for the advocate for freedom was delivered," reported a journalist for the *New York Evening Express*, that the large audience was riveted to its seats in silence, as in a "spell," when Stewart finished. After a lengthy silence, Chief Justice Joseph Hornblower adjourned the court.[92]

Stewart's argument to the court was far broader than his 1837 speech on the due process clause. He now added natural law, the common law, the Preamble to the Constitution, the Ten Commandments, European and ancient history, the constitutional requirement that guarantees to each state a republican form of government, the Declaration of Independence, the New Jersey constitution, and even the 1814 Treaty of Ghent with Great Britain to argue that the remaining New Jersey slaves should immediately be freed.[93] The *Trenton State Gazette* aptly characterized Stewart's argument as remarkable for "its powerful though disjointed reasoning, its warm appeals to the best feelings of human nature and its ingenious and copious accumulation of terms of abhorrence and contempt of slavery."[94]

Central to Stewart's exposition was his attempt to incorporate natural rights into the Constitution. While the Garrisonian wing of the abolitionist movement stressed that higher moral obligations overrode civil human laws, Stewart's strand of abolitionism interpreted positive law as never conflicting with moral code, thereby removing the positive law-moral obligation dichotomy. "Abolitionists should never make a single admission in relation to the construction of our constitution which might tell against the slave," Stewart wrote in an 1842 letter to one of Chase's close Ohio associates.[95] "We never should admit that we are under a moral obligation to do wrong, and have therefore no legal power to do right."[96] The moral-legal conflict plagued antislavery advocates: judges like Supreme Court Judge McLean believed that positive law must be obeyed even when it conflicted with natural rights; Garrisonian abolitionists who believed that the Constitution was a proslavery document argued that, to the contrary, abolitionist judges should resign because higher obligations overrode all human law and must be obeyed; Chase and his Republican Party partisans ameliorated the moral-legal dilemma by interpreting the Constitution as removing any free-state or national duty to return fugitive slaves or to extend slavery; Stewart simply obliterated the dilemma. He did so by reading broad constitutional phrases such as "all men are by nature free and independent," "due process of law," and "republican form of government" consistently with a higher law, such as the law of nature.[97] Slavery, proclaimed Stewart in his argument to the New Jersey court, was inconsistent with due process, with the guarantee to each state of a republican form of government, and with the Preamble to the Constitution, which asserts as the purpose of the document "securing the blessing of liberty." Moreover, as Chase had argued in *Van Zandt*, Stewart now claimed that the Declaration of Independence's ringing statement of equality and freedom was not a mere "rhetorical flourish"[98] but a particularized mandate, a rule on which courts could act.

Finally, Stewart eschewed legal formalism in favor of a broad political-moral argument. While he purported to be arguing a dry legal question,[99] his argument reads like a political speech or ministerial sermon. In his request for relief, he asked that the "court set the nation the shining example of doing right on this question, by acting up to the full measure of their judicial and moral power."[100]

The New Jersey Supreme Court, by a 3–1 vote, rejected Stewart's plea. The justices chose to follow the formalistic reasoning of the defense counsel, Joseph Bradley, who was later appointed to the United States Supreme Court.[101] Stewart's arguments were, according to one member of New Jersey's highest court, "rather addressed to the feelings than to the legal intelligence of the court."[102] The court interpreted the "free and independent" clause of the state constitution as a mere hortatory provision, which did not provide individual rights.[103] Only the antislavery justice Joseph Hornblower dissented, and he did so without writing an opinion.[104]

The New Jersey Slave Cases were thus consigned to history as a loser. The case did, however, accomplish the abolitionists' aim of initiating a political debate on slavery, which ended in the New Jersey legislature's formal abolition of slavery in that state several years later.[105]

Alvan Stewart and Salmon Chase, in their very different careers, share aspects of a common legacy. Both were successful lawyers who gave up the full-time practice of law to organize a political antislavery movement and political party. They both viewed their antislavery litigation as a means to further that political movement—and, in Chase's case, his own political career. They used the courts as a forum of protest in which to articulate, dramatize, and popularize their constitutional views. Both Chase in his attack on the fugitive slave law, and Stewart, in his articulation of a constitutional theory against slavery, had faith in their ability to convince the court of their position. Their cases were not mere publicity stunts. But their purposes were broader than winning or losing in court.

Both Stewart and Chase articulated constitutional theories in order to sway public opinion to support the antislavery cause. Both of their theories were ultimately grounded on the incorporation of a natural right to freedom into constitutional doctrine. Chase corresponded with Stewart in 1842 to gain his support for a moderate antislavery position, but to no avail, as Chase and Stewart parted company on the implications of their interpretation of the Constitution as an antislavery document. The use by Chase and his associates of natural law to disassociate the U.S. Constitution and free-state law from slavery touched a deep chord in Northern public opinion; Stewart and his utopian constitutionalists used natural law to argue for the total abolition of slavery, a stance that was viewed as so extreme and unrealistic that it was easy for the courts and the American people to dismiss it. Both Chase and Stewart concluded, for example, that the Fifth Amendment's due process clause prohibited slavery, but Chase hewed closer to legal precedent and political reality, arguing that the clause's prohibition applied only to areas under federal jurisdiction, such as the territories and the District of Columbia, not to the southern states. Stewart's view that the due process clause prohibited slavery in the South was implausible historically, even if persuasively and logically argued.

Chase sought a moderate position to achieve political success, albeit not courtroom victory. Stewart believed that to help the slave "we must go deep," striking at the slave system itself and not merely its intrusions into the North. For Stewart, moral purity was more important than winning, for "even without victory, you will have success."[106]

It is no great shock, therefore, that, "in the short run, radical constitutionalism was a failure."[107] Although the radicals' program was endorsed by a number of abolitionist conventions and political organizations such as the Liberty League and attracted several notable adherents such as Frederick Douglass, and James Birney, the radicals became more isolated and sectarian as the Civil War drew closer. Their theory never articulated what most Americans felt to be the essential nature of the Constitution, and thus it failed as a rallying call. No significant section of the political, economic, or legal elite adopted the radicals' legal interpretation. Northern opposition to slavery was increasingly attracted to the more moderate Free Soil and Republican efforts, and the radical constitutional program had little impact on the great constitutional debates that led to the Civil War.[108]

Despite the lack of short-term success, the radical constitutionalist had a significant long-term impact on the law. Scholars now recognize that the doctrines developed by this small brand of radicals influenced concepts and clauses that constitute Section I of the Fourteenth Amendment.[109] The doctrines of substantive due process, equal protection of the laws, paramount national citizenship, and privileges and immunities all have roots in ideas that Stewart and his radical associates introduced.[110] In 1836, Alvan Stewart set forth the tenets of what has now become accepted constitutional due process—natural rights doctrine:

> There is a class of rights of the most personal and sacred character to the citizen, which are a portion of individual sovereignty never surrendered by the citizen . . . the legislatures of the States and Union are forbidden by the constitutions of the States and Union from touching those unsurrendered rights.[111]

Yet the measure of Stewart's and his compatriots' long-term success cannot be adequately judged by our acceptance of their ideas in the twentieth century. Even more important was their impact, and that of Salmon Chase on the creation of a culture that inspired other nineteenth-century radical political movements, such as the women's and the civil rights movements, to utilize the courts and the Constitution as forums of protest. As the historian Hendrik Hartog has noted, the "contest over slavery did more than any other cause to stimulate the development of an alternate rights conscious, interpretation of the federal Constitution."[112]

The women's suffrage and African American civil rights movements of the nineteenth century built on the legacies the antislavery litigators had created. These movements also used the Declaration of Independence and natural rights theories to interpret the Constitution, and utilized the courts to inspire protest. They kept alive the flame of legal protest that the abolitionists had ignited, often drawing ideas and inspiration directly from their predecessors. And they, in turn, made possible a culture of struggle that would inspire and sustain those of us who followed.

4

"A Fine Agitation"

Women's Suffrage Goes to Court

ON FRIDAY, NOVEMBER 1, 1872, Susan B. Anthony read an editorial in the *Rochester Democratic and Chronicle* urging all citizens to immediately register to vote. The fifty-two-year-old Anthony, a feminist who had been agitating for women's suffrage for twenty years, put down her newspaper and decided to take her fight directly to the voting booth—and, ultimately, to the courts.

Anthony donned her bonnet and coat, convinced one of her sisters to join her, and briskly walked to the barber shop that served as the voting station for Rochester's Eighth Ward, where she asked a startled group of men to register her. The chief inspector tried to convince Anthony that the laws of New York did not permit women to register, but she countered by reading him the Fourteenth Amendment, which she claimed gave her a right to vote. The inspectors, recounted Anthony, were young men, "entirely unversed in the intricacies of constitutional law" and "utterly incapable" of answering her legal argument.[1] Over the lone Democrat's objections, two Republican inspectors agreed to register Anthony. She went home, rounded up fourteen more women, and marched back to the barber shop for the next round. As word of her action spread through the city, thirty-five women registered in other wards.

A few days later, on Election Day, voting inspectors in most wards turned the women away, believing newspaper warnings that they could be prosecuted under federal law if they accepted women's ballots. But Anthony, having consulted the retired appellate court judge Henry Selden, who agreed she had a right to vote and said he was willing to represent her, had promised the Eighth Ward inspectors to pay any costs resulting from action taken against them. And so, for the first time, Susan Anthony and the other registered women of Rochester's Eighth Ward cast their votes in a national election.

Anthony and her comrades created an immediate sensation around the country, earning both cheers and attacks. The *New York Times* boldly declared that "the act of Susan B. Anthony should have a place in history"; the *Toledo Blade* praised her for "keeping the public mind agitated upon the women's rights question," while the hometown *Rochester Union and Advertiser* condemned her for "female lawlessness."[2]

But Susan Anthony saw voting as a mere precursor to the main event. Encouraged by the response to her dramatic action, she hoped to launch a test case on behalf of the registered women who had been turned away from the polls. For Anthony, as for the abolitionists Chase and Stewart, litigation was both a means to win concrete rights and an opportunity to convert the courtroom into an arena for protest. A courtroom battle, she believed, would provide a dramatic forum for publicizing the cause. To her friend, the feminist leader Elizabeth Cady Stanton, she wrote about the exhilaration of casting a vote in a national election, and her expectation of the ensuing litigation: "[W]e are in for a fine agitation in Rochester on this question."[3]

Anthony could not have foreseen the course of events that was to result in one of the great state trials of the nineteenth century. The specter of a group of women voting had created quite a stir in Washington, and the Grant administration was not about to let the situation unfold as Anthony anticipated. President Grant had met with Anthony prior to the 1872 election, seeking the feminists' help in his reelection campaign; both Anthony and Stanton had been paid by the Republicans to campaign for Grant. But now that Grant had won reelection, his administration decided to take action against Anthony and her band of middle-aged lawbreakers, who had not only campaigned for Grant but had audaciously voted for him.

On Thanksgiving Day, a federal marshal asked the women voters of Rochester to turn themselves in to be prosecuted under an 1870 federal statute, grandly titled "An Act to Enforce the Right of Citizens of the United States to Vote." The statute, designed to prevent former Confederates from voting illegally and to prevent Klan intimidation of black voters, had ensnared as its first victims a respectable group of northern housewives who had voted for the Republican ticket.

The women did not surrender. As Anthony reported, "The ladies refusing to respond to this polite invitation, Marshal Keeney made the circuit to collect the rebellious forces."[4] Finely tuned to political theater, Anthony even demanded that the courteous and embarrassed marshal take her to jail in handcuffs. Eventually, all the women voters and the three election inspectors who had let them vote were indicted. The stage was thus set for a courtroom battle that would be even more dramatic than the test case Anthony had originally hoped to bring.

To grasp the significance of Anthony's actions, and the impact her trial would have, it's important to understand what Anthony's leadership represented within the feminist movement. Anthony's approach to the case was consistent with her political beliefs, which flowed directly from her personality and background. The Anthony family traced its roots in America to 1634, when John Anthony arrived in Portsmouth, Rhode Island. Susan's father, Daniel, was a sixth-generation Quaker, and the Quaker tradition of resistance to oppression and sympathy to reform movements was strong in the family. Both Daniel and his wife, Lucy Anthony, were abolitionists and supporters of women's rights. Susan, one of the couple's six children, was born in western Massachusetts in 1820 and brought up a strict Quaker.

When Daniel Anthony lost his cotton mill in the business downturns of the 1840s, he moved the family to Rochester, a hotbed of reform movements, and the household became a popular gathering place for antislavery discussions. Frederick Douglass, another Rochester transplant, was a close friend, and prominent abolitionists like William Lloyd Garrison and Wendell Phillips visited regularly. The family was active in the underground railroad in Rochester; two brothers, Daniel R. and Merritt, went to Kansas to fight against slavery in that state.

Susan's devoted father encouraged her involvement in social causes. Her first forays into reform work were in the large and growing temperance movement of the 1840s; later she worked for the abolitionist movement. In 1851, she met Elizabeth Cady Stanton, one of the organizers of the first women's convention at Seneca Falls and the drafter of the Woman's Declaration of Rights. The two quickly became good friends and collaborators, a relationship that was to last for fifty years. Theodore Tilton, the prominent editor and orator, described Anthony and Stanton as "the two sticks of a drum, keeping up what Daniel Webster called the rub-a-dub of agitation."[5]

Stanton was the writer, a brilliant theorist and the better speaker. Neither a talented writer or orator nor a polished politician, Anthony was, however, a remarkably effective organizer and strategist, and her determination, courage, and persistence made her a formidable leader.

Opponents of the women's rights movement recognized her uncompromising honesty, yet often portrayed her as hard featured, sharp tempered, and humorless. But people who knew her remarked on the warmth of her personality, her strong wit and her sense of humor.[6]

During the 1850s and 1860s, Anthony and Stanton were dedicated Garrisonian abolitionists, braving violent mobs and jeering crowds to propagate the message of immediate emancipation and equality for all. From that experience, Anthony and Stanton developed several foundational concepts that were to influence their future work. The first was the principle of absolute human equality. The second was their adoption of Garrison's uncompromising militance. Finally, and most important to their women's suffrage work, they began from the premise that fundamental social change required altering people's ideas, not just the law or political institutions.[7] Their philosophy did not bank on immediate success but focused on a long-term educational program driven by persistent agitation.

Stanton and Anthony were motivated by an optimistic faith, almost religious in nature, that people would eventually support their position. "Do all you can, *no matter what*, to get people to think on your reform," Stanton wrote in her diary, "and then, if the reform is good, it will come about in due season."[8] Early in life, Anthony developed an asceticism based on her belief that "the important thing was to forget self"[9] and to work for a cause. She recognized that women's suffrage was unlikely to be realized in her lifetime, but she took satisfaction in what she called "subsoil plowing"[10] that would bear fruit only later. A belief in the immortality of her work connected her to future generations and sustained her year after year.

When once asked if she prayed, Anthony responded, "I pray every single second of my life; not on my knees but in my work."[11] Anthony's profound spiritual commitment, which saw "in every human being . . . the indestructible . . . germ of immortal life . . . this imperishable spark of divinity,"[12] was the source of her political commitment and her leadership.

Anthony's spiritual faith inspired her to take a long-term view of success and not to be dissuaded by short-term defeats. The *St. Louis Globe-Democrat* expressed the views of many when it editorialized that

Miss Anthony is one of the most remarkable women of the Nineteenth Century—remarkable for the purity of her life, the earnestness with which she promulgates her peculiar views, *and the indomitable courage with which she bears defeat and misfortune*.[13]

But Anthony's personality was only one factor behind the events that would culminate in her dramatic trial. The political meaning of the litigation cannot be understood without also examining the state of the women's suffrage movement at the time. To begin with, Anthony's decision to register and vote was not spontaneous or individual; it was the product of a well-thought out strategy that the group she and Stanton led, the National Women Suffrage Association, had adopted three years earlier. The strategy was developed in reaction to the political climate of the late 1860s and early 1870s and included test-case litigation as one important component of a broader constitutional-political strategy.

The women's movement had emerged from the Civil War with great hopes. Most of its leaders had been ardent abolitionists who believed that the emancipation of slaves would bring civil and political rights for all, including women. But the feminists were to be deeply disappointed. Proclaiming the primacy of "the Negro's Hour," their erstwhile allies in the Republican Party and abolitionist circles largely abandoned women's suffrage. The coalition of prewar years collapsed during the bruising fight over the Fourteenth and Fifteenth Amendments, with most prominent abolitionists placing women's suffrage on the back burner to avoid complicating and possibly derailing the fight for black suffrage.

The Fourteenth Amendment, enacted in 1868 over the opposition of many feminists, including Anthony and Stanton, contained the Constitution's first explicitly sex-based distinction, basing congressional representation on the number of male citizens. The Fifteenth Amendment, which prohibited only race discrimination in voting and not also gender discrimination, was also opposed by many feminists but passed the following year. The passage of the Reconstruction Amendments without any express affirmation of women's right to vote created what appeared to be, in the words of the historian Ellen DuBois, "a strategic dead end for woman suffrage."[14]

That dead end was compounded by a split in the women's movement. In 1869, Anthony and Stanton, dissatisfied with the predominantly male leadership of the Equal Rights Association, organized the National Women's Suffrage Association. Another group, led by Lucy Stone, Julia Ward Howe, and Howe's husband, Henry Blackwell, became the rival American Women's Suffrage Association. The NWSA, with its broad demands for equality, was more militant. It opposed the Reconstruction Amendments and emphasized federal over state action to enfranchise women. The AWSA focused exclusively on women's right to vote, sought to avoid alienating influential community leaders, and concentrated its practical work for suffrage within each state.

Meanwhile, middle-class women, emboldened and politicized by their relief work during the Civil War, had begun showing up at the polls asserting a right to vote. In 1868, almost 200 women attempted to vote in the radical, spiritualist town of Vineland, New Jersey, while, a year later, Mary Olney Brown sought to vote in Washington territory. The increasing rights-oriented assertiveness was not confined to American soil; in 1868, English women brought and lost a lawsuit to obtain voting rights, a lawsuit prominently featured in Anthony's and Stanton's newspaper, *The Revolution*.[15]

By 1869, though, divisions and disillusionment brought the movement to a strategic and tactical watershed. At an 1869 women's suffrage convention, a husband-and-wife team of Missouri suffragists, Francis and Virginia Minor, proposed a radical new approach. The Minors argued that, instead of agitating for a new constitutional provision granting women the right to vote, feminists should assert that they already had the constitutional right to vote. The Minors saw a way to use the controversial Reconstruction Amendments to their advantage, asserting that voting was "a privilege or immunity" of U.S. citizenship, protected by the Fourteenth Amendment to the Constitution. Susan Anthony was taken with the approach. She and Stanton printed the Minors' argument in their newspaper and published 10,000 extra copies, sending it to all members of Congress.[16] The NWSA adopted the argument, and it became the cornerstone of the organization's work for the next half decade.

The strategy urged by the Minors and accepted by the NWSA became known as the New Departure movement and represented a basic turn toward a rights-conscious women's movement.[17] And this rights strategy inevitably led to the courthouse.

The New Departurists believed in a combination of direct action and litigation. They urged women to attempt to vote and, if prevented, to sue the officials who had denied them that right. The Minors clearly viewed litigation as a means not only of vindicating rights but also of educating the public. Francis Minor urged that a test case be brought, because "in no other way could our cause be more widely, and at the same time definitely, brought before the public. Every newspaper in the land would tell the story, every fireside would hear the news. The question would be thoroughly discussed by thousands who now give it no thought."[18]

Suffragists' political efforts had not won the vote; now litigation opened up a new arena of action. The New Departurists did not write on a blank slate but continued many of the same litigation strategies pursued by abolitionists in the 1840s and 1850s. Like Alvan Stewart and his associates, Anthony and the Minors viewed the original Constitution's guarantee of a republican form of government as requiring equal rights for all. Like Stewart and Chase before them, they insisted that the Constitution be interpreted consistently with the Declaration of Independence. As the prominent suffragist Isabella Beecher Hooker said, testifying before Congress, "in my heart my claim to vote is based upon the original Constitution, interpreted by the Declaration of Independence."[19] For these suffragists, the Fourteenth Amendment "formulated into law the Declaration of Independence,"[20] incorporating the radical constitutional abolitionists' view of equality and natural rights into the Constitution. Anthony and Stanton repeatedly quoted Republican Senator Charles Sumner's statement that "the true rule of interpretation under our National Constitution especially since its Amendments, is that anything for human rights is constitutional," which itself was a rephrasing of Stewart's view that the Constitution should always be interpreted in favor of liberty.[21]

That Anthony and Stanton would adopt the radical constitutional abolitionists' viewpoint was somewhat surprising. Stanton and Anthony had come of age as Garrisonian abolitionists, believing that the Constitution was in conflict with the people's natural rights. Now they adopted the position that human rights were not in opposition to, but incorporated within, the Constitution.

Their transformation reflected a larger change in Republican ideology after the Civil War. The ideas first proposed by a small group of abolitionists such as Stewart, dismissed as utopian, foolhardy and irrelevant in the two decades before the war, were resurrected by radical Republicans during Reconstruction. Before the war, most Republicans had supported state autonomy, thus recognizing the maintenance of slavery in the southern states while asserting the free states' refusal to recognize slavery within their own borders. After the war, Republicans viewed the Constitution and the national government, including the courts, as the protector of the people's fundamental rights.

In 1866, Senator Sumner argued in the Senate almost exactly what Alvan Stewart had urged twenty years earlier in the New Jersey slave case: that the original Constitution was antislavery and could have been utilized by the courts and Congress to eradicate slavery.[22] Now Sumner, himself an antislavery and equal-rights litigator in the 1840s and 1850s, urged Anthony to test her theories in court:

> There is not a doubt but women have the constitutional right to vote. . . . I voted for both the 14th and 15th [Amendments] under protest; would never have done it but for the pressing emergency of that hour; would have insisted that the power of the original Constitution to protect all citizens in the equal enjoyment of their rights should have been vindicated through the courts. . . . I insist that [women] shall appeal to the courts, and through them establish the powers of our American *magna charta*, to protect every citizen of the Republic.[23]

Other important Republican Party figures such as former Congressman Albert Gallatin Riddle, of Ohio, an antislavery lawyer and close associate of Chase's in the 1850s, also argued for a court test. Many, like the Republican attorney general of New York, J. H. Martindale, believed as early as 1866 that the court would find "the right to vote . . . a constitutional right appertaining to native, national citizenship."[24] And, at the apex of the federal judiciary, sitting now as chief justice of the U.S. Supreme Court, was Salmon Chase, who believed that the Fourteenth Amendment's privileges and immunities guaranteed voting rights for the freed slave and who claimed to support women's suffrage. In this ideological environment, Anthony, the Minors, and Stanton hopefully resurrected the arguments that the political abolitionists had fruitlessly made to the courts in the 1840s.

The idea that women need not demand more rights but merely take what was already theirs galvanized the women's movement. As Francis Minor put it, "We no longer beat the air, no longer assume merely the attitude of petitioners. We claim a right, based upon citizenship."[25] Anthony said she resolved to "never again beg [for] my rights, but . . . demand the recognition of them under the guarantees of the National Constitution."[26] The new approach "changed the tone of the speeches in our conventions," Stanton proudly proclaimed, "from whinings about brutal husbands, stolen babies, and special laws, to fundamental principles of human rights."[27]

Of course, resort to test-case litigation had its critics, even among supporters of women's suffrage. The famous abolitionist orator Wendell Phillips agreed with the New Departurists' claim that the Fourteenth Amendment's protection of citizens' privileges and immunities required women suffrage but believed that the legal argument was "too good a handle for agitation to be risked by a speedy contest in the courts." As Phillips prophetically argued, "an adverse decision would destroy its value as a new means of attack."[28] The Nation opined that the change the New Departurists hoped for was too momentous to occur through judicial resolution; women's suffrage, the paper editorialized, could not be achieved "by anything short of deliberate popular consent."[29] The American Women's Suffrage Association viewed the litigation effort as foolhardy, and even Stanton, while she admired much about the approach, was never enthusiastic about a court test. Yet, the Minors, Anthony, and many women across the country were determined to force the courts to address their constitutional claims.

The NWSA leaders approached their litigation optimistically. The New Departurists did recognize that the courts were "cautious and conservative" and that therefore temporary setbacks could be expected, but they had faith that "the interpretation of the Constitution which we maintain, we can not doubt, will be ultimately adopted by the courts."[30] The women and their male supporters located themselves within Republican postwar ideology, arguing that they were not making any great constitutional innovation but only restoring the historical connection between the theory of American constitutionalism and its practice.

Before a test case was brought, however, the New Departure movement made a dramatic entrance into the political arena. In January 1871, Victoria Woodhull, a well-known advocate of sexual liberation and free love, secured a hearing before the House Judiciary Committee and argued that the Fourteenth and Fifteenth Amendments guaranteed women's right to vote.[31] The New Departure leaders immediately adopted Woodhull's arguments and urged Congress to pass a law enforcing women's inalienable right to vote under the Amendments. Although the House Judiciary Committee rejected Woodhull's position, a strong dissent on the Committee continued to give hope to the New Departure leaders.[32]

The next year, the NWSA leaders obtained a hearing before the Senate Judiciary Committee. Hundreds of women attempting to gain entrance to the hearing filled the corridors of the Capitol. Stanton told the senators that Woodhull's statement had "roused wise men to thought," opened up "a new and fruitful source of litigation," and inspired women "with fresh hope that the day of [their] enfranchisement is at hand."[33]

Even as the movement's leadership agitated in Congress, women across the country were launching direct actions and litigation. By 1872, the NWSA was mobilizing women across the country to report to the polls and attempt to vote. Women voted in Detroit and in Nyack, New York; they attempted to vote in Michigan, Missouri, Ohio, Connecticut, and New York. In California, Pennsylvania, and Illinois, women unsuccessfully sued state officials who refused to let them register and vote. Seventy-two women who had marched as a group to the polls in Washington, D.C., and been turned back sued in the District of Columbia Supreme Court. The court unanimously held that, despite plaintiffs' "ingenious argument," there was no natural or inherent right to vote. "[T]he legal vindication of the natural right of all citizens to vote" would, declared Judge Cartter, "involve the destruction of civil government."[34]

This, then, was the climate in which the government indicted Susan B. Anthony and in which Anthony and the New Departurists planned their legal defense and political strategy. Anthony focused on two major aims: in the short term, she wanted to take her case to the Supreme Court for a definitive decision, while, in the long term, she hoped to use the case as a means of educating the public on women's right to vote. Her first aim immediately ran into obstacles.

After being arraigned on December 23, 1872, in a dingy courtroom that had once been used to hold runaway slaves before they were returned to their masters, Anthony refused to pay bail. Instead, she filed for a writ of habeas corpus, and she was released from jail pending a decision on the writ. On January 21, 1873, District Court Judge Nathan Hall, who had a reputation as an erratic, vindictive judge, denied her writ and increased her bail to $1,000. Anthony again refused to pay bail, preferring jail to cooperation. One of her lawyers, Henry Selden, a former lieutenant governor of New York and an old abolitionist friend of Frederick Douglass, insisted, over Anthony's objection, on paying the bail himself. When Anthony left the courtroom, her other attorney, John

Van Voorhis, explained that, by paying the bail, she had lost her chance to appeal the denial of the writ of habeas corpus to the Supreme Court. Anthony turned to Selden and angrily asked, "Did you not know that you stopped me from carrying my case to the Supreme Court?" Yes, Selden admitted, "but I could not see a lady I respected put in jail."[35] Anthony rushed back to withdraw the bail, but it was too late.[36] While Anthony appreciated Selden's excellent legal defense and his tremendous commitment to her case, she never forgave him for paying her bail.

With the habeas corpus motion decided, Anthony turned to her other goal: stirring up the "fine agitation" that she yearned for. She launched a broad speaking campaign to educate the people of Rochester on the right of all citizens to have equal access to the ballot. Over the course of the next several months, Anthony spoke in twenty-nine different post-office districts in the county, hoping, she said, "to make a verdict of guilty impossible."[37] Her campaign obviously was having an impact, for the district attorney moved to change the trial's venue to another county, and the court granted his motion.

The change of venue did not stop Anthony's agitation. In the twenty-two days before the opening of the trial, Anthony made twenty-one speeches in the new county to which the action had been transferred. Another suffrage leader, Matilda Joslyn Gage, spoke in an additional sixteen townships. Together they covered the entire county, taking the offensive and declaring that "the United States [is] on trial, not Susan B. Anthony."[38] Anthony publicized her argument that she had committed no crime but simply exercised her citizen's right to vote, as guaranteed by the Constitution.

At times, Anthony felt frustrated with the response to her case. During one such period, she discouragedly noted in her diary that "so few see or feel any special importance in the impending trial."[39] Although suffrage clubs in New York, Buffalo, Chicago, and Milwaukee sent $50 and $100 contributions to her defense fund, the contributions Anthony collected at her speeches were too small to pay her legal fees. The women activists of Rochester rallied behind her, but, except for Gage, none of the national leaders of NWSA came to Rochester to help. Resolutions were passed and supportive speeches made, but Stanton and the other leaders of the movement did not actively work on her behalf, perhaps believing that the court battle was unlikely to yield a satisfactory result.

Whatever problems she had, Anthony clearly was successful in generating nationwide publicity. Her use of the pending court proceeding as a forum on women's suffrage set off a lively debate in the press. The *Syracuse Standard* wrote that "Miss S. B. Anthony . . . is conducting her case in a way that beats even lawyers," while the *New York Commercial Advertiser* admired the "regular St. Anthony's dance she leads the District Attorney . . . in spite of winter cold or summer heat, [Anthony] will carry her case from county to county precisely as fast as the venue is changed. One must rise very early in the morning to get the start of this active apostle of the sisterhood."[40] Other papers excoriated Anthony's attempt to influence public opinion. A *Rochester Union & Advertiser* piece was headlined, "Susan B. Anthony as a Corruptionist" and angrily declared that "United States Courts are not stages for the enactment of comedy or farce."[41] A reader wrote in that Anthony was committing "a law offense known as embracery," defined as "such practices as lead to affect the administration of justice, *improperly working upon the minds of jurors*."[42]

Anthony's trial opened on June 18, 1873 before the newly-appointed Supreme Court justice Ward Hunt, described by the suffragists as "a small-brained, pale-faced, prim-looking man."[43] The packed courtroom included such notables as former President Millard Fillmore, Senator Charles Sedgwick, and former Congressman E. G. Lapham.

Justice Hunt's appearance as the judge presiding over the trial was suspicious; normally, District Judge Nathan Hall, who had handled all the preliminary hearing and change-of-venue motions, would have tried the case. But the Grant administration did not trust Hall and wanted to dispose quickly of what promised to be an embarrassing case. Hunt, recently appointed to his Supreme Court position through the influence of Senator Roscoe Conkling, of New York, an ardent foe of women's suffrage, was a more reliable jurist for the government.

Justice Hunt immediately made it clear that he was determined to limit Anthony's use of the case for political protest. He refused to permit Anthony to be a witness in her own behalf, ruling that she was incompetent, although he did allow the assistant U.S. district attorney to submit hearsay evidence of Anthony's testimony at pretrial hearings.

After Selden's three-hour argument and the district attorney's rebuttal, Judge Hunt read his prepared opinion. Written before the trial had commenced, it stated that Anthony had no right to vote under the

Constitution and that any mistaken belief she may have had about such a right did not excuse her criminal action. As a matter of law, he directed the jury to find Anthony guilty and then discharged the jury. One member of the jury later reported that he and other jurors would have voted to acquit had they been afforded the opportunity.

The court then moved to sentence Anthony and asked her whether she had anything to say. When she launched into a defense of women's suffrage, Judge Hunt ordered her to sit down and shut up, insisting that she had been "tried according to the established forms of law."[44] Anthony responded by comparing Hunt's verdict to the decisions of judges who had decided against fugitive slaves, thus highlighting the connection between the radical constitutional abolitionists and her own constitutional struggle for women's suffrage.

Hunt fined Anthony $100 and the costs of the prosecution, to which Anthony replied that she would not pay a penny and would exhort women that "resistance to tyranny is obedience to God."[45] But Anthony was not sent to prison for refusing to pay her fine. In an unusual move for such a case, Hunt said that he would not order Anthony imprisoned until the fine was paid. As Anthony's lawyer John Van Voorhis later commented, it was an adroit move, intended to deny Anthony the ability to use a writ of habeus corpus to take her case directly to the Supreme Court of the United States, where she would have had an excellent argument that her right to trial by jury had been denied. "There was a pre-arranged determination to convict Susan B. Anthony,"[46] said Voorhis. "A jury trial was dangerous and so the Constitution was openly and deliberately violated."[47] Anthony never paid the fine, the government never proceeded to enforce the fine or to jail her, the other women voters' cases were not prosecuted, and Anthony lost her chance for Supreme Court review.

For some of Anthony's colleagues, the lesson of the trial was that courts were not useful forums of struggle. Former Republican Congressman Albert Gallatin Riddle, a strong proponent of litigation who had represented the would-be women voters of the District of Columbia, wrote Anthony in despair: "There is not, I think the slightest hope from the courts; and just as little from the politicians," he concluded. "They will never take up this cause, never."[48]

But others continued to agitate and organize around the trial, springing into action again when the three inspectors who had allowed Anthony and her cohorts to vote were brought to trial and eventually jailed. The inspectors met with the same remarkable bias that Anthony had encountered: this time, Judge Hunt instructed the jury to find the inspectors guilty. When defense counsel asked Hunt why he was submitting the case to the jury, since he had already charged the jury that there was sufficient evidence to sustain the indictment, Judge Hunt answered that it was "a matter of form."[49] The jury, after lengthy deliberations, eventually voted to convict.

The inspectors' case became a national issue when Anthony, as she'd promised the inspectors before she voted, persuaded Senator Aaron Sergeant, of California, to intervene with an appeal to President Grant. During the week that the inspectors languished in jail, hundreds of local supporters visited "the boys," and the women voters of Rochester cooked dinner daily for the prisoners. On March 3, 1874, Grant pardoned the inspectors.

Altogether, Anthony's case did generate substantial public controversy. The women voters were largely portrayed with sympathy: one newspaper described the "lawbreakers" as "elderly matronly-looking women with thoughtful faces, just the sort one would like to see in charge of one's sickroom, considerate, patient, and kindly." The *Albany Law Journal* agreed with the guilty verdict and suggested that Anthony "adopt the methods of reform that men use, or better still, migrate," but criticized Hunt's decision to remove the case from the jury. The *New York Sun* attacked Hunt for violating one of the most important provisions of the Constitution, while the *Utica Observer* approved Hunt's interpretation of the Fourteenth Amendment but nonetheless condemned his seizure of jury power.[50] Virtually every newspaper in the country reported and commented on the trial, and several reprinted Anthony's arguments about women's right to vote.

More than a thousand dollars and scores of letters of support poured in to Anthony after Hunt's verdict. She used most of the money to publish a pamphlet containing a full report on the trial. Three thousand copies were sent out to libraries and newspapers all over the country, and five thousand copies of Selden's argument were also distributed.[51] The next year, one newspaper called Anthony "America's best known woman."[52] She had used litigation successfully to protest women's inequality, speaking to thousands of people about the case, engaging prominent figures in her agitation up to and including the president of the United States, and initiating debate in legal journals, as well as in the popular press of the day.

Anthony lost in court, but, as Supreme Court Justice Sandra Day O'Connor has noted, "In another respect, Susan B. Anthony was the clear victor. Her treatment at the hands of the judicial system won for her the sympathy even of those who had been opposed to her original act."[53]

The most decisive legal setbacks suffered by the New Departure movement came as a result of affirmative litigation brought in the 1870s under the Fourteenth Amendment's privileges and immunities clause. After these losses, the question for the New Departurists became whether the political gain from using the courts to publicize their cause would outweigh the high-profile legal defeats.

In 1873, the Supreme Court rejected the New Departurists' privileges and immunities argument, turning down Myra Bradwell's request to be admitted to the bar of Illinois. The case was a crippling blow to suffragists' interpretation of the Fourteenth Amendment, but its consequences had political value for the movement.

Myra Bradwell was a moderate suffragist who had strong ties to the legal and political elite of Illinois. A good friend of the late President Lincoln and his wife, Mary, she was later instrumental in rescuing Mary Todd Lincoln from the insane asylum where her son had confined her.[54] In 1869, Bradwell passed the Illinois bar examination; she was denied admission to the bar because of her sex and sued in the Illinois Supreme Court. While expressing some sympathy for Bradwell's claim, eventually the court rejected her admission "because it is not the province of a court to attempt, by giving a new interpretation to an ancient statute, to introduce so important a change in the legal position of one-half the people. Courts of justice were not intended to be made the instruments of pushing forward measures of popular reform."[55]

Bradwell appealed to the United States Supreme Court, using the New Departure argument that women's rights were a fundamental privilege and immunity of citizenship protected by the Fourteenth Amendment. Bradwell's aim was not to get admitted to the bar: indeed, by the time her case was argued, the Illinois legislature had amended the law to admit women to the bar, and Bradwell, by then the editor of a successful and well-respected legal journal, had no interest in practicing law. Bradwell retained Matt H. Carpenter, of Wisconsin, an eminent Republican U.S. senator and one of the best-known Supreme Court advocates of his era, to argue her case. It was closely followed by New Departure advocates as an indication of how much support their position could expect to receive from the courts and from the Republican Party.

The press generally viewed Bradwell's Fourteenth Amendment argument as foolhardy. The *New York World* excoriated the "preposterous" claim of a Chicago "she-attorney" that the Fourteenth Amendment granted her the right to practice law as one of the "follies" currently seeking protection under that Amendment.[56] The progressive magazine *The Nation* viewed Bradwell's claim as a "rather ludicrous illustration of the character of the woman movement" and surmised that "she must have known the court would decide against her, unless she either supposed that they were likely to be influenced by personal solicitation and clamor, or else that they were all gone crazy."[57] Sensing the uphill nature of the battle, Carpenter chose to commence his brief with a long discourse arguing that voting was not a privilege and immunity protected by the Fourteenth Amendment, but the right to practice a profession was. Although a strong supporter of women's suffrage in the Senate, Carpenter felt that the potential explosiveness and radical nature of the New Departure suffrage interpretation required him to distinguish Bradwell's claim from the women's suffrage movement. Anthony was furious with Carpenter's decision to distance the case from suffrage and termed his argument "a schoolboy pettifogging speech, wholly without basic principle."[58]

In any case, Carpenter's strategy didn't work. By an 8–1 vote the Court rejected Bradwell's claim, with only Chief Justice Salmon Chase dissenting. The majority tersely held, citing the *Slaughter-house Cases* decided the same day,[59] that the right to practice law in a state was not a privilege and immunity of U.S. citizenship protected by the Fourteenth Amendment. Justice Joseph Bradley, joined by Justices Noah Swayne and Stephen Field, concurred in the judgment because "the natural and proper timidity and delicacy which belongs to the female sex evidently unfits it for many of the occupations of civil life."[60]

Bradwell, however, claimed victory, writing, several weeks after her defeat in the high court, "Although we have not succeeded in obtaining an opinion as we hoped, which should affect the rights of women throughout the nation, we are more than compensated for all our trouble in seeing, as the result of the agitation, statutes passed in several States, including our own, admitting women upon the same terms as men. Women have since been admitted in Wyoming, Utah, the District of Columbia, Iowa, Missouri, Ohio and several other States."[61]

Upon Bradwell's death in 1894, one of her eulogists recognized the great political value of her losing legal battle. "Discussion of the *Myra Bradwell* case had the inevitable effect of letting sunlight through many cobwebbed windows." Losing cases often promote political discussion and change, because "it is not so much by abstract reasoning as by visible examples that reformations come" and Mrs. Bradwell provided a living example of the injustices of the law. That a person of Myra Bradwell's stature and learning was barred from the practice of law "was too much for the public conscience, tough as the conscience is."[62]

Even so, the *Bradwell* case was a devastating blow to the New Departurists' interpretation of the Fourteenth Amendment. Legal advocates for women's suffrage still maintained, at least in public, an optimistic view of the legal possibilities, but as a practical matter there was no way that the New Departure voting argument would win in the Supreme Court. Even Anthony's initial optimism about the Court had evaporated; she wrote to Myra Bradwell in 1873 that "the courts are so entirely controlled by prejudice and precedent we have nothing to hope from them but endorsement of dead men's actions."[63]

In 1875, the Supreme Court dealt the definitive defeat to the New Departurists' legal strategy in *Minor v. Happersett*. Virginia Minor and her husband, Francis, were co-plaintiffs in the case, reflecting their role as the architects of the New Departure approach to litigation. Descended from a distinguished, outspoken and liberal Virginia family, Virginia Minor married her cousin Francis Minor, a graduate of Princeton and of the University of Virginia Law School. The couple moved to St. Louis in 1845, and had one child, who died in a shooting accident at the age of fourteen.[64] Despite their southern backgrounds, the Minors supported the Union during the Civil War. Like many other women, Virginia Minor found that her participation in the war effort deepened her interest in public service and political affairs. To Phoeboe Couzins, a close St. Louis ally of Virginia Minor and the first woman to practice law in Missouri, the war was "the great motor which awakened her thought and roused her interest in humanity."[65]

Minor's first foray into women's suffrage came in 1866, when she organized women to send a letter to Senator Cratz Brown, of Missouri, commending him for his speech on behalf of women's suffrage given in the District of Columbia. The next year she organized a petition to amend the Missouri Constitution to permit women to vote. Later in 1867, she founded and became the president of the Woman Suffrage Association of Missouri, the first organization in the country dedicated solely to obtaining suffrage for American women.

By 1872, the Minors and the NWSA were prepared to test their constitutional theory in court. That year the NWSA undertook a major direct action voting campaign: after Anthony voted, she wrote, "I hope the morning telegrams will tell of many women all over the country trying to vote."[66] Virginia Minor had attempted to vote in St. Louis, and, after being refused, she, along with her husband (a necessary party, since married women did not have the legal status to sue on their own), filed a constitutional challenge in the Missouri courts. The Minors, as had Anthony in Rochester, sought and obtained the support of important members of Missouri's political and legal elite. Francis Minor secured as his co-counsel former Republican Senator John B. Henderson and a prominent St. Louis lawyer, James M. Krum. Henderson, a moderate Republican senator, had authored the Thirteenth Amendment, had argued for the inclusion of women's rights in the Fourteenth Amendment, and was a principal agitator for the Fifteenth Amendment.

Despite their prominent co-counsel, the Minors had little support from the established suffrage movement. In 1871, the Woman Suffrage Association of Missouri voted to affiliate with the AWSA, which thought that suffrage litigation was foolhardy, and the Minors resigned from the organization they had founded. The NWSA supported them, but without the level of activism that Anthony's case had generated.

The Minors' case reached the Supreme Court in 1874, one year after the *Bradwell* case. Chief Justice Chase, the only dissenter in *Bradwell*, had died and been replaced by Justice Morrison R. Waite.[67] Defeat seemed a foregone conclusion. Indeed, the state of Missouri did not even submit a brief to the Court.

The Minors' strategy was to rely on broad political-constitutional arguments, instead of narrow legalistic positions. Knowing the Court would almost certainly rule against them, they sought at least to force the Court to confront the basic issue of women's status as citizens. As one commentator has noted, "The language in all the Minors' briefs is both so constitutionally and politically extreme for the time that it leads one to wonder whether the briefs were written to win in court or for posterity."[68] The Minors recognized that

[m]en accept [women's disenfranchisement] as a matter of fact, and-
take for granted it must be right. So in the days of African slavery, thousands believed it to be right—even a Divine institution. But this belief
has passed away; and, in like manner, this doctrine of the right of the
States to exercise unlimited and absolute control over the elective franchise of citizens of the United States, must and will give way to a truer
and better understanding of the subject. The plaintiff's case is simply
one of the means by which this end will ultimately be reached.[69]

With dispositive victory beyond their grasp, the Minors appealed to
posterity and viewed their case as merely "one of the means," by which
public opinion would ultimately be changed.

Substantively, the Minors argued that women were citizens at the
time the Constitution was ratified and that voting in national elections
was a fundamental right of such citizenship. The Minors rejected the
possibility of halfway citizenship and, like Stewart and Chase before
them, relied heavily on the Declaration of Independence as the basis of
a republican Constitution. "Either we must give up the principles announced in the Declaration of Independence, that governments derive
their just powers from the consent of the governed," they wrote, "or we
must acknowledge the truth contended for by the plaintiff, that citizenship carries with it every incident to every citizen alike."[70] Tied, but sub-
ordinated, to this broad argument was a strong but narrow claim: that
federal rather than state law must govern the issue of the plaintiffs'
right to vote in national elections. The states could regulate the voting
process but could not arbitrarily deprive persons of their ability to vote
for president and vice president, because to do so was to interfere with
the functioning of the federal government. The Fourteenth Amendment
merely supported these propositions.

Minor v. Happersett was argued before the Court on February 5,
1875. Missouri did not send counsel to argue, and Francis Minor
adopted a peculiar position, refusing to get drawn into answering the
legal distinctions that are the grist of Supreme Court arguments. The
New York Times reported that Justice Stephen Field questioned Minor as
to whether citizenship automatically confers a right to vote. When
Minor responded that it did, Field asked whether children therefore
have the right to vote. Minor somewhat inexplicably responded, "Yes,
sir," and the *Times* parenthetically and sarcastically added "without any
further explanation." The *Times* account continues:

The court generally seemed inclined to rally the counsel but as he either did not relish the piquant interruption and therefore purposely refrained from replying, or was unable to respond to the satisfaction of their Honors, they soon ceased to ply him with questions.[71]

The general assumption was that, since Minor was a capable attorney and had had six years to think through these distinctions, he must have been trying to argue on his terms, to force the Court to deal with his politics, knowing full well that he had no chance of winning legally. He tried to goad the Court into addressing his broad arguments, concluding with his political point: "It is impossible that there can be a Republican government in which one half the citizens thereof are forever tainted."[72] As the Court clerk noted, a substantial part of Francis Minor's elaborate argument was based on "what he deemed true political grounds," with only a part "resting on legal and constitutional grounds."[73]

Minor's strategy was successful in engaging the Court. While the plaintiffs' legal claim was rejected unanimously, the Court did respond to their political and constitutional arguments. Chief Justice Waite started his opinion by noting that the Court could have dismissed the case on technical grounds but instead chose to address the central issue of whether women could be denied the right of suffrage. Perhaps troubled by Minor's charge that to establish a group of second-class citizens was despotism, the Court spent most of its fourteen-page decision responding to Minor's broad constitutional arguments.

Waite agreed that women had always been U.S. citizens and that the Fourteenth Amendment "did not affect the citizenship of women."[74] But he then undertook a lengthy analysis of the historical practice to argue that:

For nearly ninety years the people have acted upon the idea that the Constitution, when it conferred citizenship, did not necessarily confer the right of suffrage. If uniform practice long continued can settle the construction of so important an instrument as the Constitution of the United States confessedly is, most certainly it has been done here. Our province is to decide what the law is, not to declare what it should be.[75]

Although the Court was clearly troubled by the prospect of imposing second-class citizenship on women, it rationalized its decision by resorting to history, original intent, and the usual positivistic platitudes. Perhaps the law needed to be changed, it said, but the power to do so lay elsewhere. The Minors had forced the Court to adopt a jurisprudential rationale for withholding women's rights similar to the one used twenty years earlier in the *Dred Scott* decision to deny black people their rights.

And so, with *Minor v. Happersett*, the New Departurist legal strategy that had commenced with such fanfare died with a whimper. The Minor decision received little attention at the time and remains to this day virtually unnoticed outside a small circle of feminist scholars. In hindsight, the position of Congressman William Loughridge, of Iowa, seems prescient. Loughridge, arguing that the movement should not follow a litigation strategy, explained:

> In this country, on questions involving political rights the courts are generally in the rear rank; the people are mostly in advance of the courts. In my opinion the most speedy and certain victory will be acquired through the political departments of the government.[76]

Certainly, from the perspective of legal victory, the New Departure strategy was a disastrous failure. Not one judge who heard the 1870s suffrage cases agreed that the Constitution protected women's right to vote. Not one opinion concurred with the movement's legal analysis of "privileges and immunities." Not a single woman was empowered by the courts to vote.

Yet, the New Departure movement's success cannot be measured simply by short-term legal outcomes. As one historian noted, the New Departurists were not primarily "outcome-oriented" litigants but activists who believed that the real success of their strategy "must be measured in terms of the amount and kind of publicity it was able to generate."[77] Furthermore, for Anthony and her colleagues, success was never tied solely to winning, and losing was not synonymous with defeat. Asked at the age of eighty-five about her many losses, Anthony replied: "Defeats? There have been none in my life and work. All our defeats have been glorious victories, in that the cause of women has never been presented to the voters of the country without winning very many of them."[78]

From this perspective, the New Departure movement did achieve a certain success in using the courts as a political forum. Positing a constitutionally guaranteed right to vote spurred half a decade of dynamic political activity. Anthony's chief counsel, Selden, later sarcastically expressed his gratitude to the authorities for initiating her case in the form of a criminal prosecution: "If the advocates of female suffrage had been allowed to choose the point of attack to be made upon their position, they could not have chosen it more favorably for themselves."[79]

The *Anthony* case was one of the most important state trials of the second half of the nineteenth century and received a great deal of public attention. The *Bradwell* and *Minor* cases were less prominent, probably due to several factors: Anthony's stature and her ability to attract members of the elite to her defense; the massive political organizing she and her associates undertook; the rapid resolution of her trial, unlike the years-long Minor litigation; Anthony's status as a criminal defendant, rather than an affirmative litigant; and the fact that the *Minor* case was decided in 1875, after the movement had been defeated on virtually every front and the constitutional interpretation already rejected. But all of the New Departure cases, in their different ways, sparked organizing, agitation, and political change. Even the *Minor* case, which attracted the least public attention, was given serious consideration by the country's highest court at a time when, according to the eminent conservative historian of the Supreme Court Charles Fairman, "women suffrage was not taken very seriously" and thus, in Fairman's estimation "left a mark that could not be effaced."[80]

Still, the suffragists had obviously expected to win more from their legal battles. NWSA activists had hoped the *Minor* and *Anthony* decisions would do for women's suffrage what *Dred Scott* did for the abolitionists. As one biographer has noted, Anthony "asked nothing better than to become the Dred Scott of the woman movement," for, if the courts ruled against her, "a flaming brand of resentment would be kindled in women's hearts that no time and no flood would ever extinguish."[81]

It did not happen. The New Departure losses never resulted in the kind of ferment that *Dred Scott* stimulated in the 1850s or that the *Plessy v. Ferguson* decision upholding segregation did in the 1940s. Some women and men continued taking direct action: as late as 1895, Elizabeth Grannis made her eighth attempt to register to vote.[82] Two years after the Supreme Court ruled against the Minors, six California women, including Clara Foltz, who was to become the state's first woman lawyer, attempted to register and were turned away. Women's tax resistance continued into the 1870s and 1880s under the slogan "No Taxation without Representation." The Women's Taxpayers Association, formed in Rochester to organize support for Anthony's trial, actively promoted suffrage work for the rest of the century.[83] In general, though, the defeats failed to galvanize the movement.

The New Departurists continued to maintain that their constitutional position was correct. After their defeats in court, however, the NWSA generally abandoned litigation and focused on the political sphere to lobby for what would became the Nineteenth Amendment to the Constitution. As Elizabeth Cady Stanton explained, "seeing by these decisions of the courts that the theory of our government, the Declaration of Independence and recent constitutional amendments have no significance for women . . . we must fall back once more to our former demand of a sixteenth amendment to the federal constitution."[84] Two women suffrage leaders, Carrie Chapman Catt and Nettie Rogers Schuler, were more acerbic about futility of courtroom struggles for suffragists: "Again and again . . . eminently qualified lawyers with briefs in hand begged suffragists to make further appeals to the court for affirmation of their rights as set forth in the [Fourteenth] Amendment, but the women . . . steadfastly refused to waste any more time in efforts to get favorable judicial decisions to support their claim to the suffrage under the provisions of that amendment."[85]

The real contribution made by the New Departure movement turned out not to be in the area of law, where the New Departurists were soundly defeated, or even in the arena of immediate agitation, where it had a mixed impact. The early feminists realized that women's suffrage would not be seen in their lifetime and that only history would vindicate them. Anthony viewed her work as "seed-sowing"; it was in the future, and not her own era, that the fruits of her work would appear.

A quarter-century after her famous case, Anthony noted that, while she had "never started out to gain honor or notoriety for myself," she had "always longed to stand well on the page of history."[86] And history did vindicate at least some of the New Departure movement's legal theories. Anthony's articulation of an unwritten constitution incorporating certain natural or fundamental rights resurfaced in the 1960s and 1970s with the feminist legal challenge to restrictive contraceptive and abortion laws. Stanton's assertion that "the numerous demands by the people for national protection in many rights not specified by the constitution, prove that the people have outgrown the compact that satisfied the fathers"[87] was similarly vindicated by the Supreme Court a hundred years later in *Griswold v. Connecticut* and in *Roe v. Wade*,[88] where the Court held that the right to privacy, while not written into the Constitution, was nonetheless a fundamental right protected by the due process clause of the Fourteenth Amendment. And state restrictions on voting, while never held to infringe on a privilege or immunity of national citizenship, are now strictly scrutinized by the Supreme Court, which views voting as fundamental to our constitutional democracy.

But, in fact, the direct legal impact of the New Departurists on subsequent feminist litigation is questionable. The arguments made by Anthony, the Minors, and the other New Departure leaders are not mentioned explicitly in either the *Griswold* or *Roe* due process litigation, and they were not central to the legal strategies of feminists in the 1960s and 1970s. Indeed, it is hard to see how the New Departure litigation could have been relevant: *Minor v. Happersett* and *United States v. Susan B. Anthony* were simply losing cases, with not even a stirring dissent for successor litigators to cite.

Ultimately, the long-term impact of the nineteenth-century feminist litigators is much less direct. To understand the diffuse radiance of the New Departurists' success, we must view their work through a prism designed to highlight the indirect, unseen, pentimento radiances of their courtroom battles that underlie the civil rights and women's movements of post–World War II America. Seen this way, what turns out to be the main contribution of the New Departure movement is its role in developing a culture of rights.

The rights culture the movement helped form views the Constitution as an arena or forum of struggle, rather than as a static, determinative text, as a political covenant that can be read to embody the aspirations of oppressed groups, rather than as a narrow, legalistic document. The New Departurists played a crucial role in launching the women's movement in a rights-oriented mode of struggle, transforming it into one that insisted that the Constitution incorporate their aspirations and dreams. The *Minor* case's real importance, as the historian Norma Basch has observed, is that "it drew the inferiority of women's status out of the grooves of common-law assumptions and state provisions and thrust it into the maelstrom of constitutional conflict. The demands for women's suffrage . . . acquired a contentious national life."[89] With the New Departurists' decision to use litigation, women's rights became constitutional issues, to be argued on a national level, including the arena of the federal judiciary. "Individual rights," declared Stanton, "are great American ideas, underlying our whole political and religious life."[90] Reflecting the women's movement's new direction, the year after the Minors lost their case Anthony and other NWSA leaders presented a "Women's Declaration of Rights" at the centennial celebration of the American Revolution in Philadelphia.

In its fundamental principles, the rights-based women's movement launched by Anthony and the New Departurists emphasized hope, faith, and, above all, struggle.[91] Some commentators have suggested that such focus on constitutional rights, instead of on women's happiness and well-being, diluted the radical demands of the early feminists.[92] But others have praised the approach, noting the radical nature of the New Departurists' demand for universal, not merely female, suffrage. They argue that the New Departure movement treated rights "as something to be won and exercised collectively rather than individually; as the object of political struggle as much as of judicial resolution," and, above all, "as that which has greatest meaning . . . to the powerless, who have yet to have their full place in society recognized."[93] The resulting legacy, a rights-based women's movement, has engendered enormous political and legal struggle over the past century. That struggle has been premised on contesting the meaning of the Constitution, on insisting, as Elizabeth Cady Stanton did even after the Supreme Court decided the *Minor* case, that the Constitution "has no settled interpretation . . . it can be expounded in favor of many directly opposite principles."[94] Defeats in the courts therefore were not dispositive; future generations would continue to read their own interpretations into the Constitution.

The inspiration their efforts might provide for future generations was central to sustaining the leaders of the New Departure movement as they surveyed the discouraging results of their work. "Although defeated at every point, woman's claim as a citizen of the United States to the Federal franchise is placed upon record in the highest court of the Nation, and there it will remain forever,"[95] wrote Anthony, Stanton, and Gage in their *History of Woman Suffrage*. Citing Milton's *Paradise Lost*, the three feminists underscored the lesson they hoped the court defeats would yield for future activists: that success lies not merely in winning but in having "the unconquerable will and courage never to submit or yield, but to struggle on."[96] Reviewing her life's work on her eighty-sixth birthday, in 1906, Anthony could have easily looked at her recurring defeats and concluded, as one biographer put it, that she was, "like Napoleon at Waterloo, a splendid failure."[97] Yet Anthony, in her last public speech, proclaimed her faith that "with such [wonderful] women consecrating their lives *failure is impossible*."[98] As long as struggle persisted, Anthony and the New Departurists believed their long-term goal would be achieved.

5

Plessy v. Ferguson

The Fool's Last Battle

HAD THE LIKELIHOOD of success been the standard by which the members of the New Orleans Citizens Committee decided whether to test the constitutionality of the 1890 Louisiana statute segregating railway cars in court, they probably would not have brought the case of *Homer Plessy v. Ferguson*.[1] And perhaps they shouldn't have—or so Jack Greenberg, general counsel for the NAACP Legal Defense Fund, was to argue more than seventy-five years later.[2]

But, in 1892, to Rodolphe Desdunes and the other mostly light skinned, elite members of the New Orleans creole community who formed the Citizens Committee, "[i]t was necessary to resist" the imposition of state-mandated segregation "even with no hope of success in sight."[3] As Louis Martinet, a local black New Orleans attorney, leader of the Citizens Committee, and editor of the New Orleans *Crusader*, acknowledged, "the fight we are making is an uphill one."[4] Martinet did not foresee a "favorable result" but added despondently that "perhaps it is best that the battle be fought."[5]

Indeed, the political, social, and legal developments that preceded the *Plessy* litigation were ominous. The demise of Reconstruction in 1876 led to the election of conservative state governments in the South that had curtailed but not eliminated blacks' civil and political rights. By the late 1880s and early 1890s, however, the situation had taken a turn for the worse. Desperate to hold onto power in the face of a rising populist movement, southern politicians turned to more extreme versions of white supremacy. During the 1880s, four southern states enacted segregation statutes, and the Interstate Commerce Commission endorsed the principle of separate but equal.[6] In the eighteen months that followed the passage of Louisiana's railway segregation law, additional segregation measures were adopted by six southern states, and the number of lynchings soared.[7] While the total exclusion of southern blacks from the political arena was still several years in the future, the disenfranchisement campaign that gathered momentum in the early 1890s resulted in a host of voting restrictions.

Northern liberals had by and large abandoned the southern black community. While the civil rights community was encouraged by the number of northern states that had expanded or established civil rights legislation in the early 1890s, the great compromise of 1876 that ended Reconstruction had also signaled the end of northern interference in southern race relations. Racist thought was on the upswing in both the North and the South, with many northern liberals agreeing with the distinguished English observer James Bryce, who wrote in 1891 that the Negroes were "naturally inferior to whites—inferior in intelligence, in tenacity, in courage, in the power of organization."[8] The southern black community was left to fight alone.

While the political climate was so foreboding, the courts seemed unlikely candidates to strike down Louisiana's separate-but-equal law. The lower federal courts generally had applied the separate-but-equal doctrine.[9] So, too, had many state courts.[10] And the Supreme Court, in a series of decisions beginning with the *Slaughter-house Cases* in 1873, had adopted a very narrow reading of the rights granted by the Thirteenth and Fourteenth Amendments.[11]

The Louisiana black community had, prior to 1890, sought judicial intervention on behalf of integration, often with disastrous results.[12] Post–Civil War Louisiana, with a black voting majority, went the furthest of any southern state under Reconstruction in integrating public schools, public transport, and public accommodations. The Louisiana Constitution of 1868 outlawed racial segregation in public schools and public accommodations, secured to blacks the right to vote and hold office, and required all state officeholders to take an oath accepting the civil and political equality of all men. Pursuant to the Constitution, Louisiana enacted a civil rights bill prohibiting discrimination in public accommodations and adopted school integration in New Orleans at a time when such integration was virtually nonexistent throughout the South and uncommon in the North.

After Reconstruction ended in 1876, though, the schools were again segregated. A mass meeting of blacks denounced school segregation, and a committee of protestors marched on the governor's office to demand an end to segregation. When the governor refused to budge, the black creoles supported litigation to restore integrated schools.[13]

Several prominent blacks sued the school board for violating both the Fourteenth Amendment and the 1868 Louisiana Constitution. The first suit, brought in state court, was dismissed on technical grounds without yielding a ruling on the constitutional issue.[14]

The second case, *Bertonneau v. Board of Directors of City Schools*, was decided in 1878 by U.S. Circuit Judge William B. Woods.[15] Woods, elevated the next year to the U.S. Supreme Court, dismissed the case because the plaintiff had not proved the schools were unequal. Foreshadowing the Supreme Court's decision in *Plessy v. Ferguson* seventeen years later, Woods held: "Both races are treated precisely alike. White children and colored children are compelled to attend different schools. That is all. The State, while conceding equal privileges and advantages to both races, has the right to manage its schools in the manner which in its judgment will best promote the interest of all."[16]

The Louisiana black community fared no better in its attempt to use the courts to enforce equal accommodations. In 1872, a black woman named Josephine DeCuir was denied a berth in the ladies cabin of the steamboat *Governor Allen* for a trip from New Orleans up the Mississippi to Hermitage, Louisiana. DeCuir sued the captain under the 1869 Louisiana Equal Accommodations Act and won in the state courts.[17] The U.S. Supreme Court reversed, holding that even though DeCuir's trip was entirely in Louisiana, the ship operated under a federally granted license and its overall voyage was interstate—from New Orleans to Vickburg, Mississippi.[18] Therefore, application of the 1869 act to require that DeCuir receive her berth was an interference with Congress's power to regulate interstate commerce. Chief Justice Morrison Waite wrote that, although Congress had not directly regulated interstate travel on the Mississippi River, "Congressional inaction left [the captain] at liberty to adopt . . . reasonable rules and regulations for the disposition of passengers upon his boat."[19] Waite thus suggested that segregation was "reasonable." Even more ominously, Justice Nathan Clifford wrote a long concurring opinion dismissing DeCuir's claim because "it is not an unreasonable regulation to seat passengers so as to preserve order and decorum . . . equality does not mean identity as in the nature of things identity in the accommodation afforded to passengers, whether colored or white, is impossible, unless our commercial marine shall undergo an entire change."[20]

Yet, in New Orleans, in 1892, there was still a willingness to turn to litigation to resist segregation—a fact that stemmed from practical, political considerations, as well as from deeply embedded cultural factors. In part, the middle-class creole community of New Orleans felt that lawsuits would "give a dignified appearance to the resistance."[21] But there was also the fact that abolitionists had created a tradition within the black community of using litigation as part of the larger struggle for equal rights. The resulting culture undoubtedly influenced the creoles of New Orleans in their decision to turn to the courts. That tradition went back at least to the 1840s, when black and white abolitionists in Boston waged a concerted campaign to end segregation. In 1841, a number of black abolitionists, including Frederick Douglass, attempted to ride the "white" cars of various segregated Massachusetts railroads.[22] When physically removed, they often sued; yet the lower courts ruled in favor of the railroads. The abolitionists turned to the legislature, and the resulting pressure forced the railroads to voluntarily end segregated cars.[23] The Boston abolitionist community then challenged school segregation. In the 1849 case *Roberts v. Boston*, the Massachusetts Supreme Court, in an unanimous opinion written by the prominent antislavery judge Lemuel Shaw, upheld segregated schools in Massachusetts.[24] Yet, despite their loss in the courts, the abolitionist community continued its political struggle, and, five years later, the Massachusetts legislature barred segregation. So, too, New York City blacks in the 1850s formed the Legal Rights Association and, represented by future President Chester A. Arthur and other lawyers, staged a series of sit-ins against segregated streetcars, losing in court but succeeding in pressuring a number of railroads to end segregation.[25]

After the Civil War, African Americans continued this abolitionist tradition, waging an impressive campaign in the courts against racial discrimination in schools. Between 1865 and 1903, more than seventy challenges to discriminatory schools were litigated throughout the United States.[26] Blacks overwhelmingly lost the cases that were decided on Fourteenth Amendment grounds, although they were often successful on narrower state law claims.[27] Moreover, even lawsuits that lost in court often led to legislative victories. For example, New York blacks lost all six cases that they brought challenging school segregation in the nineteenth century, but the judicial battle was a springboard to victory in the local political arena; the state legislature enacted legislation securing integration. As Professor J. Morgan Kousser has written about the New York experience: "the failures of success and the ultimate success that stemmed from those failures . . . all would be missed by observers concerned only with the abstract principles embodied in printed court opinions."[28] Thus, the Citizens Committee decision to turn to the courts and the arguments that they presented in court can be understood only in the context of a developing culture of rights that used litigation as one tool in a broader political effort to attack segregation.

Despite the bleak political and social climate in the years leading up to *Plessy v. Ferguson* and the slim prospect of legal victory, the New Orleans Citizens Committee pressed on until it found its test case. On June 7, 1892, Homer A. Plessy, a thirty-four-year-old shoemaker who was one-eighth black and who was a friend of the Citizens Committee's leader, Rudolphe Desdunes, purchased a ticket on the East Louisiana Railway from New Orleans to Covington, Louisiana, a purely intrastate journey.[29] Plessy insisted on boarding a coach reserved for whites and, by prior arrangement with a sympathetic railroad company, was arrested for violating the separate-car law. Backed by the Citizens Committee, with Albion Tourgée as lead counsel, Plessy brought a suit.

The Citizens Committee was composed of descendants of the free creoles-of-color community that had existed in New Orleans prior to the Civil War. The *New Orleans Times-Democrat* described the group as "agitators."[30] It was formed at the suggestion of Aristide Mary, a creole who in 1872 had run for governor of Louisiana and who was one of the wealthiest men of any color in New Orleans. Louis Martinet was the group's unofficial leader. Born in 1849 to a Belgian father and a New Orleans creole mother, Martinet had a varied assortment of jobs and professions throughout his life. He held law and medical degrees, served in the Louisiana legislature and as a public school director, and worked over the years as a notary, a deputy U.S. naval officer, a customs clerk, a deputy surveyor, and a mail carrier. In 1890, he founded and edited the *Crusader* newspaper. Clearly a man of many talents and interests, he was described by a contemporary as "uncompromising in his ideas [and] invincible in his perseverance."[31]

The other Citizens Committee members were also from the creole elite and were deeply involved with their community. Many, like Martinet, had been active in the 1877 protest against the resegregation of the New Orleans schools. The Haitian-born Arthur Esteves, who had founded the city's leading sailmaking company, was president. C. C. Antoine, the former lieutenant governor of Louisiana, was vice president. Rodolphe Lucien Desdunes, Martinet's friend and a fellow law graduate of Straight University, was another key leader. Desdunes's mother was Cuban, and his father was a political refugee from Haiti. After graduating from law school, Desdunes could have entered his family's cigar factory, but his temperament was that of a poet, not a businessman. Later in his life, he wrote a book, *Our People and Our History*, a proud history of creoles in nineteenth-century New Orleans.[32] In 1891, he worked by day as a clerk for the U.S. Customs Service and at night wrote articles for Martinet's *Crusader*.

To understand what motivated the members of the Citizens Committee to launch a test case against segregation requires looking beyond issues of the immediate success or failure of the case. For Martinet and his compatriots, the decision to resist was not calculated the way a tort lawyer weighs the chance of success before undertaking a negligence suit but sprang from an internal predisposition to fight injustice. Desdunes criticized the majority of the black community who "believed it was better to suffer in silence than to attract attention to their misfortunate and weakness."[33] Desdunes argued that "it is more noble and dignified to fight, no matter what, than to show a passive attitude of resignation."[34] "The obligation of the people," he wrote, "is resistance to oppression."[35]

Desdunes, Martinet, and their compatriots also believed that it was important to put their views on record and to force the highest court in the land to respond. "Absolute submission," according to Desdunes, "augments the oppressor's power and creates doubt about the feelings of the oppressed."[36] A lawsuit, the members of the Citizens Committee believed, would put the rulers on notice that the black population did not accept Jim Crow. More important, they wanted to force the Supreme Court to respond to them, to explain how segregation could be consistent with the Fourteenth Amendment's command.[37] Even if the Court disagreed with them, forcing the Court to go on record with its views was in their eyes better than allowing silence to be taken as acquiescence. As their lawyer put it, they wanted "a squareout adjudication by the Supreme Court."[38]

The Citizens Committee chose as its lead counsel Albion Tourgée, a former Reconstruction-era carpetbagger and America's most vocal, militant, persistent, and widely heard white advocate of racial equality during the last two decades of the nineteenth century.[39] Tourgée's life reflected the tension between a foolhardy charge into certain defeat and the prophetic vision of a more egalitarian America. Born in Ohio, in 1838, Tourgée moved to North Carolina after fighting in the Union armies during the Civil War. Troubled by insecurity and self-doubt, Tourgée nonetheless had the brilliance and ambition to become a leader of the Radical Republicans in North Carolina. He played a central role in drafting the Reconstruction Constitution of North Carolina in 1868 and was later elected a judge.[40] His fearless stands against the Ku Klux Klan and in support of racial equality led even his enemies to admire his courage. As one leading conservative newspaper later wrote:

> His was a striking personality, and none the less so because of the fact that he was for many years the most thoroughly hated man in North Carolina. . . . With full knowledge of the dangers attending his mad course, in the face of the dire threats that were daily thrown in his face, consciously aware that there was dynamite under every foot of earth he trod, . . . he displayed the nerve of a martyr in his wild, mistaken attempt to make an Ohio of North Carolina.[41]

Tourgée's greatest fame came when he returned to the North in 1879 after the defeat of Reconstruction. That year, he published a novel, based on his experiences in the South, titled *A Fool's Errand*, whose author was originally only identified as "One of the Fools." Tourgée's book was a bestseller, and total sales may have reached 200,000 copies, a remarkable figure for the 1880s.[42] The novel was a powerful critique of both the national government, for its failure to address the fundamental issue of equality for the former slaves, and the South, for maintaining racial prejudice and for using violence against those who supported change.

Underlying Tourgée's social critique of northern vacillation and southern obduracy during Reconstruction lay a psychological self-study: the study of the fool. To Tourgée, only history's thin line separated a fool and a prophet. A fool differs from his fellow humans in that "he sees or believes what they do not, and consequently undertakes what they never attempt."[43] However, social acceptance of the fool's vision alters his status: "It is success alone that transforms the credulity of folly into acknowledged prophetic prevision."[44]

Tourgée's challenge to racial inequality stemmed from a deep, spiritual faith—one central to the psychological makeup of both fools and prophets. Tourgée wrote that the life of the fool is "full of the poetry of faith."[45] Prophets and fools are kinfolk, he argued, because both act upon a "simple, undoubting faith" that leads them to believe in the long-run value of their efforts, despite the temporary defeats they suffer.[46] As early as 1863, he had written his wife that "It is every person's duty in seeking to decide on any course of action, to ask himself, not what will bring himself most pleasure, most temporary enjoyment, but how he shall best perform his duty to God, himself and his fellows, how he shall best observe the purpose of his being."[47]

In *A Fool's Errand*, Tourgée explicitly distinguishes between martyrs and fools. While both act on principle and are prepared to accept defeat and ridicule, the martyr willingly accepts death, but the fool maintains the blind faith and hope that "in some inscrutable way the laws of human nature would be suspended, or that the state of affairs at first presenting itself would be but temporary."[48] Susan B. Anthony, Salmon Chase, Albion Tourgée, and Louis Martinet were not martyrs, but fit Tourgée's description of fools or prophets. Like the prophets of the Old Testament, these activists all rooted themselves within and not outside their communities.[49] Their solidarity with the larger community developed out of their faith that the community would change, a belief that was in the short run misplaced or foolish but that allowed them to swim against the tide of public opinion.

Despite the difference Tourgée articulated, martyrs, fools, and prophets all share some qualities. Most striking is the ability to turn what most people perceive as defeats and failures into long-term successes. While the key to a fool or prophet's ability to turn failure into success is his ability to make his life's work constitute a clarion call for future generations, a martyr requires the unusual talent of making a success of dying.[50] Thus John Brown's raid at Harper's Ferry was an unmitigated failure; yet this "seeming disaster," Brown told his family, would through his hanging "ultimately result in the most glorious success."[51] As one historian points out, "the very qualities that had caused him to fail as a businessman and as a warrior—his absolute, unyielding faith in his own righteousness and his highly developed powers of self-justification and self-deception—now made [Brown] a magnificent martyr" and redeemed a "lifetime of obstinate blunders and deadly failures."[52] To his fellow abolitionist Henry Ward Beecher, Brown's hanging displaced his "failure with a heroic success."[53]

While Tourgée was not a good organizer, and his conceit, pompous bearing, and tactlessness hindered his leadership ability, he excelled as an agitator. Known as the "Apostle of Agitation," he believed that passivity could be overcome only by persistent agitation. Despite an environment that discouraged progressive change, he argued that it was only "by constant resistance to oppression that the race must ultimately win equality of right[s]."[54]

The conflict between the arrogant prophet and the humble fool continued throughout Tourgée's life.[55] His voice of postwar radical Republican idealism was overcome by a long wave of racism, materialism, and cynicism. While *A Fool's Errand* was received as a sensation in its day, Tourgée has been aptly considered as "perhaps the most neglected figure in American literature."[56] He was influential as a civil rights lecturer and columnist, yet was never part of a successful reform movement and operated primarily on "a decisive but unjustly neglected social level."[57]

Tourgée's moods fluctuated between exuberant optimism and bitter despair. His penchant for grandiose schemes often led to depression. Tourgée's wife, Emma, once wrote that Tourgée's "life was embittered, ruined by his trying to do what he had no capacity to do."[58] Tourgée's psychological makeup was aptly described by an analyst's observation of a twentieth-century prophet: "A soul that sensitive, proud, and self-centered can find vocation only by *not* succeeding in ordinary ways, even if that means to perish."[59]

But when Louis Martinet approached Tourgée in 1891 to take on the challenge to segregation in New Orleans, the former judge, now fifty-three years old, had reached a new high in influence and activity. He was living on Chautauqua Lake, in western New York, an important cultural center that served as a base from which he gave hundreds of lectures throughout the country. His weekly editorial column, *A Bystander's Notes*, was published in the Chicago newspaper *Inter Ocean*, which claimed 200,000 subscribers, the largest circulation of any political newspaper west of the Allegheny mountains.[60] In 1891, Tourgée had launched a new multiracial organization, the National Citizens Rights Association, to agitate for civil rights and to fight segregation and other oppression through the courts. For Tourgée, litigation was tied to social action, and his new organization would utilize a variety of tactics. As he wrote to a black leader in 1891, "Protest, remonstrance, denunciation—continuous, passionate, determined—these are, in my opinion, the only things that will save your people from submissive apathy and give them hope of final equality of privilege."[61] While the

NCRA grew rapidly, within a year or so it had collapsed. But the optimism that pervaded Tourgée in 1891 carried into the legal fight that he and the New Orleans Citizens Committee waged against segregation in Louisiana.

The *Plessy* case thrust upon Tourgée the conflict between the prophetic visionary and the practical litigator. He recognized that technical legal arguments had a greater chance of success in the courts, but his interest and talent were those of a prophet or poet, rather than a lawyer. Tourgée deferred to his local counsel, James G. Walker, on the procedural legal issues, writing in reference to himself that "A man who has been substantially out of practice for half a dozen years has no right to an opinion on such points beside one who has been in the traces right along."[62]

Tourgée began the work that would culminate in *Plessy v. Ferguson* with a test case in which Rodolphe Desdunes's son Daniel purchased a first-class ticket from New Orleans to Mobile, Alabama. Tourgée was initially skeptical about his co-counsel Walker's proposal that the person arrested in the test case should hold a ticket for an out-of-state destination, thereby enabling them to narrowly challenge the Louisiana statute as a state infringement on the congressional power to regulate interstate commerce. "What we want," Tourgée wrote his co-counsel, "is not a verdict of not guilty, nor a defect in this law but a decision whether such a law can be legally enacted and enforced in any state and we should get everything off the track and out of the way for such a decision."[63] But Tourgée eventually agreed with Walker's approach, admitting that he "may have spoken too lightly of the interstate commerce matter."[64] And, in 1892, the Louisiana Supreme Court held that the segregation statute applied only to intrastate travel. Louis Martinet's newspaper, *The Crusader*, exuberantly declared that the Louisiana Supreme Court's decision meant that "Jim Crow is as dead as a door nail!"[65] While neither Tourgée nor Martinet really believed that the Louisiana court's commerce clause decision signaled Jim Crow's demise, they did think it would help undermine segregation on intrastate lines. At the very least, they had won an initial victory limiting the application of the Jim Crow law.

Tourgée offered one important tactical point regarding the selection of a plaintiff to test the constitutionality of the Louisiana statute. Over the objections of Louis Martinet and some other members of the New Orleans Citizens Committee, Tourgée urged that a Negro whose complexion was nearly white be selected to test the statute.[66] Such a test case would both highlight the arbitrariness of the statute and provide a claim that whiteness was a property right protected by the due process clause, an argument that might move a property-minded Supreme Court.[67]

The choice of Plessy to test Jim Crow highlighted the arbitrariness of racial laws. As Tourgée rhetorically argued, "Will the court hold that a single drop of African blood is sufficient to color a whole ocean of Caucasian whiteness."[68] Plessy, only one-eighth black, appeared white; his petition to the Supreme Court asserted that "the mixture of colored blood [was] not discernable."[69] As it turned out, the case that would define the African American's status for the first half of the twentieth century was brought by a man who in any nonracist society would be considered white.

The case quickly proceeded through the Louisiana courts, with Judge J. H. Ferguson ruling against *Plessy* in an opinion affirmed by a unanimous Louisiana Supreme Court. By February 1893, the case was before the U.S. Supreme Court. Tourgée secured the assistance of his old carpetbagger friend and a former solicitor general of the United States, Samuel F. Phillips, to serve as co-counsel for the Supreme Court appeal. Phillips was no stranger to civil rights, having argued and lost an important civil rights case in 1883.

Tourgée's brief to the Supreme Court reflected the influence of previous abolitionist and women's suffrage constitutional challenges. Tourgée's central, visionary argument followed Susan Anthony's and the Minors' identification of national citizenship as the key source of American's rights. While the Supreme Court focused (and continues to focus) on what Tourgée termed the restrictive provisions of the Fourteenth Amendment, which prohibit the state from denying any person due process or equal protection of the law, Tourgée challenged the Court to view the Fourteenth Amendment as an affirmative statement of a citizen's rights. To Tourgée, the provision of Section 1 of the Fourteenth Amendment conferring citizenship on any person born in the United States

> creates a *new* citizenship of the United States embracing new rights, privileges and immunities derivable in a *new* manner, controlled by a *new* authority, having a *new* scope and extent, dependent on national authority for its existence.[70]

That new national citizenship mandated "*equality* of personal right and the *free* and secure enjoyment of all public privileges."[71] Equality was not therefore merely a "comparative equality," devoid of substantive content, "but a just and universal equality whereby the rights of life, liberty, and property are secured to all—the rights which belong to a citizen in every free country and every republican government."[72] To Tourgée, this affirmative mandate of national citizenship was inconsistent with any state-imposed caste system. His brief argued that "the gist of our case is the unconstitutionality of the assortment, *not* the question of equal accommodation . . . [t]he question is not as to the equality of the privileges enjoyed, but *the right of the State to label one citizen as white and another as colored.*"[73] Tourgée claimed that the act was intended to promote white supremacy and coined what was to become an oft-cited metaphor: "Justice is pictured blind and her daughter, the law, ought at least to be color-blind."[74]

That Tourgée should follow the suffragists in focusing on the fundamental rights of citizenship was no accident. Both he and the suffragists had been deeply influenced by republican constitutional post–Civil War theories, and Tourgée was intimately connected to the women's rights movements of the 1870s. In 1878, just five years after the U.S. Supreme Court denied Myra Bradwell's claim that her privileges and immunities as a national citizen included a right to practice law, Tourgée successfully represented twenty-four-year-old Tabitha Ann Holton in her petition to take the North Carolina bar. North Carolina became the sixth state, and the first southern state, to admit a woman to the practice of law.[75]

Tourgée also drew heavily in his arguments on the abolitionists. He resurrected the abolitionist and suffragist argument that the Declaration of Independence is not a mere rhetorical flourish but that "all-embracing formula of personal rights on which our government is based."[76] In *Plessy*, Tourgée virtually repeated Alvan Stewart's position on the Declaration in the New Jersey Slave Cases. He also returned to the abolitionist and suffragist model of constitutional interpretation, arguing that the Fourteenth Amendment must be interpreted "in strict accord" with the Declaration, which "has become the controlling genius of the American people."[77] In Tourgée's final argument, he reiterated the basic republican themes articulated by the abolitionists and suffragists to urge the court to eschew "legal refinement" and to decide the case on the basis of "the fundamental principles of free government."[78]

The brief's Thirteenth and Fourteenth Amendment arguments directly attacked the Court's recent record and were unlikely to succeed. The brief "freely admitted that Cruckshank's case [a Supreme Court decision on equal rights] is squarely against us."[79] As one commentator has noted, "Hopes of so drastically altering the judicial mind would have been unrealistic."[80] Tourgée's brief in *Plessy*, like Salmon Chase's in the *Van Zandt* case, reflected his enormous ego and his expansive faith in his persuasive power, combined with an unrealistic assessment of the Court's thinking. But Tourgée, like Chase in *Van Zandt* and the Minors in *Minor v. Happersatt*, was really presenting a record for future generations. Owen Fiss, a professor at Yale Law School, notes that Tourgée's argument was "visionary" and that his "brief was striking, both eloquent and moving, but in the end, it seemed the work of a legal Don Quixote."[81]

By the time the case reached the Supreme Court, Tourgée and his associates were deeply pessimistic about their chances. Louis Martinet wrote Tourgée that he had asked himself "a thousand times" why he fought this battle in which he would gain nothing but expend "time, labor [and] money."[82] Martinet's answer was based not on the value or success of his efforts but on his own internal disposition: "[l]ike you, I believe I do it because I am built that way."[83] And, in a letter written nine months after filing the Assignment of Errors to the court, Tourgée expressed serious doubts about the case. He realized that there were five justices against *Plessy* and that a defeat would be serious. "[I]t is of the utmost consequence that we should not have a decision *against* us," since the Court had "*never reversed itself* on a *constitutional* question."[84]

He therefore counseled Martinet's committee in New Orleans to delay the case and "[t]o bend every possible energy to secure the discussion of the principle in such a way as to reach and awaken public sentiment."[85] The only hope for the case was to mobilize broad public support against segregation. "The court has always been the foe of liberty," according to Tourgée, "until forced to move on by public opinion."[86] Tourgée believed that one justice could be swayed "if he 'hears from the country.'"[87]

The Supreme Court did delay, more than three years after the appeal was filed. However, far from intensifying pressure on the Court as Tourgée had hoped, public opinion became even more unfavorable. The nascent social sciences added a veneer of expert opinion to the fast-developing racism.[88] In 1895, Frederick Douglass, symbol of militant African American struggle for equality, died. That same year, Booker T. Washington delivered his famous Atlanta address that was "widely interpreted as a sign of Negro acceptance of an inferior status."[89] Between 1892 and 1896, the number of lynchings reached new peaks, new segregation laws were adopted, and Congress repealed a host of Reconstruction-era statutes protecting equal rights.[90] In New Orleans, Louis Martinet and his newspaper were on the verge of collapse. The political and social climate boded ill.

On May 18, 1896 the Supreme Court, by a 7–1 vote, ruled against *Plessy*. The Court did not even mention Tourgée's radical national citizenship argument. Brushing aside *Plessy*'s Thirteenth Amendment claim "as too clear for argument,"[91] Massachusetts-born Justice Henry Billings Brown cited a number of cases, most prominently Judge Lemuel Shaw's 1849 opinion in *Roberts v. City of Boston*, to support the proposition that "in the nature of things" the Fourteenth Amendment "could not have been intended to abolish distinctions based upon color or to enforce social, as distinguished from political equality."[92] The Court considered "the underlying fallacy of the plaintiff's argument to consist in the assumption that the enforced separation of the two races stamps the colored race with a badge of inferiority. If this be so, it is not by reason of anything found in the act, but solely because the colored race chooses to put that construction upon it."[93] Justice Brown's vapid sociological insight led the great Yale law professor Charles L. Black Jr., commenting on the case more than fifty years later, to offer the theorem that "[t]he curves of callousness and stupidity intersect at their respective maxima."[94]

Only Justice John Harlan dissented. Harlan, a former Kentucky slaveowner and lawyer-politician who opposed secession, emancipation, and the Thirteenth and Fourteenth Amendments and who came to be the Court's most fervent defender of equal rights for blacks, understood the fallacy of Brown's opinion. "Every one knows," Harlan wrote, "that the statute in question had its origin in the purpose, not so much to exclude white persons from railroad cars occupied by blacks, as to exclude colored people from coaches occupied by or assigned to white persons."[95] Everyone, apparently, but seven other justices of the Supreme Court. "The thin disguise of 'equal' accommodations for passengers in railroad coaches," Harlan wrote, "will not mislead any one, nor atone for the wrong done this day."[96]

Harlan accepted Tourgée's position that the segregation law was caste legislation and adopted Tourgée's metaphor that justice was colorblind. However, he did so in a paragraph that revealed much about the nation's conflict over truly integrating African Americans into the political, economic, and social fabric of American life. Harlan, who maintained only limited contact with his mulatto half-brother, Robert, and who probably shared the prevailing attitude that blacks, including blood relations, were inferior to whites,[97] wrote:

> The white race deems itself to be the dominant race in this country. And so it is, in prestige, in achievements, in education, in wealth and in power. So, I doubt not, it will continue to be for all time, if it remains true to its great heritage and holds fast to the principles of constitutional liberty. But in view of the Constitution, in the eye of the law, there is in this country no superior dominant, ruling class of citizens. There is no caste here. Our Constitution is color-blind, and neither knows nor tolerates classes among citizens.[98]

Harlan's argument was visionary, both in lifting Tourgée's "colorblind" phrase and in predicting that the adoption of that concept as a constitutional principle decades later would not threaten the white race's dominance. While Harlan's comment that "our Constitution is colorblind" has become one of the most quoted words ever uttered by a Supreme Court justice, his view that holding "fast" to that principle would allow the white race's dominance to "continue" "for all time" is virtually never mentioned, an embarrassment to liberals and conservatives alike.[99]

The Citizens Committee and Tourgée had lost in court. But, unlike many of the abolitionist and suffragist cases, the *Plessy* litigation provoked neither national discussion nor a political movement to legislatively end Jim Crow.

In fact, the Supreme Court's decision received surprisingly little national attention. The typical press reports only routinely mentioned the case.[100] The historian C. Vann Woodward reports that

> the country as a whole received the news of [the Court's] momentous decision upholding the "separate but equal" doctrine in relative silence and apparent indifference.... [T]he *Plessy* decision was accorded

only short, inconspicuous news reports and virtually no editorial comment outside the Negro press.[101]

The *New York Times* included the decision in its regular page-three Tuesday column on railway news, along with one other very minor railroad decision.[102] Unlike *Plessy v. Ferguson*, three Supreme Court decisions rendered on May 18, 1896, did receive front-page coverage: a federal contract labor law dispute involving a sugar plantation owner, a challenge to a portion of an heiress's multimillion dollar inheritance, and a playwright's claim of plagiarism, which the Court refused to review.[103] It was small solace that the few newspapers that did editorialize about the case generally supported Harlan's dissent.[104]

Nor were the media alone in their silence. The Democratic and Populist Party platforms in 1896 contained strong anti-Supreme Court planks criticizing the decisions of the Court for its decisions on the income tax, the sugar monopoly, and the Pullman strike. Neither platform made mention of the recently decided *Plessy* case.[105]

That *Plessy* did not spark the broad public discussion and dialogue Tourgée had hoped for, and probably encouraged more segregation, makes the litigation appear to be an unmitigated failure.[106] Yet, one prominent historian argues that *Plessy* is "more than a tale of losers. Besides having their years in court, Martinet and his associates had their arguments displayed on the record—indeed memorialized in Justice Harlan's dissent—to instruct later generations."[107] Tourgée's original brief reemerged as the issue of segregation came again before the Supreme Court, fifty years later. Supreme Court Justice Robert H. Jackson discovered, in 1950, that Albion Tourgée had lived in a town close to Jackson's home in upstate New York. Struck by Tourgée's connection to *Plessy*, he wrote friends that

> I have gone to his [Tourgée's] old brief, filed here, and there is no argument made today that he would not make to the Court. He says, "Justice is pictured blind and her daughter, The Law, ought at least to be color-blind." Whether this was original with him, it has been gotten off a number of times since as original wit. Tourgée's brief was filed April 6, 1896, and now, just fifty-four years after, the question is again being argued whether his position will be adopted and what was a defeat for him in '96 be a post-mortem victory.[108]

Tourgée's place in history is tied to Harlan's *Plessy* dissent, and the justification for his litigation effort rests on the same rationale given for great dissents like Harlan's.[109] Judges defend the utility of prophetic dissenting opinions like Harlan's in the same manner that historians defend Martinet and Tourgée's prophetic efforts in *Plessy*: their impact on future generations. Chief Justice Charles Hughes once termed a dissent "an appeal to the brooding spirit of the law, to the intelligence of a future day."[110] Justice William Brennan used the same metaphor to describe dissents that Susan Anthony employed to depict her agitation: the best dissents "seek to sow seeds for future harvest."[111] Justice Stanley Fuld, of the New York Court of Appeals, agreed with Justice William Douglas that, although "it may serve no immediate purpose in the case at hand, the dissent 'may salvage for tomorrow the principle that was sacrificed or forgotten today.'"[112] The most eloquent judicial justification of dissenters as prophets came from Justice Benjamin Cardozo, who wrote:

> The voice of the majority may be that of force triumphant, content with the plaudits of the hour, and recking little of the morrow. The dissenter speaks to the future, and his voice is pitched to a key that will carry through the years. Read some of the great dissents . . . and feel after the cooling time of the better part of a century the glow and fire of a faith that was content to bide its hour. The prophet and the martyr do not see the hooting throng. Their eyes are fixed on the eternities.[113]

From this perspective, the success of the dissenting judge and the prophetic litigator may lie in the future, when their views are adopted and the Court later reverses itself. In this sense, Tourgée's impact would come when his arguments, incorporated into Harlan's dissent, affected the future path of the law.

But did they really? Did Tourgée's losing effort in *Plessy* have any significant impact on the *Brown* decision? Scholars question whether even great dissents influence the Court's later reversal or only provide "some quotable support for a decision that would have been the same in any event."[114] One scholar asks:

> Was the Supreme Court of 1954 dependent upon, or even substantially influenced by, the wisdom of Mr. Justice Harlan when it discovered that "separate but equal" had become a constitutional non-sequitur?

To so frame the question is to require answers that I believe to be obviously in the negative.[115]

Indeed, Chief Justice Earl Warren's opinion in *Brown* neither referred to Harlan's opinion in *Plessy* nor adopted his or Tourgée's reasoning. To this day, the Supreme Court has not adopted the affirmative argument in Tourgée's brief and Harlan's dissent that the Thirteenth and Fourteenth Amendments require the national government to affirmatively guarantee that all citizens equally enjoy the fundamental rights of citizenship.[116] Tourgée and his compatriots may have had as little impact on history as they had on their own era.

Certainly, it is hard to perceive any direct effect Tourgée had on the future path of the law, apart from his famous metaphor. But losing litigation and dissenting opinions often affect history indirectly, through pathways and byways not immediately apparent in judicial decisions.

Law can best be understood as consisting of layers of meaning embedded under the present normative reality. Law has thus been seen as narratives, or stories that are passed from one generation to the next. Those stories sometimes take the form of judicial decisions, yet they also can be reflected in a community's own understanding of its rights, even if that understanding is not accepted by the dominant elite as law.

From this perspective, losing efforts like *Plessy* keep alive an oppressed community's vision of the law, which collides and interacts with the court-made law. *Brown v. Board of Education*[117] cannot be fully understood without uncovering the efforts of Charles Houston, Albion Tourgée, and the radical abolitionists, all of whom contributed in some way to the *Brown* narrative, and *Brown* itself spurs a narrative of enforcement and disappointment that continues today. Some of these layers might have directly influenced the decision in *Brown*: Charles Houston's and Thurgood Marshall's strategy in the 1930s and 1940s comes to mind.[118] Other layers might have a more indirect, theoretical link, such as the radical abolitionist theory of equality rediscovered as an important aspect of the meaning of the Fourteenth Amendment. Some layers might influence the path of decision by a circuitous and fortuitous route, like Justice Robert Jackson's rediscovery of and fascination with Albion Tourgée's brief in *Plessy* during the course of the Supreme Court's deliberation over the constitutionality of segregation in the 1950s.[119] But they all are woven into an ongoing narrative.

Prophetic litigation arises out of an oppressed community and reflects that community's legal vision and aspirations. When the state's courts reject that legal vision, the community—if it is committed to its view—does not acquiesce in the court's ruling but rather continues to struggle through various channels to reverse the court's interpretation. The losing litigation becomes a part of the community's understanding of its view of the law and a reflection of the community's commitment to struggle for its view. The community's law exists in tension with the state's law. The Yale Law School professor Robert Cover argued in the 1980s that social or religious groups can maintain law independent from, and in opposition to, the state's law. For Cover, "within the domain of constitutional meaning," albeit not in the realm of social control, these communities "create law as fully as does the judge."[120] Their law constantly jars with the dominant law and forces the state either to adjust its law or to use force to repress the alternative law. When, and if, the state through its courts finally accepts the community's vision of law, it often does not directly incorporate the layers of struggles and narratives that constitute the community's law—but that does not mean that those struggles and narratives played no role in the ultimate reversal.

The impact of litigators such as Tourgée and Martinet must therefore be measured primarily by whether they contribute to a social group's understanding of, and commitment to, the struggle for its view of what the law ought to be—not whether a court's later adoption of that view is directly influenced by their efforts. Tourgée and Martinet were but one link in the chain that included abolitionist lawyers, as well as the post–Civil War activists who sought to provide affirmative meaning to the Thirteenth and Fourteenth Amendments. These people developed and sustained a view of the Constitution that precluded the maintenance of an inferior caste and that tied segregation to slavery. That perspective was later reiterated by Thurgood Marshall in his closing argument in *Brown*, where he claimed that segregation was based on a determination that the former slaves "shall be kept as near that stage [slavery] as is possible."[121]

In defeat, *Plessy* became a symbol of injustice and resistance for twentieth century African American activists. Charles Hamilton Houston, the dean of Howard Law School and the mentor of a generation of African American civil rights lawyers, including Thurgood Marshall and countless others, emphasized to his students that the evil they were fighting, the reason they had attended a segregated law school, was *Plessy v. Ferguson*.[122] *Plessy* was Houston's symbol of injustice. Oliver Hill, one of Houston's first students, a classmate of Thurgood Marshall who later became an important civil rights attorney in Virginia, believes that the *Plessy* decision was "what made me go to law school. *Plessy* took our rights from us and therefore we had to overcome *Plessy*."[123] Charles Thompson, dean of Howard's School of Education, argued that resort to the courts was important and that "[e]ven unfavorable decisions by the courts had some value: they dramatized Negro discontent."[124] Similarly, the early 1930s Margold Report to the NAACP viewed litigation as having "the psychological effect upon Negroes themselves . . . of stirring the spirit of revolt among them."[125] The New Orleans Citizens Committee was accurate when it declared, shortly after the decision, "In defending the cause of liberty, we met with defeat . . . but not with ignominy."[126]

In the 1930s, the NAACP launched a campaign to overturn *Plessy* and the separate-but-equal doctrine it had spawned. That campaign to overturn *Plessy* in court did not, however, rely primarily on the legal arguments that Tourgée raised in *Plessy*. Charles Houston and Thurgood Marshall, the architects of that campaign, were much more practical lawyers than Tourgée. Early on, they rejected the idea of a frontal assault on segregation, as Tourgée had waged in *Plessy* and as had been proposed by the NAACP's consultant.[127] Instead, they focused on enforcing the equality side of the separate-but-equal formula, thereby gradually seeking to undermine southern segregation.[128] Marshall and Houston did not repeat Tourgée's foolhardy charge into certain defeat, in part because the political and legal climate had changed by the 1930s and 1940s but also because they approached litigation differently. They did not want to follow the path of Tourgée's Fool. Perhaps the *Plessy* litigation and its aftermath forced Marshall and others to recognize the reality that segregation would not be dismantled by a hasty, all-out assault. Marshall won almost all of the near three dozen Supreme Court cases he argued; Tourgée lost his only High Court battle. As one of Marshall's biographers noted, Marshall was a "legal architect." Tourgée was a romantic poet.

In the 1960s and 1970s, a new wave of lawyers rediscovered some of the more radical arguments that Tourgée and Harlan had articulated. Civil rights lawyers such as Arthur Kinoy harkened back to Harlan and Tourgée's interpretation of the Fourteenth Amendment as mandating an affirmative national obligation to sweep away all the vestiges of slavery and inequality in American life.[129] They found support from some prominent judges like Judge Minor Wisdom, who sat on the Fifth Circuit Court of Appeals covering the deep South and who himself became fascinated by Tourgée and the arguments he had made in *Plessy*.[130] In the 1980s and 1990s, those arguments were rebuffed by the Supreme Court, as they had been a century earlier. But they undoubtedly will reappear once questions of racial equality again return to center stage in the national arena.

Cases like *Plessy* highlight the dialectical path of the American common law and constitutional law. The law often changes through the interaction between social groups and the judiciary, played out in a series of cases that span decades and seek what the group perceives as justice. Often the dialectical process starts with failed efforts to change the law, followed by a series of cases that distinguish the first cases or create exceptions that eventually lead to a change in the rule.[131] The initial cases are thus an integral part of the process of change. And the common law's emphasis on history, not logic—as Oliver Wendell Holmes once put it, "a page of history is worth a volume of logic"[132]—puts a premium on a broad historical understanding of the twists and turns of the law, rather than on a snapshot of the law at it exists at one moment.

Ironically, it often occurs that the initial rule adopted by the Court contains the seeds of its own demise. Thus, the separate-but-equal doctrine that *Plessy* stood for was inherently contradictory, since the southern states had no intention of developing equal facilities for African Americans. The NAACP legal campaign fifty years later relied on the separate-but-equal rule to win victory after victory in court cases that challenged unequal facilities. Those victories brought the inherent tension in the doctrine to the fore, leading the court to revisit the stark question of whether segregation itself was constitutional. Thus does failure often lead to success, and victories often contain the seeds of defeat. Indeed, the NAACP's victory in *Brown* itself contained the seeds of later failures, leading Dr. Kenneth Clark, who played a key role in the *Brown* victory, to conclude that "I am forced to recognize that my life has, in fact, been a series of glorious defeats."[133]

The fundamental contribution of Tourgée's and Martinet's efforts in *Plessy* does not lie, however, in their future effect on substantive law. Rather, their main contribution lies in the creation of a culture that promotes constitutional litigation as a means to resist oppression. *Plessy* represents a prophetic tradition that views litigation not merely as a means to achieve concrete, substantive improvements but also as a mechanism to resist oppression. As Professor Otto Olsen, the biographer of Albion Tourgée and editor of a documentary history of the *Plessy* case, has argued:

> It would be, however, a most limited appreciation of the memory of these crusaders that would identify their efforts only with a now popular and much more successful struggle for racial justice. . . . [T]he tradition of *Plessy* encompasses a great deal more. That tradition represents a determined commitment to the rights of all mankind in the face of the greatest odds. . . . The memory of *Plessy* will be properly recalled only to the extent that there are still those possessed of the conscience and the courage to fight for causes that may not achieve respectability for generations.[134]

One of the most prominent African American judges of our times, Judge Damon Keith, of the U.S. Court of Appeals for the Sixth Circuit, agreed that the great lesson of the *Plessy* litigation is its story of resistance. For Keith, "*Plessy* is a crucial case, . . . because it emphasizes a very important point—to attain what we know in our hearts is just, we must often be willing to leave the comfort zone of societal norms and dominant values."[135]

Seeking justice is thus dependent on challenging reality, even if losing is the end result. As the prominent Jewish philosopher Martin Buber once wrote: "I cannot know how much justice is possible in a given situation unless I go on until my head hits the wall and hurts."[136] The meaning of cases like *Plessy* lies in its resistance to an oppressive reality, or, as Justice Thurgood Marshall, echoing Judge Damon Keith, stated, "go[ing] against the prevailing wind."[137]

The American focus on winning suggests that *Plessy*'s loss in court should have discouraged other communities from fighting segregation in court. African Americans could have viewed *Plessy* as the nail on their Fourteenth Amendment coffin and turned to other arenas to fight for their rights.

But they didn't. Paradoxically, judicial struggle against segregation continued unabated after the 1896 *Plessy* decision. Between 1896 and 1934, when the NAACP seriously commenced its campaign against segregation, no fewer than seventy-one cases challenging segregation in public schools were litigated in appellate courts in the United States.[138] Almost thirty cases directly challenged the constitutionality of segregated education in a wide variety of southern and northern states. Every one of these cases that directly challenged the constitutionality of segregation *lost*, but nonetheless plaintiffs kept litigating the issue.[139]

The reason that blacks turned to the courts in the post-*Plessy* period cannot be the favorable reception they received. Rather, the turn to litigation reflected several factors: The first was the lack of a better alternative strategy, particularly in the South. The choice for Plessy and for the hundreds of others who challenged segregation in courts during the bleak decades following the *Plessy* decision was not primarily between litigation and other forms of resistance. The choice fundamentally was whether to resist at all. Electoral or other political strategies were no more promising than litigation, and resort to armed struggle suicidal.[140] The significance of the *Plessy* case was primarily that the New Orleans community chose to resist segregation, and only secondarily that the means they chose was litigation. When, in the 1930s, the NAACP initiated its campaign against segregation, Charles Thompson, the dean of Howard's School of Education, argued that it is "no longer a question of whether Negroes *should* resort to the courts, they must resort to the courts. They have no other reasonable, legitimate alternative."[141] Those who doubted the efficacy of judicial action emphasized accepting and improving segregated schools.

The second factor was the African American faith and hope that the Civil War Amendments would be interpreted in a manner consistent with the principles of freedom and equality, a faith justified by the plain language of the Amendments and by the abolitionist tradition of reading into the Constitution the values of human rights.[142] A third cause for the reliance on litigation was the tradition first established by the abolitionists, continued in Reconstruction and *Plessy*, to use the courts as forums for obtaining justice.

That *Plessy* can be remembered as a beacon of struggle in an otherwise bleak period does not mean that all aspirational or prophetic litigation can be justified in this way. The critical questions for this type of litigation are whether it is undertaken as an integral and organic part of a broader political movement and whether it articulates the deeply felt understanding and yearnings of that movement. *Plessy* clearly fits that description. The New Orleans Citizens Committee was but one part of a broader African American movement against segregation. Indeed, in the late 1890s and early 1900s, blacks organized boycotts in more than twenty-five southern cities to protest Jim Crow streetcars. While most of those boycotts were unsuccessful, some of the boycotts did temporarily succeed. Success, however, was only temporary. Segregation was reimposed within a few months or, at most, years. Moreover, litigation against Jim Crow was also widespread. While *Plessy* is the most remembered of the cases, other cases that challenged aspects of segregation also came before the Court in the 1890s and in the first decade of the twentieth century. Virtually all lost.

The *Plessy* decision also forces future generations to remember that African Americans resisted segregation and that the Supreme Court legitimated the practice. Lawyers for losing causes not only articulate for future generations a vision of justice unachievable in the present but also record history by creating a narrative of oppression and resistance. Lawyering in a losing cause is one way "of ensuring that the future remembers."[143] For example, lawyers who challenged the death penalty in the 1990s understood that they were likely to lose in the existing climate, yet many justified their work as making a record about poverty, abuse, and injustice that may be remembered in the future.[144] So, too, civil rights leaders often express the sentiment that the "more we appreciate the extraordinary injustice" of slavery and segregation, "the more persistent we will be in eradicating the vestiges" of those practices,[145] a view common to many oppressed cultures.

In part, though, litigation against segregation continued because *Plessy* remained such a strong beacon of struggle, one that showed how prophetic litigation works in the world. The seed that Louis Martinet, Rodolphe Desdunes, and their compatriots sowed in their battle against segregation in New Orleans did not die.

Less than three years after Homer Plessy lost his case in the Supreme Court, Alexander Pierre Tureaud was born to a black creole family in the same New Orleans neighborhood where Plessy and other members of the Citizens Committee lived. Like Homer Plessy, Tureaud was light skinned, and, like Plessy, he attended St. Augustine Church. His culture was that of the creole community that had spawned the 1877 and 1890s struggles against segregation. His heroes as a young man were Rodolphe Desdunes and Louis Martinet.[146]

Tureaud left New Orleans in 1916 and eventually landed in Washington, attending Howard Law School just as Charles Houston became dean. After law school, he went back to New Orleans and established a law practice. On his return to New Orleans in 1926, Tureaud asked Louis Martinet's widow for her late husband's *Crusader* newspaper files.[147] Tureaud was determined to follow in Martinet's and Desdunes's footsteps, and for the next fifty years he was the foremost legal advocate against segregation in New Orleans. In 1952, Tureaud filed a lawsuit on behalf of sixteen-year-old Earl Benjamin Bush, challenging segregation in New Orleans public schools. In November 1960, after almost eight years of persistent and courageous legal struggle, A. P. Tureaud's lawsuit resulted in the integration of the schools, and federal marshals escorted four young black girls into formerly all-white schools.

The spirit of Homer Plessy survived to blossom in Tureaud's successful lawsuit, as it did in the actions of so many others, because it was rooted in an activist community with a prophetic vision. *Plessy v. Ferguson* was, from the beginning, an integral and organic part of a broader political movement and articulated the deeply felt understanding and yearnings of that movement. It forced future generations to remember that African Americans resisted segregation and that the Supreme Court legitimated the practice. And it articulated for future generations a vision of justice unachievable at the time, creating a durable narrative of oppression and resistance.

6

Plant-Closing Litigation
"Youngstown Sure Died Hard"

AS STAUGHTON LYND THOUGHT about the lawsuit on behalf of steelworkers to prevent U.S. Steel from closing its Youngstown, Ohio, plants, he felt like he was a kid in Hungary in 1956, throwing bricks at the Soviet tanks.[1] And, indeed, the legal action he had filed in December 1979 had as much chance of success as the youthful Hungarian revolutionaries' efforts to overthrow Soviet rule. Both acts were desperate cries for help to an outside world bent on ignoring the victims' plight.

The plight of the steelworkers in the heartland of steelmaking in North America was becoming tragic. In the decade between 1977 and 1987, the steel industry in Pittsburgh and Youngstown would decline precipitously. In Pittsburgh, where steel had been the leading industry, three out of every four steel industry jobs would disappear.[2] A wave of plant shutdowns would end all steelmaking in Youngstown, which had been the second leading steel-producing city in the country. Whole communities would go bankrupt, the suicide rate would rise dramatically in mill towns, once-vibrant downtowns would take on the appearance of ghost towns, and workers would flee the rustbelt for low-paying jobs in the sunbelt.

Youngstown entered what Staughton Lynd characterized as a "deep sleep," a city that time had passed by.[3] The idled, aging, hulking mills that were still standing hovered over the Mahoning River like fossilized dinosaurs, remnants of a bygone era in which you could read a newspaper at night almost anywhere in Youngstown by light reflected off the clouds of smoke from the steel furnaces.[4] The city would lose more than one-fourth of its population between 1970 and 1987. By 1987, downtown Youngstown, which had been a city of more than 100,000 people, would have no hotel or department store. A number of the bridges into downtown would close because their cement was cracking.

As steel went, other manufacturing jobs dependent on the steel industry would also leave. Youngstown would lose 20 percent of all its jobs in the thirteen-year period ending in 1986.[5] In the early 1980s, it had the highest unemployment rate of any metropolitan area in the nation. "If you want to see the effect of mass unemployment on a community," one expert proclaimed, "Youngstown is probably the worst case you can think of."[6] The Youngstown city council described the city's plight as "economic genocide."[7]

To many, such as the local union president Gus Dolychronis, what had happened was "like an earthquake."[8] His metaphor suggests that natural, inevitable forces caused the disaster—forces set in play by the transition from an aging industrial economy to a new, high-tech economy where the Internet, not manufacturing, would be the engine of growth. One cannot fight earthquakes but can only hope to survive them. Yet, the people in Youngstown did fight the earthquake and did not accept their fate quietly. Theirs was a desperate, probably hopeless battle, and, in the end, like so many other struggles in the United States, it wound up in the courts.

The Youngstown steelworkers were not destined to fight for their jobs alone. Despite the long odds they faced and the lack of support from their international union, the United Steelworkers of America, the struggle to save the Youngstown mills attracted broad support from religious leaders, community activists, the local congressman, the neighborhood legal services office, and local unions in the Youngstown area. Their desperate battle also attracted the services of three nationally prominent attorneys—Staughton Lynd, Arthur Kinoy, and Ramsey Clark. All could be characterized as among the United States's most important progressive lawyers in the second half of the twentieth century. A lot of high-powered legal talent was committed to a legal struggle that was facing a steep uphill gradient. Arthur Kinoy had played a prominent legal role in the 1960s civil rights movement, represented Harlem Congressman Adam Clayton Powell in fighting his ouster from Congress, and won three important Supreme Court cases in the 1960s and early 1970s. Ramsey Clark was the son of former Supreme Court Justice Tom Clark and the former attorney general of the United States under President Johnson; after leaving government service he had represented a wide variety of David-like clients against the Goliath of the United States government. No clients were too hated, too tarnished, too poor, or too outside the mainstream for Clark to represent, as long as he felt they were victims of injustice. And Staughton Lynd was just beginning his career as a lawyer, after playing an important activist role in both the civil rights and the antiwar movements of the 1960s. Lynd was to become one of the most prominent legal voices for rank-and-file labor struggles of the last several decades of the twentieth century.

That the paths of these three well-known lawyers crossed in Youngstown was explainable. Their choice to engage in a struggle that objectively had little, if any, chance of winning reflected all three men's deeper interests in the law. For Kinoy, it was the chance to represent a labor struggle that he saw as vital to building a progressive movement in the United States, as well as the opportunity to articulate in the courts a vision of constitutional rights that went beyond traditional civil and political rights. For Clark, Youngstown represented an important case of gross injustice, which he hoped his prominent stature might call to America's or at least a judge's attention. Lynd's legal role derived from a need that he was to later describe as "accompaniment"—a term he learned from the liberation priests of Latin America.[9] This meant a duty to accompany workers in their struggle for justice, to help them articulate their interests, express their anger, and present their vision of a more just and ultimately socialistic society. It was these interests, not the weighing of victory or defeat, that brought each of these attorneys to Youngstown.

On Monday, September 19, 1977, the Youngstown Sheet and Tube Company announced that it was closing its massive, technologically obsolete Campbell Works in Youngstown, thereby throwing 5,000 steelworkers out of work. The local union responded immediately by collecting 110,000 signatures in less than three days on a petition to President Jimmy Carter and Congress to give the steel industry relief. Two hundred and fifty workers boarded buses to take the petitions to Washington the next day and unsuccessfully sought to present the petition to Carter or at least to one of his aides.

Within a week of the shutdown, Gerald Dickey, a local union official, suggested that the steelworkers and community "buy the damn place" and reopen it.[10] While many expressed skepticism about the idea, the absence of any real alternative led to a campaign to buy Campbell Works, spearheaded by a newly formed Ecumenical Coalition, consisting of leaders of the major religious denominations in Youngstown. The Coalition launched a "Save Our Valley Campaign," which in six months raised $4 million to buy the plant.[11] The Coalition sought $300 million in federal monies and loan guarantees to modernize the plant and reopen it. But in March 1979, the Carter administration decided not to furnish the monies requested, and the Coalition's efforts around Campbell Works collapsed.

Meanwhile, Youngstown Sheet and Tube had been acquired by the LTV Corporation. On December 14, 1978, LTV made public a decision to close the Brier Hill Works in Youngstown and to lay off its 1,500 workers. Those 1,500 workers were represented by Local 1462 of the United Steelworkers Union, a militant democratic local led by the forceful leaders Ed Mann, Gerald Dickey, and John Barbero. The local union organized a picket line outside the plant and filed an NLRB charge alleging that the company's refusal to bargain over the shutdowns was an unfair labor practice. The NLRB, with the international union's agreement, dismissed the charge.

In March 1979, three months after the plant had closed, the local organized what it hoped would be a massive demonstration in downtown Youngstown. The demonstration drew fewer than five hundred people, a major disappointment. The long delay between the plant's closing and the rally contributed to the poor turnout, as did the international union's lack of support for the whole effort.[12] The struggle at Brier Hill was over.

The Youngstown community now focused on its major remaining steel mills at U.S. Steel's Youngstown Works, which employed close to 5,000 workers. Staughton Lynd recalls "[f]eeling that just as George Washington's army retreated southward across New Jersey in the summer and fall of 1775, losing one battle after the other, so our little band of resisters was withdrawing north up the Mahoning Valley."[13] The Youngstown Works were aging mills, clearly in danger of closing. The mills still made steel in open hearths, a process that was technologically obsolete. At least one steam engine at those mills dated from the nineteenth century.

But U.S. Steel had, as one worker, George Denney, put it, "made a promise to the employees that as long as it's profitable they would stay open."[14] And the workers believed, on the basis of company statements and union concessions, that the Youngstown Works were profitable. Many workers were stunned on November 27, 1979, when the board of directors of U.S. Steel announced the permanent shutdown of the Youngstown Works and more than a dozen other smaller plants. "It's a betrayal," George Denney told the *New York Times*.[15] Frank Georges, a thirty-seven-year-old machinist at the Youngstown Works, was at the bank that gloomy November 27, closing on a new house. He and his wife had decided to buy the house some months before, when he heard U.S. Steel chairman David Roderick state on TV that the company had no plans to close the mill. When Georges heard the news of the closing, he "felt like someone pulled a rug out from under me. Then I got angry."[16]

Several days later, seven buses of Youngstown steelworkers and their supporters braved the cold and snow to descend on U.S. Steel's national headquarters in Pittsburgh. After several hours outside, the picketers streamed into the building, brushed past security personnel who attempted to bar their way, and surged up an escalator to a mezzanine from which elevators led to executive offices forty floors above. U.S. Steel officials, taking no chances that they might be confronted by the workers, turned off the elevators leading to the higher floors. The workers were thus prevented from going up, and the executives were trapped in their offices. No one knew what to do as the placard-carrying steelworkers walked around the mezzanine. At about four in the afternoon, the demonstrators decided that they had accomplished enough for the day, left the building, and boarded the buses for the one-and-a-half-hour ride back to Youngstown.

Before leaving the occupied mezzanine and escalator of U.S. Steel's Pittsburgh headquarters, Staughton Lynd, who was accompanying the workers, talked with the group and proposed a possible lawsuit against U.S. Steel. The gist of the lawsuit, he said, would be that U.S. Steel had made a promise to keep the Youngstown mills open if they could be made profitable. The workers had agreed to a variety of concessions, worked hard, and relied on that promise to their detriment, yet U.S. Steel had breached its promise. Under contract law, U.S. Steel's promise might be enforceable.

Bob Vasquez, the president of the Youngstown Works Local 1330 of the Steelworkers Union, and the other workers who listened to Staughton explain his theory that day were receptive. Indeed, Vasquez had asked Neighborhood Legal Services to come up with legal strategies for fighting the shutdown, and Staughton's coworker Jim Callen had thought of the contract argument. The workers had petitioned, picketed, demonstrated, and negotiated with the companies to avert shutdowns, all to no avail. Maybe litigation could help; in any event, there were no rosier alternatives.

The path that led Staughton Lynd to participate in the occupation of the U.S. Steel Building on that cold November day had taken many twists and turns. Lynd was born in New York City in the 1920s to famous parents, Robert and Helen Lynd, who had co-authored the sociology classic *Middletown*. His father was a tenured professor of sociology at Columbia University, and Lynd grew up in privileged circumstances on New York's West Side. He spent a good part of his adolescence and young manhood trying to escape what his father wanted him to become, the two key elements of which were a tenured professor at an Ivy League university and an American Lenin.

Lynd attended Harvard but dropped out in 1948 after reading Trotsky's *Literature and Revolution*. After falling in love and marrying Alice, his wife, collaborator, and comrade of now fifty years, Staughton eventually graduated from Harvard, in 1951. He then served in the army as a noncombatant medic but was given an undesirable discharge because the army said he had belonged to the leftist John Reed Society in college and his mother was a "hypermodern educator."[17] (Eventually the Supreme Court held that Lynd and others similarly discharged must be given honorable discharges.)

Between 1954 and 1957, Staughton and Alice were members of the Macedonia Co-operative Community in Northeast Georgia, where they lived in "voluntary poverty" and made decisions by consensus. Their time in Macedonia was a period of "formation, establishing values and teaching us ways of living in community which we vowed to live by for the rest of our lives."[18] Macedonia showed them, Lynd would later write, that people could live in a style different from the "dog-eat dog ambience of capitalist society."[19]

After the Lynds left Macedonia, they moved back to New York where Staughton got his Ph.D. in history from Columbia. The southern sit-ins motivated them to move back South, and Lynd got a job teaching at the all-black Spelman College in Atlanta. The Lynds actively participated in the civil rights movement and became committed Quakers. Staughton was director of the Freedom Schools in the 1964 Mississippi Summer Project. He accepted a position at Yale in 1964 and seemed destined to follow his father into a brilliant academic career, fulfilling at least the first of his father's goals for him.

But Lynd's tenure at Yale coincided with the rise of the antiwar movement, and he was "briefly notorious in the 1960s."[20] He was the chairperson of the first major march on Washington against the Vietnam War, which took place in April 1965; in December of that year, Lynd, Herbert Aptheker, and Tom Hayden traveled to Hanoi. On the way to Hanoi, the group stopped in Moscow, and Lynd had a meeting with Dang Quang Ming, the North Vietnamese ambassador to the Soviet Union. Lynd expressed his sympathy and support for the Vietnamese victims of American imperialism and suggested that American military power could destroy the Vietnamese guerrilla movement. The ambassador, a slight, elderly man, responded very softly, "You don't understand, professor, we're going to win. . . . [F]or every United States soldier who lands in Vietnam one more Vietnamese will come to the National Liberation Front."[21] Lynd drew the lesson that the Vietnamese perspective was that of a long-distance runner, one who knew that winning could be measured only in the long term. With determination and perseverance, people could triumph over apparent overwhelming power.

Lynd's Vietnam trip was highly publicized, and upon his return he spoke to thousands of people about his experience. His father's second goal was also in sight, although Lynd's role was that of a leftist political leader, instead of an American Lenin.

By the late 1960s, however, Lynd faced two difficult personal and political setbacks, which would eventually lead him to Youngstown. The first was political. The end of the sixties witnessed the demise of the Students For a Democratic Society (SDS) and the Student Nonviolent Coordinating Committee (SNCC). The movement that the Lynds so identified with was fractured and drifting. Lynd was disappointed that so many who called themselves revolutionaries in the 1960s disappeared when the movements of that decade failed to produce instantaneous, total transformation.[22] Staughton "looked askance at the pattern of behavior that expected quick results."[23] It was to him "a fast-food mentality."[24] He became "addicted to the notion that the once and future movement requires us to be long-distance runners."[25] So, he resolved to continue his movement work in grass roots communities, digging in for the long haul. The movement's collapse might not have led Staughton and Alice to Youngstown had another, more personal trauma not befallen him. After his trip to Vietnam, Yale denied him tenure. He and Alice decided to move to Chicago in 1967. Alice Lynd obtained part-time work as a trainer of draft counselors. Staughton

Lynd was offered jobs teaching history at five Chicago-area colleges, only to have each appointment vetoed by the college administration. His career as a history professor over, Lynd started anew, studying law.

In 1970, Lynd's father died, leaving a manila envelope for Lynd with his first three published articles, including two articles about a summer in 1922 he had spent as a volunteer preacher in a Rockefeller oil camp called Elk Basin, Wyoming. The articles told how his father had lived in squalid conditions with the workers and had become a pick-and-shovel laborer in the oil field. Lynd had only vaguely known of his father's experience in Elk Basin. Reading the articles for the first time left Staughton bursting with pride. He experienced what he believes is an "unconscious project" of every child, to find that part of their parents' life and work that has particular meaning for the child and to continue it and build on it.[26] Lynd wrote, later, that "[w]hat my Dad did for one summer I have tried to make into a way of life."[27]

In 1976, at the age of forty-six, Lynd received a law degree from the University of Chicago and moved to Youngstown, a move that he said was "all mixed in with his new clarity about his father's life."[28] He saw his own future as a lawyer in a working-class community as a continuation of his father's summer at Elk Basin.[29]

In Youngstown, Lynd's friends Ed Mann and John Barbero were local union officials. He found work with the town's leading labor law firm, from which he was fired two years later for displaying excessive sympathy with rank-and-file unionists. In 1978, he went to work for the Northeast Ohio Legal Services office in Youngstown. Staughton viewed his work for Legal Services, like his directorship of the Mississippi Freedom Schools, as providing glimpses into the closest thing to a socialist institution that could exist within capitalist society: democratic, egalitarian, with a mission of serving the poor.

In December 1979, in the wake of the plant closings and the Pittsburgh demonstration, Lynd was working with local steelworkers' leaders like Bob Vasquez to create a broad coalition that would file suit against U.S. Steel. They got help from an unexpected source: Congressman Lyle Williams. Williams, who before going into politics had worked as a barber in Warren, Ohio, was the first Republican to represent the Youngstown area in Congress since the 1930s. He had beaten the long-time incumbent Democrat in 1978, after voters became disenchanted with the Carter administration's failure to make good on its promises to help save the Youngstown Sheet and Tube mills. Williams invited Lynd, the local union presidents, and other attorneys to meet with him about a possible lawsuit. A coalition of plaintiffs was assembled that included Congressman Williams; the four local unions representing the workers at the U.S. Steel Youngstown Works; the local union representing the workers at the now closed Brier Hill Works, who wanted their mill to reopen as part of a reconstituted and modernized Youngstown Works; Local 1112, UAW, representing workers at the General Motors plant in Lordstown, Ohio; the Tri-State Conference on Steel, composed of clergy and steelworkers with a special interest in modernizing existing steel facilities; and sixty-five individual steelworkers at the Youngstown Works. While Lynd and the other attorneys suspected that some of the Plaintiffs lacked a sufficiently close interest in the Youngstown Works to have "standing" to sue, they wanted the judge to understand the wide variety of groups and individuals interested in keeping the mills open.

On December 21, the lawsuit to keep the mills open was filed in federal court in Youngstown. Congressman Williams admitted that victory in court was a long shot but argued that a lawsuit could buy time for government intervention. Williams noted that filing a lawsuit was in many respects a "radical" action, but U.S. Steel's action in closing the plant was to him "equally radical."[30] Desperate times called for desperate measures. "We're fighting an uphill battle," he recognized, "but we do see a way to fight."[31] Other plaintiffs made the same point.

The lawsuit was part of a broader political effort by steelworkers and their supporters to focus attention on Youngstown and to find a way to keep the Youngstown Works alive. The Youngstown City Council enacted a resolution calling for the federal government to come up with loan guarantees to keep the mills alive. The day after the lawsuit was filed, an emergency task force of the Ohio legislature appeared at the Local 1330 Union Hall to take testimony and to publicly announce its support for the lawsuit. One week later, a subcommittee of the U.S. House of Representatives Ways and Means Committee held a hearing on steel in Youngstown and voiced support for the steelworkers. The lawsuit, which asked for injunctive relief to keep the mills open, sought to buy time for these and other political efforts.

Many labor, business, and community leaders, however, were critical of the suit. The former mayor of Youngstown echoed the sentiments of much of Youngstown's elite when he told Lynd at a checkout line in the grocery store that the case was "frivolous and ridiculous." William Edwards, from the International Union's public relations department, also thought the lawsuit was futile. "I don't think we can force the company to keep the plants open," he told the press.[32]

The first action taken by the court after the case was filed provided the steelworkers with a lucky break. Judge Thomas D. Lambros was assigned to handle the case. Lambros was a liberal judge; Lynd thought Lambros had more than the ordinary share of human feeling and was likely to empathize with the steelworkers' plight and to want to help them.

Before the case got under way, though, political action erupted. The workers' strategy was to negotiate with U.S. Steel to provide more employee concessions to save the mill or, alternatively, for U.S. Steel to allow the workers to buy it and run it themselves. U.S. Steel said no, and the workers took dramatic action. On January 28, they took over and occupied the U.S. Steel Building in Youngstown. Ed Mann, the former president of the Brier Hill Works local union, expressed the sentiment of the local union leadership when he quoted Frederick Douglass' famous 1857 speech:

> Power concedes nothing without a demand. . . . Find out what people will submit to and you will find out the exact measure of injustice and wrong which will be imposed upon them. And these will be continued until they are resisted with either words or blows or with both. The limits of tyrants are prescribed by the endurance of those they oppress.[33]

The workers prepared to sleep in the building and left only after the mill superintendent, William Kirwan, promised them that if they left, the company would meet with the local union presidents the next day.

The next day Kirwan met with the local union officials and promised them the chance to buy the mills and run them. The *Cleveland Plain Dealer* colorfully summed up the meeting in its front-page headline the next day: "Buy or bye-bye, steel union told."[34] The workers were hopeful of federal help to buy the plant.

Three days later, however, on January 31, 1980, David Roderick, chairman of the board of U.S. Steel, flatly refused to sell the plant to a coalition subsidized by the federal government. The workers' hopes were dashed, and for all intents and purposes direct action against U.S. Steel and negotiations with the company ended. The only reed of hope the workers still held onto was the lawsuit.

Judge Lambros had scheduled the trial of plaintiffs' request for an injunction for March 17, 1980. U.S. Steel paid no attention to the pending court proceeding and announced that it would close down the Youngstown Works on March 11, only six days before the trial. In effect, the company was rendering the trial virtually meaningless—an act of hubris that only a company with no doubt of the outcome would contemplate.

Judge Lambros scheduled a pretrial hearing in Cleveland for February 28. Local 1330 chartered a bus to take steelworkers to Cleveland for the hearing, but only a dozen or so riders showed up. The average steelworker had given up hope; to most, the lawsuit appeared to be just one more dead end.

Those few workers who did make it to Cleveland must have been surprised at what transpired. Bob Clyde, the director of Northeast Ohio Legal Services, had persuaded Ramsey Clark, the former attorney general of the United States, to appear before Judge Lambros on the workers' behalf. Clark, a slim six-foot-three-inch former Marine, walked into the courtroom wearing corduroys, some kind of earth shoes, and a blue sports jacket. Despite his modest attire and unassuming presence, the judge took notice when Lynd brought Clark to his chambers, addressing Clark as "General."[35]

Ramsey Clark's father, Tom Clark, was President Truman's attorney general; in 1949, Truman appointed him to the Supreme Court. Ramsey graduated from the University of Texas Law School and went into the private practice of law in Dallas. In 1961, the Kennedy administration appointed him an assistant attorney general, in which capacity he supervised the federal presence at the University of Mississippi following the admission of James Meredith as the school's first black student, in 1962. In 1967, President Johnson nominated Clark, then thirty-nine years old, to be attorney general, a position he held until 1969. As attorney general, he was an outspoken advocate for civil rights, against wiretapping, and for abolishing the death penalty. Yet, as a high-ranking member of the administration, he publicly supported the Vietnam War and authorized the prosecution of Benjamin Spock for conspiring against the draft.

After leaving government, Clark had tried working at a large New York law firm and was unhappy. In 1972, he went to Hanoi and criticized the United States bombing of Vietnam. He waged two unsuccessful campaigns, in 1974 and 1976, for U.S. senator from New York. He left the large New York firm and instead practiced law out of a small, usually disheveled office in Greenwich Village.

Clark's turn towards radicalism infuriated many, such as President Carter's attorney general, Griffin Bell. The New Republic wrote a scathing attack on Clark, calling him a "legal 911" for the tawdry collection of accused terrorists and neo- or ex-Nazis that he had represented.[36]

Others, however praised him. The prominent civil rights attorney William Kunstler, a co-founder of the Center for Constitutional Rights, called him "the voice of conscience in the American bar."[37] Nicholas deB. Katzenbach, Clark's predecessor as attorney general, has called Clark a man of questionable judgment but "great courage," "absolute decency," and "total honesty and sincerity."[38] "[T]his man is an American original, . . . who really tries to speak the truth as he sees it," according to Victor Navasky, the editor of the left-wing Nation magazine and a longtime Clark friend.[39]

Many of his former colleagues viewed Clark's career after leaving the attorney general position as a failure. His former New York law firm partner Melvin L. Wulf has called him a "total enigma."[40] "He lost the opportunity to be a really effective, influential voice on the American left, such as it is, and that was a great loss."[41] Henry Schwartzchild, who worked with Clark on death penalty cases, noted that "his career has not been successful—nor would he have had it otherwise."[42]

Clark does not trouble himself with questions of his courtroom success. He views his role as employing the courts to expose injustice to the American public, not necessary to win legal victories. "You need to act," he says. "You don't measure the odds. They're all long shots."[43]

Indeed, Clark is not reluctant to bring cases he sees as important, even if they are sure losers in court. His cases at times generate controversy over the proper role of the courts. One district court found that Clark "surely knew" that his "case offered no hope whatsoever of success" but was nevertheless brought as a legitimate "public statement of protest," because federal courts "serve in some respects as a forum for making such statements, and should continue to do so."[44] The Court of Appeals, unfortunately, disagreed, sanctioning Clark because it did "not conceive it a proper function of a federal court to serve as a forum for 'protests.'"[45]

Clark's legal arguments often appealed to emotional impulse, and that emotional appeal carried the day on February 28, 1980, in Judge Lambros's courtroom. As the *Youngstown Vindicator* reported, "the heart of the [pretrial] conference belonged to Clark," whose "simple eloquence" touched everyone in the courtroom that day, including the judge.[46]

Judge Lambros started the pretrial conference with a long, extraordinary speech ruminating on the pros and cons of the plaintiffs' lawsuit. To him the case involved nothing less than "the economic fate and survival of a large segment of this state, a large segment of our civilization."[47] Obviously, this was not a routine matter.

Judge Lambros's "first reaction" was that plaintiffs had no legal claim. "At first blush . . . applying the principles of law that we have learned in law school and our experience in dealing with the regular routine business of the court . . . there is no basis for this type of a lawsuit in American jurisprudence, it is unheard of."[48]

The judge then cautioned that he did not want to do anything that would intrude on the free enterprise system and that the court's role was not to make law. But, he pointed out, the law is based on maintaining "stability and tranquility" in human relationships, in this case the relationships among U.S. Steel, the City of Youngstown, and its inhabitants.[49] Lambros questioned whether *something* hadn't "come out of that relationship," a proposition he uncovered not by reading any case but by "looking at the law as a whole."[50] For him, "[T]he judicial process cannot survive by adhering to the attitudes of the 1800s."[51] Lambros did not want to dismiss the case simply because of a lack of judicial precedent supporting the plaintiffs.

Judge Lambros then made a truly radical suggestion that astounded all of the lawyers and steelworkers in the courtroom. He suggested that the "something" that had come from the long-established relationship between U.S. Steel and the community was that the community had acquired a vested property right in U.S. Steel's not completely abandoning its obligation to Youngstown. "[I]t seems to me that a property right has arisen from the lengthy, long-established relationship between United States Steel, the steel industry as an institution, the community in Youngstown, the people of Mahoning County, and the Mahoning Valley in having given and devoted their lives to this industry."[52]

Lambros followed this startling proposition with an equally sweeping suggestion that the case belonged in state court, not federal court. He then gave the lawyers a ten-minute recess to assess his "preliminary views."

The plaintiffs' lawyers were unsure what to say when they got back before Judge Lambros. All they could agree on was that Ramsey Clark should speak first.

Clark spoke powerfully and eloquently. He spoke not primarily of law but of people. He spoke of the American dream and what it meant for Youngstown steelworkers. He spoke of plant obsolescence and the need to develop a policy that would balance property rights with "fair and humane" treatment of employees. For Clark, "this is essentially a human rights case."[53]

Staughton Lynd spoke next and filled in more of the technical details of the lawsuit and plaintiffs' contract theory. He ended with a plea that the judge not "leave us to a state remedy that isn't really there. Please help us."[54]

After Lynd's and Clark's arguments, Judge Lambros seemed less inclined to give up jurisdiction of the case. Lynd thought that Clark had spoken magnificently and impressed the judge. U.S. Steel's attorney, James Carney, presented the company's case ably and clearly and criticized Clark's "impassioned rhetoric."[55]

When everyone had finished, Judge Lambros suddenly referred to Harry Truman's famous statement "The buck stops here." He proceeded to

(1) issue a temporary restraining order enjoining U.S. Steel from closing the steel mills until further order;
(2) order that the trial take place in Youngstown; and
(3) allow plaintiffs to take the deposition of U.S. Steel chairman David Roderick.

The plaintiffs were elated. The local union president Bob Vasquez called the ruling "great"; Congressman Williams thought that those who had scoffed at the suit might "take it a little more seriously." U.S.

Steel apparently did so, replacing its local attorney with the leading litigator of a Cleveland corporate law firm. They also filed a motion to stay Judge Lambros's injunction pending appeal and asked Lambros to reconsider his decision to hold trial in Youngstown on the ground that Mr. Roderick's safety could not be ensured. Both motions were promptly denied.

What Clark had focused on in his argument, and what Lambros had recognized, was that human rights in the twentieth century had to reach into the economic realm. Just as the antislavery, women's, and antisegregation litigators had focused on extending civil rights to blacks and women even if the law of that era was against them, Lynd and Clark were attempting to extend civil rights into the economic and social arena.

It was not the first time that people had recognized that the law must change to recognize the need for economic rights in addition to civil and political rights. President Franklin Delano Roosevelt's 1944 State of the Union address called for the enactment of a second Bill of Rights to ensure that all Americans be guaranteed a decent standard of living, a home, medical care, and social security. In the 1960s, lawyers for poor people attempted to establish through litigation a right to an equal education for all, a right to decent housing, food, and other economic necessities. While they won some important early victories in the Supreme Court, in the 1970s, the Court rejected the use of the Fourteenth Amendment's equal protection and due process clauses to expand civil rights into economic rights. And, although most of the world has accepted the concept of economic rights in treaties such as the International Covenant on Economic, Social, and Cultural Rights, the United States has not ratified those treaties.

Judge Lambros's speech recognized the need to bring American law out of its nineteenth-century precepts and into the late-twentieth-century reality. It was a task that was to prove as difficult as the endeavors of Albion Tourgée, Alvan Stewart, Louis Martinet, Virginia Minor, Susan B. Anthony, and Salmon Chase to move the law off its early-nineteenth-century moorings. Unfortunately, the recognition of economic rights was not to be achieved in the United States in the twentieth century just as women and blacks did not successfully gain their civil rights in the preceding century.

The trial of *Local 1330 et al. v. U.S. Steel* opened dramatically in the Youngstown Federal Courthouse on Monday, March 17, 1980. The courtroom was packed with steelworkers, reporters, and federal marshals to protect U.S. Steel chairman Roderick from the presumably dangerous hordes that were employed in his steel mills.

Ramsey Clark flew into Youngstown by chartered plane and made an opening statement for plaintiffs. Clark has an extraordinary grasp of American history, and his opening was a brilliant exposition of the struggle between American labor and business, starting with the railroad strike of 1877. Clark's historical perspective barely made it into the twentieth century and only briefly touched on the specific legal issues involved in the case. But Clark made his point that the workers needed protection, quoting emotionally from a newspaper account of a man who killed himself when the plant he worked at closed. "Technology doesn't make moral judgments," Clark said. "Mankind, through the rule of law, has to make moral judgments."[56] U.S. Steel's attorney, Charles Clarke, retorted that, while he was impressed by Clark's eloquence, the case should be decided on its legal merits and not on his opponent's "purple prose."[57]

At the end of the first day of trial, Clark told the plaintiffs' attorneys that he was returning to New York. He had other commitments; in any event, he didn't believe he was needed; and he liked the idea of Legal Services attorneys questioning U.S. Steel's top executives. Lynd was clearly disappointed by Clark's early exit.

The trial lasted five days. For Lynd, it was a kind of "morality play," obliging the individuals who had decided to close the mills to come speak to the community they had damaged. Although the plaintiffs had taken Judge Lambros's suggestion and now claimed a violation of a community property right and also had added an antitrust claim, the testimony at trial focused on whether U.S. Steel had reneged on a contractually binding promise to keep the plants open if the workers made them profitable.

William Kirwan, the mill superintendent, testified that he had told the workers on a number of occasions that if the plant could make a profit, it would be kept open. Kirwan stated, however, that all this was simply positive reinforcement designed to exhort workers as you would prod children.[58] Kirwan and the company's Eastern Division comptroller testified that what they meant by profit was covering the direct costs of operating the mills. Under that definition, the Youngstown Works made $9 million profit in 1979. However, at trial, the company claimed that profit meant income earned after deducting all corporate expenses, such as sales and advertising costs, a calculation that yielded a $300,000 loss for the first ten months of 1979.

Lynd, the workers, and most of the reporters believed the plaintiffs had presented a compelling case. After Lynd made his closing statement on Friday, the union presidents congratulated him on a job well done. Judge Lambros met Lynd in the hall during the recess after both sides had concluded and muttered, "Great argument" as he walked past.[59]

But "great" and "winning" were not to be synonymous, and Lynd might have just as well gotten a good night's sleep instead of working until late at night on his closing argument. For, after a two-hour recess, Judge Lambros read a twenty-three-page decision he must have written prior to hearing the closing argument. In it, he held that (1) the company had made no enforceable promise to the workers to keep the mills open if profitable and (2) even if it had, the company's determination that the mills were not profitable was reasonable.[60]

Judge Lambros then turned to the community property right that he himself had suggested. Lambros made clear that his goal in making that suggestion was to prod U.S. Steel to reach a negotiated settlement to provide economic aid for the workers' "rehabilitation." Unfortunately, U.S. Steel had not done so, and, while Lambros expressed great sympathy with the workers' and the community's plight, he found that such a property right "is not now in existence in the code of laws of our nation."[61] Forced to decide the issue and not just ruminate about it, Lambros held that he was not a "legislative body and can not make laws where none exist."[62] Lambros dissolved the injunction but ordered the company to keep the mill in mothballs while the court proceeded with plaintiffs antitrust claim. Apparently, Lambros was still committed to trying to reach a settlement.

Some of the legal services lawyers who had worked on the case were devastated by what was clearly a legal defeat. Many workers, while obviously disappointed, at least publicly refused to admit that the trial had ended in defeat. The local union leader, Vasquez, said that the judge's decision still left open the possibility that the workers could buy the mills. Congressman Williams felt that "we did set a precedent in this trial that will be used more and more in this country" to fight plant shutdowns.[63] The Reverend Charles Rawlings, a leader of the Ecumenical Coalition, proclaimed that the "battlefield now has to be the legislative field."[64]

Staughton Lynd was, of course, saddened by the defeat and held out no illusions that the workers would prevail in their antitrust claims. But, addressing the workers in the posttrial meeting, he expressed a sentiment that underlay whatever hope the steelworkers still had. He told the story of how he and a handful of friends had gone to the steps of the Pentagon in June 1965, to picket against the Vietnam War. Within a few minutes of their arrival, military police arrived, incredulous that such a small group of people would undertake so obviously ineffectual an action. "You don't understand," Staughton replied. "We are just the first of thousands."

The story, which also opens Lynd's autobiographical book, *Living Inside Our Hope*, expresses Lynd's deepest underlying hope and optimism about setting out on history's path.[65] Indeed, Lynd's comments to the policeman proved prophetic. But, unfortunately, the steelworkers' movement against plant closing followed a different trajectory from that of the anti-war protestors.

The plaintiffs appealed Judge Lambros's decision. The appeal angered Lambros, who undoubtedly felt that he was still trying to help the plaintiffs get U.S. Steel to negotiate by holding the antitrust claim over its head. Shortly after plaintiffs filed the appeal, Judge Lambros encountered the Legal Services lawyer Bob Clyde and the community activist Charles Rawlings in the Cleveland federal courthouse and snapped at them, "You blew it."[66] Soon thereafter, on April 14, 1980, Lambros dismissed the antitrust claim. All that plaintiffs had left was their appeal.

Lynd and his Legal Services compatriots worked hard on their promissory estoppel claim on appeal. Lynd had always believed that contract law supported their claim, but he was queasy about asserting a community right to property. Although Lambros had raised the issue, the judge had concluded that there was no legal precedent for such a right. Lynd sadly agreed.[67]

Lynd could not write a brief on a point for which there was no precedent. It was not fear of Rule 11 sanctions (for bringing frivolous cases) that deterred him; it was a deep-seated belief in the need for radical lawyers to maintain an intellectual honesty about the limitations of the law. The role of a radical labor lawyer, Lynd thought, is to articulate the workers' feelings of injustice in a manner that the law could recognize. If the law did not recognize the workers' complaint as actionable, then the lawyer's role was to tell the workers that and to develop another strategy for fighting the injustice. Lynd spoke to the workers cautiously, without rhetorically painting a rosy picture of the plaintiffs' chances. For Lynd, "style is the man," and it was important to be "as intellectually responsible in the spoken word as in the written word."[68]

Lynd's intellectual predilection coincided with his politics. Lynd's view of socialism led him to the belief that, while he could use the law to win concrete victories and raise issues, he also felt that the limitations of capitalist laws had to be recognized, understood, and explained. While Lynd was perfectly willing to bring a "prophetic" case for which there was some legal precedent, even if for political reasons the case would likely lose, he was unwilling to argue a case with no supporting precedent.

But, though Lynd was unwilling to argue the community property right issue to the Court of Appeals, there was a respected national legal group and a prominent national lawyer willing to fill the void. The Center for Constitutional Rights submitted an amicus brief, signed by Arthur Kinoy, a professor at Rutgers Law School, that argued for a community property right to prevent a company in U.S. Steel's position from unilaterally deciding to close mills vital to that community. Michael Ratner, at the CCR, had found a line of Supreme Court cases that had held that private property, such as the Youngstown Works, that are "affected with a public interest" could be regulated for the public good. Lynd noted, however, that these Depression-era cases had upheld the *legislature's* right to take emergency action affecting private property, and not a *court's* ability to act on its own.[69]

At five feet, four inches, Arthur Kinoy could barely poke his head over some podiums, but he was a rousing orator; when he started speaking, a power, excitement, and engagement spewed forth that made him resemble a preacher more than a law professor. Kinoy's faith in the power of popular struggle was as resolute and unshakable as a priest's faith in God—and he could impart that powerful faith to others. Kinoy's style was the opposite of Lynd's low-key manner. With his high-pitched voice and his rhetorical, passionate language, Kinoy could hold audiences spellbound through lengthy speeches.

Kinoy had started his legal career in the late 1940s, during the early days of the Cold War and domestic McCarthyism. Kinoy was a young lawyer for the United Electrical Workers in 1947 when he first experienced what was to become his basic approach to the law. The union had filed an unfair-labor-practice charge that was to be heard before the

National Labor Relations Board in Cleveland. The union was not really interested in whether it ultimately would win legally, and realized that it undoubtedly would not. It needed to gain time and to retake the initiative from management. As Kinoy explained, in his autobiographical book, *Rights on Trial*,

> the test of success for a people's lawyer is not always the technical winning or losing of the formal proceeding. Again and again, the real test was the impact of the legal activities on the morale and understanding of the people involved in the struggle. To the degree that the legal work helped to develop a sense of strength, an ability to fight back, it was successful. This could even be achieved without reaching the objective of formal victory. . . . Victory or defeat that day in Cleveland would be measured not by the ultimate ruling of the NLRB but by the immediate impact of the legal proceeding upon the organization of workers at the plant.[70]

Thus, for Kinoy, the decision whether to bring a lawsuit could not be based solely on "the likelihood of success within the court structure."[71] Rather, the question was what role the lawsuit would play in the people's struggle. "If it helped the fight, then it was done, even if the chances of immediate legal success were virtually nonexistent."[72]

Yet, Kinoy felt the same uneasiness about using the NLRB and the courts to further political goals that Lynd felt about arguing for a community right to property. Since the union and its lawyers knew that there was little likelihood of success in the courts, "was this really an honest . . . use of legal techniques?"[73] But Kinoy, unlike Lynd, resolved his doubts. For Kinoy, the court system was simply one form of political expression for people in struggle. Thus, the First Amendment protected lawsuits as a means of political expression, even if the suit had no hope of success and was not based on legal precedent.

The different approaches to law and constitutional rights taken by Kinoy and Lynd reflect longstanding tensions in the radical movement's view of the Constitution that commenced with the split within the abolitionist movement over whether the Constitution, properly interpreted, outlawed slavery. Lynd sympathized with the abolitionists who had accurately viewed the Constitution as having accepted slavery and thus had called on antislavery judges to resign, as opposed to those abolitionists, such as Alvan Stewart, who had proposed radical reinterpretations of the Constitution based on theories of natural law and natural rights. Kinoy's view hued closer to that of Alvan Stewart and Senator Charles Sumner who argued that the Constitution should always be interpreted in favor of liberty, equality, and human rights.

Kinoy had endured many bitter defeats in the 1950s, including a devastating failure in his last-ditch attempt to stop the execution of Julius and Ethel Rosenberg. Kinoy vowed that, despite thoughts of giving up lawyering, "No matter what, we'll keep fighting."[74] In the 1960s, the movement's fortunes changed, and Kinoy rode the crest of the civil rights movements to legal victories in a number of crucial cases. In Danville, South Carolina, he and William Kunstler, another co-founder of the CCR, pioneered the use of the long-dormant federal removal statute to prevent state prosecutions of civil rights activists. Jack Greenberg, then the legal director of the NAACP Inc. Fund, completely rejected the idea of using this old Reconstruction-era statute to stop the state court trials of the demonstrators, calling it a crazy idea amounting to "playing with the courts."[75] But, despite the reservations of many of the lawyers, they decided to try, for there were no other good alternatives. Miraculously, this time Kinoy and the other Danville lawyers won in the Fourth Circuit Court of Appeals—at least temporarily.

Kinoy was a leading proponent of resurrecting and applying the Thirteenth and Fourteenth Amendment theories held by Albion Tourgée and the other Reconstruction-era activists to the 1960s civil rights movement. He wrote an important article in the *Rutgers Law Review* in which he argued that the Thirteenth and Fourteenth Amendments did not grant mere negative rights but provided an affirmative grant of freedom for the former slaves and their descendants. He argued that position in dozens of cases throughout the South.[76]

Kinoy developed the perspective that progressive lawyers must always imagine that victory is possible, leading many of his coworkers to term him an unredeemable optimist.[77] Kinoy's irrepressible, unshakable, and infectious optimism serves as a fountain for his boundless energy and incredible ability to motivate others.

Kinoy's approach, combined with his passion as an orator, motivated thousands of law students and other Americans to struggle for a view of the Constitution as a progressive instrument supporting a movement for radical change. In addition, during periods of mass upsurge such as occurred during the 1960s civil rights movement, Kinoy was able to convince some courts to interpret the Constitution in the spirit of justice and equality, despite the lack of precedent supporting his argument.

Kinoy's view, however, does not address the limitation of the law and the Constitution. While the Constitution has proven to be a powerful tool utilized by numerous progressive movements, the Constitution was also clearly intended to and has continued to function as a crucial bulwark to prevent radical reordering of social and property relations in this country. Despite this reactionary intent, for Kinoy, the law and Constitution are fundamentally indeterminate vessels, with their meaning determined not by legal precedent but by the political struggle of masses of people.

By 1979, Kinoy, now approaching sixty years old, was in a new stage of his political-legal career. While he still taught law, was very active with the CCR, and dispensed legal advice to young lawyers needing assistance, his main mission in life was to create a mass progressive party independent of both the Democrats and the Republicans. Two key components of that new party would be the active participation and leadership of working people and the use of constitutional rights to fight for economic justice. The plant-closing issue intrigued Kinoy on both scores. Here was an issue critical to working people, where local unions were actively engaged in struggle, raising fundamental questions of whether the Constitution protected not merely civil and political rights but also economic rights. Irrespective of whether legal precedent supported a community property right, Kinoy believed that people's lawyers had to find and use whatever they could to argue that the Constitution supported such rights—a position that would help motivate workers across America to struggle against plant closings. He hoped that a mass labor movement around plant closings would have the same impact as the civil rights movement had on the courts in the 1960s. Kinoy eagerly went to Cincinnati to argue the issue that Lynd felt queasy about.

The Court of Appeals heard oral arguments on the appeal on June 18 in a packed courtroom in Cincinnati. Ramsey Clark was unavailable, having recently returned from Iran in connection with the hostage crisis. Staughton Lynd argued the case for plaintiffs, and in an unusual decision the court allowed Kinoy to argue on behalf of plaintiffs' amicus. The Court of Appeals panel was composed of three liberal judges, Judge George Clifton Edwards, Gilbert S. Merrit, and John W. Peck.

Lynd argued the point that the workers had relied on promises that U.S. Steel had made to their detriment and asserted that those promises were legally binding. Kinoy then got up to argue for a community property right. Before the argument, he had felt that the plaintiffs had no chance of winning—but, as often happens to litigators in such situations, when he got up to argue, a wave of hope and faith overcame his pessimism. Halfway through Kinoy's impassioned argument, Chief Judge Edwards looked at his friend Arthur Kinoy and asked, "Mr. Kinoy, do you have any case, in any jurisdiction, in any period in U.S. history, that supports the recognition of such a right?"[78] Kinoy answered without hesitation—*Marbury v. Madison*.

Kinoy's answer only confirmed Judge Edwards's hunch that he had no case directly on point. For *Marbury v. Madison*, one of the oldest and most famous cases in American constitutional history, did not involve a community property right. *Marbury v. Madison* established the proposition that the Supreme Court could review acts of Congress or executive-branch officials to decide whether they were constitutional, a far cry from addressing a community's property right over a steel mill.

But, to Kinoy's way of thinking, *Marbury v. Madison* was relevant. Chief Justice Marshall, in that case, daringly asserted the broad power of the Court, despite the fact that such power was not mentioned in the Constitution's text, and relied upon no judicial precedent to support his position. Kinoy was in effect telling the court that if Chief Justice Marshall could assert such unsupported power in *Marbury*, the appeals panel could do it again—that federal judicial power is as broad as necessary to promote a just government.

But the Court of Appeals did not support Kinoy's broad view of judicial power. The court's opinion characterized the worker's suit as "a cry for help from steelworkers and townspeople in the City of Youngstown."[79] It reproduced verbatim large sections of the plaintiffs' complaint, detailing the breach of trust the company had committed. It treated plaintiffs' appeal seriously and with sympathy, writing a lengthy opinion. Yet, in the end, it dismissed the plaintiffs' main claims.

The court held that plaintiffs' detrimental reliance argument failed because the workers had not proven that the mills were profitable. The court then expressed "great sympathy for the community interest reflected" in the plaintiffs' property right claim.[80] But Chief Judge Edwards found absolutely no legal authority to support it:

Neither in brief nor oral argument have plaintiffs pointed to any constitutional provision . . . nor any law . . . nor any case . . . which would convey authority to this court to require the United States Steel Corporation to continue operations in Youngstown.[81]

The court relegated plaintiffs to the legislature for any remedy to the tragedy that had befallen them.[82]

The Court of Appeals did reverse Judge Lambros's dismissal of plaintiffs' antitrust claim. That reversal proved significant, because it meant that the case would continue, and therefore a negotiated settlement with U.S. Steel became possible. Eventually, a small part of the Youngstown Works were leased to Toro Enterprises, a corporation that intended to reopen one small mill. The plaintiffs were able to negotiate a settlement with Toro Enterprises and U.S. Steel and to win minor concessions, which ended the case. Judge Lambros called the settlement "a valuable lesson."[83] The *Warren Tribune* headline read, "[Mahoning] Valley Is the Winner in Mill Suit" and commended the USW local presidents Vasquez and De Pietro and Staughton Lynd for their roles. The *Tribune* recognized that by "most accounts the plaintiffs were the loser in the year-long battle against U.S. Steel" and got "precious few concessions in exchange for dropping its lawsuit." The plaintiffs' "victory" consisted not of achieving concrete goals but rather "in keeping alive the idea of reopening the entire McDonald Works."[84]

Those works, however, were never reopened. Toro Enterprises did keep a small mill running that employed about 100 workers—less than 2 percent of the 5,000 steelworkers employed there prior to 1980.

The "valuable lessons" learned by the lawsuit were different for each participant in the plant-closing struggle. Bob Vasquez, president of Local 1330, told Staughton Lynd a year later that he had learned not to expect fairness from the courts. For him, workers should do what they had to outside the courts, rather than rely on lawsuits.[85]

For Lynd, the "lessons" were conflicting. For him, the lawsuit was an act of resistance by the community and workers that did compel the top executives of U.S. Steel to come to Youngstown and to confront the community they had wronged. The lawsuit articulated the stories and aspirations of the Youngstown community and helped define its issues in court. And the resulting court decision left a strong and vivid record of the injustice of the plant closing. The Youngstown mills would not simply vanish into history.

But, as a mechanism for political agitation, Lynd believed the lawsuit had several weaknesses. First, it relegated the workers to the role of spectators; the main action was conducted by lawyers. Second, it fed into people's misplaced faith in the courts and the law, into their beliefs that, if they could only tell the judge their story, they could win. Finally, it tended to channel workers' anger into a more moderate form of struggle, where picketing, booing, chanting, and hissing were off limits. Staughton concluded that the lawsuit did not do much to build a popular movement.

Both in court and on the streets, the lawsuit was a failure. But desperate acts of resistance to oppression, such as the Hungarian uprising of 1956 or the Warsaw ghetto uprising against the Nazis, cannot be understood in terms of their immediate effect. So, too, the Youngstown plant-closing litigation was a desperate act of resistance that opened up another arena of struggle. That it resulted in neither court victory nor popular uprising is not surprising. Rather, the question to ask is whether it had any long-term impact.

Of course, it is often difficult to assess the ultimate effect of a struggle like the plant-closing movement. For the long sweep of history is often measured not in years but in decades or even centuries, and the ripple effects of a particular action over the long term are often imperceptible. But two contrasting, yet complementary, outlooks coexist in tension with each other.

An optimistic take on what appears to be a defeated struggle focuses on eventual vindication in the future. Staughton Lynd's comment to the police at the 1965 Washington anti-war picket best captures this view: "We are just the first of thousands." That Lynd repeated this comment to the steelworkers after their defeat in Judge Lambros' courtroom underscores his deeply held faith in the progressive march of history and in the essential goodness and redemption of humanity. It illustrates the spiritual faith that motivates people like Lynd, Kinoy, Clark, and their compatriots to continue their work. For, underlying their radical critique of existing society lies a vision of a better one, and a defeat can be located as one point in the path to that future, redeemed society.

There can be no doubt that a future humane society will treat people who have spent thirty years working hard in a factory differently from the way the workers at U.S. Steel were treated in the late 1970s. That more humane treatment will find some legal expression, as a limitation on employers' managerial discretion, as a right devolving upon workers, or as some supervening governmental obligation.

The optimistic perspective viewed the Youngstown case as a precedent for future similar struggles, a point explicitly made by Congressman Williams and others after Lambros's decision went against them. They were right. The Youngstown workers' lawsuit was the first, not of thousands perhaps, but of dozens of other lawsuits. By the late 1980s, the *Wall Street Journal* reported that factory towns throughout the United States had begun to fight back when major companies decided to close down.[86] In 1987, the town of Norwood, Ohio, filed a $318 million lawsuit claiming that General Motors' planned auto factory closing was in breach of an implied contract. The city's lawyers argued that the sixty-four-year relationship between Norwood and General Motors was analogous to a marriage; since General Motors sought a divorce, the city was entitled to alimony.[87]

In West Virginia, in 1988, Governor Archie A. Moore Jr. sued the Newell Corporation for breach of contract when it announced that the company was closing its plant in Clarksburg, West Virginia. That same year, the city of Duluth, Minnesota, joined by local unions, sued the Triangle Tool Company to force it to keep its local plant open. The city of Chicago sued Hasbro Bradley, Inc., when it decided to close its Playskool plant, which employed 700 workers; Kenosha, Wisconsin, threatened a lawsuit against Chrysler when that company announced that it was shutting down operations and laying off 5,500 workers in the community.[88] While none of these lawsuits totally prevailed in court, most resulted in a negotiated settlement between the corporation and the community.[89]

The case that progressed the farthest in court occurred more than a decade after the Youngstown lawsuit. In 1992, the city of Ypsilanti, Michigan, sued General Motors after the company closed its factory after years of tax abatements granted in return for GM's promise to keep its auto factory in the town open. The community sued General Motors in state court, making the same contract claim that the Youngstown steelworkers had raised in their suit. This time, the plaintiffs won a judgment in the trial court enjoining General Motors from shutting down the plant.[90] Ypsilanti's victory was reversed by the appellate court, and the Michigan Supreme Court denied the town leave to appeal. Nevertheless, the *Ypsilanti* case illustrates that the Youngstown struggle did inspire other communities to challenge plant closing in court and suggests that they may yet have a victorious day in court.

The optimistic view coexists with a more pessimistic outlook. Optimistic faith redefines success by enlarging its historical scope, by looking toward future redemption. The pessimistic perspective redefines success by reorienting it internally, by perceiving internal redemption in waging the good fight.

Lynd's more "pessimistic" perspective came out near the end of the litigation, during the appeals process. When asked how he felt, Lynd then answered

> I feel like a boxer between the 13th and 14th rounds of a 15 rounder. The seconds are holding the sponge under the nose, holding up a finger to see if the eyes still focus. But you answer the bell.[91]

Success was not winning the fight but answering the bell. Success in this sense is defined not in a utilitarian manner but in one's attitude toward life, particularly one's reaction to oppression and suffering. The noted psychologist and Holocaust survivor Victor Frankl notes that our search for meaning inheres in defining ourselves and maintaining our identity, even in the most difficult of circumstances.[92] Concentration camps degrade life, but even the prisoner can define him- or herself in relationship to that extreme oppression.[93] The ability to struggle and not quit defines meaning and thus success for people like Lynd, Kinoy, Clark, and the Youngstown steelworkers.

Lynd recognizes that, if success is defined as getting the community to accept his ideas, he probably would be considered a failure. But, for him, success inheres in "living out one's values," or, as he titled his quasi-autobiography, *Living Inside Our Hope*, which signifies the living out of our future hopes and dreams in the present.[94]

The steelworkers saw their fight as an affirmation of their community's identity. They did what they believed was right, and their success inhered as much in their own self-definition as in their impact on the world. As Bob Vasquez stated, "It saved people's dignity that they made that fight for the mill."[95] Or, as another union leader, John Barbero, put it, "Youngstown sure died hard."

7

Politics versus Law

Were Travelers to Cuba Trading with the Enemy?

FOR MANY BOSTONIANS, spring is a time to shed the dreadful layers of winter clothing and to contemplate the delights of a summer vacation. In the spring of 1982, Ruth Wald, a professor of biology at Harvard University, was planning an August trip to Cuba with a group of American women. Wald's group would meet with Cuban women, attend theater and dance events, and visit factories, day care centers, educational facilities, and even a psychiatric hospital in Havana. For Wald, the trip was an opportunity to renew friendships with Cuban women she had met on a prior trip and to learn more about the problems Cuban women faced.

Wald's planned trip seemed innocuous enough, not the sort of stuff that generates spy thrillers, treason charges, and important Supreme Court cases. But, while Wald was planning her summer activities, officials of the United States government were deciding to invoke the ominous-sounding Trading with the Enemy Act, enacted during World War I, to prevent Wald and thousands of other Americans from visiting Cuba. What to Wald was a trip to meet old friends and learn about Cuba was to the Reagan administration an act of consorting with the enemy, which could cost Wald five years in jail and a $50,000 fine.

Nor was Ruth Wald the only American about to be ensnarled in the net the Reagan administration was poised to cast to prevent Americans from traversing the ninety miles of ocean between Florida and Havana.

In Newton, Pennsylvania, Francis Bradley, assistant headmaster of the George School, a secondary school operated by the Quakers, was planning a trip to Cuba for twenty students and teachers. The school's purpose was educational: to promote dialogue with Cuban youth and to learn more about Cuban history, culture and education. The George School also had another goal: to establish contact with a Quaker community in a remote part of Cuba.

In Kingwood, Texas, Dan Snow was preparing for his favorite activity in life. Snow, a six-foot-two-inch, 225-pound former Marine whose favorite president was Richard Nixon, loved to fish—more precisely, loved to fish for large-mouth bass. Dan had found the best bass fishing holes in the world in the pristine lakes of mountainous Cuba. But travel to Cuba would lead to a jail sentence for Dan Snow, a bout with the Treasury Department for the teachers at the George School, and a Supreme Court case for Ruth Wald.

Nineteenth-century Americans were generally free to travel wherever they chose, with or without a passport. Until World War I, American travelers abroad seldom bothered to procure a passport. When they did obtain one, it was primarily to serve as a sort of official request to the foreign country to treat the traveler well. A passport was essentially an international form letter of introduction—useful, but not necessary.

Starting with World War I but escalating with the onset of the Cold War in the 1950s, the passport came to serve another, more insidious function—that of restricting travel. In 1952, Congress made it illegal to leave or enter the United States without a valid passport when the president had declared a national emergency. President Truman declared such an emergency in 1950, which remained in effect until the late 1970s, and the executive deprived Communists and other leftists of their passports and hence their right to travel abroad.

Various presidents also asserted the power to restrict the use of passports to travel to certain countries. In the late 1940s and 1950s, travel to Yugoslavia, Hungary, Albania, Bulgaria, the People's Republic of China, Czechoslovakia, Poland, Romania, the Soviet Union, North Korea, North Vietnam, Egypt, Israel, Jordan, and Syria was at times restricted. In 1961, Cuba was added to the list.

These passport restrictions did not go unchallenged. In 1958, the Supreme Court struck down the secretary of state's denial of passports to American citizens because they were Communists or Communist sympathizers. Justice William Douglas, writing for a narrow 5–4 majority on the Court in *Kent v. Dulles*, proclaimed that the freedom to travel is "an important aspect of the citizen's 'liberty.'"[1] Absent an explicit congressional mandate, the president could not deny a passport to a citizen because of his or her beliefs or associations.

However, in 1965, the Court upheld the secretary of state's power to impose geographical restrictions on Americans' use of passports to travel abroad—in this case to Cuba.[2] The upshot was that an American

Communist could not be barred from traveling abroad, but an American who wanted to learn about communism abroad could. Two years later, the Court rendered the legal situation even more complicated when it denied the president the power to criminally prosecute Americans for traveling to Cuba without using their passport, holding that Congress had not explicitly authorized such prosecutions.[3]

These Court decisions effectuated an uneasy truce between a citizen's right to travel and the government's attempt to restrict travel to Cuba, a truce that was to continue until 1977. Most American citizens were dissuaded from traveling to Cuba by passport restrictions; those who went to Cuba did not use their passports and could not be prosecuted. (The Cubans simply did not require an American to use his or her passport to go to Cuba.)

The 1970s thaw in relations with the Soviet Union, known as détente, aided Americans' right to travel abroad. In 1975, the United States joined European countries, including the Soviet Union, in signing the Final Act of the Conference on Security and Cooperation in Europe, popularly known as the Helsinki Accords, which called for freedom of international movement and communication. At the first scheduled compliance review provided for by the Helsinki Accords, the United States and the nations of Western Europe challenged the continued restrictions on the right to travel imposed by the Soviet Union and by Eastern European nations. The Soviets responded by pointing to our restrictions on the right to travel to various countries, such as Cuba, Vietnam, North Korea, and Albania. The State Department was embarrassed, caught in its own contradictions.

The Carter administration acted to remove this source of embarrassment. On March 9, 1977, just prior to the next compliance review of the Helsinki Accords, President Carter announced the removal of "any travel restrictions on American citizens who want to go to . . . Cuba" or to any other previously restricted country.[4]

The following year, Congress amended the Passport Act to deny the president authority to impose area restrictions on travel except during war, armed hostilities, or imminent danger to the public health.[5] Congress proclaimed that "the freedom of travel principle is sufficiently important that it should be a matter of law and not dependent upon a particular administration's policy."[6] Travel to Cuba was now perfectly legal and unrestricted.

And so it was to remain until 1982.

The day that Carter's proclamation lifted restrictions on travel to Cuba, Dan Snow wrote a letter to Fidel Castro. Snow told Castro about his desire to fish for bass in Cuba and to lead tours of American bass fishermen to the Cuban lakes.

Dan had led a relatively sedentary life for fifteen years as an independent insurance agent, his greatest distinction being his selection as the Indiana Young Agent of the Year. He often found time to slip away from his insurance business to indulge his hobby—bass fishing. Soon his hobby had become a passion and led him to quit insurance and to take a full-time job with the Bass Angler Sportsman Society.

As director of tours for the Angler Society, Snow spent weeks traveling on an old ramshackle bus from city to city, presenting seminars on bass fishing. At each stop, he and his entourage would provide rudimentary fishing instruction and show a video extolling the pleasures of bass fishing. Snow's video prominently featured 1950s film clips of an old fisherman named Wayne Dyer proudly displaying a huge, seventeen-pound large-mouth bass he had caught in Treasure Lake, located near the Bay of Pigs in Cuba. Snow and a generation of fisherman had grown up dreaming of the huge bass swimming idly in pristine Cuban lakes waiting to pounce upon the various lures of wily American fisherman. But the closest any American effort had gotten to Treasure Lake since 1960 was the ill-fated Bay of Pigs invasion in 1962.

Snow was sure that if he could get to Cuba he would break the world record of twenty-two pounds, nine ounces for the largest bass ever caught—a record set back in 1932 in Montgomery, Alabama. So Snow wrote to Castro, thus unleashing more political controversy than any other bass fisherman in the twentieth century.

Castro wrote back, inviting Snow to Cuba to fish. Once in Cuba, Snow began exploring. "I am a pioneer," he said, traversing Latin America for the "hall of fame type lakes, that will go down in history as great places to fish." He "discovered" six "hall of fame lakes" in Cuba, negotiated a contract with the Cuban authorities to lead trips there, and between 1977 and 1982 went to Cuba 120 times, taking 6,000 to 7,000 American fisherman with him. Snow also brought fish biologists down to mark, tag, and otherwise conduct scientific research on these fish. Snow treated the Cubans well, and they responded accordingly. "Finest people I've ever met in my life," he claims. "And, unlike in other countries, I never had to pay anyone off."

On April 19, 1982, Dan Snow was peacefully relaxing in a fishing boat in Lake Hanabanilla, deep in the heart of the Cuban mountains. He remembers the date because he was having "the best bass fishing" of all his trips to Cuba. Ruth Wald also remembers the date; her daughter was in Cuba working on a construction project. That day, the Reagan administration announced new restrictions that effectively prohibited most Americans from traveling to Cuba.

From the beginning, the Reagan administration cited Cuba as the source of political and economic strife in Central America. While the Carter administration had shown some signs of reaching an accommodation with the Castro government, the incoming Republican president seemed implacably hostile. The 1979 triumph of the leftist Sandinistas in Nicaragua and the 1980 offensive by leftist guerrillas in El Salvador had startled Washington, which had long supported Nicaragua's Somoza dictatorship and the oppressive regime in El Salvador. The Reagan administration was committed to rolling back what it perceived as a Communist threat in Central America. Some observers saw the wars in Nicaragua and El Salvador as indigenous fights against poverty and repression, but Reagan and his advisers insisted that Cuba and the Soviet Union were responsible for the Central American uprisings. As early as February 1981, Secretary of State Alexander Haig stated that the Reagan administration intended to go to "the immediate source of the problem [in Central America]—and that is Cuba."[7]

While the new administration's attention was at first focused on shoring up the tottering regime in El Salvador, by 1982 it was ready to strike at Cuba. The *New York Times* reported that Secretary of State Haig was pressing the Pentagon to examine a series of options for possible military action against Cuba.[8] Both the Joint Chiefs of Staff and Secretary of Defense Caspar Weinberger opposed a direct military attack on Cuba.[9] Instead, Reagan's advisers decided to tighten the screws on Cuba, to further isolate it and to weaken its economy.

Knowing that Cuba was expanding its facilities for tourists, the administration's April 19, 1982, announcement tightened the trade and financial embargo against Cuba by preventing American travelers from going to Cuba. The government's timing was curious in that, only several weeks before, a senior Cuban official had indicated that Cuba was ready for wide-ranging negotiations and agreements on "mutual restraint" in its relations with the United States.[10] It was almost as if the administration had decided to launch a preemptive strike to scuttle any chance of a negotiated settlement of the issues dividing Washington and Havana. The travel ban told the Cuban government there would be no negotiations, no letup in U.S. pressure on Cuba.

But the administration had a problem. Congress in 1977 had written the "freedom of travel principle" into law by denying the president authority to prevent U.S. citizens traveling to certain countries by invoking passport controls. Reagan's aides found a devious mechanism to circumvent Congress's 1977 mandate. The government did not technically prevent travel to Cuba or prevent Americans from using their passports to enter Cuba. Instead, the administration utilized the 1917 Trading with the Enemy Act to prohibit United States citizens from entering into any economic transactions related to travel to Cuba. Americans were barred from spending money to travel to and from Cuba and to pay for hotel rooms, meals, and other living expenses while in Cuba. Certain exceptions were made for journalists, scholars, and Cubans living in the United States, but the average American was and still is essentially precluded from going to Cuba.

Francis Bradley, Dan Snow, and Ruth Wald were not the type of people to quietly accept an infringement on their basic rights. Dan Snow, the former Marine, was determined not to let the government stop him from fishing wherever and whenever he wanted to fish. He was shocked by the new travel restriction, and as soon as he got back to Texas from Cuba he went down to the district court and filed an action to enjoin the government. (Snow felt the principle was so obvious he didn't need a lawyer: "If you could travel to China and the Soviet Union," he said, "why not Cuba?")

Francis Bradley was concerned about his students' planned trip to Cuba. Some of the students had raised their own money for this exciting adventure, and he didn't want them disappointed. Bradley thought that his trip might fall within one of the exceptions and applied to the Treasury Department for a license to travel to Cuba. "I thought the religious nature of our trip made it likely that we would receive the appropriate permission," he said. Recognizing that the administration's sympathy for religious endeavors might not suffice, Bradley mobilized political support, getting the headmaster of five Quaker schools, five congressmen, and two senators to write the Treasury Department in support of his application for a license. The Treasury Department was unmoved, so Bradley called the American Civil Liberties Union to see what could be done so that his youngsters could still carry out their summer plans.

Ruth and her husband, George Wald, also a Harvard professor, as well as a Nobel Prize–winning physicist, had a long history of struggle in peace and justice issues. But they were not as confident of her abilities as a constitutional litigator as Dan Snow seemed to be of his. So instead of immediately suing the government in federal district court, Ruth Wald called her good friend Leonard Boudin for advice.

Boudin was one of the great constitutional litigators of the post–World War II era. In the early 1940s, he and Victor Rabinowitz, another great progressive lawyer, had started a law firm that represented primarily labor unions. The firm was successful, and Rabinowitz and Boudin seemed assured of a long future representing mainly CIO unions.

In the 1950s, their practice dramatically changed. The McCarthy era and the Cold War engulfed their law firm as if it was one of a few lonely vessels seeking to rescue survivors of a terrible storm. Desperate, mostly poor people streamed through their doors—workers who had lost their jobs because they were Communists or leftist sympathizers, union activists who were subpoenaed to testify before McCarthy's committee. Some clients were well known, like the great black singer and actor Paul Robeson and the artist Rockwell Kent; more were unknown and badly in need of help. Rabinowitz and Boudin devoted their full energies to defending the constitutional rights of literally thousands of people swept up in the 1950s anti-Communist red scares. They didn't make much money, they were always tired, but it was one of the most invigorating and productive periods of their legal careers.

The road they had taken often led to the Supreme Court. Rabinowitz and Boudin handled many of the critical constitutional cases of the 1950s and early 1960s; Boudin litigated virtually every important travel case of the 1950s and 1960s. Boudin helped Paul Robeson, Otto Nathan (Einstein's best friend and the executor of his estate), Rockwell Kent, and countless other Americans whose passports the government sought to take away or restrict. And most of the time he won. Leonard Boudin was associated with the constitutional right to travel as was no other American lawyer.

But there was another reason why Ruth Wald and other outraged citizens began to search their telephone directories for Boudin's number in April 1982: his connection to Cuba. In the 1960s, the Cuban government, which had nationalized American companies' properties in Cuba, had retained Rabinowitz and Boudin to represent them in the U.S. courts against the claims being filed against them. Sugar companies, banks, producers of fine Cuban cigars, and a host of other large and small companies were rushing to the federal courthouse in New York City to sue Cuba or one of its governmental agencies. Eventually, more than two hundred cases presenting complicated legal issues were filed in federal court. In 1964, Rabinowitz, aided by Boudin, somehow persuaded the Supreme Court, in *Banco Nacional de Cuba v. Sabbatino*, that the U.S. courts ought not decide the validity of the Cuban nationalizations under international law.[11]

But Boudin was at first pessimistic about the chances of a successful lawsuit. The rightward turn of the Supreme Court in the late 1970s and early 1980s had ominous implications for the right of Americans to travel abroad. In the 1981 *Haig v. Agee* case, the Court had allowed the government to deny a former CIA agent named Philip Agee his American passport on the ground that he was a threat to national security. For the Court, "The freedom to travel abroad . . . is subordinate to national security and foreign policy considerations; as such, it is subject to *reasonable* governmental regulation."[12] That decision signaled that the freedom to travel abroad was clearly not particularly high on the Court's pantheon of rights, and Boudin was not sanguine about its invocation to protect travelers to Cuba.

Boudin was not about to litigate a case if he saw little chance of winning. For Boudin's principal motivation was winning cases and establishing himself as a winner. He was contemptuous of the Center for Constitutional Rights; he did not see its lawyers as serious litigators and scholars and considered them more interested in political goals and in publicity than in the law.

Boudin always claimed that he was apolitical—surprisingly, since he was a devoted civil libertarian who had spent his whole life representing clients who were fighting for civil liberties. But his claim was, in a sense, accurate. As his law partner and friend of forty years Victor Rabinowitz put it, Boudin had no vision of using the law as a tool to accomplish a social and political purpose. "He would say he had no such illusions," Rabinowitz remembered. "He saw law as an end in itself, as a scholarly pursuit, as an intellectual game."[13] And the point of playing the game was to win.

Boudin, as his biographer told me, was a man of "little or no faith." Although he vigorously represented Castro and the Cuban government and a host of other left-wing clients, he had none of the faith in socialism or in using the law to further progressive goals shown by his partner Rabinowitz, CCR's Arthur Kinoy, or Staughton Lynd.

But would-be challengers to the new Cuba travel restriction were also contacting the CCR, and Michael Ratner, at the CCR, had uncovered a promising legal angle on the issue. In relying on the economic embargo against Cuba, the administration had sought to avoid direct confrontation with the right to travel. However, by veering away from directly prohibiting travel and instead banning spending money in Cuba, the government had swerved headfirst into an area of executive power that had plagued presidents from Jefferson to Lincoln, Roosevelt, and Truman: emergency power. The constitutional linchpin of President Reagan's executive order prohibiting Americans from spending money to travel to and in Cuba was his power to restrict international transactions "in time of national emergency."

Such executive emergency power had expanded dramatically over the years. Most Americans of the post–World War II baby-boom generation would have been surprised to discover that they had lived a substantial part of their lives during a declared state of national emergency. The postwar imperial presidency was, in fact, dependent on emergency power. The legality of the Cuban embargo was based on the national emergency Truman had declared on December 16, 1950—in response to the Korean War—an emergency that had outlived the Korean War by more than twenty-five years.[14] As the astute political scientist Clinton Rossiter had predicted in 1948, "the use of constitutional emergency powers" had "become the rule and not the exception."[15]

In the aftermath of the Vietnam War and its escalating invocation of executive emergency power, Congress terminated all the national emergencies then in effect and imposed a series of procedural reforms designed to limit the president's broad power.[16] One of those statutes, the International Emergency Economic Powers Act (IEEPA) required that the president declare a new national emergency before he can impose new embargoes or financial restrictions against foreign nations.[17] Reagan had simply ignored those procedural limitations in barring travel-related expenditures to Cuba. Now, CCR's Michael Ratner thought there was a good lawsuit in challenging the violation of the procedural reform.

However, when Congress had enacted those reforms in 1977, it had not wanted to face the thorny political problem of whether to terminate the then-existing embargoes against Cuba, North Vietnam, Kampuchea (formerly Cambodia), and Korea and had simply grandfathered in those embargoes. The Reagan administration acted under the grandfather clause to prohibit travel-related transactions with respect to Cuba in 1982. Lurking in the background, however, was a serious problem, one that would eventually occupy the attention of the U.S. Supreme Court.

The problem was what exactly Congress had grandfathered in when it passed the procedural reforms. Did Congress mean to allow the president to continue the restrictions against Cuba that were in place as of July 1977, thus permitting the prohibitions existing as of that date and allowing no further expansion of the embargo? Or did Congress mean to grandfather in the whole ongoing Cuban program, including any new restraints that the president wanted to impose? This question was critical because, as of July 1977, American travel to Cuba *was freely permitted*, since President Carter had acted to lift all travel restrictions on travel to Cuba.

Thus, the broad rights of American citizens to travel to Cuba hinged on a technical reading of this relatively obscure grandfather clause in the International Emergency Economic Power Act.

The hostility of the federal courts to broad claims challenging U.S. foreign policy initiatives that violate treaty obligations, international human rights, or constitutional provisions forced lawyers to constantly search for some procedural or technical legal handle to use to bring the case. Often the executive made things easier, as in the Cuban situation, by ignoring clear provisions of law. But a tension constantly existed between the broad values and constitutional principles that progressive lawyers and their clients wanted to vindicate and the crabbed, technical, procedural terrain the courts were forcing them into. How would the lawyers highlight the basic constitutional and political argument that the right to travel abroad was a fundamental freedom for all Americans, yet not get lost in a maze of technical argument about the grandfather clause and the history of IEEPA? This tension remains central to the dilemma constantly faced by litigators and activists who seek to challenge U.S. foreign policy in the courts.

Ruth Wald and other would-be travelers to Cuba were motivated by several concerns. All of them wanted to vindicate their right to travel to any country they wished, whether Communist, socialist or capitalist.

Many also felt a sympathy for the Cuban revolution and deeply resented the U.S. government's tightening of the screws on Cuba. And, to Ruth Wald and others, the entire embargo was an illegitimate effort by an imperial United States to force a small Latin American country to bow to its wishes. But, as Leonard Boudin and Michael Ratner recognized, the court was not likely to be sympathetic either to Cuba or to left-wing Americans' right to travel there. The court might be more sympathetic to a claim that the administration had overreached its emergency power, as narrowly circumscribed by IEEPA and the grandfather clause. And this claim would not require the court to tell the government it could not prohibit travel to Cuba, a broad ruling the court would be reluctant to make. It would require the court only to order the president to comply with the requirements set forth by Congress in the NEA and IEEPA: that he declare a national emergency and then submit that declaration to Congress for review.

For his part, Dan Snow did not care about grandfather clauses, declarations of national emergencies, or any of the other legal technicalities that were to consume literally thousands of hours of lawyers' time. He had filed his lawsuit and flew back to Cuba.

On May 9, 1982, the fourth annual Cuban-American bass fishing tournament—organized by none other than Dan Snow—was to begin in Cuba. Snow's idea was to get the top fifteen U.S. fisherman together with Cuba's best fisherman in a once-a-year annual contest to show which country was strongest in the thing that really mattered in life—fishing. Fifteen boats would go out, each carrying one American and one Cuban fisherman. The idea of the contest was appealingly simple: whichever side caught the most pounds of fish won, and there would be no advanced weaponry used—only plastic worms, spinner worms, and other basic lures.

This year, Snow had come up with a creative idea designed to do more than prove which country had the best fisherman. He had invited Fidel Castro and Vice President George Bush to fish together in the tournament. Snow knew that both leaders "claimed to be ardent bass fisherman," and he thought maybe they'd put fishing over their political differences. He thought fishing might be to Cuba what Ping-Pong was to China: a sporting mechanism for breaking through the icy political relationship with the United States.

Snow proved to be wrong. Castro immediately accepted Snow's challenge. Bush did not, apparently, isolating Cuba and winning the

Cuban vote in Florida was more important than a week of the best bass fishing in the world.

Despite the two leaders' absence, the American fishermen had a wonderful time—at least until they returned to the United States. Upon their return, the fishermen were met by dour-looking FBI and Treasury Department agents, questioning the propriety of their trip. Everyone was released after minor hassles, but it was clear the government was determined to stop Snow's fishing expeditions.

But Snow was not a man to be easily dissuaded. "I don't intimidate easy," he said. As the government stepped up the heat on Snow's operation, he returned fire with fire. He contacted members of Congress and the news media and called the Treasury Department so many times that the lawyer in charge eventually accused him of "harassing the department" and instructed the receptionists that he wouldn't take any more phone calls from Snow.

Snow returned to Cuba again on May 23, determined to lead another group of American fishermen. But then the U.S. government got really nasty and threatened to seize any airplane that carried his group. While he made it through on the twenty-third, the airline companies got nervous, and when Snow got back on May 30, he was grounded. At least temporarily.

While Dan Snow was out fishing, all the lawyers working on challenging the Reagan administration's new restrictions met at Leonard Boudin's office on 42nd Street in New York. Michael Ratner, Margie Ratner, and Sarah Wunsch from the Center for Constitutional Rights, were there, as were Charles Sims, from the American Civil Liberties Union, and Harold Mayerson, from the National Lawyers Guild, who represented a travel agency that conducted tours to Cuba. Leonard Boudin asked me to attend the meeting and to help him on the case.

I had worked at the firm since my graduation from Rutgers Law School in 1978. While I had come to the firm interested in labor law, the firm's exciting international and constitutional law practice had enticed me. I had worked closely with Boudin on the litigation surrounding the 1979–1980 Iranian hostage crisis, which had eventually wound up in the Supreme Court.

Leonard Boudin had many great traits: he was intensely loyal to his friends, a charming and witty man and a wonderfully talented lawyer with terrific persuasive skills. Modesty and the ability to be a team player, however, did not rank high among Boudin's skills. He made it clear at the meeting that the right to travel was his bailiwick (sort of Boudin's equivalent of the Monroe Doctrine) and that everyone had to understand that he was to be lead counsel in any suit challenging the new restrictions on travel to Cuba. As Boudin put it to Michael Ratner before the meeting, he was "Mr. Travel." Boudin eagerly sought out the other lawyers' help and advice and wanted to consult with all the lawyers at the meeting—but he was to be the first among equals. The other lawyers agreed, albeit in some cases reluctantly.

The lawyers meeting in Leonard's office then turned their attention to discussion of how to divide the various research tasks confronting us and where to bring the case.

We could have brought the case in any location where any of our plaintiffs resided: New York, Pennsylvania, Boston, or Chicago. The lawyers chose Boston. Boston wasn't the most convenient of places—all the main lawyers were from New York. But it had a decisive advantage over any other locale; the Court of Appeals was likely to be sympathetic. Boston was part of the First Circuit Court of Appeals, which covers Massachusetts, Maine, Rhode Island, New Hampshire, and Puerto Rico. It was the smallest Court of Appeals in terms of cases and number of judges in the country and had only four circuit judges. The key factor was that of those four judges, three (Frank Coffin, Hugh Bownes, and Stephen Breyer) were liberal-to-moderate judges who were likely to at least be sympathetic to our claims. Since the circuit courts usually sat in panels of three unless the whole court hears the case (known as taking the case *en banc*), the odds were very high that at least two of the three judges hearing our case in the First Circuit would be open to our arguments. No other circuit court offered anywhere near those odds, so we decided on Boston.

Boudin chose Ruth Wald, the Harvard biology professor, to be our lead plaintiff. He did so probably for two reasons. First, Wald was a solid Bostonian who was likely to impress the court. Second, Wald and her Nobel Prize–winning husband were precisely the type of individuals Boudin liked to represent and associate with.

Boudin, an old friend once wrote, identified with and was fascinated by "the embattled or heroic individual who challenged the system or the law, rather than his political cause itself."[18] Boudin had represented many important figures over the preceding three decades: Dr. Benjamin Spock who was charged with conspiracy to violate the draft laws during the Vietnam War; Daniel Ellsberg, charged with purloining the Pentagon Papers and giving them to the *New York Times* and the *Washington Post*; Julian Bond, the civil rights activist who was denied a seat in the Georgia House of Representatives because of his opposition to the Vietnam War; and the great African American singer and political figure Paul Robeson. In all of these confrontations between great, heroic individuals and the law, Leonard had won. He always considered his greatest victory to be that won on behalf of the artist Rockwell Kent, when the Supreme Court ruled in *Kent v. Dulles* that the right to travel prevented the State Department from withholding passports for political reasons.[19] According to Victor Rabinowitz, "he always wore the *Kent* case like a badge of honor." With Ruth Wald, Boudin now had a perfect chance to add to his right-to-travel victories.

After the meeting broke up, Boudin assigned me the task of researching the question of what Congress had intended to grandfather in in 1977 when it enacted IEEPA. I approached research on the intent of Congress as if I were a detective seeking to solve a crime. Researching legislative history tends to be a rather dull, painstaking endeavor, more suited to a crusty old historian than to a young lawyer seeking the intellectual challenge of constitutional theory. It involves spending hours upon hours in dimly lit libraries poring over dusty old volumes (or, even worse, microfilm, microfiche, or some other micro-something, the descriptive word being "micro," meaning hard to read). Often lawyers have to read hundreds of pages of wandering and extraneous debates before they uncover a relevant passage. None of the great American lawyer folk-heroes of television, movie, or real-life lore—Perry Mason, Paul Newman in *The Verdict*, or Clarence Darrow—was ever filmed hard at work researching legislative history. If you didn't wear glasses before you began your research, a trip to the eye doctor often awaited you at the end. But, for some reason, I really liked researching legislative history. I could imagine myself a legal Colombo or Phillip Marlowe, painstakingly examining every piece of evidence in order to prove his case: a clear harbinger of my future career as an academic.

The legislative history of the grandfather clause looked promising. The dominant thrust of all the hearings, committee reports, and markup of the final bill in the subcommittee was that Congress wanted to prevent the executive from issuing new emergency regulations absent a true emergency. The grandfather clause was a narrow exception to that principle.

Moreover, there was substantial discussion in the House subcommittee that actually drafted the bill suggesting that the grandfather clause was designed merely to preserve the "existing uses" of emergency controls under the Trading with the Enemy Act and was not intended to allow the president to increase the restrictions.[20] Congressman Jonathan Bingham, the main author and the driving force of IEEPA, stated that expansion of the existing embargoes was clearly not contemplated:

> If the President has not up to now used some authority that he had under section 5(b) [of the Trading With the Enemy Act] in connection with those cases where 5(b) has been applied, I don't know why it should be necessary to give him authority to expand what has already been done. It is really going beyond grandfathering. It seems to me that grandfathering applies to what has been done to date.[21]

On the basis of this history, our case seemed very strong. But a strong case might not suffice to win. Litigating a foreign policy case against the government was not easy, since the government began with all the presumptions in its favor. What we needed was a smoking gun.

At the Center for Constitutional Rights, Sarah Wunsch was working on whether the plaintiffs were entitled to a preliminary injunction. Our plan was to go to court to seek immediate relief enjoining the administration from implementing its travel ban so that Ruth Wald and the Quaker kids could go to Cuba that summer. Preliminary injunctions are difficult to obtain, as they require showing that irreparable harm will be suffered if they're not granted—but Sarah Wunsch thought we clearly met the standard.

Meanwhile, Charles Sims, at the ACLU, had turned up important information that the Trading with the Enemy Act did not allow the president to regulate travel. A comprehensive report, issued in 1958 by the New York City Bar Association after examination of all of the administrative and legislative materials and consultation with high ranking government officials on travel control, concluded that the Trading with the Enemy Act "was never intended to be used as a device for the regulation of travel."[22] Every scholarly commentator who addressed the issue agreed with the Bar Association.[23]

Moreover, in the sixty-five years that had elapsed between TWEA's passage in 1917 and Ruth Wald's planned vacation in 1982, *not one sin-*

gle person had been prosecuted under the statute for traveling to another country. American journalists openly traveled to China in the face of a TWEA embargo similar to the general embargo on Cuba; literally hundreds of Americans openly traveled to and spent money in Cuba despite the Cuban embargo in the 1960s and 1970s; numerous opponents of the Vietnam War, including Harrison Salisbury, Ramsey Clark, Jane Fonda, and others less well known, traveled openly to Hanoi during the war despite a general trade embargo. None was ever prosecuted under TWEA.[24] Indeed, the State and the Treasury Departments abandoned plans to prosecute three American journalists who had traveled to Communist China in 1958, apparently because the government concluded that TWEA was never intended to be used as a device to regulate travel.[25]

Meanwhile, after hours of research, I caught a glimpse of a potential smoking gun. I found a passage in the legislative history in which the House Subcommittee's staff director, R. Roger Majak, was discussing the grandfather clause and mentioned a draft of the clause. That draft would have clearly allowed the president to expand the embargo against Cuba to include other restrictions not in effect in 1977. Congressman Bingham, the subcommittee chairman, objected to the draft statute. He said clearly in response to Majak that he wanted the president's authority limited to continuing "what has already been done." If the president wanted to expand the Cuban embargo, he must declare a new national emergency and be subject to the IEEPA procedures designed to ensure Congress input. Reagan hadn't done that.

Nowhere was the draft of the bill reprinted in the committee documents. But I was sure that the missing draft was the key piece of evidence we needed. If the draft had a provision that would have allowed the president to expand the existing embargoes but Congress had removed that provision, we should be able to win.

The next morning I called the subcommittee. Majak had left for a private law practice, and nobody at the committee knew where to find some old draft of a bill enacted five years earlier. It seemed to be a dead end. But I somehow cajoled Majak's new office number out of the reluctant secretary and called Majak directly. An authoritative, throaty Eastern European voice answered. When I explained the problem, Majak instantly recalled the draft, the colloquy, and the importance of the issue. He thought he had saved a copy of the draft.

Several days later, a copy of the draft bill appeared in the mail. Majak had come through. The draft contained exactly the provision I was looking for. It provided that the president could continue to exercise (1) "any authority which is currently (as of July 1977) being exercised" with respect to Cuba but also could impose (2) "*any other authority*" upon Cuba even if not then being utilized. In short, Subsection 2 would have allowed the president to expand the embargo.[26] At Congressman Bingham's urging, the offending provision, Subsection 2, was deleted. But the Reagan administration had gone ahead and expanded the embargo in clear disregard of Congress's intent. I thought we had what we needed.

On June 17, we filed our complaint and a motion for a preliminary injunction. Within minutes after the court clerk accepts a complaint and dutifully stamps all the documents with the date of filing, he or she "spins the wheel" to randomly select the judge—in 1982, in Boston, the court still used the old-fashioned method of literally spinning a roulette-style wheel.

The outcome would be decisive for Francis Bradley and the Quaker schoolkids. We had filed a motion for a preliminary injunction, hoping to get a speedy hearing. But when you really need immediate relief, an even faster procedure is to ask for a temporary restraining order ("TRO"), and we also had requested such an order preventing the defendants from restraining our eager teenagers from traveling to Cuba. If they didn't get an answer from the court by June 25, they couldn't make their plans for an early July departure.

Where the wheel stopped was thus crucial. If we drew a sympathetic judge who would grant our TRO, the kids would be on the plane to Cuba before the conservative Supreme Court could get a chance to block them. If the District Judge denied our TRO, the kids would have to be satisfied with the usual family vacation at the Jersey shore.

The wheel of fortune appeared to turn favorably for our plaintiffs that balmy morning in Boston. The case was assigned to Judge Joseph L. Tauro, a moderate Democrat appointed by President Richard Nixon. Boudin was optimistic about Tauro. But our optimism vanished overnight when Tauro, apparently too busy with a criminal trial to be bothered with this matter of a right to travel to Cuba, turned the case over to a federal magistrate, Robert Collings. (Federal magistrates—sort of but not quite judges—are on occasion utilized by district court judges to supervise pretrial evidence gathering and to recommend disposition of preliminary motions prior to trial.)

Boudin feared Collings was a disastrous choice, a premonition that proved accurate. Collings's employment before his recent elevation to magistrate was as an assistant U.S. attorney in Boston—the very office that would be defending the government.

The appointment of Collings led to a somewhat bizarre week of the procedural maneuvering and wrangling that often consume a substantial portion of federal litigators' time, but often can be decisive in a case. In this one, it was an obscure rule that made the difference.

For some reason not immediately apparent to anyone but the drafter of the magistrate's rules, a federal magistrate can recommend decisions on motions for preliminary injunctions (which recommendations are usually accepted by the district court judge) but has no power whatsoever over motions for TROs.[27] That rule, not the broad constitutional right to travel, became the decisive factor in the outcome of the dispute.

Magistrate Collings set a hearing date on our motion for preliminary injunction for June 25 at 10:00 in the morning. Boudin flew up from New York to argue the motion, accompanied by Charles Sims and myself. William Weld, the U.S. attorney for Massachusetts and, later, governor of Massachusetts, sent a young assistant U.S. attorney, Ralph Child, to represent the defendants.

The hearing opened with the magistrate stating his intentions to treat the Quakers' motion for a temporary restraining order as a motion seeking a preliminary injunction. That way, under the rules, he could issue a recommendation forthwith on whether the George School could leave for Cuba in early July. Both Boudin and the government raised strong objections, stating that the rule was clear that a magistrate could not hear a TRO motion.

Neither Boudin nor the government cared about the rule particularly; they had other concerns. Boudin thought Collings likely to be unsympathetic and reasoned that we should not let him hear anything more than we had to; instead, we should let the TRO be reassigned to the potentially more sympathetic Judge Tauro. The U.S. attorney probably wanted delay. He submitted a response to our motion that briefly argued the legal points but stated that the government wanted a delay at least to June 29 in order to have time to go Washington to prepare a fuller response. By objecting to having the magistrate hear the TRO, the government figured the case would go back to Tauro, delaying and probably thereby preventing the Quakers' trip.

The government's figuring backfired. Collings, after consulting with Tauro, decided that he could not hear the TRO over the parties' objection. But Tauro was still too busy and probably annoyed with having to hear a case he thought he had dumped on the magistrate. So the case was reassigned to another district judge who was responsible for what is known as the miscellaneous business docket. The constitutional right to travel had become "miscellaneous business."

The miscellaneous business judge that week turned out to be Judge P. David Mazzone, nominated to the federal bench by President Carter in 1978. A Godsend for us, Mazzone had both the time and the inclination to decide the TRO quickly and did so within a few hours of getting the motion. At 3:30 on June 25, Mazzone issued an order temporally restraining the government from "interfering in any way, including by threats or subsequent punishment," with the school's scheduled trip to Cuba. The kids were on their way.

The decision not to let magistrate Collings hear the TRO looked even better three weeks later when, on July 16, Collings denied the other plaintiffs' motion for a preliminary injunction. Three weeks later, Judge Tauro perfunctorily upheld the magistrate's recommendation.

But Bradley and his school kids had gone and returned. They had finally found and visited a Cuban Quaker community that they had first learned of in 1978, spawning a long-lasting friendship that has resulted in yearly visits by Cuban Quakers to Newton, Pennsylvania, and by Newtonian Quakers to Cuba. I didn't find out what happened to the George School's trip until much later. I knew they had gone and presumably came back. But I was unconcerned with their experiences, because I saw the clients and the lawsuit simply as means to litigate the broad constitutional issues we were concerned with—the right to travel, emergency power, executive compliance with law—and to help the Cuban people. Bradley was now out of the case, having traveled to Cuba. We went ahead in the late summer and fall of 1982, researching and writing our appeal briefs to the court of appeals, oblivious to the Bradley group's wonderful experience in Cuba.

The Court of Appeals was what we had been counting on ever since we decided to file our case in Boston. And we were not to be disappointed. The three-judge panel that was to hear the case couldn't have been better. Judge Breyer (now a Supreme Court justice) was a former Harvard administrative law professor and had been Boudin's colleague during the year that Boudin taught at Harvard. The other two members of the panel were Judge Bownes and Judge Pettine.

It was a cold, wintry Boston morning in January 1983 when Boudin stepped to the podium to argue *Wald v. Regan*.[28] Dan Snow, who had flown up from Houston, was "extremely impressed" with Boudin's argument and felt he had clearly beaten the government attorney. Boudin was at his best, charming the court to the point that the judges allowed him to exceed his allotted time without stopping him. First-year law students are always taught that when the little red light goes on at the podium indicating that your time is up, you politely end your argument and sit down. When Boudin's little red light went on, the judges kept on asking him questions as if Boudin were an important guest speaker who had just finished a scintillating lecture.

Ruth Wald also came to court that January 7. She had read the briefs, particularly the part on the right to travel, though she said she was "allergic to the law and court proceedings, and turned off by formalism and legalism." As she recalled later, "I tried to be interested in the other stuff," the grandfather clause, the Trading with the Enemy Act, but "what really interested me was the right to travel and the First Amendment." Unfortunately, that didn't really interest the judges; they were all concerned with the scope of the grandfather clause.

With Wald that day in court was her then twenty-four-year-old son Elijah. He remembers the court argument well.

To him, Leonard was wonderful. Boudin established "immediate rapport" with the judges, Elijah Wald said. "It was as if they said, okay, we're dealing with someone we can talk to about this problem." "My idea of a lawyer was Spencer Tracy as Clarence Darrow," he recalled, "and Leonard was it."

Four months later, the court's unanimous decision, written by Judge Breyer, was announced. Breyer's opinion was a careful, scholarly canvass of the law, rejecting the government's broad claims and masterfully interweaving the right-to-travel aspects of the case and the narrow dispute over the meaning of IEEPA's grandfather clause.[29]

Breyer first concluded that he need not decide whether the government's action violated the plaintiffs' constitutional right to travel to Cuba. A careful scholarly type, Breyer was not about to render a broad ruling when he didn't have to.

He then turned to whether IEEPA's grandfather clause was applicable to this situation, and thus did not require the president to comply with the new procedures. Breyer's opinion quickly restated what ought to have been obvious, that on July 1, 1977—the relevant grandfather clause date—the government was not restricting travel to Cuba. Thus, the only way the government could win was if the court accepted its argument that the words "authorities . . . being exercised" were meant to have a broad meaning in which the "authority" referred not to the particular restriction, such as travel, but to the broad class of restrictions, on economic transactions with Cuba. The government had argued that, since it was regulating the purchase of Cuban cigars, sugar, and toiletries on July 1, 1977, it was "exercising" the authority to regulate economic transactions and that, therefore, the authority was grandfathered. According to the government, the purpose of the grandfather clause was not to freeze the existing restrictions so that the government could make no changes whatsoever; that would be denying the government the flexibility to add a new product to the list of embargoed goods. Purchasing a hotel room or a bus ticket was like buying a Cuban cigar—thus, the authority to regulate any transaction was being exercised.

Not so, responded Breyer. "[A]s a matter of common sense and common English, restricting, say, commodity purchases and restricting travel purchases would seem to be very different 'exercises' of authority."[30] Moreover, "unlike most commercial regulations, travel restrictions raise special constitutional rights," Breyer wrote, "for they involve specially protected rights of citizens."[31] Spending money to travel to Cuba was a very different activity, entitled to special constitutional protection, from buying cigars from Cuba. After an exhaustive search of the legislative history, the court concluded that the government had not been exercising the authority to regulate travel to Cuba on July 1, 1977, and thus the Reagan administration had acted unlawfully in imposing the new restrictions without complying with the IEEPA requirements.[32] The court enjoined the enforcement of the travel restrictions.

The Reagan administration, shocked that a court of appeals could unanimously rule against it in an important foreign policy matter, played what it thought was its trump card. When faced with a serious legal question involving foreign policy, the executive branch invariably invokes the terrible, tragic, disastrous consequences that will befall U.S. foreign policy and the free world if the court decision is upheld. Usually the invocation of such draconian consequences suffices to persuade a reluctant judge. It didn't work here. Breyer and his colleagues held firm.

The government asked the Court of Appeals to rehear the case and to stay the injunction pending review. It submitted the affidavits of high-ranking Treasury Department and State Department officials who stated that, "in the opinion of those responsible for the execution of U.S. foreign policy," the court's injunction would "do significant and irreversible harm to U.S. foreign policy."[33] John Walker Jr., assistant secretary of the treasury and George Bush's cousin, stated that the court's *Wald* opinion could lead to "undermining . . . the President's authority to stop an influx of illegal foreign aliens into the United States . . . a matter of grave national concern."[34]

But the Court of Appeals was not moved and calmly replied that the government had submitted nothing new. The court reiterated that it was not preventing the president and Congress from taking whatever steps they believed necessary to conduct our foreign policy toward Cuba. As the court had already stated, "We do not arrogate to ourselves the power to make foreign policy" but only the power to "preserve the constitutional 'equilibrium' between the President and Congress and [to] insist that the executive Branch follow the laws that the legislative Branch enacts."[35] If the Reagan administration believed a serious emergency existed and wanted to impose travel restrictions on Cuba, it had merely to follow the procedures set forth in IEEPA. In short, the court said the president's beef was with Congress, and not with the First Circuit Court of Appeals.[36] The court was only doing its job of upholding the law.

The court also denied the government's request for a stay. It doubted that a "reasonable reader" would conclude that the legislative history so clearly supported the government as to warrant an infringement on plaintiffs' right to travel. "Thus, we think it unlikely that the Supreme Court will reach a different decision."[37]

The government immediately applied to the Supreme Court for a stay of the injunction and filed a writ of certiorari seeking review of the First Circuit's decision. They quickly got both granted. It was to be Boudin's last case before the Supreme Court, and in some respects the most troubling.

The few months after the Supreme Court agreed to hear the case were hectic, with teams of lawyers busily preparing briefs for the Court.

Oral argument was scheduled for April 24, 1984. Boudin spent the weeks before argument studying the case and seeking advice from lawyers and law professors around the country as to how to argue the case. He went to Boston for a practice session, known as a moot court, where Professors Larry Tribe and Charles Nesson, both of Harvard Law School, grilled him with questions they thought the justices might ask at oral argument.

Boudin was troubled by a critical question of strategy: how should he begin, and what should he focus on before the Court? John W. Davis, a great constitutional lawyer who argued against Thurgood Marshall in *Brown v. Board of Education*, once advised appellate lawyers that a key to success was to "[a]lways go for the jugular vein, . . . get right to the heart of your case."[38] For Boudin, the question was whether the key to the case was the right to travel or the grandfather clause.

For Boudin, the heart of the case from the very beginning was that the government's restrictions involved travel, a fundamental right at the heart of our constitutional liberties. His gut told him to start with travel, to emphasize it, and then to place the technical arguments about the meaning of the grandfather clause in that context. By convincing the Court that the case involved travel, not trade, Boudin would lead the Court to take a narrow interpretation of the grandfather clause. Larry Tribe, from Harvard, whom Boudin respected, agreed with that approach. So did I.

At precisely 10:06 A.M. the morning of April 24, the clerk of the Court called the case of *Regan v. Wald* (Donald Regan being the Treasury secretary responsible for enforcing the embargo). Paul Bator, the deputy solicitor general, stepped up to argue the government's case.

Born in Budapest, Bator arrived in the United States at the age of ten, at almost the exact time that Ruth Wald had landed as a refugee from Austria. But, while Wald's experiences had made her allergic to the law, Bator had risen to prominence as a legal scholar. He graduated from Harvard Law School summa cum laude in 1956 and was president of the *Law Review*, then clerked for Justice John Marshall Harlan. After a very brief sojourn in private practice, in 1959 Bator joined the Harvard law faculty, where he was highly regarded as a teacher and a scholar, co-authoring a leading text on federal jurisdiction. In 1983, the Reagan administration enticed him from Harvard with the assignment of arguing many of its most important cases before the Supreme Court.

It is unusual for oral argument to make much of a difference in an important case. The justices have read dozens of pages of briefs, exploring every nook and cranny of the case. Philip Elman, who observed the Court for seventeen years from the solicitor general's office, points out that, generally, "the greater the issues involved in a case, the less oral arguments are likely to affect it. In lesser cases, effective counsel can sway a Court that hasn't made up its mind. Overall, though, it is safe to say that you may well lose your case with a bad oral argument, but it is difficult to win it by a strong one."[39] Bator's argument that day may have been the exception.

Charles Fried, another Harvard Law professor who was to succeed Bator as deputy solicitor general in 1985, was particularly struck by Bator's argument to the Court in *Regan v. Wald*. "Everybody thought that case was unwinnable," Fried remembers. Harold Koh, who worked at the Justice Department's Office of Legal Counsel in 1983 and now is a Yale law professor, recalls that virtually everyone in his office thought the government would lose *Regan v. Wald* and had urged the solicitor general not to appeal to the Supreme Court. Reeling from their disastrous unanimous defeat in the Court of Appeals, the government's attorneys may have underestimated the sway that "national security" would have on the Court. But Bator's oral argument before the Court certainly helped the government's case.

Bator deftly presented the government's crucial argument that "the authority to regulate financial transactions incident to travel" was being exercised on July 1, 1977 and thus was grandfathered in. He cleverly propounded the Orwellian argument that when the Carter administration had opened up travel to Cuba by licensing Americans to spend money on travel to Cuba, that was "an act of regulation, not of deregulation."

Boudin had planned to start his argument by emphasizing the fundamental liberty interest in a citizen's right to travel abroad. But he was the respondent, speaking second, and a good oral advocate always maintains the flexibility to change his argument on the basis of his feel for the Court's questions of his opponent. Boudin had a hunch about Justice O'Connor's questioning of Bator and decided to play out his gut feeling.

Before the oral argument, Boudin and the rest of the legal team figured that we had three sure votes—Justices Harry Blackmun, Thurgood

Marshall, and William Brennan, all of whom highly valued civil liberties and probably favored restraining unbridled executive emergency power. We thought we could pick up Justice John Paul Stevens, considered to be a moderate civil libertarian. That left us one short of the five-justice majority needed to win. Justices William Rehnquist and Warren Burger were sure to support the government. That left Justices Byron White, Lewis Powell, and Sandra Day O'Connor. Just as presidential candidates tend to tailor their campaigns to the undecided middle, effective oral advocates seek to pitch their arguments to the crucial undecided voters on the Court. The argument before the nine-justice Court thus came down to a mini-contest for the hearts and minds of the three middle justices. Or so we thought. We had spent substantial energy researching all of White's, Powell's, and O'Connor's opinions, hoping to find some inkling of what would persuade them. Boudin thought he had uncovered Justice O'Connor's concerns in her questions to Bator.

Instead of starting with the right to travel, as he had planned, Boudin opened by stating, "I would like to address myself first to Justice O'Connor's question, what did Congress have in mind." Boudin was not above flattery, so he continued, "Justice O'Connor's question really was directed to the heart of the case."

Boudin then launched into a lengthy exposition of IEEPA and the grandfather clause: Congress was concerned with controlling emergency power, and the grandfather clause was a narrow exception. After canvassing the legislative history, the draft proposal, and Bingham's objection, he responded to Bator's general license theory of the case.

Finally, Boudin turned to the constitutional right to travel, arguing that it is one thing for the government to forbid travel in emergency situations such as a nuclear missile crisis. But, he said, prohibiting travel because American citizens would spend money in Cuba, which would then aid the development of a Cuban tourist industry, eventually allowing Cuba to subvert Latin America, "was far too tenuous" to uphold an infringement on Americans' fundamental liberty to travel.

Boudin sat down, confident that victory was within our grasp. Nothing said by either Bator or the justices at the argument had shaken his belief that we could count on Blackmun, Stevens, Marshall, and Brennan. O'Connor's questioning seemed very favorable; Boudin thought we had her vote and maybe even Powell's. Walking down the long, white marble steps that lead from the Supreme Court's lofty level to the bustling street below, Boudin turned to me and said, "I think it will be 6–3 in our favor."

Dan Snow shared Boudin's optimism as he left the courtroom. This was Snow's first trip to Washington, and he "felt that freedom would prevail." His impression of the Supreme Court—the ornate building, the formal proceedings, the justices' seemingly detached, intellectual questioning of the attorneys—was that the court was "everything it was supposed to stand for." The Court stood for justice, and Snow felt that justice was on his side. "I don't see how we can lose in a free country," he said.

The Supreme Court, by a bare 5–4 majority, overturned the decision by the Court of Appeals.[40] Justice Rehnquist, writing for Justices O'-Connor, Burger, White, and, surprisingly, Stevens, adopted the government's arguments. "[T]he authority to regulate travel-related transactions," said the Court, "is merely part of the President's general authority to regulate property transactions."[41] Rehnquist accepted the government's argument that the government was regulating travel to Cuba in 1977 by exempting travel-related transactions from the general prohibition on trade with Cuba. By permitting travel, the government was in fact exercising its authority over travel.

The Court rejected the plaintiff's argument that there was no national emergency and consequently no justification for the restriction on the constitutional right to travel. The Court responded by saying that it must defer to the executive's judgment about when such restrictions are necessary.[42] It would not make an independent inquiry as to whether an emergency actually existed.

Rehnquist also used the occasion to articulate a highly questionable mode of construing congressional intent. He found that there was a "clear, generic meaning of the word 'authorities'"—which he read very broadly.[43] This "clear statutory language" should "not be materially altered" by the congressional "colloquies," which are seldom as "precise as the enacted legislation."[44] To do so would open the door to undermine the language of the statute.

Rehnquist had turned the whole case topsy-turvy. For it was precisely the term "authorities" that was ambiguous and unclear—and the legislative history was unambiguous about Congress's intent to grandfather only the existing embargo, not its future expansion.

The majority decision also provoked a strong dissent from Justice Blackmun, joined by Justices Powell, Brennan, and Marshall.[45] The only surprise among the four dissenters was Powell, a conservative justice not known to take on the government in foreign policy matters. Even more curious was his separate, pithy, dissenting opinion,[46] with the disclaimer that its author was not questioning the political wisdom of President Reagan's policy.

Powell agreed that the majority's opinion might be in the best interests of the United States but maintained that an inquiry into the nation's best interests was not the question before the Court. The Court's role, rather, was "limited . . . to ascertaining and sustaining the intent of Congress."[47] The president and Congress were empowered to determine the political wisdom of a particular foreign policy, but the nine justices were empowered only to uphold the law. As Powell read that law, "Congress intended to bar the President from expanding the exercise of emergency authority."[48]

Only much later did I discover what may have triggered Justice Powell's curious, short discourse on the relationship between law and politics. Powell's memos and notes reveal his conflict between his political view that accepting the government's position "would be in the best interest of the United States" versus the legislative history of the statute that supported the plaintiff's position, a conflict also shared by the justices who voted with the majority.[49] Some Supreme Court clerks that year heard Justice Rehnquist state that, although the plaintiffs probably had presented a more persuasive legal interpretation of IEEPA, the Court should not enjoin the executive action toward Cuba. Powell's dissent may have been a response to that comment by Rehnquist, as well as his own political concerns. Politics, not a narrow legal interpretation of the law, lay behind the Court's decision in *Regan v. Wald*, and Powell knew it.

The Court's decision provoked strong public reaction. The *New York Times* columnist Anthony Lewis wrote that the decision's "implications" made it "the Court's most important judgment of this or any recent term."[50] The *Washington Post* editorialized that the Supreme Court had "gone much too far in order to uphold the president" and criticized the Court's "heavy emphasis" on "'deference' to the executive in all matters of foreign policy."[51]

What Lewis and others recognized was that underneath the dry lawyers' language and the technical argumentation over the scope of the grandfather clause lay a critically important reading of executive power. It was not merely that the Court had brushed aside plaintiff's right to travel; as Lewis wrote, what "really mattered" was that "[i]t did so by taking a worshipful view of executive power—by virtually assuming that anything the executive branch does under the label 'foreign policy' is lawful."[52]

The lesson of *Regan v. Wald* is that when foreign policy and the law clash, courts are willing to discard the law and defer to the executive's incantation of national security. The problem of politics triumphing over law is nothing new: in 1946, Supreme Court Justice Wiley Rutledge mockingly noted in a letter that "the *big* cases are cases in *Politics and the Law* takes a back seat."[53] Or, as the respected former Chief Justice of the Supreme Court Charles Evan Hughes once put it, "at the constitutional level where we work, ninety percent of any decision is emotional. The rational part of us supplies the reasons for supporting our predilections."[54]

That politics should interact with and even override the technical law is hardly surprising; indeed, most of the "losers" portrayed in this book lost not because their legal arguments were frivolous but because the political climate was unfavorable. For their part, many of these lawyers and activists often shared a belief in using the law as a political mechanism to radically transform society. For them, the intertwining of success and failure was linked to the connection between law and politics: a lawyer could lose in court, but the case could have a broader impact politically. For Boudin, though, the law was principally a means to defend individuals against harmful government action, not a political instrument. Unlike some of the other lawyers and plaintiffs on the team, he didn't see *Wald v. Regan* as part of a long-term struggle against U.S. foreign policy or for constitutional rights, or as a gesture in support of Cuban socialism.

Boudin took the loss in *Regan v. Wald* very hard. He petitioned the court for a rehearing, which predictably was denied. He then explored bringing a new case, challenging some other aspect of the travel ban to Cuba. His partners realized that any new case would be hopeless and said that the firm should not take it. Rabinowitz suggested that Boudin contact me (I was now teaching at the University of Pittsburgh and was deeply involved with the Center for Constitutional Rights) to take any such case. They had already spotted my proclivity to be a Don Quixote of the progressive legal world.

Dan Snow, Ruth Wald, and many other Americans did not give up after the Supreme Court's decision. Snow was disappointed by the decision but felt "we had put our best team on the field, gave it our best shot" and lost. He never "accepted this as a loss." Snow still believes that "had the Supreme Court only known the truth" it would have ruled in our favor. But Snow had always been successful in whatever he did in life and felt that eventually he would win.

He kept on traveling to Cuba to fish—thirty-five times in all between 1982 and 1987. At first, Snow argued that he fell into the exception under the regulations that allowed travel to Cuba for scholarly activities. He brought fish biologists with him to Cuba and argued that he was conducting professional research in Cuba.

The government amended the regulations to read that professional research does not include "general study tours, general orientation visits, student class field trips, . . . *travel by fishing or bird watching groups and similar affinity groups.*"[55] Just in case Snow might continue to attempt to get around the travel ban, the administration added, as an example, "the presence of a professional fish biologist who travels to Cuba to engage in professional research does not bring within the general license other persons who might travel with the fish biologist but whose principal purpose is to engage in recreational or trophy fishing."[56]

Dan Snow, undeterred, kept going to Cuba, leaving from Cancun, Mexico. But the U.S. government did not care if he was leaving for Cuba from Mexico, Canada, or Miami; as an American citizen, he couldn't spend money in Cuba. The flag, they argued, follows the citizen wherever he or she goes.

In Snow's case, the flag was not all that was following him. The FBI finally placed an agent on one of his trips, and in 1987 he was arrested and finally convicted of violating the Trading with the Enemy Act. Snow served ninety days in jail, spread out over forty-five weekends; with some pride, he notes that he's the "world's only bass-fishing felon."

Nor was Ruth Wald defeated by the Supreme Court. Unlike Dan Snow, she has not returned to Cuba. But she has returned to her other political work, marching, fund-raising, petitioning, demonstrating, and writing in the cause of peace and justice. For Wald, legal cases like *Wald v. Regan* are simply one way to tell the government "we're not going to take this"; they are only one avenue of struggle.

The right to travel to Cuba remains a critical issue. Thousands of Americans have continued to travel to Cuba, many in flagrant violation of the ban on such travel.[57] A "Freedom to Travel" campaign organized trips in which hundreds of people openly violated the travel restrictions. For those involved in such disobedience, *Wald v. Regan* serves as a symbol of the Court's insensitivity to the rights of Americans.

Moreover, despite the Court's decision in *Wald*, activists continue to proclaim that they have a "constitutional right" to travel to Cuba and look to the courts for vindication. In 1994, the "Freedom to Travel" campaign sued the government in federal district court in San Francisco, raising a number of constitutional, statutory, and international law claims. Their lawyer was Boudin's partner Michael Krinsky, who, along with Eric Lieberman, took over representing Cuba when Boudin died, in 1989 and Victor Rabinowitz retired.

Krinksy advised the Freedom to Travel campaign not to sue, believing that the case would be difficult to win in court and that litigation would siphon off energy and resources into an unproductive court battle. But the activists overruled Krinsky, and he filed a suit titled *Freedom to Travel Campaign v. Newcomb*. In 1996, the Ninth Circuit Court of Appeals ruled that plaintiffs' constitutional right to travel was not violated and that international law granted only a right to leave the United States, not to visit other countries.[58]

Both legal and political interest in defending the right to travel remain strong. In the summer of 2000, the ACLU announced that it would consider filing a class-action lawsuit on behalf of anyone fined for taking an illegal trip to Cuba.[59] There is strong support in the House of Representatives from both Democrats and Republicans for a bill overturning the Cuban travel ban.[60] The Center for Constitutional Rights has maintained a Cuba Travel project to advise would-be travelers to Cuba about their rights. Periodically, I get a call from the attorney working on this project, who is being strongly requested by right-to-travel activists to explore the possibilities of a lawsuit. I usually respond that any broad attack on the ban would have virtually no chance of success in the courts.

Nonetheless, when Americans have a deeply felt belief that they have a basic constitutional right that is being denied them by their government, whether a right to equal treatment or a right to travel, they inevitably turn to the courts for vindication, and defeat in the courts often does little to dissuade them. Just as, after *Plessy v. Ferguson*, African Americans continued to litigate the constitutionality of segregated schools despite their defeats in court, travelers to Cuba have continued to violate the ban and to argue about its constitutionality even after the

Wald v. Regan defeat. I have no doubt that one day Congress and the courts will recognize that the right to travel abroad cannot be curtailed except in time of war.

Nor does Dan Snow doubt his eventual vindication. After a hiatus following his felony conviction, Snow is back traveling to Cuba. He doesn't request a license and claims he "wouldn't want a license even if they gave me one." In July 1999, the FBI raided his office and home, but he has not yet been indicted again. He believes the government is lying about Cuba, and he is going to continue to try to prove it wrong. "You can't give up," he says. Despite his losses in court, he believes that many people respect him: "I'm their hero." "I will be vindicated at some point," he resolutely continues to believe.

The underlying essence of Ruth Wald's, Dan Snow's, and Francis Bradley's right-to-travel claims was a perspective on the nature of relations between Americans and the rest of the world that is radically different from that propounded by the government and the courts. Dialogue, and not dictates, should govern our relations with Cuba. As Francis Bradley stated in 1989 to a congressional committee that had asked him to testify about the experiences that led to his being a plaintiff in *Wald v. Regan*:

> [The] Friends . . . have found it difficult to accept war as an acceptable manner for resolving human differences. If war is difficult to accept, then dialogue is vital. In order to be faithful to the heritage of Quakers . . . [we must] try every means possible . . . to enter into dialogue with all people, but most particularly, those people perceived by our countrymen as enemies.[61]

This was certainly not the legal perspective of any of the thirteen judges who eventually heard this case. None was willing to rule that the government could not prohibit travel to Cuba, except in the midst of a dire emergency. The Court of Appeals avoided that issue, as did the four dissenters in the Supreme Court. The most that the seven judges who agreed with us were willing to say was that the president couldn't prohibit travel without following the procedures set forth by Congress in the 1977 IEEPA legislation.

In *Wald v. Regan*, the clash of broad principles occurred on very narrow terrain. The conflict over the scope of emergency power and the right to travel occurred in the context of this seemingly narrow dispute over whether IEEPA procedures should apply. But the lasting impact of *Wald v. Regan* was not procedural at all. The case—and the continuing actions by citizens, even after their defeat in court—demonstrates a faith in the eventual vindication of the constitutional rights of all Americans.

8

Challenging United States Intervention in Central America

IN AUGUST 1983, Ben Linder, twenty-four years old, and a recent graduate of the University of Washington, flew from Portland to Nicaragua to start his first engineering job. As early as high school, Ben had wanted to work in the Third World, and he arrived in Nicaragua with great excitement and hopes, as well as doubts over leaving his friends and family.

The 1979 Nicaragua Revolution, in which the Sandinista Liberation Front (FSLN) had overthrown a corrupt, U.S.-backed dictator, Anastasio Somoza, had by 1983 become a magnet for thousands of idealistic Americans. These Americans were impressed by the improvements the revolution had brought in poor people's lives—the country's literacy rate jumped from 55 percent to 88 percent after the revolution, and in 1983 the World Health Organization declared Nicaragua a model for health care in Latin America. The United States, however, was covertly funding former Somoza forces—the contras—to try to oust the Sandinista government.

Most of the tens of thousands of Americans who traveled to Nicaragua during the eighties visited for only a few weeks—long enough to be smitten with the revolutionary energy of Nicaragua and the warmth and friendliness of its people. Ben Linder stayed, committing himself to working in one of the poorest, most wartorn, and most dangerous regions of Nicaragua to bring hydroelectric power to peasants who had never known electricity. In doing so, he gave his life. As the CBS News correspondent Dan Rather reported on the national news, Benjamin Linder

> was killed with weapons paid for with American tax dollars. The bitter irony of Benjamin Linder's death is that he went to Nicaragua to build up what his own country's dollars paid to destroy—and ended

up a victim of the destruction. The loss of Benjamin Linder is more than fodder in an angry political debate. It is the loss of something that seems rare these days: a man with the courage to put his back behind his beliefs. It would have been very easy for this bright young man to follow the path to a good job and a comfortable salary. Instead, he chose to follow the lead of his conscience.[1]

At almost the same time that Ben was flying to Managua, I was, too. Like Linder, I was also at a transition point in my life—although for me the change was much less extreme. I went to Central America in be-tween leaving my job at the law firm of Rabinowitz, Boudin, Standard, Krinsky & Lieberman and moving to Pittsburgh to begin teaching at the University of Pittsburgh Law School. I was to spend only a month in Nicaragua. But that experience spent living with poor Nicaraguan fam-ilies in Managua's slums, visiting farm cooperatives, and traveling to Northern mountainous jungle war zones abutting the Honduras border was a powerful one. It launched me on an almost decade-long quest to utilize my legal skills to assist the Nicaraguan people in their effort to transform their society. I aided the Nicaraguans in drafting a new con-stitution, worked to establish a sister-city relationship between Pitts-burgh and the small, rural community of San Isidro, Nicaragua, and traveled back and forth to Nicaragua many times. I also helped bring half a dozen major legal cases that sought to place obstacles in the U.S. government's drive to overthrow the Nicaraguan revolution through its contra war.

Ben Linder and I would never meet. He did, however, become a client of mine in a lawsuit I filed challenging U.S. aid to the contras. After his death, so did Linder's family, when they sued the contra lead-ership for his murder. While I never met him, I came to feel a deep con-nection to Ben Linder; his courage, determination and spirit kept me going through difficult times.

Before I left for Nicaragua, I went to see Michael Ratner, who gave me letters introducing me to various people he knew there. While I knew Michael somewhat through our work together on the Cuba travel case, the Nicaraguan trip brought about my first, more personal contact with him.

Michael is an extraordinary fellow. Born into a well-to-do Jewish family in Cleveland, Michael attended Columbia Law School, where he graduated first in his class in 1967. Eschewing a more prestigious Court of Appeals and potential Supreme Court clerkship, Michael clerked for the first black woman federal court judge, Judge Constance Baker Motley, who had been an associate of Thurgood Marshall at the NAACP. After his clerkship was over, Michael landed a teaching job at New York University Law School and was en route to a cushy life as an academic at a prestigious law school. But Michael was too much an activist to settle into academia; after a year, he left NYU and joined the newly formed Center for Constitutional Rights. As a recent law graduate, Michael was somewhat overwhelmed by the great lawyers who had founded the CCR: Arthur Kinoy, Morty Stavis, and Bill Kunstler. After a few years, he left the CCR and went into private practice, litigating a potpourri of discrimination and civil rights claims. By the early 1980s he was back at the CCR, this time as its legal director. In 1981, he was also elected president of the National Lawyers Guild, a progressive legal organization that had been formed in the 1930s as an alternative to the then all-white, reactionary American Bar Association.

Michael was personally, politically, and culturally drawn to the leftist movements in Central America in the early 1980s. He had visited Cuba numerous times and represented the Venceremos Brigade, an organization that sent groups of idealist Americans to work in Cuba in support of the revolution there. When a leftist group called the New Jewel movement came to power in Grenada in 1979, Michael quickly visited that small island country and met with its leader, Maurice Bishop. Michael Manley, the leftist prime minister of Jamaica, was a friend of Michael's. But his closest personal ties were to the Salvadoran left, which in the late 1970s and early 1980s was fighting against the repressive oligarchic regime in El Salvador.

Michael's four-story brownstone in Greenwich Village was a mecca for the Salvadoran left in the early 1980s. Almost any time I spoke with him, at least one and sometimes many Salvadorans were staying at his house, which came to resemble a New York headquarters for the Salvadoran leftists in exile. His friendships with the Salvadorans were tinged with both exuberance and great sadness. In 1979, Michael had hosted a gathering where half a dozen of the most prominent members of the Salvadoran opposition had met with the progressive New York community; a year later, all of the Salvadorans had been massacred by right-wing death squads while at a meeting at a high school gymnasium in San Salvador.

In 1981, Michael viewed Central America as a site where U.S. imperialism could be challenged and where lasting revolution might happen. Michael perceived that Central America was a place where capitalism had failed, democracy was virtually nonexistent, and U.S. power had been unable to stave off the growth of socialist movements. Many Central American countries had strong leftist movements organized against antidemocratic regimes, and there was a spirit of struggle that made real social change seem possible for the region.

Ronald Reagan had just taken office, committed to defeating the revolutionary forces in El Salvador and overturning the Nicaraguan, Cuban, and Grenadan revolutions. The Reagan administration's immediate plan was to escalate U.S. military involvement in the Salvadoran civil war and to arm, train, and direct counterrevolutionaries (the contras) to attack the Sandinistas.[2] In early 1981, without the approval of Congress, the Reagan administration provided $25 million in military aid and fifty-six U.S. military advisers to the government of El Salvador.[3] Later that year, the CIA began covertly to arm Nicaraguan contras based in Florida and Honduras to attack the revolutionary government in Nicaragua.[4] Reagan's interventionist policy had constitutional implications at home as his administration tried to evade and eviscerate the legal restraints on executive power enacted in the wake of the Vietnam War.

Michael began to focus his energies on Central America. With Ramsey Clark and others, he formed the Lawyers Committee Against U.S. Intervention in Central America. As president of the National Lawyers Guild, Michael had made Central American support work the primary focus of that organization and also prodded the Center for Constitutional Rights to wage a major legal campaign against U.S. policy toward Central America.

Michael drew me into the Center's work, and we became good friends and colleagues. Some of the CCR's work involved defense of individual rights in the United States. The CCR set up a Movement Support Network, which foresaw that the FBI would surveil and harass people and organizations that supported the popular struggles against U.S. intervention in Central America. Through Freedom of Information Act (FOIA) requests, the CCR exposed the FBI's placement of informants in church groups believed to be providing sanctuary to Salvadoran refugees, and the FBI's surveillance against CISPES, the Committee in

Support of the People of El Salvador. The CCR and the National Lawyers Guild brought a successful class-action lawsuit against the INS to protect the rights of Salvadoran refugees to fair hearings on their claims to political asylum. The CCR also represented American travelers who were being harassed by the U.S. Customs Service when they returned from trips to Nicaragua or El Salvador.

Michael's and my primary focus, however, was a series of "offensive" cases challenging U.S. foreign policy. Some of these cases were broad challenges to U.S. policy and had virtually no chance of success. Others were framed more narrowly to increase the possibility of a court ruling in our favor. While we were able to sometimes win in the lower courts, in not one of these cases did we ultimately ever get the relief that our clients were seeking.

Nonetheless, Michael and I still consider our Central American litigation to be the high point of our legal careers. Michael's view is especially perplexing, because he certainly has litigated more important and more successful cases prior to and after our Central American cases, and from any conventional viewpoint our joint litigation was an ignominious failure.

But the Central American litigation occupies a special place in our hearts because the cases were tied to movements for radical social change that we strongly supported. The Central American litigation was not primarily about arguing the finer points of law, or about winning legal victories, or even about promoting our beliefs about the Constitution. It was fundamentally about defending the Central American peoples' efforts to alter the fundamental social structures of societies that had produced such repression, poverty, and devastation for so many years. Michael and I both believed that our cases were just one part of a broader movement for a socialist future. We were activists in that movement, both politically and legally. Our cases represented a clear vision of a better world, not simply a fight for some particular legal principle.

Both of us grew up politically in the 1960s. Those were turbulent years, in which a dynamic, expanding, often victorious, and increasingly radical civil rights movement intertwined with a massive and, at times, militant struggle against the Vietnam War. The climate made it possible to entertain delusional dreams of an impending crisis of American capitalism that would lead to a democratic socialist society. In the 1960s, the crisis seemed upon us, with riots in the streets of major U.S.

cities, mass demonstrations besieging the Pentagon, and an increasingly radicalized student, black, and Latino left swelling the ranks of such groups as SDS, the Black Panthers, the Young Lords, and the Progressive Labor Party. While even in my youthful state of utopian optimism I realized that a "revolution" was not imminent, I and thousands of other students hoped that within a few decades we might witness the coming of democratic socialism to America.

Michael and I had different paths through that time, but we shared the same basic beliefs. After his graduation from Columbia Law School, Michael fairly quickly became a "movement" lawyer, representing civil rights groups, workers who were discriminated against, and prisoners involved in the uprising at Attica State Prison, in New York. I attended New York University and had a fairly mundane career as both a student and a radical. After graduation, to the great chagrin of my parents, I eschewed graduate school, opting for a working-class life as a rank-and-file organizer, first as a cabbie in the Bronx and then, for several years, as a bakery worker in a large Wonder Bread factory. I tried to integrate myself with the group that Marxists believed would be the engine of change—the workers—although to most of my bakery compatriots I must have appeared as a Marxist more in the Groucho tradition than the Karl one. I was able to organize a group of bakery workers called the Bakers for a Democratic Union that challenged both the corrupt union leadership and oppressive management. The bakery organizing led to a host of legal battles—NLRB proceedings to protect workers fired for union activities; a Labor Department complaint filed to protest an undemocratic union election; arbitration hearings; a $600,000 libel suit filed against another worker and me by the union leadership. My encounters with the law led me to decide to go to law school after I was fired from the bakery in connection with my organizing efforts.

The job I landed after law school at Rabinowitz, Boudin, Standard, Krinsky & Lieberman allowed me to undertake pro bono representation of rank-and-file activists. I also became deeply involved in community organizing in Brooklyn. Nonetheless, the 1970s were generally a disappointing time for me as I slogged away in the trenches of labor law and organizing; the movements and hopes of the 1960s had dissipated, and American society had clearly turned more conservative.

In 1979, though, the Sandinistas triumphed in Nicaragua, and the leftist insurrection in El Salvador threatened to topple the regime. At first, I first paid little attention to the dramatic events occurring in

Central America. But I was finding my international law work at the firm exciting and challenging. I had been drawn into our Cuba work, had visited Cuba, helped represent the Central Bank of Iran during the 1979–1980 hostage crisis, and began to notice that sections of the American left were becoming reenergized by events in Central America.

By 1983, I was ready to jump on the Sandinista bandwagon. The possibility that a new democratic socialism—one different from the oppressive system in the Soviet Union—was being born in the rain forests and forbidding mountains of Central America exercised a powerful magnetic pull on my soul. I eagerly jumped at the chance to spend a month in Nicaragua before starting teaching in the fall of 1983. Like thousands of other Americans who went to Nicaragua, I entered a struggle with the U.S. government. It would lead me to join with Michael Ratner and others in a series of cases—our Central America litigation—that I still consider the high point of my work as a lawyer.

In early 1981, shortly after Ronald Reagan's inauguration, Congressman George Crockett, of Michigan, a prominent member of the National Lawyers Guild with a history of involvement in popular movements, asked the Center for Constitutional Rights to file a lawsuit challenging the dispatch of fifty-six U.S. military advisers to El Salvador without congressional approval.

Congressman Crockett, a black lawyer then in his seventies, was a hero to the CCR lawyers. In the 1950s, he had been jailed for six months for contempt of court because of his vigorous defense of Smith Act victims in a communist conspiracy trial in New York. He was one of the key northern lawyers who went south in the late 1950s and 1960s to defend civil rights advocates. Subsequently, he became a judge in Detroit. A radical black activist, Crockett had battled the odds and became a congressman. Now he was again prepared to do what he had done so often in his life: fight an uphill battle for justice.

Crockett was angered by the dispatch of U.S. armed forces to El Salvador because he saw the United States intervening to defend a repressive and unjust oligarchical government and because President Reagan had not received congressional approval before sending troops. Today, the unilateral dispatching of fifty or so military advisers by a U.S. president to aid a government fighting insurgents would raise little protest. But this was 1981, and the memories of Vietnam were less than a decade old. Senator Kennedy and many others in Congress protested; White

House mail was reportedly running ten to one against the president's policy.[5] Members of Congress and the public were afraid of another Vietnam in El Salvador, whereby advisers and aid would escalate into full-blown military intervention in a civil war. Crockett knew that the War Powers Resolution had been enacted precisely to avoid such a scenario. Jacob Javits, a main drafter of the Resolution, said it was intended to "provide an important national safeguard against creeping involvement in future Vietnam style wars."[6]

Michael and Peter Weiss, from the CCR, met with Crockett, but were at first reluctant to pursue the case, knowing full well the failure of the courts to strike down executive unilateral war-making during the Vietnam War era. But Crockett argued forcefully that the Reagan administration was violating the War Powers Resolution. That Resolution, enacted over President Nixon's veto in 1973,[7] imposed a sixty-day limit on executive authority to introduce U.S. troops into hostilities or "situations where imminent involvement in hostilities is clearly indicated by the circumstances," after which the president must obtain congressional authorization or withdraw the troops.[8]

The advisers in El Salvador were drawing "hostile fire pay," accompanying Salvadoran troops on combat missions and aiding one side in an ongoing, bloody civil war.[9] Yet, the administration had not sought the required congressional approval, instead claiming that the advisers were not in imminent danger. As Senator Thomas Eagleton, another drafter of the WPR, put it, Congress was being "snookered by the hair-splitting interpretations of the executive branch."[10] Here, unlike the Vietnam War cases, the plaintiffs could point to a congressional enactment that the president was clearly violating. CCR agreed to file what would be the first major test of the War Powers Resolution.

Michael also wanted to challenge the United States's provision of military aid to a country in which violations of human rights had reached epidemic proportions.[11] As Michael would later write:

CCR attorneys believed that a broader challenge to U.S. military support to the government of El Salvador was also important as a means of demonstrating how intimately the U.S. was involved in the war effort. We wanted a lawsuit that would reflect the reality and horror of the war in El Salvador. There was strong evidence that the government and its military in El Salvador was indiscriminately killing thousands of civilians; it was executing prisoners of war, carrying out political assassinations of unnamed civilians including church people and disappearing and torturing those the ruling junta considered dissidents.[12]

Again, the Reagan administration appeared to be violating a post-Vietnam statute—the Harkin Amendment to the Foreign Assistance Act—which prohibited the provision of any security assistance "to any country the government of which engages in a consistent pattern of gross violations of internationally recognized human rights."[13] As Michael said, "Only an ostrich could avoid seeing that the government of El Salvador was engaged in a consistent pattern of torturing, murdering and disappearing its citizens."[14] The Archdiocese of El Salvador reported that in an eight-month period, from January to September 1980, the military had assassinated 4,000 people. Church people were particular targets of right-wing, government-backed death squads: the Roman Catholic archbishop Oscar Romero had been brutally murdered, as had four American churchwomen, yet Reagan kept increasing American military aid to the Salvadoran government. While the CCR lawyers knew that the human rights claim would be even more difficult to litigate than the war powers claims, they felt that an important part of the lawsuit was educating the public about the atrocities occurring in El Salvador and the U.S. government's complicity with the Salvadoran army. They convinced Crockett, who initially was against filing the human rights claim, to include it in the lawsuit.

On May 1, 1981, eleven members of Congress—ultimately joined by eighteen others—filed Crockett v. Reagan. The filing date was deliberately chosen for symbolic purposes: May 1 is Law Day, and the lawsuit argued that the president was not above the law. It is also International Workers Day, and the suit was an effort to express solidarity with the poor people of El Salvador.

The lawyers and some of the congressional plaintiffs held a press conference the day the lawsuit was filed. The members of Congress were surprisingly militant. Two future senators, Barbara Mikulski and Tom Harkin, attacked the human rights record of the Salvadoran government, while Congressmen Crockett, Frank, and Lowry focused on the War Powers Resolution violation. Although local TV and the major wire services attended the press conference, CCR lawyers were disappointed that the suit failed to attract the national papers like the *New York Times* and the *Washington Post* or network TV.

The complaint requested extremely strong relief in the form of an injunction ordering the immediate withdrawal of all U.S. troops, weapons, military equipment, and aid from El Salvador. Some critics argued that requesting narrower relief, such as simply requiring the president to file a report pursuant to the War Powers Resolution, would have made the case easier to win.[15] Indeed, it was unthinkable that a court would order immediate withdrawal, and the intrusiveness of the requested relief may have politicized the case in the judge's mind. The CCR's interest, however, went beyond winning: the lawyers wanted to publicize illegal conduct by the U.S. and El Salvadoran governments. Crockett, a former judge and a part-time professor, expressed the contradictions of the complaint well when he told the CCR lawyers: "If you were in my civil procedure course, I would flunk you, but, given the political nature of the case, I understand why we're doing this."[16]

District Court Judge Joyce Hens Green granted the government's motion to dismiss the case.[17] Green, a fairly liberal judge, held that the human rights claim based on the violation of the Foreign Assistance Act was barred by the equitable discretion doctrine, which counsels judicial abstention where a congressional plaintiff's dispute is primarily with his or her fellow legislators.[18] Congress had enacted a statute allowing aid to El Salvador if the president certified that the Salvadoran government was making a concerted effort to comply with internationally recognized human rights principles.[19] The president had done so twice, although those certifications had been challenged by some members of Congress as "akin to calling night, day or a duck, an eagle."[20] In these circumstances, Judge Green found plaintiffs' dispute to be primarily with their fellow members of Congress.[21] Indeed, to emphasize that point, the conservative Washington Legal Foundation had intervened in the *Crockett* case on behalf of sixteen senators and thirteen representatives, asking that the case be dismissed.

The War Powers Resolution claim was more difficult for the court to resolve. Green agreed that the complaint's factual allegations were "at a minimum disturbing."[22] The court, however, could not engage in the fact-finding necessary to determine whether U.S. forces had been introduced into hostilities in El Salvador. Therefore, the case presented a nonjusticiable political question.

Nonetheless, Judge Green left the door slightly ajar for a future case. According to Green's opinion, were the United State to be involved in a major military conflict, a court could enforce the War Powers Resolution, at least to the extent of ordering the president to report to Congress.[23] Attempting to get any case through that crack, however, would prove to be daunting. The *Crockett* decision, affirmed the next year by the Court of Appeals, signaled that the courts would not enforce the War Powers Resolution absent a full-scale war.

What had the litigation gained? It had helped build the popular movement against U.S. intervention in El Salvador. Despite the absence of national media coverage, the CCR used the lawsuit as a vehicle for organizing a major effort against U.S. intervention in El Salvador. The CCR published a pamphlet detailing the executive branch's violations of law; spoke at fora and bar association meetings around the country; and continued its support of the domestic anti-intervention movement.

The CCR turned next to Nicaragua. By 1982, the contras—former National Guardsman who had been part of Somoza's defeated army—were being armed and trained by the CIA and had begun attacking Nicaraguan villages from Honduras. Alarming reports of human rights violations committed by the contras were beginning to surface. The contras attacked villages, murdered, tortured, raped, and kidnapped civilians and brought them back to contra camps. Despite these abuses, President Reagan referred to the contras as "freedom fighters" and said they were "the moral equal of our Founding Fathers."[24] As part of its aid to and training of the contras, the CIA produced and distributed a 134-page manual, which recommended the use of assassination, kidnapping, blackmail, and mob violence and explicitly violated the legal ban on CIA involvement in, or encouragement of, assassination.[25]

Facts were hard to come by. The contra attacks against civilians were taking place deep in the mountainous jungle areas of Nicaragua, far from the gaze of the international media, and support for the contras was covert. While there had been reports of CIA involvement in the *New York Times* and other newspapers, the story of what was really happening in northern Nicaragua was only beginning to emerge. Michael and other CCR lawyers thought a lawsuit would be a good way of exposing and publicizing what the U.S. government was doing to the Nicaraguan people and their revolution.

Michael contacted the people he knew and began an investigation in Nicaragua. He often traveled by helicopter or military jeep and visited victims of contra attacks, going to hospitals and to villages that had no passable roads. Eventually, seven Nicaraguan citizens agreed to become plaintiffs for Michael and to file a lawsuit in American courts against President Reagan for supporting the contras.

Among the seven was Dr. Myrna Cunningham, a Miskito Indian doctor who, on December 28, 1981 was abducted from the hospital in a small town on Nicaragua's Atlantic Coast where she worked. She was beaten and taken by the contras into a paramilitary camp inside Honduras, where she was repeatedly raped. Her attackers boasted of the support they received from the American government and threatened her with death for being a Sandinista and for working with the Nicaraguan government.[26] When she was finally released by her captors, she returned home to find that the hospital administrator had been seriously wounded by the contras and that the hospital, which had served almost 18,000 people, would have to close because it could not be protected. As Cunningham stated:

> Because I was kidnaped, beaten, raped, because I have seen so many Nicaraguan mothers crying because they lost their children, because I have seen and I have heard about hundreds of Nicaraguans who have been kidnaped, I have joined the lawsuit against the Reagan Administration, hoping this would help stop the attacks against Nicaragua and protect other Nicaraguans from these brutalities.[27]

Brenda Isabel Rocha Chacon, who at fifteen lost an arm during a paramilitary attack on her village, and Jose Santos Baireira Valez, whose son was murdered by the contras during an attack, were among the other Nicaraguan plaintiffs who joined the lawsuit.

The main legal theory that Michael used to bring this case, eventually entitled *Sanchez-Espinoza v. Reagan*, was based on a recent, important human rights precedent decided by the Court of Appeals for the Second Circuit. In 1980, the Second Circuit had held, in *Filartiga v. Pena-Irala*,[28] that a Paraguayan citizen could bring a civil action in a U.S. court against a Paraguayan police chief for torture committed in Paraguay. The plaintiffs in *Filartiga* had invoked the 1789 Alien Tort Act, which allows foreign nationals to sue in U.S. courts for tortious violations of international law. The *Sanchez* plaintiffs structured their claims to resemble the claim upheld in *Filartiga*. Only the defendants were different: the plaintiffs in *Sanchez* were suing American, rather than Paraguayan officials. As David Cole, a law student who worked on the case, wrote, it seemed "a common sense proposition . . . that United Stated courts should apply principles of international law as rigorously to United States officials as to foreign officials."[29] Unfortunately, such common sense was to elude the federal courts that heard *Sanchez*.

Michael and the CCR were urged not to bring the case by some within the human rights community. They felt that an attempt to apply the path-breaking *Filartiga* precedent to claims against the U.S. government in the politicized context of the covert war against Nicaragua was too risky. A prominent human rights activist told Michael that the CCR shouldn't bring the case; "it will ruin the law." Michael's response was that "people are being killed, we have to do something, let's not worry about precedent." As Michael put it, "what's the use of precedents, unless you use them?"[30]

The human rights activist was clearly right as a matter of prudent legal strategy: the *Filartiga* precedent was newly minted, and a wise strategy was to follow it up with clear, easy cases against brutal human rights abusers from foreign countries until the law became firmly established. But Michael was not merely a lawyer but a political activist. He had found a legal handle to sue the Reagan administration in U.S. courts—and he intended to use that hook for all it was worth. If the case helped slow Reagan's drive to overthrow the Sandinistas, if it saved even a few Nicaraguan lives, it was worth it.

Michael and the other CCR lawyers also decided to follow the *Crockett* example and to join the human rights claims to separation-of-powers issues in one lawsuit. Therefore, Congressman Ron Dellums was added as a plaintiff, claiming that the executive branch was conducting a covert war in Nicaragua in violation of the Constitution and applicable statutes. As Michael explained, we were "throwing everything into the kitchen sink." The result was an omnibus suit against the Reagan administration.

The CCR was again criticized by some within the human rights community for presenting too many claims in one case, thus allowing the court to sidestep the Nicaraguan plaintiffs' human rights tort claim.[31] Moreover, like the *Crockett* case, the *Sanchez* complaint requested broad relief—an injunction against continued U.S. aid to the contras, as well as damages—that a court was unlikely to grant.

However, the CCR was developing a theory that the two issues were in fact linked. The Reagan administration interventionist policies in El Salvador and Nicaragua had no respect for law: constitutional law, statutory law, or international human rights law. Moreover, and more important, U.S. intervention was fundamentally undemocratic, as evidenced by its lack of popular support.[32] Continuation of the intervention therefore required both circumventing the democratic process here and terrorizing the population there. Human rights violations and war powers subterfuge were integral and related aspects of the policy.

The complaint in *Sanchez* was filed on November 30, 1982. Michael's and the CCR's attention turned to publicizing its allegations. The case was one of the earliest attempts to tell the story of what was happening in Nicaragua and to portray the contras as terrorists who were attacking the civilian population. The complaint was published in a book on Nicaragua,[33] and got the Nicaraguan's story heard in the United States at a time when the mainstream media were still largely ignoring it. Michael and others spoke about the case around the country and used it to mobilize literally thousands of people against the covert war. The CCR, in conjunction with the prominent actress Susan Sarandon and other artists, film makers, poets, and writers, organized a multimedia event about the case titled "Talking Nicaragua," which was performed at New York University in the summer of 1983. Dr. Myrna Cunningham traveled to New York and Washington in connection with that event and met with Senator Ted Kennedy and other congressional figures.

The *Sanchez* complaint also had an impact in Nicaragua. While the mainstream U.S. press paid little attention to the case, *Sanchez* was front-page news in Nicaragua. That U.S. lawyers had filed a legal challenge to U.S. policy in U.S. courts served, at least in a small way, to strengthen the resolve of the Nicaraguans fighting the contras.

While the CCR lawyers felt that they had a solid legal case, they knew that getting the court to hear the merits of the claim would be difficult. Indeed it was. The district court dismissed all of the claims as presenting nonjusticiable political questions.[34] To adjudicate those claims would require the court to "determine the precise nature and extent of the U.S. government's involvement in the affairs of several Central American nations."[35] The court relied on the *Crockett* precedent to dismiss, holding that the "covert activities of CIA operatives in Nicaragua and Honduras are perforce even less judicially discoverable than the level of participation by U.S. military personnel in hostilities in El Salvador."[36] The court's analysis was not altered by the fact that the plaintiffs' human rights were involved: the war powers and the human rights claims were equally subject to the political question doctrine's broad sweep.

The Court of Appeals affirmed, using different language but nonetheless articulating the same basic principle.[37] Then-Judge Antonin Scalia found that the doctrine of sovereign immunity protected the federal officials from suit for damages under the Alien Tort Statute. Scalia denied plaintiffs' request for injunctive relief because in "so sensitive a foreign affairs matter as this"[38] a court should exercise its discretion to withhold equitable relief. Scalia's opinion relegates to a footnote its response to the *Filartiga* analogy that the CCR had relied upon:

> Since the doctrine of foreign sovereign immunity is quite distinct from the doctrine of domestic sovereign immunity that we apply here, being based upon considerations of international comity rather than separation of powers it does not necessarily follow that an Alien Tort Statute suit filed against the officer of a foreign sovereign would have to be dismissed. Thus, nothing in today's decision necessarily conflicts with the decision of the Second Circuit in *Filartiga*.[39]

Scalia's attempt to construct a legalistic distinction between *Filartiga* and *Sanchez* made no sense. Why should considerations of international comity be less weighty than those presented by separation of powers? Nor is it obvious that U.S. courts ought to be less reluctant to adjudicate damage actions against foreign officials accused of torturing aliens abroad than to adjudicate similar actions against executive branch officials, with whom the courts share the task of governing. Scalia had simply come up with a distinction without content.

The defeat in *Sanchez* was total. At no point in the litigation did the courts look at the human consequences of U.S. policy in Central America.[40] And, unlike *Crockett*, *Sanchez* left not even a slight crack through which future plaintiffs might attempt to wriggle.

Moreover, many in the human rights community renewed their questioning of whether *Sanchez* should ever have been brought. They focused on the bad precedent created and questioned, "[H]ow successful is a highly publicized case if the legal result presents a new hurdle for future litigants?"[41] After *Sanchez*, some opined that a broad range of questions formerly open for adjudication could be considered nonjusticiable. As one participant in a 1985 human rights conference argued, "If the primary goal of those who brought the suit was simply to direct public and media attention to the situation in Nicaragua . . ., congressional trips to Nicaragua could have produced a positive dramatic effect without creating bad precedent."[42]

For Michael, *Sanchez-Espinoza*, despite the almost certainty of defeat, was the case he was the most committed to of all the Central American litigation. "I knew all the plaintiffs, I had visited the hospitals, saw the victims." To Michael, "the case was not about an abstract legal issue, it was about real people, real suffering." Moreover, by tying the human rights violations to executive warmaking, the case reflected Michael's radical approach to politics: to him, "it was like putting the United States on trial as a defendant."

While the *Crockett* and *Sanchez* cases were prophetic, the way they were framed made them virtually impossible to win. I recently asked Michael whether in hindsight he would still have brought *Sanchez*. "Definitely," he answered, "although I know so much more about international law that I would have much more precisely framed the complaint. I would have taken out much of the rhetoric that made the case seem one simply about policy and not law." In the end, however, it undoubtedly would not have made much difference: *Sanchez* was destined to lose in court.

I joined the CCR's Central American legal team in the summer of 1983. After I returned from Nicaragua in August 1983, the CCR asked me to become the lead attorney in a new Nicaraguan suit it wanted to bring.

The new case was a much narrower challenge to the covert war against Nicaragua and sought more limited relief. Our aim was to avoid the broad political question problems raised in *Crockett* and *Sanchez* and to obtain a court ruling declaring that, if the facts alleged in press accounts were accurate, the president was violating the law. Three of the *Sanchez* plaintiffs—Congressman Ron Dellums, Dr. Myrna Cunningham, who had been kidnapped and raped by the contras, and the Florida ACLU president Eleanor Ginsberg, who lived close to the contra training camps in Florida—wrote a letter to Attorney General William French Smith requesting an investigation of whether top administration officials had violated the Neutrality Act in aiding the contras.[43] The Neutrality Act, enacted in 1794, declares that:

> Whoever, within the United States, knowingly begins or sets on foot or provides or prepares a means for or furnishes the money for, or takes

part in, any military or naval expedition or enterprise to be carried on from thence against the territory or dominion of any foreign . . . state . . . with whom the United States is at peace, shall be fined under this title or imprisoned not more than three years, or both.[44]

From a literal reading, it appeared that the administration had violated the Neutrality Act. Administration officials had unilaterally provided at least $19 million to finance covert paramilitary operations against the Nicaraguan government and had trained and organized the contra forces, at least in part, in Florida.[45] Thus, unless Congress had implicitly repealed or superseded the Neutrality Act, the CCR had a good claim.

The procedural device the CCR employed to get the case to court was the Ethics in Government Act.[46] That Act, passed in the wake of Watergate to ensure that "no one, regardless of position, is above the law,"[47] required the attorney general to conduct a preliminary investigation upon receipt of specific information from a credible source that a high-level executive official had engaged in nonpetty criminal conduct.[48] Dellums, Cunningham, and Ginsberg sent a letter detailing their allegations and requesting a preliminary investigation of seven high government officials, including President Reagan, Secretary of State Alexander Haig, and CIA Director William Casey. The Justice Department responded with a short letter refusing to initiate the requested investigation, and the plaintiffs sued in the Northern District of California, Dellums's home district.

I was asked to litigate this case because I had written an article arguing that the administration was violating the Neutrality Act; the case was structured along the lines suggested in that article.[49] The case reflected my predilection as an academic: it was legalistic, focusing on the abstract question of the applicability of the two-century-old Neutrality Act to the contra war against Nicaragua. Moreover, the relief asked for in *Dellums v. Smith* was very narrow. We did not seek a court injunction against U.S. aid to the contras, as had been requested in *Sanchez*. Nor did we even seek the appointment of a special prosecutor. All we requested was that the attorney general conduct the preliminary investigation that he was required to undertake under the Ethics Act. The relief requested was therefore embarrassingly minimal, almost purely symbolic. Had the attorney general conducted the investigation and concluded that no special prosecutor was warranted, that probably would have dispositively ended the case. But the Reagan administration was in no mood to do so, preferring rather to boldly assert executive power rather than perfunctorily comply with the law.

Judge Stanley Weigel, a maverick Republican judge appointed by President Kennedy in 1962 to the District Court for the Northern District of California, was assigned to hear the case. I flew to San Francisco and prepared with our excellent and creative legal team: Mark Van der Hout, a nationally prominent San Francisco immigration attorney represented the National Lawyers Guild; David Cole, a brilliant law student at Yale who was a CCR intern and who would become one of the great appellate lawyers of our generation, first with the CCR and then as a professor at Georgetown Law School; and Ellen Yaroshevsky, who was a key lawyer at the CCR and a great trial lawyer. We discussed the legal intricacies of the case until late at night, arguing over minor technical issues with the intensity of Talmudic scholars parsing the Torah's text for its true meaning. But we all realized it would take a miracle to actually win. Despite the narrowness of the requested relief, in essence we were still asking a court to hold that top administration officials might be committing crimes in their covert war against Nicaragua.

The argument before Judge Weigel focused not on the human rights abuses in Nicaragua but on the legal interstices of long-forgotten laws and ill-defined doctrines. The administration argued that this case, like *Sanchez*, presented a political question.[50] Not so, answered the court; we had structured the complaint to avoid the political question pitfalls.[51] Judge Weigel held that:

> Unlike the complaints in *Crockett* and *Sanchez-Espinoza*, the complaint in the case at bar does not directly challenge the legality of any action take by the President. . . . The case before this Court does not require any assessment by the Court as to the accuracy of the data reported by plaintiffs to the Attorney General. The sole issue is whether the report is sufficient to trigger the preliminary investigation plaintiffs contend is required by the Ethics in Government Act. The limited task requested of the Court is thus judicially manageable, unlike those requested in *Crockett* and *Sanchez-Espinoza*.[52]

The court ordered the attorney general to conduct a preliminary investigation.[53] Judge Weigel had turned out to be no ordinary judge.

The Justice Department, probably confident that it would win on jurisdictional grounds, had not argued the merits—namely whether the

Neutrality Act applied to covert paramilitary activities undertaken with the president's approval. After Weigel's opinion came out, the government made a motion to alter the court's judgment, arguing for the first time that the Neutrality Act does not apply to actions authorized by the President.[54] The district court held another hearing and rejected the government's argument, holding that the conclusion that the Neutrality Act requires universal obedience and applies to the President is "well supported by the history" of the Act.[55] The language, history, and judicial precedents, the court said, made plaintiffs' reading of the Act "at least as persuasive as defendants"[56] and demonstrated the "reasonableness of the view that the Act applies to all persons, including the President."[57]

Judge Weigel's ruling received prominent attention both in Nicaragua and in the mainstream U.S. media, focusing national attention on the question of the lawfulness and legitimacy of covert warfare. Stuart Taylor, a *New York Times* legal correspondent, wrote an in-depth story on the case and noted that while there was "virtually no chance that Mr. Reagan or anyone else will be prosecuted" for Neutrality Act violations, the *Dellums* case illustrated the "legal ambiguities that arise whenever the President supports guerrilla operations amid dispute as to whether Congress has authorized them."[58] To Taylor, the "ultimate issue" in the case was not whether the President was violating the Neutrality Act but whether a covert war violates the "exclusive power of Congress under the Constitution to declare war."[59] As Judge Weigel had recognized, one of the Neutrality Act's "major purposes was to protect the constitutional power of Congress to declare war or authorize private reprisal against foreign states."[60]

The attorney general appealed Weigel's decision, and in January 1984 the Ninth Circuit stayed the lower-court judgment and ordered an expedited appeal. The Justice Department sent one of its top political appointees, Carolyn Kuhl, to argue the case. The government seemed concerned about the case—at least, that is what a senior Justice Department official privately told Congressman Dellums. And it had reason—on April 9, 1984, a majority of the Democratic members of the House Judiciary Committee, invoking section 595(e) of the Ethics Act, requested the appointment of a special prosecutor to investigate violations of the Neutrality Act. The attorney general refused to do so.

Almost two and one-half years after the expedited appeal was argued, the Court of Appeals issued a terse opinion dismissing the case.[61]

The court declined to address the district court's ruling on the scope of the Neutrality Act and failed to respond to the government's political-question argument. Instead, it held that the plaintiffs lacked standing to challenge the attorney general's refusal to investigate.[62] The court relied on two analogous D.C. Circuit cases[63] to find that Congress "did not intend to create procedural rights in private citizens sufficient to support standing to sue."[64]

The panel, composed of Judges Betty Fletcher, Thomas Fairchild,[65] and William Canby, left a small opening in its opinion for future litigation. The court stated that its opinion did not render the Ethics in Government Act meaningless because the attorney general's compliance with the Act remained subject to oversight by members of the congressional judiciary committees.[66] Maybe those committees had standing to sue. We prepared to go that route.

We never had an opportunity to try the opening left by the court. When the Court of Appeals issued its opinion in *Dellums*, we urged the committee members to renew their request of April 9, 1984, for a special prosecutor. On October 17, 1986, two months after the Court of Appeals's decision, a majority of Democrats on the House Judiciary Committee again requested the appointment of a special prosecutor. Had the attorney general again denied their request, we would have sought to intervene on behalf of the committee members, requesting reargument in the court of appeals. Still, I suspect that the appearance of the Judiciary Committee at the court's doorstep undoubtedly would have led to the invocation of some other doctrine—perhaps executive-branch discretion—to avoid confrontation with a popular president over foreign policy.

However, by this time, the allegations in our lawsuit had received massive confirmation. The Nicaraguans had shot down a plane carrying an American, Eugene Hasenfus, and evidence was mounting that the administration was evading recent congressional restrictions on aid to Nicaragua in addition to those imposed by the 200-year-old Neutrality Act.[67] Attorney General Edwin Meese was forced to set in motion the investigation that led to the Iran-contra scandal and the appointment of Special Prosecutor Lawrence Walsh. We called a press conference and declared political victory and thus ended the *Dellums v. Smith* case.

Despite the loss in the Court of Appeals, Judge Weigel's rulings were very useful in the political battle against Reagan's support to the contras. For more than two years, during the height of U.S. aid to the contras, a district court ruling strongly suggesting that the president was violating the Neutrality Act stood untouched. As supporters of the contras recognized, the *Dellums* case was "widely cited by opponents of U.S. policy in Central America" as demonstrating the illegality of U.S. policy.[68] The National Lawyers Guild and CCR actively mobilized around the case. Judge Weigel's decision received significant attention in the U.S. mainstream media, meriting attention by the *New York Times*, the *Washington Post*, the *McNeil-Lehrer News Hour*, and other, smaller papers and broadcasts around the country.[69] The case also prompted two House Judiciary Committee requests for a special prosecutor and contributed to the growing demand for accountability that eventually exposed the Iran-contra scandal.

By framing the *Dellums* case narrowly and requesting minimal relief, we were able to win in the district court, which thrust the case into the mainstream media, gave our arguments much more legitimacy, and allowed us more access to the broader community. *Dellums* taught us the valuable lesson that courts are more willing to intervene in difficult cases where the relief sought is least intrusive to the government. I came to see our cases as essentially asking the courts to declare what the law was and then to allow the political branches to work out a political remedy. The *Dellums* court did leave us an opening by suggesting that the Judiciary Committee might have standing even though individual members of Congress did not.

Yet framing *Dellums* narrowly also had some negative consequences. To a certain extent, the *Dellums v. Smith* case lost the passion, human connectedness, and prophetic quality of *Sanchez* and *Crockett*. While *Dellums* did receive mainstream media attention, my sense was that the political organizing around the *Sanchez* case was stronger and that the impact of that case on political activists in the United States and Nicaragua was deeper. With *Dellums*, we were drawn into an argument about citizen standing under the Ethics Act and the meaning of the obscure 1794 Neutrality Act. Our connectedness to the situation in Nicaragua was becoming more attenuated; *Dellums* was a more academic case than *Sanchez*. We had found a technical handle to get somewhere in the courts—albeit not very far—but it came at the cost of diluting our basic critique of U.S. policy and our compassion for and solidarity with the Nicaraguan people.

The quest for judicial relief was appearing more Sisyphean with each passing case. The lesson we were drawing was that the courts were extremely reluctant to interfere with U.S. foreign policy, no matter how strong our case appeared or how narrowly tailored the relief requested.

By 1984, the CCR began to narrow its complaints to be more legalistic and procedurally oriented, rather than to present the type of broad legal-political challenge to U.S. foreign policy made in *Sanchez* and *Crockett*. In part, this trend was a reaction to the defeats suffered in those cases and to the at least temporary victory in *Dellums*.

The CCR revisited the Salvadoran human rights issue in a more legalistic form in *Barnes v. Kline*. That case challenged President Reagan's pocket veto of legislation that would have required a certification that human rights were improving in El Salvador.[70] After the December 1980 brutal murder of four American churchwomen in San Salvador, and in the face of escalating reports of human rights violations, Congress imposed a requirement that the president certify that the Salvadoran government was improving its human rights record before he could transfer U.S. aid to that country. President Reagan had so certified in both 1982 and 1983, although independent observers generally agreed that the Salvadoran government's human rights record was still atrocious. When Congress re-enacted the certification requirement for the 1984 budget, President Reagan apparently tired of the phony certification shell game that he and Congress were playing. But, instead of vetoing the bill, which would have allowed Congress to override his veto, Reagan simply did not return the bill either signed or vetoed—an act known in constitutional parlance as a pocket veto. We believed that the "pocket veto" was unconstitutional.

Congressman Michael Barnes and a number of other Democrats asked Michael to file a lawsuit, which he did. This lawsuit, which the entire House of Representatives and Senate eventually joined as plaintiffs, was a challenge to the constitutionality of a presidential pocket veto. Unlike *Crockett v. Reagan*, the complaint in *Barnes* raised only the separation of powers issue—the constitutionality of the president's pocket veto—and not the broader political-legal question of the human rights violations being committed by the Salvadoran government with our aid.

Barnes v. Kline was an important case because the human rights community in the United States viewed the congressional mandate that the president certify human rights improvement in El Salvador as critical. The CCR's challenge to Reagan's pocket veto initially attracted considerable interest and support both from members of Congress and from the activist community.

Michael, though, felt somewhat conflicted about *Barnes*. While the certification was an important political issue, the Reagan administration had made a mockery of the certification process in the past and would certainly continue to do so in the future if the Court struck down the pocket veto. A win in court would not achieve the legal result we really wanted. On the other hand, it would be symbolically and politically important in stopping the Reagan administration from riding roughshod over Congress. And this was a case we thought we could win.

The district court ruled against us, and Michael filed an appeal.[71] But timing became critical. The certification requirement that Reagan had "vetoed" was attached to the 1984 budget and would expire after that budgetary year was complete. It was therefore critical to get a definitive court ruling before the budgetary year was up and the case became legally moot. Michael therefore petitioned the Court of Appeals for an expedited appeal, requesting that it hear the case quickly before it became moot. The Court of Appeals refused the request—and at that point our fate was sealed. Michael was both furious and dejected, but he doggedly proceeded with the appeal.

The Court of Appeals did, however, rule in the plaintiff's favor before the budget year was over, holding that Congress had standing to sue and that Reagan's use of the pocket veto was unconstitutional.[72] The government appealed to the Supreme Court, and the High Court agreed to hear the case.

For almost any other lawyer, the way the *Barnes* case was playing itself out should have been the crowning achievement of a legal career. We had won in the Court of Appeals, and the stage was set for a dramatic showdown over important constitutional issues in the Supreme Court. Most lawyers—even most excellent ones—never get a chance to argue in the Supreme Court. Attorneys, even those without the legal capability to do so, jump at the chance to argue before the Supreme Court. My old boss Leonard Boudin lived for Supreme Court arguments. It is the greatest challenge of one's legal career. While Michael and I had both been involved in litigation before the Supreme Court, neither of us had ever argued a case in that court. Here was Michael's chance.

But Michael told me that he was not going to argue the *Barnes* case before the court, that he would defer to Morgan Frankel of the Senate

Counsel's office, also an excellent lawyer. Michael's decision not to argue the case reflected his growing dissatisfaction with the case, which had started out strongly connected to the human rights movement but had lost much of its political meaning as the lawsuit dragged on. The abstract constitutional question of whether a president could pocket veto legislation had become paramount and the political nature of the legislation he had vetoed all but forgotten. In fact, the case was in danger of being declared moot, as the budgetary period was running out and the 1984 certification therefore virtually irrelevant. Michael's interest was stopping U.S. aid to the oppressive El Salvador government, not in arguing whether legislators had standing, whether a pocket veto was constitutional, or about the rules governing mootness. To Michael, "the idea that I would put aside weeks or months to brief and argue this highly technical case while I was at the height of my political organizing was absurd." I respected, even admired, his decision, but it seemed as if he were throwing away the chance of a lifetime.

After the Supreme Court took the case, the budgetary period did run out. The Court heard the argument but eventually decided that the case was moot and therefore vacated the Court of Appeals' decision without reaching the merits of the constitutional issues.[73] The Court of Appeals's refusal to expedite the case had deprived us of a chance for victory.

As *Barnes* was too slowly winding its way up the appellate ladder, Michael, David Cole, and I turned back to Nicaragua and brought a fairly narrow, technical case challenging new Reagan policies toward that country. In this new case, the Reagan policy affected me personally.

In April 1985, I had returned to Nicaragua for the third time, leading a National Lawyers Guild delegation studying the human rights situation there. By then, the contra war had escalated dramatically; "the [contra] FDN was engaged in numerous kidnappings, torture, and murder of unarmed civilians, mostly in villages and farm cooperatives."[74] While Congress had at times attempted to cut the flow of funds to the contras, by 1985 more than $20 million had reportedly been spent to build and maintain a force of from 10,000 to 15,000 contras.

Early in 1985, the Reagan administration turned the pressure up one more notch on the Sandinista government. On May 1, 1985, as our NLG delegation was nearing the end of its stay in Nicaragua, President Reagan announced a trade embargo against Nicaragua and the termination of the Treaty of Friendship, Navigation, and Commerce between the United States and Nicaragua. The most immediate impact of the embargo was that flights between the two countries were suspended. We were stranded in Nicaragua, and I anxiously fretted about getting back home. It took us several days before we were able to leave by way of El Salvador.

I spent many hours over those few days on the phone to Michael at the CCR—always with a bad connection—planning litigation against the embargo. The embargo, along with the contra war and U.S. efforts to pressure international economic institutions, such as the Inter-American Development Bank and the World Bank, to refuse providing loans to Nicaragua, was undermining the already severely weakened Nicaragua economy.

President Reagan imposed the trade embargo under a statute that Michael and I knew well from our Cuba travel litigation—the International Emergency Economic Powers Act (IEEPA). As the Cuban travel litigation had demonstrated, Congress was reluctant to accord the president untrammeled emergency power. The IEEPA was a reform statute that required the president to find the existence of "an unusual and extraordinary threat to the national security and foreign policy of the United States"[75] before imposing an embargo against another nation. IEEPA and a companion statute, the National Emergencies Act, also allowed Congress to veto the president's determination of emergency and required that Congress vote every six months on whether to continue the emergency. Congress had enacted these requirements in response to embargoes such as the Cuban which had gone on and on and on despite the lack of a real emergency and without congressional participation.

We thought the administration legally vulnerable on several points. First, what was the unusual and extraordinary threat to the United States posed by tiny, militarily and economically weak Nicaragua? As former Congressman Jonathan Bingham, the principal drafter of the IEEPA, wrote in the *New York Times*, the ongoing tension with Nicaragua was not the type of situation that Congress had in mind when it limited the president's emergency power to situations involving "unusual and extraordinary" threats.[76] Of course, most courts were unlikely to second-guess a presidential declaration of emergency and would relegate such a determination to the realm of nonjusticiable "political questions" with which we were already so familiar.

But we had another sound legal argument, one that Michael and David Cole thought was a sure winner, and very technical. The legislative history of the emergency power statutes clearly indicated that Congress would not accord the president the power to authorize trade embargoes unless it had the ability to "legislatively veto" what the president did. Congress had enacted the National Emergencies Act and IEEPA but had refused to give the president unilateral power. However, the Supreme Court, in a case entitled *INS v. Chadha* had later held the "legislative veto" mechanism found in the NEA and many other statutes to be unconstitutional.[77] Thus, since one part of IEEPA was probably unconstitutional, the narrow legal question became whether the legislative veto could be severed from the whole statute. Supreme Court case law held that a whole statute had to be struck down as unconstitutional if its unconstitutional provision was so integral that Congress would not have enacted the statute without it. We thought the legislative history was clear that Congress would have been unwilling to enact IEEPA without some veto power over the president. Michael believed that "we had a slam-dunk winner."

I also wanted to challenge President Reagan's notice of termination of the friendship treaty with Nicaragua, which he had done without any congressional participation. The Constitution requires the Senate to ratify any treaty the United States enters into, and, while the document is silent about how we get out of treaties, the views of the Constitution's framers clearly indicate that Senate or House consent is necessary before a treaty can be terminated. Indeed, some years before, Senator Goldwater and a number of other conservative senators had challenged President Carter's unilateral termination of our treaty with Taiwan. The Supreme Court had refused to decide Goldwater's constitutional claim.

The CCR had located several progressive businessmen who conducted business with Nicaragua. One made some kind of industrial molds, and the other was a specialty coffee distributor who had concluded that Nicaraguan coffee was terrific and was selling it in the States. Both had standing to assert that their private rights under the treaty were being affected. We thought that this point distinguished the case from *Goldwater v. Carter*, in which only legislators with no private rights had sued.[78]

We filed the case, titled *Beacon Products v. Reagan*, in the fall of 1985, returning to Boston, our old stomping grounds from the Cuba travel case and a city rich in its history of revolt against imperial economically repressive measures. And we drew a good judge—Judge W. Arthur Garrity, a fairly liberal judge who was known primarily for his courage and determination in ordering the desegregation of the Boston public schools. Our "slam-dunk" case was getting better, although the Cuba travel case loomed as a warning that law and legislative history would play second fiddle to politics when it came to foreign policy.

The oral argument before Judge Garrity took place in a courtroom packed with spectators, reflecting the chord the case had struck among anti-interventionist political activists. Our case was an important piece of the solidarity movement, which emphasized personal, economic, and cultural ties between Nicaragua and the United States. In fact, because of the strength of that movement, the Reagan administration never moved to bar travel to Nicaragua, as it had done with respect to Cuba.

The argument that day before Judge Garrity was not particularly memorable, focusing as it did on fairly dry legal points. One irony of the argument, though, remains fixed in my mind. I argued our treaty claim, treating Judge Garrity and the spectators to a rather academic historical exposition on the original intent of the constitutional framers and early leaders of the American Republic. After I finished, David Anderson, the Justice Department lawyer sent from Washington to argue the case, rose to respond. Before he could say much, Judge Garrity asked him pointedly, "What's your response to all this history propounded by Professor Lobel?" Anderson responded that it was essentially irrelevant, given the twentieth-century history of presidential termination of treaties. Some in the audience snickered, for Anderson appeared blithely unaware that Attorney General Edwin Meese had recently given a major, well-publicized speech arguing that the Constitution had to be interpreted according to the original intent of the framers. I had just provided the Justice Department the opportunity to apply Meese's theory. But, apparently, the attorney general's doctrine did not apply to foreign policy but only to domestic issues like abortion or gay rights. In foreign policy, the administration argued for a flexible modernist interpretation of the Constitution, adapting the eighteenth-century document to the needs of a twentieth-century world, the opposite of its argument against abortion rights. We argued that the intent of the framers should be respected, a position in tension with the CCR argument on such issues as race, sex discrimination, and gay rights. The search for a neutral, apolitical jurisprudence seemed illusory; law and politics were inextricably linked, as our cases so clearly demonstrated.

It was not that we believed that the words of the framers should be accorded the same reverence that fundamentalists ascribe to the statements of the biblical prophets. Rather, we saw our country's early history as anti-interventionist; the new republic was trying to fend off European intervention and defend its newly won sovereignty. Therefore, both the Constitution and early laws placed a great reliance on international law and separation of powers to restrain executive adventurism that could result in potentially disastrous wars with stronger European powers. Many of the tools we deployed in our modern Central American cases—the Neutrality Act, the Alien Tort Claims Act, the war powers clause of the Constitution, and the Constitution's supremacy clause, which accorded treaties the status of law—were from the 1780s and 1790s. What we were really trying to do was to recall the country to its early revolutionary, noninterventionist history—a history that had been obscured and discarded because it conflicted with the realities of American imperial power.

In April 1986, Judge Garrity ruled against us, holding that the legislative veto was severable from IEEPA, that the question of whether an unusual and extraordinary emergency existed was a political, not a judicial, question, and that *Goldwater v. Carter* barred our treaty claims, despite our private-businessmen plaintiffs.[79]

We made the mistake of appealing to the Court of Appeals. We fervently believed Garrity wrong, but, as the case dragged on, the political activists lost interest. Moreover, Congress amended the National Emergencies Act and IEEPA to remove the unconstitutional legislative veto and therefore forced us to make more and more technical arguments that were totally divorced from any important political reality. The friendship treaty terminated after a year and our treaty claim became moot. Moreover, it became clear that Congress would not challenge the president on the embargo issue: indeed, the National Emergencies Act and IEEPA *required* Congress to vote *every* six months on whether to continue the emergency, yet Congress *never* voted on the Nicaraguan embargo. Congress preferred to punt the ball to the president, in utter disregard of the law it had enacted less than a decade earlier. The Court of Appeals turned down our appeal.[80] What had begun with a big bang thus died with a whimper. In the end, the only significant result of the *Beacon Products* litigation was to demonstrate conclusively that two key reform statutes of the post–Vietnam era—the National Emergencies Act and the International Economic Emergency Powers Act—had been eviscerated by Congress and the courts.

I had by this time immersed myself in local efforts in Pittsburgh to organize against Reagan's policies, and in many ways it was more satisfying than my legal work. I joined the board of the Thomas Merton Center, an ecumenical peace group that had been founded by several Catholic activists during the Vietnam War. We organized rallies, sit-ins at the Federal Building, and meetings with senators in opposition to the U.S.-sponsored war against Nicaragua. One sit-in at the Federal Building led to my arrest, along with dozens of other peace activists, and I testified as an expert legal witness for us. Along with a group of predominately Catholic religious activists who were opposed to the embargo and the contra war, I organized a sister-city organization to pair Pittsburgh with a similar city or town in Nicaragua to develop people-to-people ties with and to have a specific focus for humanitarian and economic aid. We did not find another steel city but were paired with San Isidro, a sleepy little rural town, located astride the Pan American highway between the capital and the northern town of Esteli. We adopted a wonderful, very poor farm cooperative in San Isidro and made a number of trips there, carrying humanitarian supplies; San Isidrians visited us in Pittsburgh. It was our nonlegal, people-to-people answer to the embargo.

But I nonetheless had one last major legal campaign to fight. That campaign led me to Benjamin Linder, the slight, soft-spoken, and thoughtful twenty-four-year-old young man who wanted to be an engineer in a socialist Third World country. Linder had told his father that "you could count on the fingers of one hand the number of engineers in the entire world who go to Third World countries with a socialist base and make life better."[81]

When he arrived in Managua, a sprawling city of 800,000 mostly poor people, Linder tried to get a fulfilling job as an engineer. He found that it was not going to be easy to deal with a frustrating government bureaucracy, bouts of illness that resulted in vomiting and diarrhea, the stifling heat in his tiny cement-block bedroom, and the loneliness of being separated from his girlfriend from Seattle. Linder's moods fluctuated from elation at being in Nicaragua and observing firsthand the revolution's progress to depression growing out of his loneliness and frustration. His letters home reflected these mood swings. "I kept wondering if I really want to do this. . . . I feel better, then worse, then better, then worse."[82] He also wondered why he was in Managua, writing, "So why am I here? Adventure is part of it. Proving myself is also a part. Doing good is a very large part. The rest, I guess, will be known in time."[83]

Linder's decision to immerse himself in Nicaragua and to work and live among the poor was consistent with his character, upbringing, and values. As a boy he had not placed much emphasis on success and winning as traditionally defined. He loved playing chess, although he usually lost. He was a member of a swim team that always lost. His mother, Elisabeth, recalls that, unlike many children, "Ben didn't care about winning."[84]

Like Michael and me, Ben Linder had deeply Jewish cultural values and roots that attracted him to the Nicaraguan revolution. His mother had fled Czechoslovakia to escape the Nazis during World War II, and his parents had raised him as a "cultural Jew," emphasizing a nonreligious but deeply ethical tradition and heritage. "For Ben, it's [being Jewish] who he was," said his friend, Dr. Anne Lifflander, "the ethical basis for everything he did."[85] In Nicaragua, he attended a Yom Kippur service that touched him greatly. He wrote in his journal,

When justice burns within us like a flaming fire, when love evokes willing sacrifice from us, when to the last full measure of selfless devotion, we demonstrate our belief in the ultimate triumph of truth and righteousness, then your goodness enters our lives; then you live within our hearts, and we through righteousness behold your presence.

The bush is burning, but the Voice has not yet spoken aloud; we can only feel, guess, hope; we cannot yet hear. But it may be that we must act in order to hear.

. . .

I must not cower from the task ahead. In Nicaragua I was shown the trail ahead. Tonight I vow to set forth upon the trail.

It is in our love that I find the strength to carry on. Great is the eternal power at the heart of life: mighty the love that is stronger than death.[86]

Nonetheless, after several months in Nicaragua, a country desperately in need of skilled engineers, Linder still had no work. But he had other talents; he juggled, rode a unicycle, and was a clown. So he joined the circus. Linder wrote home, "I go to school for five years, I go to some godforsaken country to save the world with my newly acquired skills and what happens. The only work I can do is clowning around."[87]

Finally, after more than three months, Ben landed a job with the state-run National Institute of Energy (INE) in Managua, where he was assigned a job designing a piping system for a geothermal plant. He moved in with a large Nicaraguan family in Barrio Riguero, a working-class neighborhood of Managua, and became very popular in the community, being invited to perform at children's birthday parties and neighborhood festivals and in health and nutrition campaigns. In the summer of 1984, he began working on an INE pilot project to construct a very small hydroelectric plant that would provide energy to the remote town of El Cua, in northern Nicaragua and to its surrounding communities. The project was stalled by myriad problems, but Linder was intrigued by the challenges of finishing the plant and by its potential for spurring development in the region.[88]

El Cua lies in the rugged mountains of northern Nicaragua, forty-five miles from the nearest significant town, Jinotega, a three-hour drive along a rugged dirt road. Linder once said:

> Going into El Cuá is a lot like going into a small town in the western United States in 1830. The main street is dusty, two bars, one hotel, a military command post that looks like it came right out of a western. A dusty road comes into town. The bar and bank both have diesel generators so you can get your money out of the bank and buy a cold beer.[89]

The 2,000 residents of El Cua had no electricity, no running water, no sanitation system, and no industry. Sixty-eight percent of the region's children under five suffered from malnutrition.[90]

The El Cua-Bocay area, located near the Honduran border where the contras were based, was beset by contra attacks. One of the first things Linder noticed about El Cua was that "It's a war zone . . . the most striking thing you see is the military presence."[91] As early as 1983, the contras had attacked El Cua. That same year the contras assassinated a West German doctor, Albrecht Pflaum, in a small community thirty miles southwest of El Cua and ambushed and burned El Cua's only ambulance. As a result of the assassination, the other West German doctors were removed from the area. Several teachers were murdered on the road coming into El Cua. The nearby agricultural cooperative of El Cedro suffered forty-three deaths in the course of three contra attacks, and of the twenty-six schools established in the Cua-Bocay area by 1982, seventeen had to be closed because of the war. Throughout the mid-1980s, attacks in the El Cua area were common, and residents of El Cua were awakened often at night by bursts of machine gun fire in the mountains surrounding the town.

Despite the danger, Ben Linder decided to spend a good deal of time in El Cua working on the hydroelectric project. He felt good there, felt that he had found his home. He told his friends that, if he died, he wanted to be buried in El Cua.[92] To his father, David, Linder "was passing through that wonderful moment when a person finds a meaning to his life. But I think as regards the danger, he also made a pact with destiny."[93]

Linder's mother said that her son, while often described as idealistic, was also "very realistic. He knew what he could do. . . . You don't change the world. But you can make changes in small places, and that is worthwhile."[94] People who knew him recognized Linder as "a humanely motivated revolutionary."[95] "I see the kids," Linder wrote, "and I feel like taking them all away to a safe place to hide until the war stops and the hunger stops. . . . The pied piper of El Cua. But I can't do that. . . . So instead, I try to put in light, and hope for the best."[96]

Despite Linder's best efforts, it was incredibly difficult to get the small hydroelectric plant to work. "I finally decided," he wrote, "that this really is what I'm here for, like it or not, and that I just have to keep fighting."[97]

After more than a year of working on the project, Linder and his coworkers succeeded in getting the plant to work. It was the first small hydroelectric plant completed since the Sandinistan revolution in 1979, and it meant electricity for El Cua. For Ben, it was the overcoming of a challenge, and conquering challenges was one key to what made Ben tick. He wrote, "Ever since I left home I keep finding myself challenged and being unsure if I can meet the challenges. . . . Will I keep doing this to myself? Probably I will. Who knows why."[98] When he returned home to Portland in 1986 after the plant was completed, he wrote, "I felt like I had come back a somebody."[99]

In 1986, the contra war in El Cua and other northern regions of Nicaragua escalated. In June 1986, the House of Representatives narrowly approved $100 million dollars in new aid to the contras, a substantial increase over the aid provided in 1985. Around the same time, the contras began to plant U.S.-made land mines on roads in the northern part of Jinotega provinces, causing the death of many civilians. In the worst incident, on July 2, 1986, thirty-two civilians, including twelve children, were reportedly killed when their vehicle exploded on a mine on the road from San Jose de Bocay to El Cua, a road Linder frequently traveled.

The Nicaraguan government fought the contras and their U.S. patrons on the military, political, and diplomatic, but also legal fronts. In 1984, at the urging of its foreign minister, Miguel DeScoto, a Catholic priest who had lived in the United States, the Nicaraguan government brought a lawsuit against the United States in the World Court. The lawsuit was filed after the disclosures that the CIA had been mining Nicaraguan harbors, leading to the damage and destruction of commercial vessels entering Nicaraguan ports.

Nicaragua alleged that U.S. support for the Nicaraguan contras constituted both an impermissible intervention in Nicaragua's internal affairs and a use of armed force that contravened the UN and OAS charters and general principles of international law. The United States contested the court's jurisdiction. After considering extensive briefs filed by both sides and hearing several days of oral argument, the court ruled that it had jurisdiction and competence to adjudicate Nicaragua's claims.[100] The United States thereupon formally withdrew from the proceeding and later decided to withdraw from the World Court's compulsory jurisdiction altogether. The United States was in essence saying to the court, if you don't rule the way we want you to, we won't play in your game.

The case nonetheless went forward, and, on June 27, 1986, the court issued its opinion on the merits. By a 12–3 vote, the court found that by training, arming, equipping, financing, and supplying the contra forces, the United States had violated its obligations under international law not to use force against another state and not to intervene in the internal affairs of another state.[101] Nevertheless, Congress thereafter authorized $100 million in new aid.[102]

Walter Hoffman, the executive director of the World Federalist Association, a national organization founded in the aftermath of World

War II to advocate the abolition of war through just and enforceable world law, called me to pursue a case against the U.S. government for violating the World Court decision. I was interested, as was the CCR. The World Federalist Association, however, clearly had no standing to bring this lawsuit; in a series of cases, the Supreme Court had rejected standing for generalized injuries suffered by all citizens.[103]

But Benjamin Linder and other American citizens who lived or worked in the war zones of northern Nicaragua were suffering grave, particularized injury from their government's violation of the World Court's decision and order. I had met with Jim Goff, the president of an organization called the Committee of U.S. Citizens Living in Nicaragua (CUSCLIN), and he had expressed an interest in the lawsuit the World Federalists now wanted to bring. The CCR sent Reed Brody, a human rights lawyer who had written an important and well-publicized report on contra atrocities in Nicaragua, to meet with potential plaintiffs who lived or worked in northern Nicaragua. CUSCLIN found him five individuals who agreed to be plaintiffs to bring this challenge to U.S. policy. One of them was Ben Linder.

Linder met with Brody and drew a map of El Cua and Bocay, marking X's where the contras had attacked in the past few months. The map was full of X's. "[O]f all the people that I could identify, Ben was the furthest out and the least protected," said Brody.[104]

Before Brody left Nicaragua, Linder signed an affidavit in which he prophesied that if the United States continued to support the contras in violation of the World Court decision, "I will be subject to personal danger to life and limb as I carry out my work." Using legal parlance, Linder wrote that "I may suffer irreparable physical harm as a result of the unlawful activities of the U.S. government."

On September 23, 1986, we filed the new case, entitled *Committee of U.S. Citizens Living in Nicaragua v. Reagan (CUSCLIN)*, together with a motion for a preliminary and permanent injunction. We included the affidavits of Ben Linder and the other plaintiffs. In addition to CUSCLIN and five American citizens living in Nicaragua, the plaintiffs included the World Federalist Association, the like-minded Campaign for UN Reform, and a number of Nicaraguan solidarity groups whose work was being hindered by the contra attacks. Our complaint alleged that (1) the executive branch was violating Article 94 of the UN Charter, which mandates obedience to a decision of the World Court, and customary international law; and (2) that the executive branch had violated the Fifth Amendment by providing aid to the contras, whose policy and practice was to kill, wound, kidnap, and detain civilians, thus threatening the lives and liberty of plaintiffs living in Nicaragua. Moreover, we alleged that the imminent threat to the American citizen plaintiffs was arbitrary and unreasonable in that it violated Article 94 of the UN Charter and customary international law as set forth by the World Court (ICJ) decision.[105] Not only did the American plaintiffs living in Nicaragua have standing, but also the threat to their individual constitutional rights would make it more difficult for a court to dismiss the case as presenting a political question since, as one court had stated "an area concerning foreign affairs that has been uniformly found appropriate for judicial review is the protection of individual or constitutional rights from government action."[106] We requested bold relief: the enjoining of a major foreign policy initiative supported by both the president and a majority of Congress.

From a legal perspective, *CUSCLIN* was probably the most utopian case we brought in our whole Central American litigation campaign. "I didn't think we would win," said one lawyer, Reed Brody, "but I thought we were right."[107] Of the several cases we had brought, this one most directly attacked the entire U.S. policy toward Nicaragua. To say that the case would be an "uphill battle," as I conceded at the press conference announcing the suit's filing, was a serious understatement.

A little before the *CUSCLIN* case was filed, I attended a panel discussion at the annual meeting of the American Society of International Law on whether the president could violate international law. I asked the panel whether Congress and the president, even acting jointly, should be constitutionally permitted to violate basic norms of international law. A very well-known professor of international law answered that he doubted that any court would hold to the contrary in my lifetime.[108]

For more than a century, the federal courts had given effect to congressional statutes even when those statutes conflicted with U.S. treaty obligations or customary international law.[109] Here Congress had enacted a statute explicitly providing aid to the contras; precedent required the courts to give effect to that statute despite the UN Charter and the World Court decision. Nevertheless, like our nineteenth-century abolitionist forebears, we relied heavily on fundamental principles of justice to argue for an exception to the general rule, one in which fundamental norms of international law would be binding on Congress. We also, however, relied on the constitutional framers' intent that Congress not be accorded the power to violate fundamental principles of international law.

In fact, we had rejected a possible technical ground for arguing the case. In appropriating the $100 million, Congress had not directly mentioned the World Court decision. We might have argued that Congress's appropriation had to be construed consistently with our treaty obligation to obey the ICJ. Indeed, a leading human rights casebook later questioned why we did not take that approach.[110] However, both we and our clients wanted to challenge directly the U.S. policy violating the ICJ decision, and we did not believe that narrowing our claim would significantly help our chances of success; it might only cloud the issue.

In the district court argument before Judge Charles Richey, the government argued that the plaintiffs lacked standing and that the suit presented a nonjusticiable political question. The defendants asserted that the plaintiffs were simply standing in the shoes of the Nicaraguan government and thus that the whole case should be dismissed. I countered by arguing that the plaintiffs' *own* lives were in danger.

Judge Richey, while impressed with the "extensive and learned briefing" on the issues (a clear indication that we were going to lose), dismissed the case on February 6, 1987, as presenting a nonjusticiable political question.[111] Noting that the court had "never shirked its duty to render decisions that make bureaucrats more than ordinarily squeamish,"[112] the opinion identified the potential for "embarrassment"[113] to the political branches as justifying invocation of the political-question doctrine. The distinction between judicial decisions that simply make bureaucrats "squeamish" and those that present "embarrassment" was not to be gleaned from Judge Richey's opinion. While the court was "painfully aware that plaintiffs claim to be in danger because of actions taken by the United States . . . the proper forum for airing these grievances is not their Court but the Congress and the voting booth."[114] Indeed, the vigorous and widespread opposition to U.S. intervention in Central America eventually did convince Congress to end aid to the contras, but it would come too late for Benjamin Linder.

We appealed. While the appeal was pending, the danger to Benjamin Linder increased. In December 1986, Linder moved permanently from the relative safety of Managua to El Cua. He resigned from INE to work full time on a model project, the Cua-Bocay Development Project, in which the construction of hydroelectric plants in the region was to serve as the driving force to development of the region. Linder and his coworker Mira Brown had big dreams for the project, thinking that it could serve as a model not just for Nicaragua but for development in the Third World in general. Ben wrote home to his parents:

> Here in El Cua I'm faced with very challenging work, a dismal social life, unforeseen as well as foreseen problems, and more responsibility than I ever imagined I'd have. Also, and most important, I have the good fortune to start one of the most exciting hydroelectric projects perhaps in the world. The technical excitement is part of it but really only a part. The concept of social development on a revolutionary context, especially in the outback, is an amazing idea. Key in all plans for Cua-Bocay is where the electricity is. Key in that is me.[115]

Ben's dream was to teach people to build and operate their own power plants, which would spur other development such as machine shops, a lumber mill, and a rice-processing plant. He wanted to empower people, to give them control over their lives. In El Cua, once the plant was operational, Ben and his coworker Don Mcleay taught classes to poor Nicaraguans to become electricians. Linder told a visiting journalist a story that expressed his dream:

> One day it was very hot, so I went down to the stream behind my house with my calculator and my papers. A peasant woman comes down, takes the laundry out and starts washing it on the rocks. Behind, the horses are grazing. I started thinking about my work in Nicaragua. I try to explain as much as I can about what we're doing. But until those people from the community get so they can repeat what I do, not have someone from Managua repeat it, or a gringo like me, then the work isn't done. That poor peasant woman washing her clothes on the rocks, what will it take for her kid to be the one sitting by that stream, fiddling with his calculator? It's far away, maybe, but it's imaginable.[116]

To dream what to most people is unimaginable and to attempt to make it reality is the essence of a revolutionary. Giving people control over their lives "was his idea," his father claimed "of the revolution."[117]

In El Cua, Linder lived in the house of Cosme Castro, an elderly man who had fought with the Nicaraguan patriot Sandino in the 1930s. Linder slept on a cot in a partitioned room. The house had no running water; drinking water had to be saved from rainwater or carried from the river and boiled. Cooking was done on a smoky wood stove. But, despite the hardships and dangers, Linder enjoyed his life in El Cua. He was dedicated to his work and inspired by the commitment and hope of the Nicaraguans with whom he lived and worked.

As in Managua, his role in the community transcended his technical job as an engineer. He was known by virtually everyone, not only as a result of his work with the project but also as a neighbor. The children, in particular, came to love him. He juggled tomatoes or lemons or whatever came to hand, fascinating children who had never before seen a juggler. Just three weeks before his death, the local doctor asked him to assist in a measles vaccination campaign, so Linder dressed as a clown covered with measles and rode his unicycle through El Cua followed by dozens of screaming children. Shouting "Death to measles!," he went from house to house and told people to come to the health clinic the next day for vaccinations.

March 1987 brought a large number of contra attacks to the El Cua-Bocay region. Backed by U.S. money, the contras were making a desperate effort to establish a permanent foothold in northern Nicaragua. On March 19, 1987, the contras raided El Cedro, a nearby agricultural settlement. This was the third attack on El Cedro. The community fled while four men defended the settlement. All four were killed. One of them was Don Luis, a friend of Ben's who had worked with him on the hydroelectric plant. The contras retreated, but not before burning down the medical clinic and the grain and coffee warehouse.

Less than a week later, on March 24, 70 to 100 contras tried to destroy the hydroelectric plant in El Cua while Linder was away in Managua. The plant was successfully defended by ten militiamen and Oscar Blandon, the chief plant operator and Linder's closest friend, but Blandon's house was practically destroyed by the contras. When Linder returned to El Cua the next day he asked first about Oscar's family and the plant and then the "next most important thing . . . Oscar's guitar," which, unfortunately, the contras took.[118]

His friend Don Mcleay left El Cua on March 24, in large part because he felt it was too dangerous to continue. But Linder and his coworker Mira Brown stayed. While they, too, must have thought of leaving, his brother, John, said of him, "I think Ben felt that all around him Nicaraguans were taking greater risks than he."[119] At the beginning of April, twenty-four people, including thirteen local militiamen from

El Cua, were killed while guarding a nearby road construction site. One of them was the son of Don Cosme, in whose house Ben was living.

A journalist asked Linder about the wisdom of continuing his work. Linder responded that the contras had said that everyone working on the hydroelectric project was a target for assassination and that's when he started carrying a gun for protection. "Sometimes I think about dying and the friends I've had who have died," but he then shrugged and said no more.[120]

On April 21, 1987, Linder and Mira Brown drove to San Jose de Bocay to begin work building a small hydroelectric plant for that community. Bocay was where the road ended, with only jungle villages to the north. The area had been the scene of much fighting between the contras and Sandinistas, and the atmosphere exuded fear. Brown and Linder selected a small stream about a mile from Bocay to start building a small weir to measure the water flow of the stream; Ben began work, and Mira returned to El Cua for more supplies.

On April 28, Linder and his team of six Nicaraguan were ambushed by the contras as they started work. Linder, Sergio Hernandez, a skilled mason, and Pablo Rosales were killed in the attack; the other workers escaped. Hernandez, thirty-three years old, who had moved to Bocay because of repeated contra attacks, was killed by a bullet wound to the head. He was survived by his widow and their seven children, ranging in age from ten months to thirteen years. Rosales, an unarmed member of the construction team, received multiple wounds and was then fatally stabbed in the chest.

While the contras claimed that Linder and his coworkers were killed in a firefight, the evidence suggests otherwise. An autopsy done by Nicaraguan military doctor concluded that Linder died from a gunshot wound to the head fired at very close range—a conclusion concurred in by two prominent U.S. medical examiners, Dr. Michael Baden, of New York, and Dr. Werner Spitz, of Detroit, who reviewed the autopsy. It appeared that Linder was first immobilized by injury to his legs and arms and then killed by a gunshot wound to his head. As his father, Dr. David Linder, a pathologist with more than thirty years' experience, concluded, the contras "blew his brains out at point-blank range as he lay wounded. . . . This is murder."[121]

We at the CCR and the country as a whole were shocked by Linder's death, the first of an American civilian killed in the contra war. I had taken an academic approach to the *CUSCLIN* case. Ben Linder's death reminded me that the harm caused by our government's policies was not merely the abuse of process or disregard of abstract formalities.

Linder's death refocused national attention on the contras' human rights abuses. Every major newspaper in the country and many around the world ran stories on the ambush. The day after Linder's killing, six members of Congress, led by Representative Les AuCoin, sent a letter to Secretary of State George Shultz calling for an investigation of the attack and a judgment on whether to extradite the killers.[122] Congressman Peter Kostmayer called Linder "a national hero, the kind of person of whom our country can be very, very proud."[123] Congressman Tom Downey said that Linder's "death is a textbook example of that assassination manual," referring to the CIA's instructions to the contras on how to "neutralize" Sandinista supporters.[124] Mayor Andrew Young, of Atlanta, compared Ben Linder to civil rights workers in the South and said "the intensity of his dedication is really one of the finest examples of the prophetic and service tradition of Judaism in the world today."[125]

The Linder family, the CCR, and many Americans opposed to U.S. aid to the contras placed responsibility for Ben's death on the Reagan administration. David Linder testified before Congress that "I consider the United States government and its effectors—the contras—guilty of this crime. This was not an accidental result of U.S. policy; it is the essence of the U.S. policy, as Ben witnessed before he himself was killed."[126]

The administration attempted to shift the blame for his death onto Linder himself. White House spokesman Marlin Fitzwater said that the hundreds of American volunteers working in Nicaragua "certainly understand that they put themselves in harm's way."[127] Vice President Bush also expressed regret but noted that Linder was "on the other side."[128] Supporters of Washington's policy justified him as a "legitimate target" and asked, "Was he a Communist?"

On April 30, 1987, Ben Linder was buried in Matagalpa, a small city north of Managua. The funeral procession included Nicaragua's president, Daniel Ortega, walking arm in arm with Linder's parents, David and Elisabeth, followed by family members, friends, clowns from the Nicaraguan National Circus, and thousands of other Nicaraguans and foreigners. Linder was laid to rest in a Matagalpa cemetery with a tombstone inscribed with a unicycle and the phrase "Internacionalista Benjamin Ernest Linder." Above the unicycle is a circle of juggling balls, a dove, and the inscription "La luz que encendió brillará para siempre" (the light he lit will shine forever).

Several weeks later, a packed congressional hearing took place in which the tensions and emotions occasioned by Linder's death overflowed. Assistant Secretary of State Elliott Abrams told the subcommittee that Linder should have known not to go into a "combat zone." In a stormy exchange with one congressman, he said that Linder "was in the middle of a group of armed men, which would be an appropriate target."[129] Michael testified on behalf of the CCR that Nicaragua's economic infrastructure was not a legitimate target of war. Congressman Connie Mack, a right-wing Republican, launched into an abusive tirade against Elisabeth Linder. "I just cannot understand how you can use grief that I know you feel, use it to politicize this situation. . . . I guess the reason I find this so difficult is that I don't want to be tough on you, but I really feel you have asked for it."[130] Elisabeth Linder, a small woman sitting a few feet from Mack, quietly answered, "That was about the most cruel thing you could have said."[131]

The CCR decided to make an emergency appeal in the *CUSCLIN* case to emphasize the danger civilians faced in Nicaragua. Predictably, the court declined to hear our emergency petition. In November 1987, I argued the *CUSCLIN* appeal before a liberal panel of the D.C. Court of Appeals: Circuit Judges Aubrey Robinson and Abner Mikva[132] and District Judge Gordon, sitting by designation. In a scholarly forty-six page opinion issued early in 1988, Judge Mikva, a liberal internationalist, dismissed our claims. The Court of Appeals did not hide behind the political question doctrine, as the district court had done.[133] The court was, in fact, particularly troubled by the political-question dismissal of the individual plaintiffs' Fifth Amendment claims. Judge Mikva noted, "[a]s Appellants point out, the Supreme Court has repeatedly found that claims based on such rights are justiciable, even if they implicate foreign policy decisions."[134]

As expected, the court followed precedent in finding that the congressional violation of a treaty commitment or rule of customary international law by funding the contras was binding, as a matter of domestic law, on the judiciary. We had, however, sought to create an exception to this precedent by arguing that certain *fundamental* norms of international law are binding on both Congress and the president. The Nuremberg judgment rejecting the Nazis' argument that they were only obeying domestic law, the holding of the Second Circuit, in *Filar-*

tiga v. Pena-Irala,[135] that foreign officials could be sued in U.S. courts for violations of certain fundamental norms, and the views of the framers of the Constitution all seemed to require that certain international legal norms be accorded constitutional stature that ought to be binding on Congress.

The D.C. Circuit was sympathetic to this argument. It agreed that "if Congress and the President violate a peremptory norm (or jus cogens), the domestic legal consequences are unclear."[136] The court expanded on this idea:

> Such basic norms of international law as the proscription against murder and slavery may well have the domestic legal effect that appellants suggest. That is, they may well restrain our government in the same way that the Constitution restrains it. If Congress adopted a foreign policy that resulted in the enslavement of our citizens or of other individuals, that policy might well be subject to challenge in domestic court under international law. Such a conclusion was indeed implicit in the landmark decision in *Filartiga v. Pena-Irala.*[137]

Ultimately, though, the court concluded that the obligations created by Article 94 of the UN Charter and customary international law had not reached the stature of fundamental or peremptory norms of international law.[138] Finally, the court of appeals found that governmental recklessness could give rise to a constitutional tort but that, in the foreign policy context, the standard for finding reckless conduct was very high—and we had not met it.[139]

This foolhardy, radical case brought by organizations of mostly aging post–World War II international government types and American citizens living in Nicaragua was not particularly newsworthy. Most of the coverage followed the lead of the *New York Times* in describing the ICJ decision as purely "hortatory" and unenforceable. *CUSCLIN* clearly had only a very limited impact on the movement to end contra aid.

CUSCLIN, unlike *Reagan v. Wald, Dellums,* and *Beacon Products,* directly challenged an important norm of current U.S. constitutional law—that the U.S. government can do anything it wants abroad without being subjected to judicial scrutiny. I may have been fighting a losing battle, but at least we forced the circuit court in *CUSCLIN* to focus on our serious constitutional and international law claims and not primarily on procedural issues such as standing, ripeness, or mootness.

But, as Walter Hoffman, then-executive director of the World Federalists, pointed out, "the main reason for doing the case was for the future." Although we lost the case, we did receive a serious, analytical opinion that left hope for the future. The court had accepted our argument that fundamental norms of international law could potentially restrain the president and Congress[140] and that individual rights challenges to U.S. foreign policy should not be dismissed as political questions. The *CUSCLIN* case is one precedent from our era that a future court might use to restrain U.S. government actions in violation of international law.

While *CUSCLIN* was wending its way through the appeal process, we met with the Linder family and decided to sue the contra leadership for damages for Linder's death. Linder's brother, a militant activist, strongly urged us to also sue the U.S. government for complicity in Ben's murder. While we were sympathetic to his argument and believed that U.S. officials should be held responsible, we knew that suing the government was the quickest way to get the case dismissed on political-question or some procedural ground. So we convinced the family to sue only the contras.

I was impressed by the Linders' quiet determination to continue their son's work, both in building a hydroelectric plant in Cua-Bocay and in opposing American aid to the contras in the United States. While David Linder was retired from the practice of medicine and had been looking forward to a more peaceful, relaxed life, he and Elisabeth and their son, John, and daughter, Miriam took upon themselves the task of raising hundreds of thousands of dollars to ensure that the project Ben had started would be completed. They toured the country, speaking in dozens of cities to publicize the circumstances of Linder's work and death. These speaking tours raised thousands of dollars to complete Ben's project and reached thousands with the message urging opposition to aid for the contras. The CCR set up a Ben Linder Justice Committee to help educate the public about Ben Linder's life and death and the lawsuit filed by his family against the contras for killing him.

The Linders believed a lawsuit could force the contras and the U.S. government to testify in court as to what really had happened on April 28, 1987 and why. Equally important, it was a very useful adjunct to the Linders' political work. But they knew, Elisabeth Linder said, that the lawsuit "wasn't going very far."

After meeting with the Linders, Michael and I decided we needed a more in-depth investigation of the circumstances of Ben's death. Michael sought to obtain cooperation from the U.S. Embassy in Honduras so that we could interview the contras involved in Linder's death, but they stonewalled. Embassy officials refused to help arrange interviews with the contras who killed Linder and denied the CCR's request to interview the embassy personnel who had debriefed them.[141] The embassy refused to provide CCR investigators with any notes it had prepared concerning interviews with the contra attackers or with the contras' sketches of the attack site. When the family made a formal request for these materials, the State Department claimed it had destroyed them.

Michael arranged for Beth Stephens, an American lawyer working in Nicaragua who had known Linder, and Lois Wessel, another American living in Nicaragua, to gather information about Linder's death. Stephens interviewed various former contras but could obtain almost no useful information. She also made repeated unsuccessful efforts to obtain from the Sandinista government or military the results of their own investigations and the names of former contras who had information about the attack.

Because of the paucity of information as to who ordered the April 28 attack and the reasons behind it, and our general inclination to use the lawsuit to expose the contras' policy and practice of killing civilians, we drafted a broad complaint against the contra leadership. We claimed that Benjamin Linder was wounded in the attack and then tortured and executed at close range by the contras. Since we were interested in suing not the individual contra soldiers who carried out the attack but, rather, the higher-up contra leadership, we had to tie the leaders to the killing. We did so by alleging that the torture and execution of Linder was carried out in compliance with the contras' policies, approved and authorized by the defendant leadership, of executing wounded and defenseless persons; or, alternatively, that these leaders had knowledge of this widespread contra practice and failed to take steps to stop it. We also alleged that the leadership authorized the attack that killed Benjamin Linder and approved or at least did nothing to prevent attacks on civilians and development projects like the one that killed Benjamin Linder. We sued for wrongful death, battery, the intentional infliction of emotional distress, and violations of the Geneva Convention.[142] We sued both the contra organizations and their top leaders.

On April 20, 1988, almost a year after Linder's death, we filed the lawsuit, titled *Linder v. Calero Portocarrero*, against the contras, seeking $50 million. As Elisabeth Linder said, "The best way to remember Ben is by changing the policy that killed him. We will do that by bringing his killers to justice, by ending—once and for all—the war of terror that the U.S. government has carried out against Nicaragua." She also announced that she and her husband would soon travel to Nicaragua carrying $250,000 contributed by thousands of people to keep Linder's work alive. The filing of the complaint received significant media attention, with articles appearing in the *New York Times*, *USA Today*, and other papers around the country.

The defendants moved to dismiss, and the court ordered a stay to discovery, which meant that our attempt to question the defendants was on hold. The contras were represented by John Kirkpatrick, whose main claim to fame was that he was the son of Reagan's ambassador to the United Nations, Jeane Kirkpatrick. Michael and I went to Miami to argue the case before Judge Stanley Marcus, a former U.S. prosecutor. The argument was lengthy, focusing primarily on whether the case should be dismissed as a nonjusticiable political question.

Judge Marcus took his time ruling on the motion to dismiss, and in October 1989 we received our first big break in the case. Maritza Peña Cortes, a Nicaraguan journalist writing a book on the war, had interviewed a former high-level contra named Fermin Cardenas Olivas, whose pseudonym was "Cain," on tape. Cain fought with the contras from 1981 until 1988 and was a member of the Juan Castro Regional Command, the command that killed Linder. At the time Linder was murdered, Cain claimed to have been head of operations for the regional command.

Cain stated that Enrique Bermudez, a key defendant and the commander of the contras' armed forces and head of its Strategic Command, directly ordered Linder's murder. Bermudez and the Strategic Command ordered Linder murdered because they said he was a Sandanista adviser and his murder would be a defeat for the Sandinistas.

Cain, who appeared quite knowledgeable regarding the circumstances of Linder's murder and who claimed to have knowledge of the whole plan of attack, also stated that Linder was caught alive and then killed before he fired a shot. Cain also stated in the interview that, upon the return of the contra unit that conducted the ambush, its leader, "Mapachin," had been congratulated by the defendant Enrique Bermudez, who gave him a reward of approximately 2,500 Honduran lempiras for having killed Linder. We immediately amended our complaint to allege not only that the contra leadership had ordered the attack and that the contras had a policy and practice of killing civilians but that the defendant Bermudez had directly ordered the attack with *the intent* of killing Benjamin Linder and stopping his development project. We also asked for reargument to address this new allegation, which in our minds was a bombshell, because for the first time we could directly tie the defendants to Linder's murder.

It was decided that I should travel to Nicaragua as soon as possible and attempt to reinterview Cain and, if possible, get a sworn affidavit. On December 12, 1989, I flew to Managua with Cain's transcribed interview in my briefcase.

Upon my arrival in Managua, I met with Maritza, the journalist who had interviewed Cain. She agreed to vigorously attempt to interview other former contras to try to corroborate Cain's statement. I then attempted to interview Cain.

Cain was then living in a small mountainous area in the war zone known as Plan de Grama, in the northern jungle area of Nicaragua. There was no way to get there by road, so the plan was for the Nicaraguan military to fly me by helicopter to interview Cain. The military headquarters in charge of that zone was in Matagalpa. Ani Whibey, a fifty-year-old American nun who had been a friend of Linder's, volunteered to drive me in her jeep to Matagalpa. She and other friends had been trying to firm up plans for my flight with the Sandinista military officials, but nothing had materialized.

We arrived in Matagalpa and finally got word that a helicopter would take me the next day into the mountainous area where Cain lived. The next day, when I arrived at the home of the colonel in charge, he informed me that the trip was not possible, because they had just learned that Cain had been killed by the contras in an ambush on December 1, 1989, less than two weeks before I had arrived in Nicaragua.

Driving back to Managua with Ani Whibey, I asked her about her humanitarian work in northern Nicaragua, which led her to travel roads that were often mined and rife with ambushes and other dangers. Was she worried about her safety? She calmly answered that she knew that Jesus Christ was watching out for her and wouldn't let anything happen. As a nonreligious Jew with only a morsel of spirituality, I was deeply affected by her answer. Ani's faith in her God enabled her to do things to help people that I could never do because I feared the danger.

Back in Pittsburgh, I submitted an affidavit to the court describing my trip. Judge Marcus accepted our amended complaint and granted our motion to reargue the motion to dismiss. Michael and I again tromped down to Miami. But it was to no avail.

In September 1990, more than two years after we filed our lawsuit, Judge Marcus dismissed our complaint. In a lengthy opinion, Marcus held that the Linders' complaint presented a political question. The crux of his opinion claimed that there were no "discoverable and manageable standards to adjudicate the nature and methods by which the contras choose to wage war in Nicaragua."

> The realm of issues determinable by a court or jury with reference to Florida tort law simply does not include issues such as these arising out of conflict between belligerents in the midst of a foreign civil war. Among other things, we would be required to discern between military, quasi-military, industrial, economic and other strategic targets, and rule upon the legitimacy of targeting such sites as hydroelectric plants on Nicaraguan soil in the course of civil war. We would be called upon to inquire into whether and under what circumstances Defendants were justified in targeting such sites with knowledge that civilians, or paramilitary or military personnel would be present at the sites. Indeed, we would be called upon to discern between military and paramilitary personnel guarding a strategic dam and engineers building or maintaining such a site during time of war. In short, we would necessarily be required to measure and carefully assess the use of the tools of violence and warfare in the midst of a foreign civil war. Nothing in Florida's law of torts adequately prepares us for so daunting an undertaking.[143]

By the time Judge Marcus dismissed the case, the political situation in Nicaragua had fundamentally changed. The Nicaraguan people, all of whom were tired of war and many of whom were weary of the Sandinistas' authoritarian style, voted for the opposition candidate, Violeta Chammorro, in a free national election. The Sandinistas turned over governmental power to Chammorro as they had promised to do, and the contra war ended, except for some small pockets of contras who continued to fight.

The Nicaraguan revolution had suffered a devastating defeat, which dramatically changed the nature of the anti-interventionist movement's support work and the CCR's political focus. We felt as if the United States intervention in Nicaraguan had won: the U.S.-supported contra war and economic embargo had so worn down the Nicaraguan people and economy that a majority were willing to abandon the revolution for peace.

Many internationalists left Nicaragua over the next few years, and interest in that country among American progressives and the U.S. government quickly waned, though the Linders' campaign of continuing their son's work providing electricity to rural Nicaraguan communities kept going. One key motivation for the lawsuit—to use it as a tool for seeking an end to aid to the contras—was no longer relevant. But, for Michael and me, getting at the truth of why and how Ben was killed, forcing the contras and the U.S. government to be held accountable, and trying to get justice for Ben's family all were still very important.

We appealed the district court's dismissal of the case. Michael argued the case in the Eleventh Circuit Court of Appeals. At oral argument, he kept hammering away at the narrow allegation in our amended complaint based on the "Cain" interview: the defendants, acting from Florida, directly targeted and ordered the murder of a U.S. citizen working in Nicaragua. That allegation, Michael persistently argued, could not constitute a nonjusticiable political question because, even during wartime, the torture and summary execution of civilians or prisoners was strictly prohibited.

The Eleventh Circuit Court of Appeals, usually a very conservative court, agreed with us. On June 27, 1992, more than five years after Linder was killed, the Court of Appeals issued its decision reversing the district court. While the appellate judges concluded that the district court had properly dismissed our broad claims of contra violations, they focused on Michael's argument that our narrow allegation that Linder was targeted, tortured, and executed while he was a noncombatant civilian in the process of constructing a dam could be resolved in court.[144] The court held that, "contrary to the district court's conclusion, there is no foreign civil war exception to the right to sue for tortious conduct that violates the fundamental norms of the customary laws of war."[145] The court cited our century-old Supreme Court precedent for that proposition. Moreover, the court found that the political question doctrine was inapplicable because our narrow allegation challenged "neither the legitimacy of the United States foreign policy toward the contras, nor does it require the court to pronounce who was right and who was wrong in the Nicaraguan civil war. On the contrary, the complaint is narrowly focused on the lawfulness of the defendants' conduct in a single incident."[146]

We were ecstatic. While the court had sidestepped thorny jurisdiction issues that we had spent hundreds of hours analyzing and briefing, such as whether we could sue directly under international law and the Geneva Convention, and had focused on our narrow allegations under Florida tort law, we were back in business at least against the individual contra leaders. (The court did dismiss our allegations against the contra organization.) And the appellate court had not precluded our raising our broad claims that the contras deliberately attacked civilians but, as we read the opinion, had simply required that any such evidence be offered to prove that the defendants had ordered Linder's murder.

We refocused on proving our case. The obstacles to getting at the truth were formidable. John Kirkpatrick, the defendants' lawyer, was uncooperative: at one point he didn't even show up to a status conference before Judge Marcus, claiming that he was changing offices, had no answering machine, and was living at his parents' house. Michael, who had flown to Miami to attend the conference, was astounded by Kirkpatrick's no-show. Michael submitted an affidavit claiming that he was "simply tired of chasing Mr. Kirkpatrick and angry at his dissembling" and requested attorneys' fees, which the judge awarded us.

Several of the defendants, including the key defendant, Bermudez, died while the case was proceeding, and we never got a chance to depose them. When, after years of delay, we finally got responses to our requests for documents, the defendants answered that every document in their possession had been destroyed. When we deposed the defendant Calero, he had virtually no useful information to provide. Our investigators in Nicaragua turned up almost nothing of much value.

Our last hope for evidence lay hidden in the files of various U.S. government agencies. In 1993, we requested the thousands of pages on files at the CIA, FBI, National Security Agency, Defense Department, and State Department that were relevant to our lawsuit. The government agencies refused outright to comply, and we had to get a district court judge to order compliance. Not until 1995 did we receive any documents, and those were either so heavily redacted as to be virtually use-less or incredibly meager, given what we knew the agencies had. For ex-ample, the National Security Agency acknowledged that it had exten-sive communication "intercepts" relevant to our case but still refused to release *any* information at all, claiming that the intercepts were all clas-sified for national security reasons. As Beth Stephens, who had left Nicaragua and was now working at the CCR in New York, wrote to the Linders in April 1995:

> What are they [the U.S. government] hiding and why? We would like pressure on the agencies to change their whole attitude and ap-proach to this case, to one which sees revealing the truth as the cen-tral goal.

By 1995, the lawyers unfortunately concluded that we had virtually no realistic chance of winning the case and wrote to the Linders asking them to think about whether it was time to drop the lawsuit. I carefully informed Judge Marcus that we were evaluating the evidence and de-ciding whether we could proceed. The Linders felt strongly that we should continue as long as there was some chance of proving our case. We agreed that, as long as there was some, albeit small chance of getting at the truth, we should pursue it. So we decided to press hard on the one final avenue for getting information: our discovery requests against the U.S. government agencies.

As the case pressed inexorably forward at a snail's pace, the Lin-ders doggedly pursued their plan to continue Ben's work. Rebecca Leaf, a mechanical engineer who had been helped by Ben when she first arrived in Managua in 1984, volunteered to replace Ben on the project to bring electricity to San Jose de Bocay. She stayed after the Sandinistas' electoral defeat to continue work on the small hydroelec-tric plant. The Linders' Ben Linder Memorial Fund raised more than $800,000 to complete the project and to aid other small communities in Nicaragua. In May 1994, seven years after Ben's death, the Linder fam-ily attended the inauguration ceremony marking the completion of the San Bocay hydroelectric plant. The access to electric power has made it possible to fulfill another of Ben's dreams—constructing a rice milling machine that has enabled small farmers to get a higher price for their crops.

Unfortunately, our case in the end was unsuccessful. We spent many years litigating against the federal agencies, seeking the documents they had. After several appeals, some court victories, and some defeats—all on questions involving how much material agencies had to turn over—the court finally ordered the release of some thousands of pages of materials, but only if we paid $100,000 or so to cover the government's costs. We had nowhere near that kind of money, nor were we sanguine that the documents would turn up anything really useful. So we called it quits, accepted our legal defeat, and requested the court to dismiss our case.

The lawsuit was over, the San Jose de Bocay hydroelectric power plant built. Benjamin Linder remains in the memories of many Americans who sought to help the Nicaraguans construct a new society and defeat U.S. intervention. Some have named their children after him; others continue to view him as a role model; still other North Americans moved to El Cua to continue Ben's work.

At times, I still think of Linder's commitment and the terrible sadness and tragedy of his death, particularly when I am evaluating or questioning my own commitment. In September 1987, about five months after Linder was killed, Michael and I were invited to attend a conference on Nicaragua dedicated to his memory, in Portland, Oregon. In a very moving and spiritual ceremony, the conference participants adopted a Nicaraguan revolutionary tradition to remember the dead, repeating aloud, "Ben Linder presente" [Ben Linder is here]. I felt a stirring deep in my soul as if Linder actually were there that night.

Linder and I had dreamed of and attempted to do what was probably impossible—he to build a power plant in the most dangerous area in wartorn Nicaragua, I to challenge U.S. intervention in American courts. Linder's commitment was to work among the Nicaraguan people, to live their lives, to attempt to concretely help them, and, to risk danger in doing so. My commitment seemed almost inconsequential in comparison: I had poured hundreds of hours of pro bono legal work into cases, with the price of failure mainly a feeling of having wasted my time. The achievements of both of us, though, are likely to be measured not by the immediate success of our actions but by the long-term impact our work has on others who follow in our footsteps.

Reflecting on the time and energy I expended on aiding a revolutionary process in Nicaragua that ultimately failed, in representing a man who was killed before his dream could be realized, and in litigating cases that eventually lost in court, I am often comforted by a thought best expressed by a good friend I met in the course of my Nicaragua work. Gioconda Belli, a Nicaraguan poet, novelist, and Sandinista, has also thought much about the success and failure of a revolutionary process for which she, like Ben Linder, risked her life and has concluded that "I am the same Quixota who learned, through life's battles, that defeat can be as much of an illusion as victory."[147]

9
End of an Era
Fighting U.S. Action in Kosovo

ON APRIL 12, 1999, Representative Tom Campbell, a Republican from California's Fifteenth District, embarked on a quixotic campaign to enforce the Constitution of the United States. Despite the opposition of both the Republican and the Democratic leadership of the House of Representatives, Campbell had just introduced resolutions to force Congress to vote either to declare war against Yugoslavia or to terminate the air war that the United States and its NATO allies had been waging against that country since March 24. Campbell's constitutional campaign was to become the effort that he would be most proud of in his almost ten years as a member of Congress. My involvement with Campbell proved to be intellectually gratifying, yet also the most personally troubling of all the foreign policy cases I had litigated.

Campbell's actions were directly descended from the example of Ron Dellums' 1990 challenge to President George H. W. Bush's unilateral decision to go to war against Iraq. Like Dellums, Campbell was prepared to buck his party's leadership and ask the courts to decide the question of whether the president could go to war without congressional authorization.

Campbell and Dellums, though, were very different men. Dellums, an African American social activist with a master's in social work from Berkeley, represented the poor, overwhelmingly black Oakland district in which he had grown up. Campbell, a Stanford Law professor who had received a Ph.D. in economics from the University of Chicago and who had graduated near the top of his class at Harvard Law School, was first elected in 1988 to represent the predominantly white, hi-tech, Silicon Valley district anchored by San Jose. Dellums was a left-wing Democrat who believed in government spending and programs to help the poor, Campbell an iconoclast Republican, a social liberal and economic conservative, was pronounced by the National Taxpayers Union in 1999 the congressman "least willing to spend money."[1]

Both were very thoughtful men, but Dellums was a dynamic and emotional speaker who once, in the heat, of an argument challenged Newt Gingrich to "to call off the dogs." Campbell was a less than forceful lecturer: measured and refined, he was most comfortable speaking with a chalkboard behind him.[2] Both men were political mavericks, but Dellums combined his radical politics with a determined effort to work within the system, eventually rising to the chairmanship of the powerful House Armed Services Committee. Campbell's actions, such as his vote against Newt Gingrich's re-election for Speaker of the House, had left him fairly isolated within his party. But, when the war in Yugoslavia came, he was ready to take action.

Tom Campbell's life and career had been characterized by taking long shots, elevating principle over success. He grew up in Chicago, in an upper-middle-class neighborhood near Lake Michigan, the youngest of eight children in a devout Roman Catholic family. Campbell's father was a prominent New Deal democrat appointed to a federal judgeship by Franklin Roosevelt in 1940.

Campbell followed in his father's footsteps, voting for the Democratic presidential candidate, George McGovern, in 1972 and graduating from Harvard Law School in 1976. However, his studies in the conservative, free-market economics department at the University of Chicago, where he earned his B.A., M.A., and, at the age of twenty-eight, Ph.D., led him to become a Republican precinct captain in Mayor Richard Daley's Democratic Chicago. Campbell was terrified to tell his father about his conversion, but, when he found the courage to do so, his Catholic father was relieved. "[T]hat's okay," he responded. "You can become a Republican. Just don't become an Episcopalian."[3]

Campbell clerked for Supreme Court Justice Byron White and then served for several years in a variety of posts within the Reagan administration. In 1983, he became, at the age of thirty-one, a professor at Stanford University's Law School.

In 1988, despite his relative political inexperience and tender age of thirty-six, Campbell decided to run for Congress, a decision that perplexed his colleagues at Stanford, who enjoyed the good life of the academic elite. Campbell defeated an incumbent congressman in the primary (the only challenger to do so that year) and was elected to Congress. In 1992, his ambition led him to run for the U.S. Senate, but he was defeated in the Republican primary by a wealthy conservative, Bruce Herschensohn, who eventually lost to Barbara Boxer in the general election.

Campbell viewed his 1992 defeat in the Senate race as "a tremendously valuable religious experience." It was, he said, a turning point for him. "I was supposed to win in 1992," says Campbell. "By losing, I narrowly escaped great danger."[4]

A practicing Roman Catholic, Campbell was tempted to rail against God for dealing him a terrible defeat. He chose not to take that route and instead decided to see his defeat as a sign that God had a much better, grander, and more fulfilling role for him to play. He vowed that if he ever got back to Congress, he would do things differently than he had his first four years. Prominent among his regrets was his failure to join Congressman Dellums's lawsuit in 1990.

Campbell was determined, if he was elected again, not to value power over principle, to eschew trading votes or making compromises to stay in office—even if that meant not having much influence. He would see his role as a beacon on the Hill, a model of how a member of Congress should act. And, if he ever got a chance, he thought he would do things he had not done the first time—such as sue the President to stop an unconstitutional war.

One year after his U.S. Senate loss, Tom Campbell returned to the political arena and won election to the California State Senate. In 1995, he won a special election called when an incumbent died unexpectedly. He was back in Congress.

His role in Congress made him, in the words of one commentator, "a compulsive maverick."[5] In his soft-spoken, courteous, rationalistic manner, he frequently bucked the majority. He opposed the income tax, preferring a nationwide sales tax, opposed the "war on drugs," took a pro-choice stand, and was the only moderate Republican to sign onto a bill to investigate whether Clinton should be impeached at a time when the Republican leadership in the House was not ready to take that step. He joined only eight Republican Congressmen in voting against Newt Gingrich's reelection as Speaker in 1997. Campbell later explained, "I did not take an oath of office to be smart. I did not take an oath of office to be popular. But I did take an oath of office to uphold the Constitution."[6]

If Campbell does not look at polls to decide his position, neither does he engage in the usual mechanisms politicians use to be successful. He does not trade votes to get things accomplished, nor is he a backslapper. His Republican colleague Mark Sanford described Campbell as "one of the smartest and most principled folks I know on earth."[7] On the Democratic side, Congressman Barney Frank said of Campbell's efforts within the Republican party that "he is kind of swimming upstream. And he is not making much headway."[8]

In 1999, Campbell was contemplating giving up his House seat and running for the Senate—this time against the Democrat Dianne Feinstein—in 2000. He believed he could win, although virtually every California observer saw his defeat as certain. For Campbell to win the Senate race, declared the *California Journal*, "would redefine the term 'upset.'"[9]

But then came the bombing of Kosovo. The administration had accused the Serbs and the Yugoslav government of committing gross human rights violations against the Albanian population in Kosovo, which was a province of Serbia. At negotiations in Rambouillet, France, in February 1999, Slobodan Milosevic, the president of Yugoslavia, refused to accede to NATO's demands. The Clinton administration, backed by NATO, then decided to use military power to force the Serbs to cease committing human rights abuses against the Kosovars (the Albanians in Kosovo). On March 24, 1999, U.S.-led air strikes commenced against Kosovo and the rest of Yugoslavia. The U.S. Senate quickly endorsed the bombing, but the House of Representatives took no position.

Campbell decided he had one last major battle to fight before leaving the House—to uphold the constitutional principle that only Congress could declare war. As he worked on the resolutions he planned to introduce in Congress, he also began searching for a lawyer to handle the case he intended to file after Congress voted on his resolutions. While he admitted that he could be wrong on what the correct U.S. policy should be in Kosovo, he was certain that he was right that Clinton was violating the Constitution by launching and continuing the air war against Yugoslavia without congressional authorization. And he was confident that the courts would agree.

In early April, Campbell called an attorney named Lee Halterman. Campbell knew Halterman as one of Dellums's chief aides during the more than twenty years that Dellums served in Congress. Halterman, in turn, called Michael and me at the CCR.

Michael Ratner and I were not so confident. Campbell was right that, in the *Dellums* case, Judge Greene had held that members of Congress had standing to sue the president for going to war unilaterally. He was also correct that our constitutional claim appeared strong: this clearly seemed to be a war for constitutional purposes. Moreover, we also felt Campbell had a very strong argument under the 1973 War Powers Resolution, which required the president to seek explicit congressional approval if he kept American troops in hostilities for more than sixty days. American troops were clearly involved in hostilities, and it appeared that the air war would continue for more than sixty days.

However, we also knew that, in 1997, seven years after Judge Greene decided *Dellums*, the Supreme Court had held, in *Raines v. Byrd*, that members of Congress generally do not have standing to sue the president.[10] Members of Congress, the court said, do not suffer personal injuries when the president violates the Constitution, and the institutional injury to their roles as representatives is not sufficient to accord them standing.[11] Aggrieved legislators, the court felt, should use the political process to obtain relief. Given this, Michael and I worried that, though we might have a great case against the president, we could not get a court to hear our claim.

Raines v. Byrd, however, did contain an exception. The Court did not overrule an old case, *Coleman v. Miller*, which stood for the proposition that "legislators whose votes would have been sufficient to defeat (or enact) a specific legislative act have standing to sue if that legislative action goes into effect (or does not go into effect), on the ground that their votes have been completely nullified."[12] In short, if a member of Congress votes for a bill but the president refuses to give it effect, the congressperson can claim that the president has "completely nullified" his or her vote. Maybe we could fit within that exception if Campbell's resolution to withdraw the troops was passed by the House and the president refused to comply.

Michael and I were ambivalent about bringing Campbell's case. First, we doubted we could win on standing. We called Alan Morrison, the lawyer who had argued *Raines v. Byrd* for the members of Congress, and he thought a new case was futile. His view was that, if we somehow fell within the *Coleman* exception the Supreme Court would simply close the exception, and get rid of legislative standing completely. If he was right, then even if Congress voted the right way, we would accomplish nothing.

Moreover, the political situation facing us was grim. If we took this case, we would not be doing so in conjunction with a broad political movement. A major reason that Michael and I had undertaken the Central America and Persian Gulf litigation was that in both situations we were supporting a broad progressive and liberal movement that opposed U.S. policy. Even if we ultimately lost those cases, we believed we were helping the political movement that we supported.

Not so with respect to Kosovo. Michael and I opposed Clinton's bombardment of the Serbs, as did Tom Campbell. We thought it illegal and unwise: we were very suspicious of the United States's so-called humanitarian motives and did not believe that the air attack would actually help the Kosovars. We thought that the administration, particularly Secretary of State Madeline Albright, had been too trigger-happy and had abandoned real diplomacy in order to present Milosevic with an ultimatum. To us, the war against Yugoslavia represented U.S. imperial bullying in NATO and "humanitarian" garb.

But many progressives and most liberals, particularly human rights activists, argued that something had to be done to help the Kosovars against Milosevic's repression. They thought NATO's use of force necessary to cure an awful situation. Even the CCR was somewhat divided. Thus, if we took Campbell's suit, we would not be suing on behalf of a united progressive movement. Indeed, our clients would be predominantly conservative Republican congressmen who hated Clinton and his foreign policy. It was an odd position for Michael and me to be in.

Nonetheless, despite our ambivalence, Michael and I decided to represent Campbell, if—and this was a big if—he could get a favorable vote in the House against the war. We agreed with him on the basic principle that only Congress could authorize war. It was an important principle that we had a long history of litigating. We were outraged by Clinton's air war, even if many of our friends felt differently. And Campbell was a very compelling client, an intelligent, persuasive man of deep principle and convictions. If he was able to get support from the House, we were willing to go ahead.

But nobody, with the possible exception of Tom Campbell, felt that he could get and win a vote. The House Republican leadership was desperately trying to derail a vote in the House on Campbell's resolutions. They did not want to confront Clinton on these issues, nor did they want to endorse the air war. They wanted to do what Congress usually does—remain silent and then either criticize Clinton when things go bad or take some credit when things go well.

But Campbell refused to back down. When the leadership grumbled that he was putting them on the spot, Campbell replied, "As to putting folks on the spot, that's our job. . . . There's a reason the Constitution requires that Congress declare war . . . and if we go to war, it's with a lot of popular support."[13] And Campbell had a legal mechanism to force a vote: the War Powers Resolution provides that any resolution introduced in the House or Senate shall be given priority and voted on in a timely fashion by that body.[14]

The leadership was angry. Majority leader Dick Armey diplomatically described Campbell's refusal to back down: "He is a man of what seems at times unbending resolve."[15] Others were less circumspect. As one leadership aide put it, "Everybody's really ticked off at him about it."[16] But House Speaker Dennis Hastert reluctantly promised Campbell a vote on his resolutions.

But winning that vote seemed impossible. Everyone expected the House to overwhelmingly vote down Campbell's first resolution calling for a declaration of war, but a court would be unlikely to give that vote much significance. Everyone knew that most legislators, including Democrats, simply thought it unwise and unnecessary to declare war, even if they supported the war. A declaration of war has simply become an anachronism. The real test—or so we thought—was Campbell's second resolution, H. Con. Res. 82, directing the president, pursuant to the War Powers Resolution, to remove U.S. armed forces from their positions in connection with the present operations against the Federal Republic of Yugoslavia. In the twenty-five-year history of the War Powers Resolution, no Congress had ever directly voted to remove U.S. forces from overseas action. And this one was equally unlikely to do so.

The vote on the resolutions was scheduled for April 28. A few last-minute and important surprises occurred in the few days just before the vote. First, some members of Congress came up with a compromise resolution that required the president to receive specific authorization before any ground troops were introduced into Yugoslavia. Next, the Democrats decided to offer their own resolution—S. Con. Res. 21—which specifically authorized the president to conduct military air operations and missile strikes against the Federal Republic of Yugoslavia. Congressman Sam Gejdenson, the ranking Democrat on the House International Affairs Committee, introduced that resolution, which had already passed the Senate, obviously believing that the House would also adopt it.

Despite Democratic objections, all four resolutions were considered on April 28. Campbell and Congressman Dennis Kucinich, Democrat of Cleveland, worked all day long, attempting to convince legislators to vote against authorizing the war. The first three votes were fairly predictable. The House voted 427–2 not to declare war, resoundedly defeated Campbell's resolution to remove the troops by a vote of 290–139, and voted 249–180 to require President Clinton to obtain congressional authorization before using ground troops in Yugoslavia. Late at night they were still debating S. Con. Res. 21. I went to sleep, sad that Campbell had not prevailed, yet relieved that I was not going to have to work like crazy to file and litigate yet another losing case.

I was shocked when I was awakened after midnight by a call from Joel Starr, Campbell's legislative aide, telling me that the House had deadlocked on S. Con. Res. 21, 213–213 on a vote taken at almost midnight on April 28. The tie vote meant that the resolution had failed—the House had voted not to authorize Clinton's air war. Campbell and Kucinich and their supporters had pulled off a miracle.

The result was political confusion. The House had voted not to require the president to remove the troops but also not to authorize the president's use of troops. Apparently, many members were not willing to tell the president to get out of Yugoslavia, but neither did they want to go on record supporting the war.

Legally, we thought the situation was clearer: the War Powers Resolution and the Constitution both required the president to receive explicit authorization or else terminate the war. The defeat of S. Con. Res. 21 meant that Clinton did not have the required authorization. It also meant that Congress had acted to defeat a legislative act giving the president authorization. If the president acted on his own, anyway, we thought that maybe members of Congress would have standing to sue. A long-shot to be sure—but not hopeless.

Campbell was fired up and wanted us to file a complaint the next day. But that was impossible, as he quickly recognized. We had done some work drafting a complaint but had not expended a huge amount of energy on an issue that we felt was unlikely to go forward. Now, we cranked up our legal team and went to work around the clock. Lee Halterman, in California, was a great help; he combined tremendous political savvy with legal acumen. Joel Starr, an air force reserve and a lawyer from Campbell's office, helped enormously with the facts and researching legislation. Jim Klimaski, our local Washington, D.C., lawyer, provided good advice; Franklin Siegel, from CCR, did an excellent job assembling the facts and putting the documents together in a coherent fashion. Campbell read everything, was involved every step of the way, and gave us great feedback on the work we had prepared. Working as a team was both fun and a tremendous learning experience, totally unlike the mythological image of the heroic individual lawyer.

We filed our complaint on April 30, just two days after the historic vote. Campbell had rounded up seventeen plaintiffs to sign onto the complaint—fifteen Republicans and two Democrats. Among them were figures from the far right of the Republican Party—Bob Barr, Phil Crane, Dan Burton—who never had supported any of our war powers claims against Republican presidents. The two Democrats were Dennis Kucinich and Marcy Kaptur. Kucinich, a progressive Democrat whose economic policies are the opposite of those of the free-marketer Campbell, had made a remarkable comeback from electoral defeat and was the co-leader of the congressional plaintiffs, along with Campbell. The eldest son of a truck driver, Kucinich won election to the Cleveland City Council in 1969 at the age of twenty-three. By 1977, at the age of thirty-one, he was elected mayor of Cleveland, the youngest person ever elected mayor of a major American city. Kucinich courageously thwarted a plan to privatize the city owned electric system, incurring the wrath of the banks, which thereupon refused to extend the city credit. Cleveland thus became the first major American city to go into default since the Great Depression. Kucinich lost the 1979 mayoralty election[17] and spent the next fifteen years out of political office.

However, eventually the people of Cleveland recognized that Kucinich's principled stand had saved the city-owned electric company and the rate-payers a bundle of money, and in 1996 he was elected to Congress. Considered by many to be a very effective congressman who works with members from all political spectrums, Kucinich was an early, vigorous opponent of the NATO bombing.[18]

Marcy Kaptur was a welcome addition to our suit. She was the only member of Congress to have signed on to both the *Dellums* case and the *Campbell* case. She had voted against the Campbell resolution to withdraw the troops and had voted in favor of authorizing the Kosovo war. Indeed, it was unclear whether she had standing to sue, even if the court accepted the theory of the case. Kaptur was an incredibly principled, soft-spoken, and courageous women, and she wanted to join our lawsuit because she deeply believed that the Constitution requires Congress to authorize warfare—and Congress had not done so. She was the only plaintiff who was in favor of both the Kosovo war and the defense of constitutional principle.

Drawing a good judge to hear this case was critical. Lee Halterman and Jim Klimaski came up with a clever idea to file *Campbell v. Clinton* as a related case to *Dellums v. Bush* and thus have the case assigned to Judge Greene, who we thought would be sympathetic. I was dubious about whether we could do this, since *Dellums v. Bush* had ended more than eight years earlier. But Klimaski found the local rule for the federal district court of the District of Columbia and technically one could argue that the cases were still related. Unfortunately, Judge Greene was quite ill, and the case was reassigned to Judge Paul Friedman.

Friedman was a decent judge for us to draw. Fifty-five years old, Friedman had been a partner at the large D.C. law firm White & Case before being appointed to the federal bench in 1994. Jim Klimaski had known him when he was president of the D.C. Bar Association and had appeared before him in court. He found Freidman to be quite thoughtful and well reasoned, someone who was willing to stick his neck out a little bit.

Michael and I expected that Campbell would hold a press conference when we filed the complaint. While we did not think we could get the kind of major press attention that we had received when we filed the *Dellums* case, we were hopeful that maybe the case could draw media attention to the important constitutional and statutory questions we were raising. That, in our view, was probably the most important role of the case, since we did not really think we could win.

But Campbell said no to a press conference. He and the CCR sent out a press release, but Campbell did not want to appear to the court to be seeking publicity. I believe that he really expected to win, was dubious that we would get much press, and did not want to do anything that could hurt our chances in court. In any event, unlike the *Dellums* filing, the initiation of Campbell's lawsuit drew little mainstream media attention.

We wanted to move the case along fast, but, on a conference call the week after we filed, Congressman Campbell and our legal team decided not to seek a preliminary injunction. No court would ever grant an injunction ordering a halt to a war in progress. But we thought a court might declare that an ongoing war was unconstitutional and unlawful, a much less intrusive remedy. Congress and the president could then decide how to proceed with the military action in Kosovo. We wanted declaratory relief, not an injunction.

We decided to seek summary judgment and requested an expedited schedule. Lawyers use summary judgment to resolve a case when the facts are not in dispute. In this case, the facts were quite clear. Using the government's own sources, it was clear that the United States and the rest of NATO were engaged in a substantial military action that to all looked and acted like war. Siegel and Starr had gathered the materials showing that, by early May, the United States had committed more than 800 warplanes to Operation Allied Force, flown more than 20,000 sorties, and had dropped almost 10,000 bombs on almost 2,000 targets. And the air war was escalating.

The administration's attempt to deny that we were at war turned almost comical at times. The administration's official position was that we were involved in an "armed conflict" not a war, and top State Department officials, such as Undersecretary of State Thomas Pickering, refused to answer Campbell's question whether we were involved in hostilities in Yugoslavia, claiming not to know the legal consequences of answering that question. Nonetheless, military officials, as well as President Clinton, could not help referring to the "armed conflict" as war. When Major General Charles Wald, the operations director for the Joint Chiefs of Staff, referred to the Kosovo action as "war," he immediately realized his legal mistake and attempted to correct himself by stating that it was "combat."[19] President Clinton declared at a press conference that "the air *war* has accomplished quite a bit," but when reporters later asked his press secretary, Joe Lockhart, whether they should now refer to the Yugoslov conflict as an "air war," Lockhart replied, "No, you can use 'campaign' or 'conflict.'" His answer provoked laughter.[20]

On May 20, 1999, after two weeks of working furiously, we filed our motion for summary judgment with a supporting brief. We also filed an amended complaint, adding new plaintiffs and a motion for an expedited hearing schedule.

Our motion was timed fortuitously—just before the sixtieth day of bombing, when President Clinton would be required to end the military hostilities by the terms of the War Powers Resolution. On May 25, the War Powers alarm clock rang, and no one listened. Campbell did hold a major press conference with a number of other plaintiffs in the lawsuit, and some newspapers briefly noted the date. Meanwhile, the bombing continued to escalate, with no apparent end in sight.

Our brief in support of summary judgment made several key points. First, we emphasized the uniqueness of this case. Not since the Vietnam War and the passage of the War Powers Resolution had a president engaged in an armed conflict of such length, magnitude, and duration without the consent of Congress. Nor since that war had a president engaged U.S. armed forces in such massive and prolonged hostilities in the face of a congressional vote, explicitly on point, refusing him the authority to do so. Indeed, this would be the first time that a president had continued open offensive hostilities against another country for more than sixty days in flagrant disregard of the War Powers Resolution.

Second, we argued that the Constitution gave Congress the power to authorize war, and a war by any other name was still a war. The constitutional command that Congress authorize war cannot be negated by presidential semantics. As the prominent international law professor John Basset Moore once wrote:

> There can hardly be room for doubt that the framers of the Constitution, when they vested in Congress the power to declare war, never imagined that they were leaving it to the executive to use the military and naval forces of the United States all over the world for the purpose of actually coercing other nations, occupying their territory, and killing their soldiers and citizens, all according to his notions of the fitness of things, so long as he refrained from calling his action war or persisted in calling it peace.[21]

The Supreme Court had long ago reached the same conclusion when it stated that "no name" given to the Civil War by the president or Congress could change "the fact" that it constituted war.[22] So too had Judge Greene in *Dellums v. Bush*.[23] Even the administration had recognized, in a 1994 letter to Congress on the Haiti military action, that, where substantial U.S. forces attacked another country without the consent of the recognized government, leading to prolonged hostilities, inflicting substantial casualties on the enemy, and involving such "extreme" uses of force as sustained air "bombardment," the United States was engaged in "war" for constitutional purposes.[24]

We next argued that there could really be no dispute that the president was violating the War Powers Resolution. Even if the government disputed whether we were at "war" or merely in an "armed conflict," we clearly were involved in hostilities, which was the legal term that triggered the sixty-day period under the War Powers Resolution. While Secretary of State Madeline Albright had skirted Congressman Campbell's question as to whether we were involved in hostilities in Kosovo by merely stating that "there is a conflict going on," Secretary of Defense William Cohen had admitted the obvious in his testimony before the Senate: "We're certainly engaged in hostilities."[25] A violation of the War Powers Resolution could not be clearer.

Finally, we turned to justiciability. We argued that the members of Congress had standing to sue under the *Coleman* exception to the *Raines v. Byrd* holding. Furthermore, under the case law in the D.C. Circuit, including *Dellums v. Bush*, the question of whether the president was violating the Constitution and the War Powers Resolution did not present nonjusticiable questions. By deemphasizing the justiciability questions, we sought to turn the court's attention to the merits of our claim. We hope that the court would recognize the president's clear violation of the War Powers Resolution and the Constitution.

But the Justice Department was too clever for us. Instead of responding to our motion for summary judgment, the defendants filed a motion to dismiss our complaint that virtually ignored the constitutional war power issues. In addition, they asked the court to hold our summary judgment motion in abeyance and to first address their motion to dismiss. While we wanted both motions to be heard together, they did not even want to respond to our summary judgment motion.

In support of this procedural move, the Justice Department submitted a telling affidavit by Undersecretary of State Thomas Pickering. Pickering declared that for the court to even *hear* the merits of our case could create confusion in NATO, lead Milosevic to miscalculate U.S. resolve, worsen the plight of refugees, and "significantly hamper the ability of the United States to obtain a resolution to the crisis." If the dire consequences of merely giving our claims a fair hearing were not sufficient to frighten the court, Pickering added threats of an even more draconian fate that would befall the United States should the court rule in our favor. By ruling in our favor, the court would cede victory to Milosevic, split NATO, vindicate ethnic cleansing, and put the stability of southern Europe in grave jeopardy. We were disturbed by the implications of Pickering's bold assertions: they suggested that constitutional debate and the rule of law itself should be suspended at the political convenience of the administration as harmful to the Kosovo war efforts.

On May 26, Judge Friedman accepted the defendants' arguments, and we knew then that all hope for winning the case was gone. While initially Friedman had felt that both motions should be heard together, he had obviously been swayed by defendants' warnings of the terrible implications of a hearing on the merits. From that point on, it was virtually unthinkable that he would rule in our favor. The one consolation was that he had ordered an expedited schedule for hearing the motion to dismiss, with oral argument set for Thursday, June 3, at 10:00 A.M. Both sides quickly filed opposing briefs, and Lee Halterman rounded up two supporting amicus briefs by different groups of prominent law professors, one supporting us on the constitutional merits, another supporting us on standing.

The argument before Judge Friedman on June 3 was not particularly memorable. Set against the backdrop of both escalating bombing of Yugoslavia and increasing rumors that Milosevic was seeking peace, the legal argumentation taking place in Friedman's courtroom seemed a minor distraction. Certainly, the press viewed it that way, showing little interest in the courtroom proceedings. Even Campbell unfortunately could not be there, having a prior commitment in California. He did call from California and predicted victory—a view he appeared to genuinely believe.

Friedman appeared to be a thoughtful judge. He listened attentively and asked good questions. The argument focused on congressional standing to sue and the War Powers Resolution. Friedman seemed to be genuinely grappling with our argument that to deny standing to these members of Congress was to essentially eviscerate the War Powers Resolution, since the House had defeated the two measures that would have constituted legislative authorization under that Resolution. Our hopes rose slightly when the Justice Department lawyer arguing the case appeared to stumble under Friedman's questioning. But the lawyer did not need to be all that good; he was representing the president in a war powers case.

Friedman told us that he would issue a decision early the next week. But the next day a political bombshell hit that caused Friedman to reconsider: the press reported that the United States, its NATO allies, and Milosevic had struck a deal to end the bombing. Friedman's clerk frantically called us requesting that we allow him to consider the case moot and hold off doing anything until the peace negotiations played out. We refused, wanting to force Friedman to decide the case—even though we thought we would probably lose.

On Tuesday, June 8, just two days before NATO suspended the bombing of Yugoslavia, Friedman issued his decision. His technical, legalistic decision focused virtually exclusively on congressional standing and had none of the majestic sweep of Judge Greene's decision nine years earlier refuting the president's view of war powers. Friedman held that Congress had acted inconsistently by refusing to authorize the war but nevertheless subsequently voting for supplemental appropriations for the Kosovo war and also voting against terminating the war. Therefore, there was no true constitutional impasse that could give members of Congress standing.[26] Friedman agreed with us that the War Powers Resolution affirmatively required explicit authorization but argued that congressional inconsistency denied these members of Congress standing to assert their claims.[27]

Friedman had, by way of footnotes, rejected two positions that the government had forcefully argued. In a footnote, he held that the president was wrong to argue that every case brought by a legislator alleging a violation of the war powers clause raises a nonjusticiable political question.[28] In another footnote, he rejected the president's argument that members of Congress should be denied standing because Congress has available such political remedies as impeachment or the withholding of funds to stop a war.[29] The footnotes were a small consolation.

Our defeat before Friedman was generally not considered newsworthy. While Judge Greene's decision in *Dellums* had generated a significant article in most newspapers around the country, Friedman's technical dismissal on standing produced a short Associated Press wire story that was generally ignored.

Two days later, on June 10, the United States and its NATO allies reached an agreement with Milosevic and suspended the bombing campaign. Yugoslavia agreed to withdraw from Kosovo, and on June 20, after that withdrawal was virtually completed, the Kosovo air war was officially terminated.

Michael and I preferred not to appeal Friedman's decision. We had litigated the case hoping that it would provoke some debate over the constitutionality of Clinton's actions and maybe even the wisdom of the Kosovo war. It had for the most part failed to do so. Now the war was over, and the only purpose left to the litigation was to vindicate the constitutional principle that only Congress could take us to war. We felt strongly about that principle, but the Court of Appeals would almost certainly affirm Friedman's decision on standing. In addition, the government now had yet another procedural argument: the case was moot. We would have to spend hours researching that point, all to no avail. An appeal would be totally divorced from any political movement, any urgent moral or ethical necessity, and any likelihood of legal success; it was not likely to yield even a useful legal defeat. Moreover, we were already exhausted. Why do it?

But Tom Campbell wanted to appeal. He deeply believed in the constitutional cause and wanted to take the fight as far as we could. Moreover, he was sure that we were right on the law and that some judge would see that. Campbell had a profound faith in the power of rational discourse. He was also a deeply religious man, and I think he deeply believed that if you were morally, ethically (and in this case legally) right, you could convince others to see that truth.

Campbell also had a practical argument. Now that the war was over, it might be easier for a court to reach the merits of our action. A court could declare Clinton's actions unconstitutional without interfering with an actual war and bringing about all of the allegedly terrible consequences Pickering had mentioned. Of course, such a course looked like the kind of advisory opinion that federal courts generally did not render. But there was some precedent for such a course of action. In *Brown v. Board of Education*, the Supreme Court essentially declared that the Constitution prohibited school segregation, yet provided no immediate relief, allowing the branches of government affected by the decision to remedy the violation. Other courts issued decisions even where a case had become moot when the issue was capable of repetition, yet evading review. Maybe we fit within that doctrine.

Michael and I were unconvinced. We totally agreed with Campbell on constitutional principle, but our view of the legal and political reality was that further litigation was hopeless. But Campbell's faith had led him to force a vote under the War Powers Resolution and to actually defeat the authorization required under that statute. Campbell had taken on both the Republican and the Democratic leadership of the House and had at least partially won. To have done so was no small feat—and required perseverance under tremendous odds. Maybe he was right, and we could take on the judiciary and win. In any event,

Campbell was our client, he was a very principled man who had coura-geously taken a stand, and I thought we owed him the duty to appeal. Michael agreed.

We also agreed that we wanted to move quickly while the issue was still current events and not history. Jim Klimaski filed a notice of appeal on June 16, and we asked for an expedited briefing schedule and oral argument before the court. Michael was worried that, if the court granted our request, we would be in a real jam to file a brief by July 2. I told him not to worry; they would never grant our motion for an expe-dited schedule, now that the war was over.

With that, my wife, Karen, and I left for Alaska. We were running the Anchorage marathon to raise money for the Leukemia Society. I thought that running 26.2 miles would be a difficult challenge, but much easier than winning *Campbell v. Clinton* on appeal.

When I returned a week later, Michael had astounding news. The court had agreed to our briefing schedule; the government had not re-ally opposed it but had requested summary disposition of the case without oral argument. Our brief was due in a week.

I agreed to write the brief. Michael was going out of town, and, any-way, it was clear to me that he would take a secondary role on the ap-peal. While we shared the same political-legal orientation, Michael's guy wires were more closely tethered to the political movement and to political cases; I was more the legal academic who could be intrigued by intellectual issues. In my heart, I felt that Michael was probably right: the importance of and interest in this case had vanished once the bomb-ing stopped. But, for some reason, which I began to suspect was egotis-tical, I still retained my interest in plowing ahead.

I quickly wrote the appellate brief, essentially just lifting large sec-tions of our district court briefs and adding a critique of Friedman's opinion. We filed our brief and appendix in a timely fashion and waited for the president's reply.

The Justice Department's reply predictably argued that not only did the plaintiffs have no standing to sue and that the issues were po-litical questions but that the case was moot: the air war against Yu-goslavia was by now over. Our reply brief responded by arguing that the case was capable of repetition yet evading review because, since passage of the War Powers Resolution, presidential uses of force have all been of such short duration as to be over before litigation could be completed. Therefore, in modern warfare, war powers legal issues are "typically" of such short duration as to evade appellate review. In addition, we argued that we were challenging a longstanding executive policy and practice of ignoring Congress when initiating warfare. Such policies could be litigated even after a specific challenge was rendered moot. Finally, we quoted from a decision by then-judge (now Justice) Ruth Bader Ginsburg when she sat on the D.C. Circuit, which held that a soldier's challenge to an army medical policy during the Persian Gulf War was not rendered moot by the war's end. A court, Ginsburg said, can consider the challenge the soldier "tenders most calmly and effectively after the battle fire is extinguished and before it is rekindled."[30] That was precisely our point in this case.

Campbell was very helpful throughout the process. He was always supportive, complimenting us on our briefs. At times his law professor persona peeked through: once he went over our brief as if he were back at Stanford grading papers. Generally, he was a most wonderful and kind client, perceptive and helpful, not overbearing or superinterventionist. I felt it both a treat and an honor to represent him.

By late August, the briefs were all written, and we were just waiting to see whether the court would grant oral argument. I was dubious, believing that the court would probably summarily dismiss the appeal. The Court of Appeals, however, again surprised me and granted oral argument. Hope welled up inside me: maybe Campbell was right; the court did seem interested.

Oral argument is the exhilarating part of appellate litigation. It is what experienced appellate lawyers live for, particularly arguments before a good Court of Appeals panel or the Supreme Court. While the written brief the lawyer presents to the court is most important in framing and developing his or her argument, the written word can be dry and impersonal. Oral argument is where you get to engage the judges and answer their questions. If you get a hot bench—one where the judges have read the lawyers' briefs carefully and pepper the advocate with questions—oral argument can be an intense intellectual experience, full of high anxiety and ecstasy. You have to think fast on your feet, be quick witted, have the whole case at your fingertips; you have to engage the judges, charm them, and occasionally change their minds. The pressure is increased by the short time you have to convince judges—usually fifteen minutes to half an hour to argue.

So I eagerly awaited the chance to argue the case—even though it meant that I would have to expend more time and energy on what to any rational person was a sure loser. I decided to use the case as an educational experience for the class on foreign affairs and the Constitution I was teaching at the University of Pittsburgh Law School. As the students' project for the semester, I assigned them issues in the case that they would have to brief and argue before a panel of their peers and myself. Then, they would moot me (that is, the students would serve as mock judges while I argued) as preparation for the appeal, and they would all come to Washington to hear the D.C. Circuit oral argument. They enthusiastically agreed; it was a more practical, hands-on experience than the typical law school assignment.

For me, having twenty students discussing case law and legal strategy made the case a more collective experience. It also increased the pressure; if I did poorly at oral argument, I would be exposed as a fraud before my students and, eventually, through the gossip mill, the whole law school. A psychologically oriented friend of mind told me the whole idea was nuts, the risks of failure too great.

I spent the weeks before the argument with delusions of grandeur dancing inside my head. I fantasized that we would win before the Court of Appeals, thus forcing the Supreme Court to confront for the first time in the twentieth century the question of who had the constitutional authority to place the United States at war. I would argue before the Supreme Court; the case would be the most important case of the Supreme Court's next term. I would be rescued from the relative obscurity with which I labored at the University of Pittsburgh; the case would propel me to the center of the national stage. While publicly I maintained my rationalistic stance that there was virtually no logical chance of winning (and a few of the best student briefs further convinced my rational side that the court would rule against us), my emotional side was swirling in a dreamlike state of imagined glory, heroic accomplishments, and miraculous victories. Why, I asked myself continuously, would the court have granted oral argument if it was certain to dismiss?

On October 7, several weeks before oral argument was scheduled, I plummeted back to reality. The court granted us fifteen minutes to argue our case, a paltry amount of time that conflicted with my visions of grandeur. In my previous experience, an important, complicated case would be allotted thirty minutes per side; I could not imagine the court ruling for us without a full hearing. Maybe they were giving us oral argument solely as a courtesy to the members of Congress who were our plaintiffs.

We also found out who our panel of judges would be: Lawrence Silberman, David Tatel, and A. Raymond Randolph. Lawrence Silberman was an extremely conservative judge, appointed by President Reagan in 1985, who had a reputation as a very smart judge with an acerbic tongue. He had reportedly once threatened one of his colleagues that "if you were ten years younger, I'd be tempted to punch you in the nose!"[31] He also had served as President Ford's ambassador to Yugoslavia in the 1970s and as a foreign policy adviser to Ronald Reagan during his 1980 election campaign. He was unlikely to rule for us, unless his hatred of Clinton outweighed his support of a strong executive in foreign policy, which I doubted it did. Judge Tatel was a fairly liberal judge, appointed by President Clinton, who was totally blind, the first blind judge ever appointed to the federal bench. He had a long history of support for civil rights and was also reportedly a very smart judge. Raymond Randolph was a moderate, conservative judge, appointed by President Bush, who reputedly was very well prepared and lawyerly during oral argument.

On Friday morning, October 22, after several nights of restless sleep, I stepped up to the podium to argue the appeal of *Campbell et al. v. Clinton* before Judges Silberman, Tatel, and Randolph. I was accompanied by my co-counsel, Michael Ratner, Joe Starr, Jim Klimaski, Franklin Siegel, and Lee Halterman; Tom Campbell and a number of other members of Congress, my wife Karen; and about fifteen students.

Michael recalls the argument as being probably the hardest, most difficult oral argument he has ever witnessed. The judges were all incredibly well prepared and sharp, asking difficult, very technical questions. They knew the cases well, probing for weaknesses in my argument, as Michael recalled, "to trip me up." The argument focused not on the broad political-legal themes of who had constitutional authority over warfare but on very technical distinctions about standing, mootness, and, occasionally, political-question or justiciability issues.

While the argument was difficult and technical, the judges were clearly deeply engaged. I had been disappointed by the fifteen minutes they had allotted for each side. Now I was elated by the almost one hour that they kept me arguing, peppering me with questions after my time was up.

The tone was set right from the beginning. I decided to start by forthrightly recognizing that courts had avoided deciding war powers cases, even though the president had repeatedly violated the War Powers Resolution, and to argue that such abstention strikes at the heart of the rule of law and constitutional democracy. If there ever was a war powers case that was appropriate for judicial review, I said, this was it.

I had waded only several sentences into my prepared opening when Randolph abruptly interrupted and asked who else besides President Clinton had violated the War Powers Resolution. I immediately sensed the trap Randolph had set. Our brief had highlighted that this was the first time in the twenty-five years since the Resolution had been adopted that U.S. troops had been involved in a war that had lasted more than sixty days. But a case like ours was moot unless it was capable of repetition, and Randolph was trying to get me to admit that this scenario had occurred only once in twenty-five years and thus was unlikely to reoccur. I quickly avoided being snagged by pointing out that various other presidents had violated the Resolution—for example, President Reagan, in sending advisers to El Salvador and U.S. naval vessels to the Persian Gulf—but none had done so as openly and flagrantly as Clinton in Kosovo. Randolph later returned to that theme and cited a case that he believed read "capable of repetition" to mean "likely" to reoccur and tried to turn our point, that modern wars were generally very short, against us. I cited several key cases that said that "capable" meant just that—that there is a reasonable possibility that the problem would reoccur.

After I answered Randolph, I tried to get back on track, but Tatel immediately jumped in and asked a hypothetical that came crashing down on me. Tatel asked whether our case was not identical to a situation in which Congress defeats an appropriations bill, but the president still spends the money anyway. Should Congress have standing in that hypothetical case? Visions of Bob Boehm, the eighty-year-old president of the CCR board, flashed through my mind. Several months earlier, he had wanted Michael and me to bring a case challenging just such a scenario, when the Pentagon was continuing to develop a weapon system that Congress had refused to fund. Michael and I had both told Boehm no, that members of Congress undoubtedly would be denied standing. Later, I realized that our war powers case was similar to Boehm's proposed case—and I worried that if a judge asked us about it, we'd be in trouble. Michael had agreed, but on this and several other tough questions he tried to relieve my anxiety, telling me that it was highly un-likely that a judge would ask that question. These were just questions for academics, he said.

Now Tatel had asked the dreaded question, and I gave the best an-swer I could. I said that his hypothetical would present a more difficult case than ours because here Congress had enacted a statute that set up a specific procedure to enforce the constitutional authority to declare war and then taken a vote pursuant to that procedure. It was that vote, the 213–213 tie, that distinguished our case from the hypothetical Tatel had posed.

The answer brought me only a temporary respite. Silberman im-mediately blindsided me with a question I had not anticipated. Focus-ing on a footnote in the Supreme Court's *Raines* standing opinion, he asked me whether the *Coleman* case that we were relying on could be read to give standing only to state legislators and not to members of Congress. I verbally stumbled for a short while, then gave an answer that satisfied neither of us.

On and on it went like that. After about ten minutes—when my al-lotted time was almost up—I felt comfortable and at ease, almost as if I were in front of my class. I developed a colloquial conversational style with the judges and at times even came up with witty responses. Ran-dolph continued to press me on whether this violation of the War Pow-ers Resolution was really likely to reoccur and finally came up with a hypothetical that he thought would snare me: what if the presidential candidates in the upcoming election, he asked, all agreed to abide by the War Powers Resolution—would the case then be moot? If I an-swered no—which Randolph undoubtedly thought I probably would—then he could say that my definition of "capable of being re-peated" was absurd. I thought a minute—and said, okay, I agreed with him. If all the candidates agreed to abide by the Resolution, then, I would agree that the case was moot—but the unlikeliness that his sce-nario would occur demonstrated why the case was not moot. The whole courtroom laughed, and Silberman interrupted to say that he "admired my concession." "It is always wise when lawyers give away nothing"—drawing more laughter. At another point, Silberman and I disputed whether a particular passage in a case was mere dicta—which was his view—or critical to the holding—which I believed. After going around and around a few times and getting nowhere, I said, "Why should we quibble? Let's just say it's more than dicta and less than a holding," again drawing laughter from the spectators and from Silberman.

The government's attorney, William Schultz, was smooth and sharp. If my style seemed that of a Jewish customer in a New York delicatessen, bantering, arguing, kibitzing, and philosophizing with whomever would listen, Schultz reminded observers of an immaculate lawyer carefully explaining his proposal to some corporation's board of directors. He immediately faced some tough questions from Judge Tatel and responded that, fundamentally, the only congressional remedy for a president who is bent on violating the law is impeachment, to which Silberman responded, "I think that is exactly the right answer." It was clear we were unlikely to win his vote. Schultz made his salient points clearly and cogently and then sat down.

I focused my reply on explaining why judicial resolution, not impeachment, ought to be the preferred remedy for longstanding separation-of-power disputes between the president and Congress. This was a situation not of a corrupt president but of the executive branch taking a constitutional position at odds with Congress. Why put the country through the trauma of impeachment when the duty of the court was precisely to articulate what the Constitution says? I argued that history supports judicial review, the impeachment and Senate trial of President Andrew Johnson after the Civil War was over a constitutional separation of powers issue, which the Supreme Court decided almost one half century later in the executive's favor. Would it not have been better to avoid that traumatic experience and for members of Congress to seek judicial review of the executive's actions? Again, I was barraged with questions. I finally ended by another technical distinction, trying to draw a line between a president who refuses to enforce a law and a president who refuses even to recognize a legislative act as having any legal significance, which I believed was our case. Silberman said "he understood our argument," "that it was a tough line to draw," but that we did have the *Coleman* case. With that the argument ended.

I was ecstatic. The judges had taken us seriously, and I thought I had done well. Campbell, who had clerked for Justice White on the Supreme Court, thought that both sides had presented their arguments, and said to my students afterwards that "it was one of the best oral arguments that he had ever heard." I thought that Campbell was being overly generous, but it was clear that he was pleased. Michael and the other lawyers also thought I had done well. But it turned out to make little difference.

Four months later, on February 18, 2000, the court decided against us. Each judge wrote a separate opinion. Silberman and Tatel denied plaintiffs' standing primarily on the basis of their conclusion that members of Congress always had political remedies, such as legislation to cut off funds or impeachment, to challenge the president's prosecution of the war.[32] Randolph wrote a sarcastic, angry denunciation of the majority's standing analysis, claiming that it was "tantamount to a decision abolishing legislative standing."[33] Such a decision, claimed Randolph, ought to be made openly by the Supreme Court and not by the Court of Appeals "under the cover of" a "misinterpretation" of precedent.[34] Randolph held, however, that our War Powers Resolution case was moot. Silberman and Tatel also wrote sharply conflicting separate opinions on whether our case presented a nonjusticiable political question. Silberman's position was that a case challenging a presidential war was inherently nonjusticiable in that there are no standards to decide the constitutional or statutory issues presented therein. Tatel wrote a lengthy opinion to the contrary, arguing that, had plaintiffs had standing, the court could have decided the merits of the case.

Reading the fifty-four pages of judicial decisions contained in three separate decisions was a frustrating experience: at the end of the day, the court had unanimously dismissed our claim but for reasons that were at best unclear and muddled. No judge had agreed with District Judge Friedman's reasoning. The court split 1–1 with one judge abstaining on the political-question doctrine. With respect to standing, Judge Randolph was undoubtedly correct; the majority's opinion seemed to eliminate any possibility of congressional standing. That was clearly Silberman's position at oral argument: our technical arguments had probably forced Judge Tatel to realize that our case could not so easily be distinguished from *Coleman* and therefore to agree to Silberman's more global approach. While I was still proud of my oral argument, its only real achievement, apart from ego-strengthening, had been to push Tatel into Silberman's embrace.

Like a punch-drunk boxer who had taken on too many blows to the head, I was ready to stay in my corner and quit. Neither Michael or I wanted to petition for a writ of *certiorari* to the Supreme Court, which was the only avenue to appeal. The Court takes only a small percentage, probably around 2 to 3 percent, of all the cases in which an appeal is sought. It had shown no interest in war powers cases, and there was no clear split among circuit courts that the Supreme Court might want to resolve. Our case was a total loser. And, anyway, as my friend and Supreme Court litigator David Cole pointed out, if the Court did take the case, it would undoubtedly affirm presidential power. If we got through the first, virtually impossible hurdle, we would only make bad law.

Again, Campbell was forceful that we had to petition for cert. He explained in a telephone conference how important it was that we give it one final shot, that we not leave the field without knowing we had given it our all. Moreover, he was convinced that there were potentially four justices who would vote to take the case, which was all we needed. He went down the list of justices and explained his reasoning as to why four might support us.

I got off the telephone conference and scratched my head, wondering whether Campbell could really believe that the Supreme Court might grant our appeal. It seemed absurd, but again I returned to the thought that he had clerked for the Supreme Court, and maybe he had some insight that I didn't.

Campbell later told me that all along he had believed that we would win in the district court or the Court of Appeals, or that the Supreme Court would take cert. He did believe that victory was possible, and that belief allowed him to really imagine victory. Campbell described himself as the happy warrior in the tradition of Alfred Smith, the 1928 Democratic, and first Roman Catholic, candidate for president. In essence, Campbell was able to imagine the miraculous, and that image made it real and imperative that we try to achieve it. To Campbell, the only real failure was not to try. Campbell told me of a scene that had stayed with him, from the movie *Gandhi*, in which Gandhi is attempting to vote in South Africa in the early 1900s. He is being beaten severely, and it is clear that he will not be allowed to vote. Nonetheless, lying prostrate on the ground, Gandhi rises slightly and attempts to crawl toward the voting booth, only to be beaten again and again. Campbell took away the powerful message that the essence of success is the struggle, the attempt, the effort in trying. And, now, he was not about to give up short of a Supreme Court denial. He convinced himself and, through the force of his personality and argument, convinced others that what was hypothetically possible—or maybe just short of impossible—was in fact achievable.

Campbell's optimism was infectious, and I agreed to draft the petition. I did it partly out of a sense of obligation to him. But for me to convince myself to throw myself into this work required psychological imagery of a different order and kind than Campbell's. I could more relate to the image of a solitary, determined man dreaming the impossible and achieving it. The likelihood of failure increased in direct proportion to the grandiosity of the goal. But it was dreaming big dreams and trying to achieve them that motivated me—even if failure was the likely result.

The very slight hope that Campbell had ignited within me that the Court would grant cert made me conjure up dreams of herodom. I was smitten by a story line that runs deep in both American and Jewish mythology: that of the tiny David who slays Goliath, of the inexperienced lawyer who wins a huge verdict against an insurance company, of the 1969 Mets making their implausible run to the World Series. It is not success itself that is valued in this story; it is triumphing over great odds. Now Campbell and I were going forth against great odds, on an important national issue, and Campbell had allowed me to imagine victory—however implausible that result was.

Michael had no such delusion, and he played only a minor role in drafting the petition. Luckily for me, Lee Halterman, who is a much better writer than I, took a major role in editing the petition, making it very readable. The rest of the team, including, as always, Tom Campbell, helped out.

A petition for certiorari ought to be short. We relied heavily on Judge Randolph's critique that the Court of Appeals majority had misread Supreme Court precedent, hoping that the Court would want to revisit congressional standing in the war powers context. The emotional, intellectual, and physical energy expended in writing the petition furthered my delusions; I became even more convinced that we were right and that the Court might just grant the petition.

In September, we were notified that the Court had, predictably, turned down our petition, along with hundreds of others. Over the past three decades, a clear consensus has existed on the Court to avoid these war powers issues and to let the lower courts continue to dismiss these lawsuits. Our case was to be no different from the rest.

In a conference call postmortem, Congressman Campbell thanked us all for our work and told us that this case represented the effort of which he was most proud in all his years in Congress. I was grateful for his kind and gracious words but thought to myself that this case, in which we had achieved essentially nothing, could not possibly rank particularly high on the list of accomplishments of an almost ten-year stint on Capitol Hill.

But, later, when I talked to Campbell at greater length, I understood what he meant. When he decided to act on a purely principled basis, he realized that the congressional leadership would undoubtedly limit his influence and ability to accomplish much legislatively. "I wasn't going to be the person they let sponsor major legislation," he recognized. Indeed, after more than nine years on the Hill, he has no idea whether "he changed anything major" and can't point to any specific difference he made. But he can say he lived out his principles on the floor of Congress and served as a model for others. One Republican colleague once told him, "I wish I had your guts." From this perspective, the effort against the bombing was undoubtedly one of Campbell's finest moments: he stood up for principle, got Congress to take a vote that he partially won, and litigated the issue all the way to the Supreme Court. Campbell's effort stands as a testament to political courage and principle and will, I hope, be remembered and acted upon by future generations of legislators.

Campbell was extremely happy with his effort, despite the loss: "You have to care about what you are doing so much that it is secondary whether you win or lose." Campbell, who had never given up his tenured position at Stanford Law School, returned happily to teaching after losing the Senate race to Dianne Feinstein in the 2000 election.

For me, the disappointing, albeit expected, end to the *Campbell v. Clinton* case renewed my soul searching as to what I should be doing with my legal skills. I was proud of my representation of Tom Campbell, who, along with Ron Dellums, was undoubtedly one of the most honorable and principled individuals to serve in Congress. I also still continued to believe that our legal work mattered, that we were litigating these cases to generate public debate on important issues, that our cases would serve as a record to instruct and inspire future generations to struggle, and that we were doing what we could to stop U.S. wrongdoing abroad.

But greater doubts began to intrude on my thoughts. I was particularly disturbed by what I considered the egotistical or grandiosity motivations that welled up inside me during the appellate process in the *Campbell* case. I thought that maybe I should work on more local issues, where I could win specific improvements for particular individuals.

For Michael and me, the Kosovo case represented the end of an era. For almost twenty years, we had tried to make the democratic promise of the War Powers Resolution and the Constitution a reality through the courts. We had lost. The courts bought into the prevailing sentiment among the country's elite that the president must be accorded great flexibility in using the U.S. military to protect American hegemony abroad. I have no doubt that, at some time in the future, that consensus will come crashing down under the weight of a constitutional crisis occasioned by a president's imperial overseas adventures. But Michael and I agreed that the time had come to move on. We vowed that we were done with war powers cases.

10

Conclusion

AMERICANS WORSHIP SUCCESS, yet are haunted by failure. While American society glorifies success stories and celebrates winners, we also seem obsessively drawn to losers. *Peanuts*, the most popular comic strip of the twentieth century, has as its hero Charlie Brown, the quintessential loser. As *Peanuts'* creator, Charles Schulz, once said, "The loves in the strip are unrequited, all the baseball games are lost, all the test scores are D minuses; the Great Pumpkin never comes; and the football is always pulled away."[1] This sense of failure pervading the underside of the overtly winner-dominated American culture touches us all, because it stems from common human feelings of inadequacy.

This book may be my attempt to justify and come to grips with my own sense of failure. But, while my psychological proclivities often lead me to look for the personal flaws responsible for my losses in court, my lawyer/political activist outlook drives me to turn to history, political science, sociology, and theology to seek meaning in those failures. From that perspective, my failures in court are not reflective of individual character weaknesses but are a part of the broader struggle for a more just society.

My search for meaning in defeat leads me to three basic conclusions. The first is that success and failure are not mutually exclusive, clear-cut opposites but are intertwined in a dialectical tension. Thoreau's view that "all the past is equally a failure and a success" and Emerson's comment that his "entire success, such as it is, is composed of particular failures" reflect that understanding.[2] The interconnectedness of defeat and victory are illustrated by the many cases that lose in court, yet succeed in inspiring political movements. Salmon Chase's fugitive slave cases usually lost, but his legal arguments became a critical component of the Republican Party platform. Susan B. Anthony's trial, the desegregation cases in Boston and New York in the nineteenth century, the plant-closing litigation, my own Persian Gulf litigation, and

264

some of the Nicaragua cases litigated by the Center for Constitutional Rights and National Lawyers Guild helped spur political activism. The intertwining of defeat and victory is also apparent in cases such as *Dellums v. Bush*, *CUSCLIN v. Reagan*, and Salmon Chase's fugitive slave case, *Watson v. Hoppess*, where judges issued a decision that was a technical legal defeat but affirmed principles the losers were seeking to vindicate. Indeed, American history is replete with similar examples, such as the famous case of *Marbury v. Madison*, where the Court decided for the president but used reasoning that dealt the executive branch a serious ideological defeat.

Similarly, just as some defeats are successful, some courtroom victories (e.g., *Brown v. Board of Education*) can ultimately fail to guarantee the rights they articulated. My friend Michael Krinsky, whose firm represents Cuba in U.S. courts, believes that the firm's great victory, a case titled *Sabbatino v. Banco Nacional de Cuba*, has failed to protect Cuba's interests, whereas a subsequent case in which the Supreme Court held against Cuba nonetheless articulated principles that proved critical to advancing Cuban interests. Thus have victories often proven to be as illusory as defeats.

The sharp divide that mainstream culture posits between winning and losing reflects the theoretical wall constructed between law and politics. Both separations are illusory. Nongovernment organizations in countries such as Nigeria, Chile, and Argentina often use litigation to document and expose institutionalized injustices, even where the lawsuit is unlikely to succeed in court.[3] In Chile, for example, the Vicariate of Solidarity repeatedly filed mostly unsuccessful lawsuits during the years of military rule to seek the release of prisoners and "created a powerful record of abuses that over time acquired political importance."[4] In Nigeria, the Constitutional Rights Project brought case after mostly unsuccessful case challenging governmental abuses; these cases served as a vital tool for educating people in Nigeria and abroad about official crimes.[5] As a Ford Foundation study about public-interest litigation worldwide concludes,

> Even if a lawsuit fails to change an unjust law, the act of going to court can influence or even change attitudes about the law and contribute to a climate for reform. Unorthodox arguments can serve to suggest innovative uses of the law; complaints can present a cumulative record that documents mistreatment.[6]

Of course, it often happens that the defeat in the courtroom merely mirrors a political defeat. My Kosovo case is an example of such a total defeat, in which it is difficult to find a silver lining. Moreover, as some scholars have noted, litigation can often channel the public dialogue into a very narrow discourse and may in fact stifle a political movement by channeling its energy into a courtroom clash between lawyers. My experience that losing litigation sometimes seems to have performed no immediately useful function leads to my second conclusion.

That second conclusion is a rejection of the dominant American view that success and failure can be measured by short-term consequences. Emerson excoriated "this shallow Americanism with its passion for *sudden* success."[7] We need to redefine success and failure temporally, recognizing that victory or defeat can be understood only historically. Mao Tse-Tung got it right when he was he was asked to evaluate the significance of the French Revolution and reportedly responded, "It's too early to tell."[8]

Viewed through history's lens, great courtroom victories can turn out to be less successful than at first anticipated. The historical legacy of *Brown v. Board of Education* is now much disputed. Public schools in cities across the country have become increasingly resegregated, while the Supreme Court has used the vision of a color-blind society to strike down affirmative action and other programs designed to ensure racial diversity, leading Kenneth Clark, a central participant in the NAACP's victory in *Brown*, to term that case one of his "glorious defeats."[9] Similarly, a great legal victory of the 1960s, *Miranda v. Arizona*, which imposed the *Miranda* warning requirement on the police, is now often viewed as having failed to protect criminal suspect's rights, and the data suggest that the decision has had essentially no effect on the percentage of incarcerated defendants who confess.[10] As one prominent scholar argues, both *Brown* and *Miranda* resulted in "short-term gains" but have over the longer term "led us into a trap."[11]

So too can short-term defeat lead to long-term success. In some of the cases in this book, historical redemption and vindication have come relatively quickly. Staughton Lynd's observation that he and his handful of anti–Vietnam War protestors would be the first of thousands and Salmon Chase's successful rise to become chief justice of the Supreme Court, responsible for enforcing the Thirteenth Amendment, are examples. For others, such as Albion Tourgée, redemption comes only decades or centuries later.

In American political life as in law, defeats can pave the way for later victories. Barry Goldwater ran for president in 1964 knowing that he would lose but championing a principled conservative position.[12] He viewed his overwhelming defeat—the most lopsided in the history of American presidential elections—as a repudiation of his ideas. Yet his campaign prefigured, and could even be said to have launched, Ronald Reagan's successful campaign based on Goldwater's principles a mere fifteen years later. Similarly, Senator Paul Douglass and a handful of Senate liberals fought a stubborn and lonely fight for civil rights legislation in the 1950s, knowing that they would lose but believing the principle was worth fighting for. They paved the way for the enactment of their legislation a decade later. As Douglass would write, "even if every battle was unsuccessful, constant but peaceful struggle would hasten the ultimate coming of needed reforms."[13]

At this moment in history, the United States is at the height of its imperial might and is governed by leaders whose great power is challenged only by their arrogance. It seems unlikely that the principles I have fought for in the courtroom and in the streets—obedience to international law, prohibition of unilateral presidential war making, a respect for other nations' sovereignty and peoples, a foreign policy truly based on human rights—will be established in my lifetime. Nor am I sanguine that, when those principles are eventually accepted by the courts at some future date, it will be my efforts and cases that have had a direct effect. The cases my colleagues and I litigated will likely be premonitions rather than causes of eventual political change in America.[14]

This leads me to the third and most crucial lesson I draw from my reflection on losing cases: success and failure must be radically redefined. Instead of measuring success and failure in terms of achievements, we should view success as the living out of values, persistence in the face of great odds, and the strength to stand up for principle even when defeat seems inevitable. The people I write about—Susan B. Anthony, Ron Dellums, Staughton Lynd, Tom Campbell, Ruth Wald, Michael Ratner, Benjamin Linder, Albion Tourgée—all defined success in this way. Their contributions to a culture of resistance to injustice provide the essential meaning of their actions. Their narratives contribute to and keep alive a culture of struggle, and that, not whatever victories they may have achieved, is what fundamentally gives meaning to their lives. Their main contribution, therefore, lies in the realm of process, not substantive outcomes.

This understanding is, for me, inextricably connected to my own upbringing in a Jewish cultural setting. The preservation of the memory of historical trauma and resistance to oppression serves as a primary focus of Jewish faith and the source of Jewish strength and perseverance. Jewish history is littered with defeats and desperate struggles against long odds—the most salient for me being the failed Warsaw ghetto uprising against the Nazis that began on Passover eve in 1943. The Jewish prophetic tradition emphasizes redemption, not merely reform, a passionate call for justice, and a duty to speak to the people, whether they hear or refuse to hear. Many of the prophets were often regarded as mad, deluded fools and were the object of scorn and reproach. The prophets recognized defeat and disaster, yet at the same time held out an optimistic, redemptive view of the future. Abraham Heschel explains that the prophetic vision of justice and law calls forth the image of a mighty cascading river, "a fighting challenge, a restless drive, a never-ending surging, fighting movement," in which meaning comes from being *in* the river.[15]

Many other cultures besides my own Jewish tradition remember and honor their defeats. Australia marks its national holiday in remembrance of the battle of Gallipoli, a disastrous military defeat, to commemorate the values of perseverance, determination and bravery.[16] Japan has a powerful tradition of remembering and celebrating the tragic hero, who represents the antithesis of an ethos of accomplishment.[17] Polish romanticism has utilized the memory of its martyrs as a central pillar around which national memory and identity are defined.[18] The 1389 battle of Kosovo Field, in which the Serbs were defeated by the Turks and lost their nation, lies at the heart of the Serbian national identity.[19]

But for those of us working in America, a culture that reveres success, it is a very difficult and troubling time. For progressive lawyers, the past thirty-five years represent a period when the Supreme Court and lower federal courts have become steadily and increasingly reactionary, making it more and more difficult to win significant public-interest litigation. For peace and justice activists, the establishment of the United States as the world's sole superpower, unrestrained by international law, is truly frightening. For all of us, the widening gap between rich and poor and the absence of a strong progressive alternative portends badly for America and for the world.

While I remain optimistic about the long-term ability of the human race to achieve a more just and peaceful world, I have fears about the immediate future. In this period, it is particularly important to be willing to struggle for peace and justice in the face of obstacles and to persevere in the face of defeat—to continue to dream the impossible and to act on those dreams. Our actions are neither isolated nor forgotten but rather take place in the context of a long tradition and culture of resisting oppression. It is through those acts that we remain a part of the river of struggle, give meaning to our lives, and provide hope for the future.

Notes

NOTES TO CHAPTER 1

1. Alfie Kohn, *No Contest: The Case against Competition* (Boston: Houghton Mifflin, 1986), 3. Lombardi later regretted the comment, as seeming to advocate the crushing of human values in the quest for victory. But his comment took on a life of its own, being repeated in sports, literature, and mass entertainment. In a John Wayne movie, *Trouble Along the Way*, Wayne's co-star, Donna Reed, asks the Duke one day, "Is winning everything to you?" Wayne replies, "No, Ma'am. Winning isn't everything. It's the only thing." William Burns and Thomas Tutko, *Winning Is Everything and Other American Myths* (New York: Macmillan, 1976), 4.

2. Jack Greenberg, "Litigation for Social Change: Methods, Limits and Roles in Democracy," in *Record of the Association of the Bar of the City of New York* 29 (1974): 320, 349.

3. Martha Banta, *Failure and Success in America: A Literary Debate* (Princeton: Princeton University Press, 1978), 157 n. 4.

4. Ralph Waldo Emerson, "Success," *The Complete Works of Ralph Waldo Emerson* (New York: AMS Press, 1968), 436.

5. Derrick Bell, *Confronting Authority: Reflections of an Ardent Protestor* (Boston: Beacon Press, 1994), ix–x.

6. William J. Brennan Jr., "In Defense of Dissents," *Hastings Law Journal* 37 (1986): 427, 437.

7. Richard Huber, *The American Idea of Success* (New York: McGraw-Hill, 1971), 16.

8. Robert N. Bellah, Richard Madsen, William Sullivan, Ann Swidler, and Steven Tipton, *Habits of the Heart: Individualism and Commitment in American Life* (New York: Harper and Row, 1985; Berkeley: University of California Press, 1996), 153.

9. Helmut James Von Moltke, *Letters to Freya 1939–1945*, ed. and trans. Beate Ruhn von Oppen (New York: Knopf, 1990) 270.

10. Abraham Heschel, *The Prophets* (New York: Harper and Row, 1962), 212.

11. Victor Frankl, *Man's Search for Meaning* (Boston: Beacon Press, 1984), 127.

NOTES TO CHAPTER 2

1. "Ronald V. Dellums," *Current Biography* (1972), 101, 102.

2. Ibid., 102.

3. Interview by author with Congressman Ronald V. Dellums (Washington, D.C., October 1996). That interview is the source of many of the quotes from Dellums in this chapter. See also Ronald V. Dellums and H. Lee Halterman, *Lying Down with the Lions* (Boston: Beacon Press, 2000).

4. Ibid., 101.

5. Bill Hewitt, Luchina Fisher, and Fort Lee, "Soldier," *People Weekly*, 3 December 1990, p. 143.

6. Interview by author with Dorothy Brooks, November 1996.

7. "President's News Conference on the Persian Gulf Crisis," *Weekly Compilation of Presidential Documents* 26 (8 November 1990): 1790.

8. Ibid., 1792–3.

9. William Eaton and Michael Ross, "Bush Says War Is Not Imminent," *Los Angeles Times*, 15 November 1990, sec. A, p. 1.

10. Senate Committee on Foreign Relations, *U.S. Policy in the Persian Gulf: Hearings*, 101st Cong., 2d sess., 5, 20 September and 17 October 1990, 107–9; see ibid., 91–3.

11. Stephen L. Carter, "Going to War Over War Powers," *Washington Post*, 18 November 1990, sec. C, p. 1.

12. Edward T. Hearn, *States News Service*, 30 October 1990; see also David Evans, "A Declaration Can Be a Potent Weapon in the War of Words," *Chicago Tribune*, 2 November 1990, sec. C, p. 27.

13. Robert M. Cover, "The Supreme Court, 1982 Term—Foreword: Nomos and Narrative," *Harvard Law Review* 97 (1983): 4, 52. Cover notes that groups such as the Quakers and the Amish create a "jurisprudence that orders the forms and occasions of confrontation, a jurisprudence of resistance that is necessarily also one of accommodation."

14. Complaint ¶ 21.

15. Max Farrand, *The Records of the Federal Convention of 1787*, Vol. 1 (New Haven: Yale University Press, 1911), 316; Julian P. Boyd, *The Papers of Thomas Jefferson*, Vol. 15 (Princeton: Princeton University Press, 1958), 397; Farrand, *Records*, Vol. 2, 319.

16. Jonathon Elliot, *The Debates in the Several State Conventions on the Adoption of the Federal Constitution in 1787*, Vol. 2 (New York: B. Franklin, 1974, 1888), 528.

17. Abraham D. Sofaer, *War, Foreign Affairs and Constitutional Power: The Origins* (Cambridge, Mass.: Ballinger, 1976), 32.

18. Alexander Hamilton, "Pacificus No. 1," in *Papers of Alexander Hamilton*, ed. Harold Syrett, Vol. 15 (New York: Columbia University Press, 1969), 40.

19. Senate Committee on Foreign Relations, 107.

20. *Orlando v. Laird*, 443 F.2d 1039 (2d Cir. 1971), *cert. denied*, 404 U.S. 869 (1971); *Berk v. Laird*, 429 F.2d 21 (D.C. Cir. 1985).

21. *Barnes v. Kline*, 759 F.2d 21 (2d Cir. 1970).

22. *Moore v. U.S. House of Representatives*, 733 F.2d 946 (D.C. Cir. 1984), *cert. denied*, 469 U.S. 1106 (1985).

23. See, e.g., *Blum v. Yaretsky*, 457 U.S. 991 (1982).

24. Federal News Service, Press Conference with Representative Ronald Dellums and others, 20 November, 1990, p. 2.

25. Ibid., 3.

26. Ibid., 5.

27. Ibid., 6.

28. Thomas L. Friedman, "How U.S. Won Support to Use Mideast Forces," *New York Times*, 2 December 1990, sec. A, p. 11.

29. Thomas L. Friedman, "Lighting the Fuse?" *New York Times*, 30 November 1990, sec. A, p. 11.

30. Anna Quindlen, "Consent of Congress," *New York Times*, 6 December 1990, sec. A, p. 27.

31. Editorial, "Who Can Declare War," *New York Times*, 15 December 1990, 26; Susan F. Rasky, "House Democrats Caution Bush on War," *New York Times*, 5 December 1990, sec. A, p. 22; Ethan Bronner, "Democrats Argue the Case in Court for Congressional Approval of War," *Boston Globe*, 5 December 1990, p. 10.

32. *Ange v. Bush*, 752 F. Supp. 509 (D.D.C. 1990).

33. *Dellums v. Bush*, 752 F. Supp. 1141 (D.D.C. 1990).

34. Ibid., 1146.

35. *Nightline*, "Persian Gulf Peace/War See-Saw," 14 December 1990, 13. For other news commentary on Greene's rejection of the Justice Department's war powers claims, see Ethan Bronner, "Judge Turns Back Bid to Force Bush to Consult Congress before Attack," *Boston Globe*, 14 December 1990, p. 17; David G. Savage and Michael Ross, "U.S. Judge Refuses to Block Bush from Starting a War," *Los Angeles Times*, 14 December 1990, sec. A, p. 22.

36. Harry Stoffer, "Judge Finds Bush Can't Go to War Alone," *Pittsburgh Post-Gazette*, 14 December 1990, p. 3.

37. Ibid.

38. *Marbury v. Madison*, 5 U.S. 137 (1803).

39. "Remarks of President George Bush before the Texas State Republican Convention Dallas," *Texas Federal News Service*, 20 June 1992, 3.

40. Stoffer, 3.

41. David G. Savage and Michael Ross, "U.S. Judge Refuses to Block Bush from Starting a War," *Los Angeles Times*, 14 December 1990, sec. A, p. 1.

42. Neil A. Lewis, "Lawmakers Lose a Suit on War Powers," *New York Times*, 14 December 1990, sec. A, p. 15.

43. Anne-Marie Burley, "Book Review: Constitutionalism, Democracy, and Foreign Affairs by Louis Henkin," *American Journal of International Law* 86 (1992): 415–7.

NOTES TO CHAPTER 3

1. Abraham J. Heschel, *The Prophets* (New York: Harper and Row, 1955), 204–5. The prophetic model "is characterized by the principle of solidarity." Johannes Lindblom, *Prophecy in Ancient Israel* (Philadelphia: Fortress Press, 1962), 344; Michael Waltzer, *Interpretation and Social Criticism* (Cambridge: Harvard University Press, 1987), 80.

2. Hendrik Hartog, "Aspiration and the Rights That Belong to Us All," in "The Constitution of American Life: A Special Issue," *Journal of American History* (1987): 1013, 1027.

3. Joel Kovel, *History and Spirit: An Inquiry into the Philosophy of Liberation* (Boston: Beacon Press, 1991), 2–3.

4. Albion Tourgée, *A Fool's Errand*, ed. John Hope Franklin (Cambridge: Harvard University Press, 1961; Boston: W. H. Thompson & Co., 1880), 6.

5. Hartog, 1016.

6. See, e.g., Sanford Levinson, *Constitutional Faith* (Princeton: Princeton University Press, 1988).

7. Stephen Middleton, *Ohio and the Antislavery Activities of Attorney Salmon Portland Chase 1830–1849* (New York: Garland, 1990), 96; John Niven, *Salmon P. Chase: A Biography* (New York: Oxford University Press, 1995), 50–1.

8. Albert Bushnell Hart, *Salmon Portland Chase* (New York: Houghton Mifflin, 1899), 23.

9. Ibid.

10. Frederick J. Blue, *Salmon P. Chase: A Life in Politics* (Kent, OH: Kent University Press, 1987), x.

11. Hart, 435.

12. G. Edward White, "Reconstructing the Constitutional Jurisprudence of Salmon P. Chase," *Northern Kentucky Law Review* 21 (1993): 41, 43–5.

13. Jacobus TenBroek, *Equal under the Law* (London: Collier, 1964), 33.

14. Robert M. Cover, *Justice Accused: Antislavery and the Judicial Process* (New Haven: Yale University Press, 1975), 160.

15. Blue, xi.

16. Niven, 48.

17. Blue, 31.

18. Hart, 49.

19. Blue, 31.

20. Middleton, 83.

21. Ibid., 86–7.

22. Niven, 78.

23. Eric Foner, *Free Soil, Free Labor, Free Men: The Ideology of the Republican Party before the Civil War* (Oxford: Oxford University Press, 1995), 74.

24. Middleton, 97.

25. Ibid., 97.

26. Niven, 51.

27. Niven, 53; Blue, 32.

28. *Speech of Salmon Portland Chase in the Case of the Colored Woman Matilda,* March 11, 1837 (Cincinnati: Pugh and Dodd Printers, 1837), 7–8.

29. Ibid., 32.

30. Ibid., 38.

31. William M. Wiecek, *The Sources of Antislavery Constitutionalism in America, 1760–1848* (Ithaca: Cornell University Press, 1977), 193.

32. Foner, 74.

33. Middleton, 102.

34. J. W. Shuckers, *The Life and Public Services of Salmon Portland Chase* (New York: Da Capo Press, 1970), 42–3.

35. Hart, 74; Shuckers, 43–4; Chase's argument is printed in *James G. Birney v. The State of Ohio, 8 Ohio Reports* (1837): 230, 231.

36. Niven, 84.

37. Ibid., 89.

38. *The State v. Hoppess,* 2 W.L.J. 279, 285 (1845).

39. Ibid.

40. Ibid., 285–6.

41. Ibid., 286–7.

42. Ibid., at 292.

43. "Address and Reply on the Presentation of a Testimonial to S. P. Chase by the Colored People of Cincinnati," reprinted in *Fugitive Slaves and American Courts,* Vol. 1, ed. Paul Finkelman (New York: Garland, 1988), 235, 240, 248.

44. Shuckers, 77. Read's decision had been foreshadowed by his earlier 1841 decision freeing a former slave because the warrant for her arrest had not stated that she had escaped from Kentucky to Ohio.

45. Shuckers, 78.

46. Address and Reply, 252. Almost a quarter of a century before the Fourteenth and Fifteenth Amendments were enacted, Chase claimed that all "legal distinctions between individuals of the same community, founded on any circumstances of color, origin and the like are hostile to the genius of our institutions and incompatible with the true theory of American liberty" and specifically criticized the Ohio Constitution's exclusion of blacks from voting. His comment on voting was used against Chase in his election campaign for Ohio governor ten years later. Chase refused to disavow his views and won the election. Judge Read, despite his "conversion," attracted the ire of the antislavery

forces in Ohio because of his decision in the *Watson* case and lost his bid for re-election as a Supreme Court judge. Shuckers, 79.

47. Ibid., 263.

48. Hart, 424–5.

49. White, 60.

50. *Jones v. Van Zandt*, 13 Fed. Cas. 1040, 1045 (Circuit Court Ohio 1843).

51. Ibid., 1047.

52. Shuckers, 66 n. 1.

53. Shuckers, 65.

54. *Prigg v. Pennsylvania*, 41 U.S. 539 (1842).

55. Cover, 173.

56. S. P. Chase, *An Argument for the Defendant Submitted to the Supreme Court of the United States at the December Term 1846 in the Case of Warton Jones v. John Van Zandt* (Cincinnati R. P. Donogh & Co. 1847), 5.

57. Hart, 77.

58. Ibid.

59. Chase, *Argument*, 82.

60. Chase, *Argument*, 76.

61. Ibid., 77.

62. Ibid., 82–3.

63. Ibid., 93.

64. Ibid., 107.

65. Ibid.

66. Hart, 72. Chase was one of the most effective antislavery constitutional advocates. He grounded his constitutional theory both in moral principle and in practical politics. One of his biographers notes that "hundreds of men on both sides liked to make the Constitution a partner in their speeches; hardly any other rendered such services as Chase in defending victims of slavery who got across the line into the free States. It was his courage as counsel in those cases, his use of all possible legal technicalities and expedients in behalf of his client, and his fearless and widely circulated speeches, which have made him best known as an antislavery man." Hart, 73.

67. *Jones v. Van Zandt*, 46 U.S. (5 How.) 215, 231 (1847).

68. Chase, disappointed with the result, recognized that the deck had been stacked against him. In a letter to the future senator Charles Sumner, of Massachusetts, he stated, "I do not suppose that the judges of the Supreme Court regarded the arguments as worth much attention. I have reason to believe that the case was decided before they received it." Middleton, 127.

69. Blue, 247.

70. Middleton, 121.

71. Blue, 38.

72. Foner, 136.

73. New Jersey Constitution, Art. 1, ¶ 1 (1844).

74. Daniel R. Ernst, "Legal Positivism, Abolitionist Litigation, and the New Jersey Slave Case of 1845," *Law and History Review* 4 (1986): 337, 343.

75. Ibid., 337–8.

76. Ibid., 340.

77. Ibid., 343.

78. Cover, 43–55.

79. Gerald Sorin, *The New York Abolitionists: A Case Study of Political Radicalism* (Westport, CT: Greenwood, 1971), 48.

80. Ernst, 346.

81. Ibid., 347.

82. Luther Rawson Marsh, *Writings and Speeches of Alvan Stewart on Slavery* (New York: A. B. Burdick, 1860), 36.

83. Ibid., 38.

84. Sorin, 49.

85. Marsh, 16.

86. Ibid., 28.

87. TenBroek, 67–72.

88. Ibid., 66–7.

89. Sorin, 51.

90. Ibid.

91. Cover, 56.

92. Marsh, 26; Ernst, 336.

93. Stewart's argument is reproduced in Paul Finkelman, *Introduction to Abolitionists in Northern Courts: The Pamphlet Literature*, ser. 3 (New York: Garland, 1988), 442–92.

94. Ernst, 349 n. 45.

95. Marsh, 266.

96. Ibid., 257.

97. Finkelman, 463, 478, 482.

98. Ibid., 469–70.

99. Ibid.

100. Ibid., 470.

101. Justice Bradley's most famous civil rights decision was his opinion in *The Civil Rights Cases*, 109 U.S. 3 (1883), in which he articulated a formalistic reading of the Fourteenth Amendment to deny Congress the power to prohibit segregation in public inns, accommodations, and transportation.

102. *State v. Post*, 20 N.J.L. 368, 369 (N.J. Sup. Ct. 1845).

103. Ibid., 372.

104. The abolitionists appealed to the New Jersey Court of Errors and Appeals, which affirmed the decision of the Supreme Court by a 7–1 vote without issuing written opinions. *State v. Post*, 21 N.J.L. 699 (N.J. 1848).

105. In Massachusetts, Charles Sumner litigated and lost the Boston School desegregation case, *Roberts v. City of Boston*, 59 Mass. (1 Cush.) 198 (1849). In both New Jersey and Massachusetts, abolitionists eventually obtained politically, through legislative action, what they had failed to win in the courts. Harold H. Hyman and William M. Wiecek, *Equal Justice under Law: Constitutional Development 1883–1875* (New York: Harper and Row, 1982), 90, 96, 97 (racial segregation was prohibited in Boston by statute in 1855); Ernst, 364 n. 109 (abolitionists won a partial victory in 1846, when the New Jersey legislature formally abolished slavery but declared the slaves to be apprentices for life).

106. Sorin, 50, 51 n. 98.

107. Wiecek, *Sources of Antislavery*, 274.

108. Ibid.

109. TenBroek, 89; see also Cover, 155.

110. TenBroek, 29, 116–29.

111. Wiecek, *Sources of Antislavery*, 274.

112. Hartog, 1017.

NOTES TO CHAPTER 4

1. Elizabeth Cady Stanton, Susan B. Anthony, and Matilda Joslyne Gage, *The History of Woman Suffrage*, Vol. 2 (New York: Fowler and Wells, 1882; New York: Arno and The New York Times, 1969), 627.

2. Alma Lutz, *Susan B. Anthony: Rebel, Crusader, Humanitarian*, Vol. 2 (Boston: Beacon Press, 1959), 200; see also Ida Harper, *The Life and Work of Susan B. Anthony*, Vol. 1 (Indianapolis: Hollenbeck Press, 1898), 424–5.

3. Stanton, 934.

4. Ibid., 628.

5. Miriam Gurko, *The Ladies of Seneca Falls: The Birth of the Woman's Rights Movement* (New York: Macmillan, 1974; New York: Schocken Books, 1976), 155.

6. Ibid., 113.

7. Ellen Dubois, "Women's Rights and Abolition: The Nature of the Connection," in *Antislavery Reconsidered: New Perspectives on the Abolitionists*, ed. Lewis Perry and Michael Fellman (Baton Rouge: Louisiana State University Press, 1979), 247.

8. Ibid., 248.

9. Kathleen Barry, *Susan B. Anthony: A Biography of a Singular Feminist* (New York: New York University Press, 1988), 83.

10. Ibid., 80.

11. Ibid.

12. Ibid., 121.

13. Rheta Childe Dorr, *Susan B. Anthony: The Woman Who Changed the Mind of a Nation* (New York: Frederick A. Stokes, 1928), 268.

14. Ellen Dubois, "Outgrowing the Compact of the Fathers: Equal Rights, Woman Suffrage and the United States Constitution, 1820–1878," in *A Less Than Perfect Union*, ed. Jules Lobel (New York: Monthly Review Press, 1988), 121.

15. "The British Courts on Women Suffrage," *The Revolution*, 17 December 1868.

16. Stanton, 411.

17. Joan Hoff, *Law, Gender, & Injustice: A Legal History of U.S. Women* (New York: New York University Press, 1991), 146–50.

18. Stanton, 408.

19. Ibid., 505.

20. Ibid., 596 (argument of Francis Miller, a lawyer for the suffragists).

21. Ibid., 646.

22. David Herbert Donald, *Charles Sumner*, Vol. 2 (New York: Da Capo Press, 1996), 151.

23. Stanton, 635.

24. William E. Nelson, *The Fourteenth Amendment: From Political Principle to Judicial Doctrine* (Cambridge: Harvard University Press, 1988), 68.

25. Stanton, 408 (letter from Francis Minor to *The Revolution* on October 14, 1869).

26. Harper, 411.

27. Stanton, 511.

28. "Woman Suffrage before the Courts," *The Revolution*, 11 June 1871.

29. *The Nation*, 26 June 1873, 426.

30. Stanton, 487.

31. Victoria Woodhull, "Address to the Judiciary Committee of the U.S. House of Representatives" (11 January 1871), in Stanton, 444–48.

32. House Committee on the Judiciary, *Report No. 5*, 41st Cong., 3rd sess. (1871), in Stanton, 464–89.

33. Ibid., 511.

34. Ibid., 598.

35. Barry, 252.

36. Godfrey D. Lehman, "Susan B. Anthony Cast Her Ballot for Ulysses S. Grant," *American Heritage*, December 1985, p. 27.

37. Stanton, 630.

38. Ibid.

39. Lutz, 205.

40. Stanton, 936.

41. Ibid.

42. Ibid., 937.

43. Stanton, 647.

44. Stanton, 688.

45. Katherine Anthony, *Susan B. Anthony: Her Personal History and Her Era* (New York: Doubleday and Co., Inc., 1954), 299.

46. Ibid., 299.

47. Lehman, 31.

48. Harper, 455–6.

49. Stanton, 695.

50. Lehman, 30.

51. Anthony, 301.

52. Sandra Day O'Connor, "The History of the Women's Suffrage Movement," *Vanderbilt Law Review* 49 (1996): 657, 662.

53. Ibid., 662.

54. Jane Friedman, *America's First Woman Lawyer* (Buffalo: Prometheus Books, 1993), 47.

55. *In re Application of Bradwell*, 55 Ill. 535, 540 (1876).

56. Jane Friedman, Myra Bradwell. "On Defying the Creator and Becoming a Lawyer," *Valparaiso University Law Review* 28 (1994): 1287, 1300.

57. "The Supreme Court Righting Itself," 16 *The Nation* 280, 24 April 1873, in Friedman, *Defying the Creator*, 1287.

58. Letter from Susan B. Anthony to Myra Bradwell, 30 July 1873, in Friedman, *Defying the Creator*, 1294.

59. *The Slaughter-house Cases*, 83 U.S. (16 Wall.) 36 (1873). Ironically, Carpenter had argued the state's position in *Slaughter-house*.

60. *Bradwell v. State*, 83 U.S. (16 Wall.) 130, 141 (1873).

61. Friedman, *Defying the Creator*, 1302.

62. Ibid., 1304.

63. Ibid., 1294.

64. Mary K. Dains, ed., *Show Me Missouri Women: Selected Biographies* (Kirksville, MO: Thomas Jefferson University Press, 1989), 234.

65. Anna Kelly Koetting, *Four St. Louis Women: Precursors of Reform* (1972), 18.

66. Lutz, 200.

67. Even had Chase lived, it was unclear whether he would have dissented as he had done in *Bradwell*. In an 1873 letter, Chase suggested that Susan B. Anthony was moving, "a little too fast, in her demand for the vote." John Niven, *Salmon P. Chase: A Biography* (New York: Oxford University Press, 1995), 528 n. 64.

68. Hoff, 171.

69. Plaintiff's Argument and Brief, *Minor v. Happersett*, 88 U.S. 162 (1875), reprinted in Stanton, 719.

70. Ibid., 730.

71. *New York Times*, 10 February 1879, p. 8.

72. Stanton, 734.
73. *Minor v. Happersett*, 88 U.S. 162, 164 (1874).
74. Ibid., 170.
75. Ibid., 177–8.
76. Stanton, 720.
77. Karen O'Connor, *Women's Organizational Use of the Courts* (Lexington, MA, D. C. Heathe, 1980), 43.
78. Lynn Sherr, *Failure Is Impossible: Susan B. Anthony in Her Own Words* (New York: Random House, 1995), 329.
79. Norma Basch, "Reconstructing Female Citizenship: *Minor v. Happersett*," in *The Constitution, Law and American Life: Critical Aspects of the Nineteenth Century Experience*, ed. Donald G. Nieman (Athens: University of Georgia Press, 1992), 58.
80. Charles Fairman, *Reconstruction and Reunion, 1864–1868 Part Two* (New York: Macmillan, 1987), 224.
81. Dorr, 227.
82. Ellen Dubois, "Taking the Law into Our Own Hands: Bradwell, Minor and Suffrage Militance in the 1870's," in *One Woman, One Vote: Rediscovering the Woman Suffrage Movement*, ed. Marjorie Spruill Wheeler (Troutdale, OR: New Sage Press, 1995), 97.
83. Nancy A. Hewitt, *Women's Activism and Social Change: Rochester, New York, 1822–1872* (Ithaca: Cornell University Press, 1984).
84. Stanton, Vol. 3, 84.
85. Carrie Chapman Catt and Nettie Rogers Shuler, *Woman Suffrage and Politics; The Inner Story of the Suffrage Movement* (New York: C. Scribner's Sons, 1923), 106.
86. Sherr, 290.
87. Dubois, "Outgrowing the Compact of the Fathers," 131.
88. *Griswold v. Connecticut*, 381 U.S. 479 (1965); *Roe v. Wade*, 410 U.S. 113 (1973).
89. Basch, 56.
90. Stanton, Vol. 2, 508.
91. Hoff, 149.
92. Hoff, 179–82.
93. Dubois, *Taking the Law*, 83.
94. Dubois, "Outgrowing the Compact of the Fathers," 131; see also Adam Winkler, *A Revolution Too Soon: Woman Suffragists and the "Living Constitution"* N.Y.U. L. Rev. 76 (2001): 1456.
95. Stanton, 755.
96. Ibid.
97. Dorr, 4.
98. Sherr, 324.

NOTES TO CHAPTER 5

1. 163 U.S. 537 (1896).

2. Jack Greenberg, "Litigation for Social Change: Methods, Limits, and Role in Democracy," *Record of the Bar Association of the City of New York*, Vol. 29 (1974): 320, 326.

3. Rodolphe L. Desdunes, *Our People and Our History: Fifty Creole Portraits* (Baton Rouge: Louisiana State University Press, 1973), 141. This book was originally published in 1911 as *Nos Hommes et Notre Histerie*.

4. Louis A. Martinet to Albion W. Tourgée, letter, 4 July 1892, in *The Thin Disguise: Turning Point in Negro History, A Documentary Presentation*, ed. Otto H. Olsen (New York: Humanities Press, 1967), 64.

5. Ibid., 63.

6. Ibid., 8. See generally C. Vann Woodward, *The Strange Career of Jim Crow* (New York: Oxford University Press, 1955), 69–71.

7. Olsen, *The Thin Disguise*, 11. The civil rights community was encouraged by a number of victories in the North against racial injustice in the early 1890s. Between 1891 and 1895, at least eleven northern states improved or established civil rights laws, and, in 1892, New York and Michigan state courts ruled against public segregation.

8. Charles A. Lofgren, *The Plessy Case: A Legal-Historical Interpretation* (New York: Oxford University Press, 1988), 97; quoting James Bryce, "Thoughts on the Negro Problem," *North American Review* 153 (1891): 654.

9. Stephen J. Riegel, "The Persistent Career of Jim Crow: Lower Federal Courts and the 'Separate but Equal Doctrine': 1865–1896," *American Journal of Legal History* 28 (1984): a 17, 27–8. Riegel writes that "[d]istrict and circuit court rulings in other public accommodations cases showed a remarkable uniformity of principle summed up by a phrase in *Logwood*: '*Equal* accommodations do not mean *identical* accommodations.'" Ibid. (quoting *Logwood v. Memphis & C.R.*, 23 F. 318, 319 (C.C.W.D. Tenn. 1885)).

10. Lofgren, 79. The *judicially defined* Amendment, as it emerged in the state and lower federal case reports, remained quite hospitable to the principle of separate-but-equal.

11. See *The Slaughter-house Cases*, 83 U.S. 36 (1873); *The Civil Rights Cases*, 109 U.S. 3 (1883). In the 1883 civil rights cases, the Court declared the 1875 act of Congress prohibiting discrimination in public accommodations unconstitutional because the Fourteenth Amendment proscribed only state-imposed discrimination. By outlawing private discrimination, Congress had transgressed into an area reserved to the states.

12. Roger A. Fischer, *The Segregation Struggle in Louisiana: 1862–77* (Chicago: University of Illinois Press, 1974). In New Orleans, with its cosmopolitan mix of whites, slaves, and a sizable community of free blacks of varying

shades, segregation imposed by law had been a source of tension even prior to the Civil War. Segregated streetcars in which Negro riders could only board only cars marked with a large black star were a particular source of discontent; a group of Negroes mounted an armed attack in July 1833 on a white streetcar that had refused to carry them. During the Civil War, the Union general Benjamin Butler ordered the streetcars desegregated, a decree challenged by the car companies and set aside by a local court.

13. Ibid., 139–40.

14. Ibid., 140–1.

15. *Bertonneau v. Board of Directors of City Schools* 3 Fed. Cas 294 (Circuit Ct, D. La 1978).

16. Ibid., 296.

17. Fischer, 142–3.

18. *Hall v. DeCuir*, 95 U.S. 485 (1878).

19. *Hall v. DeCuir*, 490. Curiously, Chief Justice Waite ignored the 1875 Civil Rights Act, enacted after Mrs. DeCuir's unhappy voyage, guaranteeing equal access to public carriers and accommodation. The oversight was portentous, since the Court invalidated the congressional Civil Rights Act five years later as exceeding Congress's power under the Thirteenth and Fourteenth Amendments. Lofgren, 132–3.

20. *Hall v. DeCuir*, 503. See also Lofgren, 131–2, which discusses the *Hall* case.

21. Desdunes, 141. While Desdunes had at first suggested and preferred a boycott of the railroads in protest against the separate case law, Martinet and other committee members supported litigation, and the boycott apparently never materialized.

22. Leon F. Litwack, *North of Slavery: The Negro in the Free States, 1790–1860* (Chicago: University of Chicago Press, 1961), 107–8; J. Morgan Kousser, "The Supremacy of Equal Rights: The Struggle against Racial Discrimination in Antebellum Massachusetts and the Foundations of the Fourteenth Amendments," *Northwestern University Law Review* 82 (1988): 941, 954.

23. Kousser, "The Supremacy of Equal Rights," 955.

24. *Roberts v. Boston*, 59 Mass. 198 (1849); Leonard W. Levy and Douglas L. Jones, eds., *Jim Crow in Boston: The Origin of the Separate but Equal Doctrine* (New York: Da Capo Press, 1974), xi.

25. Donald G. Neiman, "The Language of Liberation: African Americans and Equalitarian Constitutionalism, 1830–1950," in *The Constitution, Law and American Life: Critical Aspects of the Nineteenth-Century Experience*, ed. Donald G. Nieman (Athens: University of Georgia Press, 1992), 67, 71.

26. See J. Morgan Kousser, *Dead End: The Development of Nineteenth Century Litigation on Racial Discrimination in Schools* (Oxford: Clarendon Press, 1986), 5.

27. Only one judge involved in the thirty-three cases involving the Fourteenth Amendment "squarely ruled that school segregation *per se* contravened the Fourteenth Amendment." Ibid., 9.

28. Ibid., 14.

29. Liva Baker, *The Second Battle of New Orleans: The Hundred-Year Struggle to Integrate the Schools* (New York: Harper Collins, 1996), 36.

30. Ibid., 34–5.

31. Desdunes, 147.

32. See generally Desdunes.

33. Ibid., 147.

34. Ibid.

35. Charles B. Roussève, *The Negro in Louisiana: Aspects of His History and His Literature* (New Orleans: Xavier University Press, 1937), 158, quoting Desdunes.

36. Desdunes, 147.

37. The prominent African American historian John Hope Franklin has noted that it was to Plessy's "credit that he forced the hand of his state and nation and made his compatriots show themselves for what they were." Elizabeth Mullener, "Early Activist Celebrated in Lecture, Historians Discuss Plessy Decision," *New Orleans Times-Picayune*, 18 May 1996, sec. B, p. 3; available from WESTLAW at 1996 WL 6421009.

38. Albion Tourgée to James Walker (undated); in Albion Tourgée Papers (Chataugua County Historical Society; microfilm tape 6502.

39. Otto M. Olsen, *Carpetbagger's Crusade: The Life of Albion Wingar Tourgée* (Baltimore: Johns Hopkins Press: 1965), 298.

40. Tourgée was elected delegate to the Constitutional Convention on a platform that included equal civil and political rights for all citizens; no property qualification for jurymen; blanket voter eligibility for every office; popular election of all state legislative, executive, and judicial officials; free public schools from the primary to university level; equalization of property taxes; and abolition or at least reduction of poll taxes. Ibid., 89.

41. Ibid., 182, quoting Andrew Joyner, *Raleigh News and Observer*, 28 May 1905.

42. John Hope Franklin, *Introduction to Albion W. Tourgée, A Fool's Errand*, ed. John H. Franklin (Cambridge: Harvard University Press, 1961), xxi.

43. Ibid., 5.

44. Ibid., 5–6.

45. Ibid., 5.

46. Ibid., 6. His extraordinary courage and persistence stemmed from Tourgée's sense of history and of his place in a cosmic drama. Michael Kent Curtis, "Albion Tourgée: Remembering Plessy's Lawyer on the 100th Anniversary of *Plessy v. Ferguson*," *Constitutional Commentary* 13 (summer 1996): 187.

47. Albion Tourgée to Emma Tourgée (his wife), letter, 6 September 1863, in Olsen, *Carpetbagger's Crusade*, 284 n. 4.

48. Albion Tourgée, *A Fool's Errand*, ed. John H. Franklin (Cambridge: Harvard University Press, 1961), 134–5.

49. "[Prophets] place themselves *in confrontation with* the power structure, and almost always from within the community or the people." See J. Severino Croatto, *Exodus: A Hermeneutics of Freedom* (Maryknoll, NY: Orbis Books, 1981), 40; Prophets are "rooted . . . in their own societies." Michael Waltzer, *Interpretation and Social Criticism* (Cambridge: Harvard University Press, 1987), 81.

50. Richard O. Boyer, *The Legend of John Brown: A Biography and a History* (New York: Alfred A. Knopf, 1973), 4 quoted in Lacey Baldwin Smith, *Fools, Martyrs, Traitors: The Story of Martyrdom in the Western World* (New York: Alfred A. Knopf, 1997), 229.

51. Smith, 258.

52. Ibid., 251.

53. Ibid.

54. Olsen, *The Thin Disguise*, 11.

55. Tourgée's work after 1879 continued to reveal hope and frustration. He met James Garfield at the Republican National Convention in 1880, and the then presidential candidate agreed to implement certain key programs urged by Tourgée. Garfield wrote to Tourgée expressing the "hope that the day may come when our country will be a paradise for all such fools." Franklin, *Introduction to Tourgée, A Fool's Errand*, xxii. However, shortly after being elected president, Garfield was assassinated.

56. George J. Becker, "Albion W. Tourgée: Pioneer in Social Criticism," *American Literature*, Vol. 19, no. 1 (March 1947): 59; Edward Wilson, *Patriotic Gore: Studies in the Literature of the American Civil War* (New York: Oxford University Press: 1962), 536.

57. Olsen, *Carpetbagger's Crusade*, 294.

58. Ibid., 263. His wife Emma's diary is constantly punctuated with despair. "Albion [is] in despair over his work. Life does not seem worth the struggle anyhow," she wrote. Ibid., 267. See also Roy F. Dibble, *Albion W. Tourgée* (Port Washington, NY: Kennikat Press, 1921), 93–4.

59. Erik H. Erikson, *Gandhi's Truth: On the Origins of Militant Nonviolence* (New York: W. W. Norton, 1969), 153.

60. Olsen, *Carpetbagger's Crusade*, 281.

61. Ibid., 309.

62. Lofgren, 40 n. 22, quoting Tourgée to Walker, 14 January 1892.

63. C. Vann Woodward, "The Case of the Louisiana Traveler," in *Quarrels That Have Shaped the Constitution*, ed. John A. Garraty (New York: Harper and Row, 1987), 157, 164.

64. Ibid.

65. Olsen, *Carpetbagger's Crusade*, 327.

66. Louis A. Martinet to Albion W. Tourgée, letter, 5 October 1891, in Olsen, *The Thin Disguise*, 56–57.

67. Lofgren, 31; Greenberg, 324. In addition, *Plessy* challenged a train official's legal ability to determine a person's race. In addition, Tourgée and his co-counsel included various other narrow challenges to the Louisiana law, such as an attack on the statute's immunization of railways and train officials from liability for damages for refusing to carry passengers who objected to their assigned seats. Assignment of Errors, *ex parte Homer A. Plessy*, 5 January 1893, in Olsen, *The Thin Disguise*, 76; see also Lofgren, 56.

68. Owen M. Fiss, *Troubled Beginnings of the Modern State, 1888–1910*, Vol. 8, *History of the Supreme Court of the United States* (New York: Macmillan, 1993), 360, quoting Plaintiff's Brief at 31.

69. *Plessy v. Ferguson*, 163 U.S. 537 (1896), Plaintiff's Brief in Error, *Landmark Briefs and Arguments of the Supreme Court of the United States: Constitutional Law*, Vol. 13, ed. Philip B. Kurland and Gerhard Casper (Arlington, VA: University Publications of America, 1975), 1, 57.

70. Ibid., 39.

71. Ibid., 41.

72. Ibid., 50.

73. Ibid., 56.

74. Ibid., 46.

75. Laura N. Gasaway and Judith W. Wegner, "Women at UNC and in the Practice of Law," *North Carolina Law Review* 73 (1995): 705, 705–6.

76. *Landmark Briefs*, 61.

77. Ibid., 61.

78. Ibid., 63.

79. Ibid., 53.

80. Olsen, *The Thin Disguise*, 85.

81. Fiss, 354, 360.

82. Olsen, *The Thin Disguise*, 64.

83. Ibid.

84. Albion W. Tourgée to Louis A. Martinet, letter, 31 October 1893, in Olsen, *The Thin Disguise*, 78.

85. Ibid., 79.

86. Ibid., 78.

87. Ibid. Curiously, in March 1892, just prior to the test case's initiation, Tourgée urged his clients to "make no clamor at all about the case." Tourgée, letter to Walker, 1 March 1892.

88. A speech given to the American Association for the Advancement of Science by its president, Daniel G. Brinton, typified the prevailing attitude on the eve of the Supreme Court's decision in *Plessy*. Brinton argued that each race

and ethnic group had its "own added special powers and special limitations . . . and were not 'equally endowed.'" Lofgren, 104–5.

89. Olsen, *Carpetbagger's Crusade*, 328.

90. Ibid. There were some major protests and victories, particularly in the northern states, in the period 1895–1896. Olsen, *The Thin Disguise*, 8; Woodward, "The Case of the Louisiana Traveler," 168–9.

91. *Plessy v. Ferguson*, 542.

92. Ibid., 544.

93. Ibid., 551.

94. Richard Kluger, *Simple Justice: The History of* Brown v. Board of Education *and Black America's Struggle for Equality* (New York: Alfred A. Knopf, 1976), 80.

95. *Plessy v. Ferguson*, 557.

96. Ibid., 562.

97. Tinsley E. Yarbrough, *Judicial Enigma: The First Justice Harlan* (New York: Oxford University Press, 1995), 139–43.

98. *Plessy v. Ferguson*, 559.

99. Curiously, a number of important writers on the *Plessy* case have totally omitted Harlan's view of white dominance. Richard Kluger, in his Pulitzer-prize-winning book *Simple Justice*, extensively quotes the relevant paragraph but omits Harlan's prediction that the white race would remain dominant if it held true to a color-blind constitution. Kluger, 82. Charles Lofgren, in his authoritative book on the *Plessy* case, also quotes and cites the "color-blind" paragraph but again fails to mention the critical predictive sentence. Lofgren, 192–3.

100. Lofgren, 196; Olsen, *The Thin Disguise*, 25; Riegel, 17.

101. C. Vann Woodward, "*Plessy v. Ferguson*: The Birth of Jim Crow," *American Heritage*, Vol. 15, no. 3 (April 1964): 52, 103.

102. Lofgren, 196–7.

103. Ibid., 197.

104. Ibid., 196–7. Lofgren writes that, "[a]mong editors outside the South who judged the judges, hostility to the decision overshadowed approval by perhaps three to one." Ibid., 196.

105. Olsen, *The Thin Disguise*, 25; Lofgren, 197. Early-twentieth-century scholars also generally ignored the case. Charles Warren's 1926 book, *The Supreme Court in United States History*, did not discuss *Plessy*, nor did other constitutional histories published before 1950. Even Henry Steel Commager's *Documents of American History*, released in 1934, omitted *Plessy*. Lofgren, 5.

106. Lofgren, 5. The primary reason that *Plessy* was ignored for so long was that, for white America, its holding was not controversial. Most whites accepted the compromise of 1877 ending Reconstruction, and the lower federal

courts and state courts had virtually unanimously adopted the "separate but equal" doctrine. Tourgée's central and most radical arguments on the meaning of the Thirteenth and Fourteenth Amendments had already been rejected by the Supreme Court in the preceding two decades. Ibid.

Many scholars have viewed *Plessy* as triggering a second wave of Jim Crow segregation. See John H. Franklin, *Racial Equality in America* (Chicago: University of Chicago Press, 1976), 65; see also Riegel, 19 n. 10 (citing other sources that support this proposition). One scholar has argued that it was only after the Court's decision in *Plessy* "that rigid segregation-in-fact began to run rampant." Paul Oberst, "The Strange Career of *Plessy v. Ferguson*," *Arizona Law Review* 15 (1973): 389. Another commentator agrees, maintaining that *Plessy* and the *Civil Rights Cases* "constitutionally encouraged the Jim Crow laws." Charles A. Miller, "Constitutional Law and the Rhetoric of Race," in *Perspectives in American History*, Vol. 5, ed. Donald Fleming and Bernard Bailyn (Cambridge: Harvard University, 1971), 147, 196. More recent scholarly commentary treats the effect of the *Plessy* decision more modestly, as merely encouraging existing trends. "[T]he evidence of Plessy's direct role is slight." Lofgren, 203. *Plessy* was "not a turning point . . . [but] rather an affirmation of the dominant legal concept." Riegel, 39.

107. Lofgren, 208.

108. Woodward, "Case of the Louisiana Traveler," 173–4.

109. Both Supreme Court dissenting opinions and prophetic litigation often have no impact on their era and therefore are frequently described as useless. As one noted legal philosopher argued, dissents have "no consequences within the system: no one's rights or duties are thereby altered." H. L. A. Hart, *The Concept of Law* (Oxford: Clarendon Press, 1961), 138. See, for example, Harlan F. Stone, "Dissenting Opinions Are Not without Value," *American Judicature Society Journal* 26 (1942): 78. Even the "Great Dissenter," Justice Oliver Wendell Holmes, once noted that he generally found it "useless and undesirable" to write a dissent. *Northern Security Co. v. United States*, 193 U.S. 197, 400 (1904). In a 1937 study of the attitudes of lawyers and judges toward dissenting opinions, Judge Evans, of the Seventh Circuit Court of Appeals, discovered that a large majority found dissents to be useless or undesirable.

110. Charles E. Hughes, *The Supreme Court of the United States* (New York: Columbia University Press, 1928), 68.

111. William J. Brennan Jr., "In Defense of Dissents," *Hastings Law Journal* 37 (1986): 427, 431.

112. Stanley H. Fuld, "The Voices of Dissent," *Columbia Law Review* 62 (1962): 923, 928, quoting William O. Douglas, "The Dissent, A Safeguard of Democracy," *American Judicature Society Journal* 32 (1948): 104, 107.

113. Benjamin Cardozo, *Law and Literature and Other Essays and Addresses* (New York: Harcourt, Brace, 1931), 36.

114. Martin Kelman, "The Forked Path of Dissent," *Supreme Court Review* (1985): 227, 255.

115. Karl M. ZoBell, "Division of Opinion in the Supreme Court: A History of Judicial Disintegration," *Cornell Law Quarterly* 44 (1959): 186, 211 n. 129.

116. See, for example, T. Alexander Aleinikoff, "Re-Reading Justice Harlan's Dissent in *Plessy v. Ferguson*: Freedom, Antiracism and Citizenship," *University of Illinois Law Review* (1992): 961.

117. 349 U.S. 294 (1954).

118. See Kluger.

119. Woodward, "The Case of the Louisiana Traveler," 173–4.

120. Robert M. Cover, "The Supreme Court 1982 Term: Foreword: Nomos and Narrative," *Harvard Law Review* 97 (1983): 4, 28.

121. Leon Friedman, ed., *Argument: The Oral Argument before the Supreme Court in* Brown v. Board of Education *of Topeka, 1952–55* (New York: Chelsea House, 1969), 239–40, quoted in A. Leon Higginbotham Jr., *Shades of Freedom: Racial Politics and Presumptions of the American Legal Process* (New York: Oxford University Press, 1996), 83.

122. *The American Experience: Simple Justice*, prod. Aron Kirkland et al., 140 min., PBS, 1993.

123. Oliver Hill, telephone interview by author, Pittsburgh, Pennsylvania, February 2000.

124. Kluger, 171, paraphrasing Thompson.

125. Margold Report, reprinted in Jack Greenberg, "Judicial Process and Social Change," *Cases and Materials on Judicial Process: Constitutional Litigation* (St. Paul: West, 1977), 51.

126. Lofgren, 208.

127. Kluger, 133–4, 186.

128. See ibid., 212.

129. Arthur Kinoy, "The Constitutional Right of Negro Freedom," *Rutgers Law Review* 21 (1967): 387, 426–7.

130. Higginbotham, 111–2.

131. Edward H. Levi, *An Introduction to Legal Reasoning* (Chicago: University of Chicago Press, 1949), 1–19. I am indebted to my colleague Vivian Curran for pointing out the dialectical path of common law decisions.

132. Higginbotham, 189.

133. James T. Patterson, Brown v. Board of Education: *A Civil Rights Milestone and Troubled Legacy* (New York: Oxford University Press, 2001), xxix.

134. Olsen, *The Thin Disguise*, 27–8.

135. Judge Damon Keith, "Speech: One Hundred Years after *Plessy v. Ferguson*," *University of Cincinnati Law Review* 65 (1997): 853, 856.

136. Maurice Friedman, Abraham Joshua Heschel, and Elie Wiesel, *You Are My Witnesses* (New York: Farrar, Straus, Giroux, 1987), 88.

137. Carl T. Roman, *Dream Makers, Dream Breakers: The World of Justice Thurgood Marshall* (Boston: Little Brown, 1993), 453–4.

138. This statistic and those that follow are culled from a study by Glady Tignor Peterson of cases involving separate schools from 1865 to 1934. Gladys Tignor Peterson, "The Present Status of the Negro Separate School as Defined by Court Decisions," *Journal of Negro Education* Vol. 4, no. 3 (July 1935): 351–74.

139. Blacks were able to win most cases where they alleged that segregation was not sanctioned by state law (mostly in northern states), challenging separate taxation of blacks and whites for the support of their respective cases, and they won some cases in which they challenged unequal conditions at segregated schools.

140. In the late 1890s and early 1900s, blacks organized boycotts in more than twenty-five southern cities against Jim Crow streetcars. While most of those boycotts were unsuccessful, boycotts did defeat Jim Crow in a number of southern cities, but success was only temporary; segregation was reimposed within a few months or at most years. Catherine A. Barnes, *Journey from Jim Crow: The Desegregation of Southern Transit* (New York: Columbia University Press, 1983), 11–2.

141. Charles H. Thompson, "Court Action the Only Reasonable Alternative to Remedy Immediate Abuses of the Negro Separate School," *Journal of Negro Education*, Vol. 4, no. 3 (July 1935): 419, 422.

142. This "vision has justified continued struggles by groups in the face of (presumably temporary) judicial and political defeats." Hendrick Hartog, "The Constitution of Aspiration and 'The Rights That Belong to Us All,'" *Journal of American History*, Vol. 74, no. 3 (December 1987): 1013, 1016.

143. Austin Sarat, "Between (the Presence of) Violence and (the Possibility of) Justice: Lawyering against Capital Punishment," in *Cause Lawyering: Political Commitments and Professional Responsibilities*, ed. Austin Sarat and Stuart Scheingold (New York: Oxford University Press, 1998), 317, 324.

144. Ibid., 336. For these lawyers, making this record

is our way of acting in the world, our way of struggling against the system. We create these papers that we write. . . . And I think that someday somebody will look at this, maybe a hundred years from now, but someone will look and say, "Oh my God, it was true that the death penalty was really just an engine of discrimination." Even if it seems fruitless now, it is worth doing because we are making a record of who is getting the death penalty. . . . I've talked with enough other people to describe the work as a witnessing sort of function. Ibid., 337–8.

145. Higginbotham, 206.

146. Baker, 51.

147. Ibid., 54.

NOTES TO CHAPTER 6

1. Staughton and Alice Lynd, interview by author, Pittsburgh, Pennsylvania, August 1993.

2. Staughton Lynd, "The Genesis of the Idea of a Community Right to Industrial Property in Youngstown and Pittsburgh 1971–1987," *Journal of American History*, Vol. 74, no. 3 (1987): 926; William K. Stevens, "New Pennsylvania Governor Seeks an Economic Partnership," *New York Times*, 21 January 1987, sec. A, p. 16 (steel industry jobs declined from 90,000 to 22,000 in Pittsburgh).

3. Associated Press, "Youngstown Learns to Live without Steel, But It's Grim," *Los Angeles Times*, 23 August 1987, part 1, p. 2.

4. Susanna McBee, "Desperate Jobless City Seeks to Buy Failing Steel Plant," *Washington Post*, 9 May 1978, sec. A, p. 2.

5. Associated Press, "Youngstown Learns," part 1, p. 2.

6. Ibid.

7. Staughton Lynd, *The Fight against Shutdowns: Youngstown's Steel Mill Closings* (San Pedro: Singlejack Books, 1982), 145, quoting the City Council of Youngstown Resolution 79–153.

8. Haynes Johnson, "The Heartbreak of Ohio's Steel Valley," *Washington Post*, 26 October 1980, sec. G, p. 1.

9. Staughton Lynd, *Living Inside Our Hope: A Steadfast Radical's Thoughts on Rebuilding the Movement* (Ithaca: Cornell University Press, 1997), 7.

10. Lynd, *The Fight against Shutdowns*, 26–7.

11. Ibid., 40.

12. Ibid., 123–30.

13. Ibid., 131.

14. Ibid., 132.

15. Ibid.

16. Ibid., 137.

17. William Serrin, "Anti-War Leader of the 60's Now Helps Workers as a Lawyer," *New York Times*, 29 November 1982, sec. A, p. 16.

18. Lynd, *Living Inside Our Hope*, 48.

19. Ibid., 50.

20. Jane Slaughter, "Staughton Lynd," *The Progressive*, February 1994, 33.

21. Lynd, *Living Inside Our Hope*, 7–8.

22. Ibid., 64.

23. Staughton Lynd, telephone interview by author, Pittsburgh, Pennsylvania, June, 2000.

24. Ibid.

25. Lynd, *Living Inside Our Hope*, 25.

26. Ibid.; Staughton Lynd, interview, June 2000.

27. Lynd, *Living Inside Our Hope*, 25.

28. Staughton Lynd, interview, June 2000.

29. Ibid.

30. Lynd, *The Fight against Shutdowns*, 142.

31. Ernest Brown Jr., "Steel Closures Suit Is Filed," *Youngstown Vindicator*, 21 December 1979, p. 1.

32. Ibid.

33. Lynd, 154.

34. Ibid., 158, quoting *Cleveland Plain Dealer*, 30 January 1980.

35. Ibid., 162.

36. John Judis, "The Strange Case of Ramsey Clark: How Far Left Can You Go? Farther," *New Republic*, Vol. 204, no. 16, 22 April 1991, p. 23.

37. David Margolick, "The Long and Lonely Journey of Ramsey Clark," *New York Times*, 14 June 1991, sec. B, p. 9.

38. Ibid.

39. Josh Getlin, "For a Politician, Former U.S. Attorney General Ramsey Clark Took a Road Less Traveled," *Los Angeles Times*, 18 February 1990, sec. E, p. 1.

40. Margolick, sec. B, p. 9.

41. Ibid.

42. Ibid.

43. Susan Aschoff, "Thinking Globally, He Acts That Way Too," *St. Petersburg Times*, 5 April 1999, p. 1D.

44. *Saltany v. Reagan*, 702 F. Supp. 319, 322 (D.D.C. 1988).

45. *Saltany v. Reagan*, 886 F.2d 438, 440 (D.C. Cir. 1989) (*per curiam*) (Buckley, D. H. Ginsburg & Sentelle), *cert. denied*, 495 U.S. 932 (1990). Legal commentators have criticized the Court of Appeals's decision. Anthony D'Amato, "The Imposition of Attorney Sanctions for Claims Arising from the U.S. Air Raid on Libya," *American Journal of International Law* 84 (1990): 705–11; Carl Tobias, "Rule 11 Recalibrated in Civil Rights Cases," *Villanova Law Review* 36 (1991): 105, 118–9. But other judges, even critics of the D.C. Circuit's decision in the Libyan case, agree that courts do not exist as public forums. At the same time that Ramsey Clark was being sanctioned by the D.C. Circuit, the prominent civil rights attorney William Kunstler was sanctioned by the Fourth Circuit Court of Appeals for filing a civil rights case whose "central purpose," in their opinion, was not to vindicate rights through the judicial process. *In re Kunstler*, 914 F.2d 505, 520 (4th Cir. 1990). Yet, from the early history of the American Republic onward, courts have been utilized by political movements to further public debate on important constitutional issues. Indeed, as one commentator noted, a "considerable amount of civil rights litigation" is in some sense a "public statement of protest." Tobias, 118, quoting *Saltany v. Reagan*. Courts are not merely forums to settle private parties' disputes but can function, and have functioned, as forums in which broad public issues are debated, as attested by

the enormous press coverage given to, and public fascination with, the Supreme Court.

46. Paul Hurley, "Clark Tells the Story Like It Is," *Youngstown Vindicator*, 29 February 1980, p. 1.

47. Lynd, *The Fight against Shutdowns*, 163.

48. Ibid.

49. Ibid., 164.

50. Ibid., 165.

51. Ibid.

52. Ibid., 166.

53. Hurley, "Clark Tells the Story Like It Is."

54. Paul Hurley, "Action Held up 1 Week," *The Youngstown Vindicator*, 29 February 1980, p. 1.

55. Greg Garland, "U.S. Judge's Edict Could Be Appealed," *Warren Tribune Chronicle*, 29 February 1980.

56. "U.S. Steel Decided Last May Not to Invest," *Warren Tribune Chronicle*, 18 March 1980, p. 1.

57. Ibid.

58. See Lynd, *The Fight against Shutdowns*, 175.

59. Ibid.

60. *United Steelworkers of America et al. v. United States Steel Corp.*, 492 F. Supp. 1, 4–10 (N.D. Ohio 1980).

61. Ibid.

62. Ibid., 10.

63. Paul Hurley, "Steel Workers Retain Hope on Mill Purchase," *Youngstown Vindicator*, 23 March 1980, sec. A, p. 1.

64. Ibid.

65. See Lynd, *Living Inside Our Hope*.

66. Lynd, *The Fight against Shutdowns*, 177.

67. One law professor termed Lambros's statement of a property right "utter nonsense." "A Tightening Vise on Plant Shutdowns," *Business Week*, 17 March 1980, p. 38.

68. Staughton Lynd, interview, June 2000.

69. Lynd, *The Fight against Shutdowns*, 178.

70. Arthur Kinoy, *Rights on Trial: The Odyssey of a People's Lawyer* (Cambridge: Harvard University Press, 1983), 57–8.

71. Ibid., 71.

72. Ibid.

73. Ibid.

74. Ibid., 125.

75. Ibid., 193.

76. Ibid., 192–93.

77. Kinoy's view is akin to the spiritual perspective that the "impossible must be imagined if it is to be realized." Joel Kovel, *History and Spirit: An Inquiry into the Philosophy of Liberation* (Boston: Beacon Press, 1991), 13.

78. Lynd interview.

79. *Local 1330, United Steel Workers of America v. United Steel Corp.*, 631 F.2d 1264, 1265 (6th Cir. 1980).

80. Ibid., 1280.

81. Ibid.

82. Ibid., 1282.

83. Lynd, *The Fight against Shutdowns*, 186, quoting "Judge Calls Steel Suit Lesson For Nation," *Youngstown Vindicator*, 14 November 1980.

84. *Warren Tribune Chronicle*, 14 November 1980, sec. A, p. 1.

85. Lynd, *The Fight against Shutdowns*, 187.

86. Joseph B. White, "Workers' Revenge: Factory Towns Start to Fight Back Angrily When Firms Pull Out," *Wall Street Journal*, 3 March 1988, sec. A, p. 1.

87. Jacob M. Schlesinger, "General Motors Sued by Town for $318.3 Million over Breakup of Sixty-Four-Year Marriage," *Wall Street Journal*, 21 August 1987, sec. A, p. 1.

88. Merrill Goozner, "Cities Win Round in Plant Case," *Chicago Tribune*, 29 June 1988, sec. C, p. 1; Neal R. Peirce, "Plant Closings Force States to Seek Retribution," *National Journal*, Vol. 20, no. 14, 7 May 1988, p. 1207.

89. See Denis Collins, "Plant Closings: Establishing Legal Obligations," *Labor Law Journal*, Vol. 40, no. 2 (February 1989): 67, 72–3; Fran Ansley, "Standing Rusty and Rolling Empty: Law, Poverty, and America's Eroding Industrial Base," *Georgetown Law Journal* 81 (1993): 1757, 1819–30.

90. *Charter Township of Ypsilanti v. General Motors Corp.*, No. 92-43075-CK, 1993 WL 132385 (Michigan Circuit Court, February 9, 1993).

91. Lynd, *The Fight against Shutdowns*, 177.

92. Victor Frankl, *Man's Search for Meaning* (New York: Pocket Books, 1984).

93. See ibid.

94. By so living, one can pass his or her values and ideas on to future generations. Lynd recounts the story of Arthur as told by the feminist author Marion Zimmer Bradley. As Arthur lies dying, he asks whether all he attempted amounted to a failure. His sister, Morgana replies that they "did not fail" because they did what they did so that "those who came after us might bring her ["the Mother"] into this world." Lynd, *Living Inside Our Hope*, 16, quoting Marion Zimmer Bradley, *The Mists of Avalon* (New York: Knopf, 1982), 868, 876.

95. *Shout Youngstown*, prod. Carol Greenwald and Dorry Krauss, 45 min., Media Works, 1984, video cassette about Youngstown struggle.

NOTES TO CHAPTER 7

The quotes in this chapter attributed to Dan Snow, Ruth Wald, Elijah Wald, and Victor Rabinowitz are from interviews with the author.

1. *Kent v. Dulles*, 357 U.S. 116, 127 (1958).
2. *Zemel v. Rusk*, 381 U.S. 1 (1965).
3. *United States v. Laub*, 385 U.S. 475 (1967).
4. "President's News Conference of 9 March 1977," *Weekly Compilation of Presidential Documents* 13 (14 March 1977): 328–9, microfilm.
5. Public Law 426, 95th Cong.; *U.S. Statutes at Large* 92 (1978): 971; *U.S. Code*, Vol. 22, sec. 211a (1978).
6. Senate Committee on Foreign Relations, *Foreign Relations Authorization Act*, Fiscal Year 1979, 95th Cong., 2d sess., 1978, S. Rept. 842, 14.
7. "Excerpts From Haig's Briefing about El Salvador," *New York Times*, 21 February 1981, sec. 1, p. 6.
8. Leslie H. Gelb, "Haig Is Said to Press for Military Options for Salvador Action," *New York Times*, 5 November 1981, sec. A, p. 1.
9. Michael Getler, "U.S. Pumps in Arms, Widens Training to Rescue El Salvador," *Washington Post*, 5 March 1982, sec. A, p. 1.
10. Barbara Crossette, "U.S., Linking Cuba to Violence, Blocks Tourist and Business Trips," *New York Times*, 20 April 1982, sec. A, p. 1.
11. *Banco Nacional de Cuba v. Sabbatino*, 376 U.S. 398 (1964).
12. *Haig v. Agee*, 453 U.S. 280, 306 (1981).
13. Victor Rabinowitz, *Unrepentant Leftist: A Lawyer's Memoir* (Urbana: University of Illinois Press, 1996), 324.
14. President, Proclamation, "Proclaiming the Existence of a Natural Emergency, Proclamation 2914," *Federal Register* 15, no. 245 (19 December 1950): 9029, microfiche.
15. Clinton L. Rossiter, *Constitutional Dictatorship: Crisis Government in the Modern Democracies* (Princeton: Princeton University Press, 1948), 297. The United States was legally in a perpetual state of emergency. Dean Gerhard Casper, of the University of Chicago, noted that in this era of emergency "[t]here is no such thing as normal times any more." Senate Special Committee on the Termination of the National Emergency, Constitutional Questions Concerning Emergency Powers: Hearing, 93d Cong., 1st sess., 11–12 April 1973, 83.
16. Senate Committee on the Termination of the National Emergency, *Emergency Powers Statutes: Provisions of Federal Law Now in Effect Delegating to the executive Extraordinary Authority in Time of National Emergency*, 93d Cong., 1st sess., 1973, S. Rept. 549; National Emergencies Act, *U.S. Code*, Vol. 50, sec. 1601.
17. Congress wanted to ensure that the executive emergency power would only be "utilized in time of genuine emergency, and not to address ongoing

foreign policy problems." See Senate Committee on National Emergencies and Delegated Emergency Powers, *National Emergencies and Delegated Emergency Powers*, 94th Cong., 2d sess., 1976, S. Rept. 922. *U.S. Code*, Vol. 50, sec. 1701. *U.S. Code*, Vol. 50, sec. 1622(b).

18. Jonathan Mirsky, "Obituary, Leonard Boudin," *The Independent*, 4 December 1989.

19. 357 U.S. 116.

20. Subcommittee on International Economic Policy and Trade of the House of Representatives, *Trading with the Enemy Reform Legislation: Hearing*, 95th Cong., 1st sess., 9 June 1977, 189 (statement of Representative Bingham); ibid., 147.

21. Ibid., 167.

22. Association of the Bar of the City of New York, *Freedom to Travel* (New York: Dodd, Mead, 1958), 72.

23. William B. Gould, "The Right to Travel and National Security," *Washington University Law Quarterly* 1961: 334, 364 n. 135; Note, "Constitutional Protection of Foreign Travel," *Columbia Law Review* 81 (1981), 902, 930–1; Peter M. Levitt, "Legality of the Ban of Travel to Iran," *Columbia Human Rights Law Review* 12 (1980): 91, 99–100.

24. Americans Back from Cuba," *New York Times*, 29 April 1970, p. 3, col. 2; "Developments in the Law—The National Security Interest and Civil Liberties," *Harvard Law Review* 85 (1971): 1130, 1144 n. 48; *United States v. Laub*, 385 U.S. at 485; Theodore Shabad, "Ramsey Clark Joins a Group Leaving Moscow to See Dikes," *New York Times*, 28 July 1972, p. 3, col. 5; Bernard Gwertzman, "Kissinger Holds Another Session with Hanoi Aides," *New York Times*, 15 August 1972, p. 1, col. 6. A substantial number of U.S. citizens have traveled abroad to hostile areas such as North Vietnam without ever being prosecuted. See Mr. Ichord, Committee on Internal Security, "Restraints on Travel to Countries or Areas Engaged in Armed Conflict with the United States," 93d Cong., 1st sess., 1973, H. Rept. 248.

25. Association of the Bar of the City of New York, 72.

26. *Regan v. Wald*, 468 U.S. at 253 n. 4 (Blackmun, dissenting).

27. *U.S. Code*, Vol. 28, sec. 636(b)(1)(B) and (C)).

28. *Wald v. Regan*, 708 F.2d 794 (1st Cir. 1983).

29. Ibid.

30. Ibid., 796.

31. Ibid., 797.

32. Ibid., 801.

33. Affidavit of James Michel, Acting Assistant Secretary of State for Inter-American Affairs, Joint Appendix of Regan v. Wald, p. 182, on file with author.

34. Affidavit of John M. Walker Jr., Assistant Secretary of the United States Department of Transportation, Joint Appendix of *Regan v. Wald*, p. 186, on file

with author. James Michel, an acting assistant secretary of state, raised the possibility that the members of "law-abiding public" "will conclude that the entire embargo program is eroding." Affidavit of James Michel, 180. If being responsible for the collapse of the "embargo program" and an influx of illegal foreign aliens was not sufficient to cause the court to reconsider, yet another assistant secretary of state informed the court that its injunction "would assist Cuba in the conduct of its foreign policy" of "attempting the overthrow of democratic governments." Affidavit of Thomas Enders, Foreign Services Officer, Joint Appendix of *Regan v. Wald*, p. 177, on file with author.

   35. *Wald v. Regan*, 708 F.2d at 800.

   36. Ibid., 802.

   37. Ibid., 803.

   38. Richard Kluger, *Simple Justice: The History of Brown v. Board of Education and Black America's Struggle for Equality* (New York: Alfred A. Knopf, 1976), 552.

   39. Ibid., 551.

   40. *Regan v. Wald*, 468 U.S. 222 (1984), *rehearing denied*, 469 U.S. 912 (1984).

   41. U.S. at 232.

   42. Ibid., 243.

   43. Ibid., 237.

   44. Ibid.

   45. Ibid., 244.

   46. Ibid., 262.

   47. Ibid.

   48. Ibid.

   49. Memo from Lewis F. Powell Jr. to his clerk Joe Neuhaus, 16 April 1984. Lewis F. Powell Jr. Papers, Powell Archives, Washington and Lee University School of Law, Lexington, VA. Powell's notes on the justices' conference that discussed the case also indicate the role politics played in the decision. He writes that Chief Justice Burger thought that the solicitor general's argument "is plausible," and that the "legislative history is consistent with Respondent's [plaintiffs'] view." Burger felt that the "Executive Branch *should* have authority," adding that "this is a close case." Justice O'Connor also felt, according to Powell, that this was a "very close call" but that the "Solicitor General's analysis is *rational* and we should accept it." (Emphasis added.) Powell's notes on the conference held 27 April 1984. Lewis F. Powell Jr. Papers. The underlying theme seems to be that as long as the solicitor general's argument was plausible or rational, U.S. interests required according the executive branch the power to act as it had.

   50. Anthony Lewis, "Abroad at Home," *New York Times*, 2 July 1984, sec. A, p. 15.

   51. "The Right to Travel to Cuba," *The Washington Post*, 1 July 1984, sec. C, p. 6.

   52. Lewis, "Abroad at Home."

53. Sidney Fine, *Frank Murphy: The Washington Years* (Ann Arbor: University of Michigan Press, 1984), 459.

54. Ibid., 592.

55. "Cuban Assets Control Regulations: Travel-Related Transactions: 31 C.F.R. § 515.560 (1982)," *Federal Register* 47 (23 July 1982): 32060, sec. (h)(3).

56. C.F.R. § 515.560(h)(4).

57. Medea Benjamin, "Cuba Travel Will Continue Despite U.S., Helms' Sanctions," *San Francisco Chronicle*, 15 March 1995, sec. A, p. 23. In 1994, more than 600 people traveled to Cuba openly and illegally; Terri Langford, "Students Aren't Detained on Return Trip from Cuba," *Austin American-Statesmen*, 1 July 1995, sec. A, p. 20.

58. *Freedom to Travel Compaign v. Newcomb*, 82 F.3d 1431 (9th Cir. 1996).

59. Mark Wegner and Shawn Zeller, "A Last-Minute Tiff over Cuba Trade," *National Journal*, 30 September 2000.

60. See "Cuba Ban: Restrictions on Travel Ought to Go," *Dallas Morning News*, 2 September 2002, sec. A, p. 26; Alfredo Corchado, "House Votes to Allow Americans to Travel to Cuba," *Dallas Morning News*, 24 July 2002.

61. Subcommittee on Courts, Intellectual Property, and the administration of Justice of the House of Representatives, *Free Trade in Ideas Hearing*, 101st Cong. 1st sess., 3–4 May 1989, 137.

NOTES TO CHAPTER 8

1. Joan Kruckewitt, *The Death of Ben Linder: The Story of a North American in Sandinista Nicaragua* (New York: Seven Stories Press, 1999), 12.

2. See Jim Morrell, "Back Door Aid Abroad," *New York Times*, 1 April 1981, sec. A, p. 31.

3. Ibid., "U.S. Envoy Stresses Commitment to Salvador Junta," *New York Times*, 17 June 1981, sec. A, p. 13.

4. "U.S. Said to Authorize Anti-Nicaragua Forces," *New York Times*, 10 March 1982, sec. A, p. 7; "The Worst-Kept Secret War," *New York Times*, 8 December 1982, sec. A, p. 30; "Florida Reported Site of Anti-Sandinista Action," 20 December 1982, available at LEXIS Nexis.

5. Edward Walsh, "Reagan Gets First Public Opinion Backlash—On Salvador Policy," *Washington Post*, 27 March 1981, sec. A, p. 9.

6. Statement of Senator Javits, *Congressional Record*, 93 Cong., 1st sess., 1973, Vol. 119, p. 1400.

7. Public Law 148, 93rd Cong. (7 November 1973); *U.S. Statutes at Large* 87 (1973): 555; *U.S. Code*, Vol. 50, secs. 1541–8 (1988).

8. *U.S. Code*, Vol. 50, sec. 1541(a) (2002); *U.S. Code*, Vol. 50, sec. 1544(b) (2002), giving the president the power to extend the authority for one additional thirty-day period, after which it would automatically terminate.

9. See Raymond Bonner, *Weakness and Deceit: U.S. Policy and El Salvador* (New York: Times Books, 1984), 274–75.

10. Judith Miller, "Once Again Power Pendulum Swings Toward the Executive Branch," *New York Times*, 22 March 1981, sec. 4, p. 5.

11. For a description of the wave of terror unleashed by the Salvadoran government, see Robert Armstrong and Janet Shenk, *El Salvador: The Face of Revolution* (Boston: South End Press, 1982), 137–81.

12. Michael Ratner, *Crockett v. Reagan*, unpublished manuscript, on file with author.

13. *U.S. Code*, Vol. 22, sec. 2304(a)(2) (1988).

14. Ratner, *Crockett v. Reagan*.

15. John H. Ely, "Suppose Congress Wanted a War Powers Act That Worked," *Columbia Law Review* 88 (1988): 1379, 1416–17, relying on *Crockett* in reaching the conclusion that a suit for immediate withdrawal of troops requires an inquiry that is inappropriate for judicial determination.

16. Peter Weiss, telephone interview by author, June 2002.

17. Crockett v. Reagan, 558 F. Supp. 893 (D.D.C. 1982).

18. Ibid., 902–3.

19. Ibid., 902.

20. Ibid.; see also Barbara Crossette, "Congress Sends Three Study Teams to El Salvador," *New York Times*, 12 February 1982, sec. A, p. 1.

21. *Crockett v. Reagan*, 902.

22. Ibid., 898.

23. Ibid., 899.

24. Gerald Boyd, "Reagan Terms Nicaraguan Rebels 'Moral Equal of Founding Fathers,'" *New York Times*, 2 March 1985, sec. 1, p. 1.

25. Joel Brinkly, "Playing by the Wrong Book on Nicaragua," *New York Times*, 21 October 1984, sec. 4, p. 5.

26. Sara Miles, *Talking Nicaragua* (1983), 29 and Sara Miles, *Talking Nicaragua: A Dialogue with Susan Saradon and Myrna Cunningham* (1983).

27. Ibid., 29.

28. 630 F.2d 876 (2d Cir. 1980).

29. David Cole, "Challenging Covert War: The Politics of the Political Question Doctrine," *Harvard International Law Journal* 26 (1985): 155, 156; see also Jules Lobel, "The Limits of Constitutional Power: Conflicts Between Foreign Policy and International Law," *Virginia Law Review* 71 (1985): 1071, discussing the *Filartiga* decision.

30. Interview with Michael Ratner, March 2002. Other quotes from Michael Ratner in this chapter are from that interview.

31. Deborah R. Gerstel and Adam G. Segall, "Conference Report: Human Rights in American Courts," *American University Journal of International Law and Policy* 1 (1986): 137, 140.

32. Lou Cannon, "Two Objectives, Polls Apart," *The Washington Post,* 10 June 1985, sec. A, p. 2.

33. Peter Rosset and John Vandermeer, eds., *The Nicaragua Reader: Documents of a Revolution under Fire* (New York: Grove Press, 1983), 228–36.

34. *Sanchez-Espinoza v. Reagan,* 568 F. Supp. 596, 601 (D.D.C. 1983).

35. Ibid., 601.

36. Ibid., 600.

37. *Sanchez-Espinoza v. Reagan,* 770 F.2d 202 (D.C. Cir. 1985).

38. Ibid., 208.

39. Ibid., 207 n.5 (citations omitted).

40. Mark Gibney, "Courts as 'Teachers in a Vital National Seminar' on Human Rights," in *World Justice? U.S. Courts and International Human Rights,* ed. Mark Gibney (Boulder: Westview Press, 1991), 81–105.

41. Gerstel and Segall, 144.

42. Ibid.

43. *Dellums v. Smith,* 573 F. Supp. 1489, 1492 (N.D. Ca. 1983), reproducing part of plaintiffs' letter.

44. U.S. Code, Vol. 18, sec. 960 (2002) amended by Public Law 322, 103rd Cong. (13 September 1994); *U.S. Statutes at Large* 108 (1994): 2147.

45. *Dellums v. Smith,* 1492.

46. *U.S. Code,* Vol. 28, sec. 591, et seq. (2002) amended by Public Law 270, 103rd Cong. (30 June 1994); *U.S. Statutes at Large* 108 (1994): 735–6.

47. *Committee on Judiciary, Special Prosecutor Act of 1978,* 95th Cong., 2d sess., 1978, H. Rept. 1307, 3 (statement of Pres. Carter).

48. *U.S. Code,* Vol. 28, sec. 591 (2002).

49. Jules Lobel, "The Rise and Decline of the Neutrality Act: Sovereignty and Congressional War Powers in United States Foreign Policy," *Harvard International Law Journal* 24 (1983): 1.

50. *Dellums v. Smith,* 1493.

51. Ibid.

52. Ibid., 1502 (footnote and citations omitted).

53. Ibid., 1055.

54. *Dellums v. Smith,* 577 F. Supp. 1449, 1451 (N.D. Ca. 1984).

55. Ibid., 1453.

56. Ibid., 1452.

57. Ibid., 1454.

58. Stuart Taylor, "War Powers: Back in Court," *New York Times,* 13 January 1984, sec. A, p. 9. The *National Law Journal* did a similar story later on the case. John Riley, "Neutrality Act Violated in Nicaragua? Controversy Looms on Enforcement," *National Law Journal* 3 November 1986, p. 3.

59. Taylor, sec. A, p. 9.

60. *Dellums v. Smith*, 577 F. Supp. 1453, *rev'd on other grounds*, 797 F.2d 817 (9th Cir. 1986).

61. *Dellums v. Smith*, 797 F.2d 817 (9th Cir. 1986). A year after the Ninth Circuit issued its decision, I received information that the delay was the result of a dispute over the rationale. Presumably, there was some sentiment on the court supporting a broader holding than the narrow dismissal based solely on standing.

62. Ibid., 823.

63. Ibid., 819, 823, citing *Banzhaf v. Smith*, 737 F.2d 1167 (D.C. Cir. 1984) and *Nathan v. Smith*, 737 F.2d 1069 (D.C. Cir. 1984).

64. *Dellums v. Smith*, 797 F.2d 823.

65. The Honorable Thomas E. Fairchild, Senior Circuit United States Judge for the Seventh Circuit, sat by designation. Ibid., 817.

66. Ibid., 823. Dellums, although a member of Congress, was not on the Judiciary Committee and was suing as a private citizen.

67. See Milt Freudenheim et al., "Trial of American in Managua Stirs Allegations on Aid," *New York Times*, 26 October 1986, sec. 4, p. 2.

68. John N. Moore, "The Secret War in Central America and the Future of World Order," *American Journal of International Law* 80 (1986): 43, 92 n. 197.

69. "Lawsuit on Contras Dismissed in California," *New York Times*, 22 August 1986, sec. A, p. 5; Taylor, "War Powers," sec. A, p. 9; "Nicaragua Aid Probe Resisted," *Washington Post*, 12 January 1984, sec. A, p. 17.

70. 479 U.S. 361 (1987).

71. *Barnes v. Carmen*, 582 F. Supp. 163 (D.D.C. 1984).

72. *Barnes v. Kline*, 759 F.2d 21 (D.C. Cir. 1985).

73. *Burke v. Barnes*, 479 U.S. 361 (1987).

74. Peter Rosset and John Vandermeer, *Nicaragua: Unfinished Revolution: The New Nicaragua Reader* (New York: Grove Press, Inc., 1986), 266, quoting *America's Watch Report of April 1984*.

75. *International Emergency Economic Powers Act, U.S. Code*, Vol. 50, sec. 1701 et seq. (1977).

76. Jonathan Bingham, "Why Nicaragua was Labeled a Threat," *New York Times*, 12 May 1985, sec. 4, p. 22.

77. *INS v. Chadha*, 462 U.S. 919 (1983).

78. *Goldwater v. Carter*, 444 U.S. 996 (1979).

79. *Beacon Products Corp. v. Reagan*, 633 F. Supp. 1191 (D. Mass. 1986).

80. *Beacon Products Corp. v. Reagan*, 814 F.2d. 1 (1st Cir. 1987).

81. Andrew Nachison, "U.S. Parents Still Question Why Son Died in Nicaragua," *Los Angeles Times*, 3 May 1992, sec. B, p. 6.

82. Kruckewitt, *The Death of Ben Linder*, 16.

83. Ibid., 18.

84. Interview with Elisabeth Linder. Quoted letters to the Linder family, and family statements are in the author's possession.

85. Kruckewitt, 59.

86. Ibid., 85.

87. Ibid., 32.

88. "The Killing of Benjamin Linder," *Center for Constitutional Rights Report* (April 1988): 4.

89. Quoted in testimony of David Linder, House Subcommittee on Western Hemisphere Affairs, *United States Volunteers in Nicaragua and the Death of Benjamin Linder: Hearings*, 101 Cong., 1st sess., 13 May 1987, 11.

90. Kruckewitt, *The Death of Ben Linder*, 93.

91. Ibid., 64.

92. John Lantigua, "Fatal Calling," *Washington Post*, 31 May 1987, sec. W, p. 14.

93. Ibid.

94. Michelle Cole, "Ben Linder's Legacy: Ideals Turn into Reality in Nicaragua," *The Oregonian*, 22 February 2000, sec. C, p. 4.

95. Kruckewitt, *The Death of Ben Linder*, 225.

96. Ibid., 94.

97. Ibid., 126.

98. Ibid., 125.

99. Ibid., 225.

100. *Military and Paramilitary Activities in and against Nicaragua (Nicaragua v. United States)*, 1984 I.C.J. 392 (26 November 1984).

101. *Military and Paramilitary Activities in and against Nicaragua (Nicaragua v. United States)*, 1986 I.C.J. 14 (27 June 1986).

102. Public Law 500, 99 Cong., 2d sess., 18 October 1986, sec. 206(a)(2); *U.S. Statutes at Large* 100 (1986): 1783–300 (military appropriations).

103. *United States v. Richardson*, 418 U.S. 166 (1974); *Valley Forge Christian College v. Americans United for Separation of Church and State*, 454 U.S. 464 (1982).

104. Kruckewitt, *The Death of Ben Linder*, 222.

105. Plaintiff's Complaint at ¶ 34, on file with author; *Committee of United States Citizens Living in Nicaragua v. Reagan*, No. 86-2620 (D.D.C. 24 March 1987), available at Westlaw at 1987 WL 9238.

106. *Flynn v. Shultz*, 748 F.2d 1186, 1191 (7th Cir. 1984), *cert. denied*, 474 U.S. 830 (1985); see also *Pangilinan v. INS*, 796 F.2d 1091, 1096 (9th Cir. 1986) (individual rights claims justiciable in immigration context), *rev'd*, 486 U.S. 875 (1988); *Eain v. Wilkes*, 641 F.2d 504, 516 (7th Cir. 1981) (courts are cautious when invoking political question doctrine where individual rights involved), *cert. denied*, 454 U.S. 894 (1981); *American Jewish Congress v. Vance*, 575 F.2d 939, 950 n. 14 (D.C. Cir. 1978) (Robinson, J., dissenting in part) (the fact that a case deals

with international affairs does not preclude judicial review if the claim is one of unconstitutional action); *Allende v. Shultz*, 605 F. Supp. 1220, 1223 (D. Mass. 1985) (judicial review particularly appropriate in cases involving fundamental rights of U.S. citizens); *Sharon v. Time*, 599 F. Supp. 538, 552–53 (S.D.N.Y. 1984) (political question doctrine improperly invoked when individual rights involved and absent clear guidance from a political branch); Charles Alan Wright et al., *Federal Practice and Procedure*, Vol. 13A, 2d ed. (St. Paul: West Publishing, 1984), sec. 3534.1; Warren F. Schwartz and Wayne McCormack, "The Justiciability of Legal Objections to the American Military Effort in Vietnam," *Texas Law Review* 46 (1968): 1033, 1044. Indeed, the very quote upon which the government relied, from *Marbury v. Madison*, 5 U.S. (1 Cranch) 137, 166 (1803), applies by its terms only to "political" questions which "respect the nation, *not individual rights.*"

107. Kruckewitt, *The Death of Ben Linder*, 223.

108. American Society of International Law, "The Authority of the United States Executive to Interpret, Articulate or Violate the Norms of International Law," in *Proceedings of the 80th Annual Meeting* (1986), 297, 306.

109. *Diggs v. Shultz*, 470 F.2d 461 (D.C. Cir. 1972), *cert. denied*, 411 U.S. 931 (1973); *Whitney v. Robertson*, 124 U.S. 190, 194 (1888); *Edye v. Robertson*, 112 U.S. 580 (1884). *Tag v. Rogers*, 267 F.2d 664 (D.C. Cir. 1959), *cert. denied*, 362 U.S. 904 (1960).

110. Frank Newman and David Weissbrodt, eds., *International Human Rights: Law Policy and Process* (Cincinnati: Anderson Publishing, 1990), 627 (questions whether appellants would have had a stronger case if they had alleged that Congress had not intended to break Article 94 of the UN Charter). See, e.g., *United States v. Palestine Liberation Organization*, 695 F. Supp. 1456 (S.D.N.Y. 1988). The argument would have been that Congress meant to appropriate the money simply for humanitarian and not for military aid.

111. *Committee of U.S. Citizens Living in Nicaragua*, Civil Action No. 86-2620, slip op. A225, A226 (D.D.C. filed Feb. 6, 1987).

112. Ibid., A230.

113. Ibid.

114. Ibid.

115. Kruckewitt, *The Death of Ben Linder*, 243.

116. Lantigua, "Fatal Calling," sec. W, p. 14.

117. House Committee, *The Death of Benjamin Linder*, 7.

118. Lantigua, "Fatal Calling," sec. W, p. 14.

119. Ibid.

120. Ibid.

121. House Committee, *The Death of Benjamin Linder*, 13, quoting Autopsy report of Dr. Francisco Valladores; letter of Dr. Michael Baden dated June 10, 1987; letter of Dr. Weiner Spitz dated June 15, 1987. A third forensic specialist,

Dr. Vincent J. M. Di Maro, of Texas, concluded that the head wound was not caused by a bullet fired at very close range; letter dated June 18, 1987.

122. Elaine Sciolino, "U.S. Groups Lay Blame for Killing of Volunteer on Administration," *New York Times*, 30 April 1987, sec. A, p. 12.

123. Joanne Omarg, "Republican Lawmakers, Contra Victim's Parents Trade Charges," *The Washington Post*, 14 May 1987, sec. A, p. 36.

124. Lais Eric Nelso, "An American *is* Neutralized," *New York Daily News*, 1 May 1987.

125. Mayor Andrew Young Memorial Service, Decatur, Georgia, 3 May 1987, http://www.rtfcam.org/martyrs/fullness_of_life/ben_linder.htm.

126. House Committee, *The Death of Benjamin Linder*, 9.

127. Mike Mills, "American Slain in Nicaragua Aware of Risks, U.S. Says," *Los Angeles Times*, 30 April 1987, part 1, p. 1.

128. Gerald M. Boyd, "Bush Debates with Brother of American Slain By Contras," *New York Times*, 1 August 1987, sec. 1, p. 1.

129. House Committee, *The Death of Ben Linder*, 59.

130. Ibid., 44.

131. Ibid.

132. Judge Mikva had been a liberal congressman before being named to the bench by President Carter. He had been a member of the World Federalists in its early years. Judge Robinson had been a NAACP lawyer prior to his appointment to the bench.

133. *Committee of United States Citizens Living in Nicaragua v. Reagan*, 859 F.2d 929, 933 (D.C. Cir. 1988).

134. Ibid., 935.

135. 630 F.2d 876 (2d Cir. 1980).

136. *Committee of United States Citizens Living in Nicaragua*, 935.

137. Ibid., 941.

138. Ibid., 942.

139. Ibid., 950.

140. Chief Judge Wald of the D.C. Circuit Court recognized that *CUSCLIN* "left open the possibility that 'peremptory' norms might supersede domestic law." *Antolok v. United States*, 873 F.2d 369, 394 n. 17 (D.C. Cir. 1989); see also *Siderman de Blake v. Argentina*, 965 F.2d 699, 714–17 (9th Cir. 1992), citing *CUSCLIN* extensively for the proposition that *jus cogens* is the highest form of international law and that prohibition against torture had *jus cogens* status, *cert. denied*, 507 U.S. 1017, 113 S. Ct. 1812 (1993).

141. Center for Constitutional Rights, 19.

142. Plaintiffs Complaint, ¶¶ 56–8, on file with author.

143. *Linder v. Portocarrero*, 747 F. Supp. 1452, 1460 (S.D. Fla. 1990).

144. See *Linder v. Portocarrero*, 963 F.2d 332, 336 (11th Cir. 1992).

145. Ibid.

146. Ibid., 337.
147. Gioconda Belli, *The Country Under My Skin* (New York: Alfred A. Knopf, 2002), 369.

NOTES TO CHAPTER 9

1. George Will, "Uphill for a California Republican," *Washington Post*, 27 August 2000, sec. B, p. 7.
2. Judith Lewis, "My Life as an Underdog," *Los Angeles Weekly*, 27 October 2002, p. 22.
3. Vincent Schodolski, "New California Congressman Doesn't Fit Republican Mold," *Chicago Tribune*, 8 February 1996, p. 16.
4. Tom Campbell, telephone interview by author, 2001.
5. Lindsay Sobel, "Rep. Tom Campbell: California Moderate Republican Goes against the Grain without the Zeal of a Rebel," *The Hill*, 1 April 1998, p. 41.
6. Ibid.
7. Ibid.
8. Ibid.
9. Lewis, quoting *California Journal*, 1 October 2000.
10. *Raines v. Byrd*, 521 U.S. 811 (1997).
11. Ibid.
12. Ibid., 823.
13. Faye Fiore, "Crisis in Yugoslavia: Maverick Lawmaker Trying to Force Colleagues to Take a Stand on Kosovo," *Los Angeles Times*, 15 April 1999, sec. A, p. 18.
14. *U.S. Code*, Vol. 50, sec. 1545-6 (2002).
15. Fiore, 18.
16. Ibid.
17. Melvin G. Holli, *The American Mayor: The Best and Worst Big-City Leaders* (University Park: Pennsylvania State University Press, 1999), 16.
18. Kucinich says it was his own political battles in the 1970s that reinforced the lessons of his Catholic upbringing that war should be taken only as a last resort. Tom Brazaitis, "Political Warrior Wants U.S. to Give Peace a Chance," *Cleveland Plain Dealer*, 1 May 1999, p. 2A.
19. U.S. Department of Defense, News Briefing, 15 May 1999, 14, available at http://www.defenselink.mil/news/May 1999/t05151999_t0515asa.html.
20. Remarks by President Clinton and King Abdullah II of Jordan, available at 1999 WL 314931, 18 May 1999; Press briefing by Joe Lockhart, 18 May 1999.
21. John Bassett Moore, "The Control of the Foreign Relations of the United States," in *The Collected Papers of John Bassett Moore*, Vol. 5 (New Haven: Yale University Press, 1944), 196.

22. *The Prize Cases*, 67 U.S. 635, 669 (1863).

23. *Dellums v. Bush*, 752 F. Supp. 1141 (D.D.C. 1990).

24. Letter of Assistant Attorney General Walter Dellinger, 27 September 1994, reprinted in Marian Nash, "U.S. Practice: Contemporary Practice of the United States Relating to International Law," *American Journal of International Law* 89 (1995): 96, 122, 126.

25. *House Committee on International Relations, Situation in Kosovo: Hearings*, 106th Cong., 1st sess., 1999, 30–1.

26. See *Campbell v. Clinton*, 52 F. Supp. 2d 34, 43–4 (D.D.C. 1999)

27. Ibid.

28. Ibid., 40 n. 5.

29. Ibid., 45 n. 11.

30. *Doe v. Sullivan*, 938 F.2d 1370, 1379 (D.C. Cir. 1991).

31. Neil Lewis, "The 1992 Campaign, Selection of Conservative Judge Insures a President's Legacy," *New York Times*, 1 July 1992, sec. A, p. 13.

32. See *Campbell v. Clinton*, 203 F.3d 19 (D.C. Cir. 2000).

33. Ibid., 32.

34. Ibid.

NOTES TO CHAPTER 10

1. Sarah Boxer, "The Man Who Created the Kid in Us All," *New York Times*, 20 February 2000, sec. IV, p. 2.

2. Martha Banta, *Failure and Success in America: A Literary Debate* (Princeton: Princeton University Press, 1978), 160.

3. Helen Hershkoff and Aubrey McCutcheon, *Public Interest Litigation: An International Perspective in Many Roads to Justice, the Law-Related Work of Ford Foundation Grantees Around the World*, ed. Mary McClymont & Stephen Golub (New York: Ford Foundation, 2000), 287.

4. Ibid.

5. Ibid., 288–9.

6. Ibid., 295.

7. John G. Cawelti, *Apostles of the Self-Made Man* (Chicago: University of Chicago Press, 1965), 290 (emphasis added).

8. Thomas Friedman, "Half a Loaf," *New York Times*, 5 July 1995, sec. A, p. 21.

9. James T. Patterson, Brown v. Board of Education: *A Civil Rights Milestone and Troubled Legacy* (New York: Oxford University Press, 2001), xxix.

10. Michael Seidman, "*Brown* and *Miranda*," *California Law Review* 80 (1992): 673, 744; Welsh S. White, *Miranda's Warning Protections: Police Interrogation Practices after Dickerson* (Ann Arbor: University of Michigan Press 2001); Welsh S. White, "Miranda's Failure to Restrain Pernicious Interrogation Prac-

tices," Michigan Law Review (2001) 99: 1211 (*Miranda* provides only minimal safeguards) at 1217.

11. Seidman, 753.

12. Barry M. Goldwater, *With No Apologies: The Personal and Political Memoirs of United States Senator Barry M. Goldwater* (New York: Morrow, 1979), 163.

13. Robert Caro, *Master of the Senate* (New York: Alfred A. Knopf, 2002), 793.

14. The *New Yorker* writer Louis Menand viewed the Goldwater campaign in this fashion. Louis Menand, "He Knew He Was Right: The Tragedy of Barry Goldwater," *The New Yorker*, 26 March 2002, p. 92.

15. Heschel, 212.

16. Interview with Peter Weir, from Cinema Papers, August 1990 at http//www.peterweircave.com/articles/articlelc.html.

17. Ivan I. Morris, *Nobility of Failure, Tragic Heroes in the History of Japan* (New York: Holt, Rinehart, and Winston, 1975).

18. James E. Young, *The Texture of Memory: Holocaust Memorials and Meaning* (New Haven: Yale University Press, 1993), 115.

19. Editorial, "NATO Strike Is against a Criminal," *Sunday Star-Times* (Auckland), 21 March 1999, p. 10.

Index

CRITICAL AMERICA

GENERAL EDITORS:

Richard Delgado AND Jean Stefancic

Moral Imperialism: A Critical Anthology
Edited by
Berta Esperanza Hernández-Truyol

In the Silicon Valley of Dreams:
Environmental Injustice,
Immigrant Workers, and the
High-Tech Global Economy
David N. Pellow and
Lisa Sun-Hee Park

Mixed Race America and the Law:
A Reader
Kevin R. Johnson

Critical Race Feminism:
A Reader, Second Edition
Edited by Adrien Katherine Wing

Murder and the Reasonable Man:
Passion and Fear
in the Criminal Courtroom
Cynthia K. Lee

Success without Victory:
Lost Legal Battles and the Long Road to
Justice in America
Jules Lobel

About the Author

JULES LOBEL is Professor of International Constitutional Law at the University of Pittsburgh Law School. He is also Vice president of the Center for Constitutional Rights, a national civil and human rights organization. On behalf of the Center, he has been one of the foremost legal challengers of unilateral presidential warmaking for the past two decades.

About the Author